A Reporter's Lincoln

Walter B. Stevens

edited by
Michael
Burlingame

University of Nebraska Press
Lincoln and London

© 1998 by the University of Nebraska Press
All rights reserved
Manufactured in the United States of America
⊗ The paper in this book meets the minimum
requirements of American National
Standard for Information Sciences—Permanence
of Paper for Printed Library
Materials, ANSI Z39.48-1984.
Library of Congress Cataloging-in-
Publication Data
Stevens, Walter B. (Walter Barlow), 1848–1939.
A reporter's Lincoln / Walter B. Stevens ;
edited by Michael Burlingame.
p.   cm.
"A Bison original" — Cover.
Includes bibliographical
references and index.
ISBN 0-8032-9253-8 (pa)
1. Lincoln, Abraham, 1809–1865 – Anecdotes.
I. Burlingame, Michael, 1941–
II. Title.
E457.15.S84   1998
973.7′092 — DC21   98-21423
CIP

For Lloyd

Contents

Part 2: Supplementary Material
    from the St. Louis Globe-Democrat

Acknowledgments

I am grateful to James A. Rawley, who encouraged me to undertake this project.

I have been the fortunate beneficiary of the kindness of librarians at many institutions, foremost among them Brown University, where Samuel Streit, Jean Rainwater, Mary Jo Kline, Andrew Moul, Pat Sirois, and their colleagues have made the John Hay Library a most congenial home away from home. To them go my heartiest thanks. I am also grateful to their counterparts at the Missouri Historical Society, the Library of Congress, and Connecticut College.

Anita Allen and Gina Foster cheerfully and efficiently helped type the manuscript.

The R. Francis Johnson Faculty Development Fund at Connecticut College helped defray some of the costs incurred in doing the research for this volume.

To David Herbert Donald, my mentor at Princeton and Johns Hopkins Universities, I owe a special debt of gratitude.

Providing indispensable support, encouragement, and forbearance, Lois McDonald has for many years patiently endured my quest for the historical Lincoln.

Editor's Introduction

In 1886, the chief of the Washington bureau of the *St. Louis Globe-Democrat*, Walter B. Stevens, began interviewing people about Abraham Lincoln. Over the next twenty-three years, in his spare time, Stevens pursued Lincoln informants in the nation's capital, in Illinois, and in Missouri. As the centennial of Lincoln's birth drew near, the *Globe-Democrat* gathered together many of these articles for a series entitled "Recollections of Lincoln," which ran in the paper's Sunday Magazine between 3 January and 11 April 1909. Readers were informed that "[u]nder a commission from the *Globe-Democrat* Mr. Stevens has visited and is still visiting the homes and haunts of Lincoln in search of new facts, new light on old facts—the recollections of people who knew Lincoln more or less intimately, some of whom were closely associated with the great president, but whose knowledge of the man and of events connected with his life has never spread beyond the circle of their friends." Stevens, the *Globe-Democrat* declared, "has succeeded in collecting a vast amount of exceedingly interesting and delightfully entertaining information which will add much to our knowledge of Lincoln's personality and to that popular affection which is the strongest characteristic of his memory."[1]

In addition to interviews conducted by Stevens, "Recollections of Lincoln" contained Lincoln materials owned by a St. Louis businessman, William K. Bixby, as well as reminiscences gathered by the Lincoln Centennial Association of Springfield, Illinois, and by the Historical Society of Bloomington, Illinois.[2] At times it is difficult to tell whether Stevens interviewed an informant or whether he simply reproduced statements given to others. He sometimes leads the reader to think he interviewed an informant when he in fact merely reproduced a written record. A case in point is the letter by John F. Mendonsa. On at least two occasions he falsely claimed to have interviewed a subject when in fact he copied the words from another source. In 1887 Stevens asserted that he "had the pleasure of an interview with Mr. Dennis Hanks. . . . Mr. Hanks is now eighty-eight years of age, well preserved, and never tires of speaking of the many virtues and excellences of his relative."[3] Stevens's account of Hanks's words replicates several paragraphs from an interview that had run in the *Chicago Tribune* in 1885.[4] Similarly, Stevens's "interview" with Adlai E. Stevenson contains

passages lifted verbatim from Stevenson's autobiography.[5] The reminiscences of George Schneider and several other delegates to the Bloomington
Convention of 1856 originally appeared in *Meeting of May 29, 1900, Commemorative of the Convention of May 29, 1856, That Organized the
Republican Party in the State of Illinois*, edited by Ezra M. Prince.[6]

In 1916 about half of the material in "Recollections of Lincoln" appeared in Stevens's brief book, *A Reporter's Lincoln*, published by the Missouri Historical Society. This rare volume (only six hundred copies were
printed) is valuable, for it contains much information about Lincoln un-
available elsewhere. It deserves a place alongside such works as Francis B.
Carpenter's *Six Months in the White House with Abraham Lincoln*, Francis Fisher Browne's *The Every-Day Life of Abraham Lincoln*, Jesse W.
Weik's *The Real Lincoln*, Douglas L. Wilson and Rodney O. Davis's *Herndon's Informants*, William Ward Hayes's *Abraham Lincoln: Tributes of
His Associates*, and Alexander T. Rice's *Reminiscences of Abraham Lincoln by Distinguished Men of His Time*.

In preparing this reissue of Stevens's slender work, I have combed the
Globe-Democrat files for the original articles about Lincoln, some of
which were reproduced *in toto* in *A Reporter's Lincoln*; others were given
only in excerpted form; still others were left out altogether. From the articles that were either omitted or only partially reproduced in *A Reporter's
Lincoln*, I have compiled a supplement nearly as long as the original book.

One of the most revealing of the interviews was conducted in 1892,
when Joseph B. McCullagh, editor-in-chief of the *Globe-Democrat*, directed Stevens to speak with a prominent Illinois congressman, Robert R.
Hitt, who had covered the 1858 Lincoln-Douglas debates as a shorthand
reporter for the *Chicago Tribune*. Stevens recalled that "Hitt was not willing to be quoted in direct narration. He had preserved much that was
printed at the time of the debates." To this material Hitt added "his recollection of many incidents connected with the historic meetings." When
Stevens finished his long account of the debates based on Hitt's memory
and archives, he visited the congressman and went over the article with
him: "The narrative was read at length. Mr. Hitt made some further suggestions which were noted. In this form, approved by Mr. Hitt, the story of
the debates is given."[7] Only portions of the original article appeared in *A
Reporter's Lincoln*. I have included the entire article, folded into the text of
the original book at the point where the author deals with the Lincoln-
Douglas debates.

Hitt's account casts doubt on Harold Holzer's version of those debates.[8]

Holzer maintains that the Democratic newspaper, the *Chicago Times*, rendered Lincoln's words more accurately than did the Republican *Chicago Press and Tribune*, whose editors allegedly applied cosmetic retouching to make Lincoln sound smoother than he really was on the stump. Hitt denies Holzer's basic premise, contending that the *Times*'s shorthand reporter deliberately garbled Lincoln's words in order to make the Republican standard bearer sound inarticulate. Materials preserved in the Hitt Papers at the Library of Congress, including Hitt's 1858 journal, strongly support that conclusion.[9]

Other revealing materials in this volume include Mrs. Benjamin S. Edwards's curious account of Mary Todd Lincoln's child-rearing habits. After declaring that Mary Lincoln "was one of the kindest of mothers," Mrs. Edwards then relates a tale belying that claim: "I remember that a new clock was brought home. Mrs. Lincoln told the boys they must not touch it. A short time afterward she went into the room and found that two of them had taken the clock to pieces. She whipped them. Almost immediately afterward she felt so sorry for what she had done she told the boys to take the clock and do what they pleased with it." This undermines the assertion by Jean Baker, one of Mary Todd Lincoln's biographers, that "some women berated their children in unseen outbursts of temper inside their homes, but Mary Lincoln's fury appeared in unladylike public displays against hired girls and greengrocers."[10] Included as an appendix is an unpublished letter by Mrs. Edwards that provides insights into the circumstances surrounding the Lincolns' wedding. Mrs. Edwards doubted "that it was really a love affair between Mr. L and Mary T, but think it was through mutual friends (?) that the marriage was made up." Mrs. Edwards's contention that Lincoln "was deeply in love with Matilda Edwards" is supported by many other sources, as the innovative and thorough scholar Douglas L. Wilson has shown.[11]

In Hancock County, Illinois, Stevens gathered a great deal of information on Lincoln's cousins, who shared with him family traditions about Lincoln's ancestry. Stevens also visited Charleston and Petersburg, Illinois, where he spoke with many who had known Lincoln and his family well.

The reminiscences gathered by Stevens should be used cautiously, for memory plays tricks, and sometimes informants may deliberately fabricate stories. John Easton, for example, claimed to have served in the Illinois state legislature with Lincoln, but records show that although he ran for a seat in that body, he never won election. I have not included Easton's improbable reminiscences.[12] Ira Haworth's description of Lincoln's role in the formation of the Republican Party in Illinois is also suspect. When Stevens passes along other misinformation, such as his account of Lincoln's "leap" from a window to avoid a legislative quorum call, a note calls attention to the error.[13] Calvin Coolidge was amazed at people in his hometown who "remember some of the most interesting things that never happened."[14] Lincoln scholar James G. Randall observed that "[t]he vagueness of reminiscence given after many years is familiar to all careful historical students; if, in the haste of general reading, this matter is disregarded, the essence of the subject is overlooked. Huge tomes could be written to show the doubtfulness of long-delayed memories." Randall acknowledged that historians "must use reminiscence," but counseled that they "do so critically." Even some "close-up evidence is fallible," he noted. When evidence "comes through the mists of many years some of it may be true, but a careful writer will check it with known facts. Contradictory reminiscences leave doubt as to what is to be believed; unsupported memories are in themselves insufficient as proof; statements induced under suggestion, or psychological stimulus . . . call especially for careful appraisal."[15]

But as Douglas L. Wilson has sensibly argued, reminiscences cannot be dismissed simply because they would not be admissible in court: "Observing the evidentiary safeguards of a criminal trial would, after all, bring a substantial portion of historical inquiry to a halt, for much of what we want to know about the past simply cannot be established on these terms. Abraham Lincoln's early life is a perfect example. Virtually everything we know about Lincoln as a child and as a young man—his incessant reading and self-education, his storytelling, his honesty, his interest in politics, and so forth—comes exclusively from the recollections of the people who knew him. Non-contemporary, subjective, often unable to be confirmed even by the recollections of others, to say nothing of contemporary documents, this evidence is sheer reminiscence." Despite the problems raised by reminiscent material, "the historian or biographer has no alternative but to find a way to work with it and, indeed, with anything that may be indicative of the truth."[16]

Donald Ritchie, a pioneer in the recent oral history movement, offers sensible advice for readers of this volume: "Treat oral evidence as cautiously as any other form of evidence. Documents written at the time have an immediacy about them and are not influenced by subsequent events, and yet those documents can be incomplete, in error, or written to mislead." Ritchie notes that a "statement is not necessarily truer if written down at the time than if recalled later in testimony. Whether written or oral, evidence must be convincing and verifiable."[17]

In reproducing Stevens's text, I have silently corrected obvious misprints and have corrected misspellings of proper names by inserting the proper spelling within square brackets. All material within such brackets is mine and not Stevens's. In his section on the Lincoln-Douglas debates, Stevens enclosed within brackets the crowd responses to the orators. Here those responses are enclosed within rounded brackets.

Walter B. Stevens achieved renown as a "peerless Washington correspondent" and "[o]ne of the world's greatest newspaper men." A contemporary thought he deserved to be ranked with "the great reporters of the past, McGahan, 'Bull Run' Russell, Amos Cummings, Julian Ralph, Frank R. O'Neil." Compared to Stevens, none of those eminent journalists "had the *flair* for news better developed, none had more of the genius for inspiring confidence in men with news to give." He "never betrayed a confidence and never faked a line for a newspaper." As an investigator, he was "a fiend for facts," searching them out with "the ardor of a scientist." Once he had unearthed facts, he arranged "them without ornamentation in the most effective fashion." He "could ride through a county on a fast train and write seven columns of interesting stuff about it" or "could walk through a cornfield and write a better article than most writers with a city of a million inhabitants from which to draw their inspiration." With a facility for assembling "dry things" and giving them "juice," he could "make anything interesting, a trade report, a real estate bulletin, a bunch of statistics." Stevens as a Washington correspondent for the *Globe-Democrat* from 1884 to 1901 "was at the head of the profession."[18] His by-line "came to be regarded as an absolute guarantee that the matter was readable and reliable."[19]

In his sixties and seventies, Stevens concentrated on writing history and became known as "Missouri's most popular and prolific historian." Though short and "weak in voice," and though his "modest, almost timid" personality gave him the reputation of a "grey man in his neutral grey atmosphere," he was "a mighty man when engaged in the cause of Missouri history."[20] A St. Louis civic leader declared that "[v]ery few men are more generally esteemed in St. Louis than Mr. Stevens—whose ability, energy, integrity, laborious researches and painstaking accuracy are fully and deservedly appreciated."[21]

Born in 1848 in Meriden, Connecticut, Stevens at the age of seven moved with his family to Newton, Iowa, and a year later to Peoria, Illinois, where his father spent a quarter-century as the pastor of the First Congregational Church. After leaving the University of Michigan in 1872 with both a bachelor's and a master's degree, Stevens joined the *St. Louis Times* as a reporter. A year later he became city editor of the *St. Louis Post-Dispatch*; in 1881 he assumed that same position on the *St. Louis Globe-Democrat*. Three years thereafter he was appointed head of the *Globe-Democrat's* Washington bureau, a post he held till 1901. When Congress was out of session, Stevens traveled widely, writing on such topics as "Black Labor in the South," "Convict Camps in the South," "Among the Mormons," "The New States," "Missouri Minerals," "Washington Topics," "Through Texas," "Ozark Uplift," and "In the Silver Country." Like his articles on Lincoln, some of these series were collected and published between hard covers.

In 1901 Stevens became secretary of the Louisiana Purchase Exposition Company. After stepping down in 1907, he concentrated on writing books. Ten years later he was chosen president of the Missouri Historical Society, a position he held till 1925. Fourteen years later he died, at the age of ninety-one.[22]

Stevens's account of the recollections of several informants is based on their letters, statements, and reminiscences located in the files of the Lincoln Centennial Association of the Illinois State Historical Library in Springfield. Those informants and the dates of their letters or statements are as follows: Jonathan H. Cheney (7 July 1908), John Hitt (1 July 1908), Luman Burr (25 January 1908), Judith Bradner (27 June and 1 July 1908), Martin L. Bundy (26 December 1908), Stephen R. Capps (17 July 1908), John Carmody (undated), James D. Conner (6 July 1908), William Fisher (22 September 1908), Mrs. Annie C. Fox (14 January 1909), J. F. Humphreys (3 July 1908), James T. Jones (6 July 1908), Lyman Lacey (18 June 1908), Edward F. Leonard (8 January 1909), Mrs. James Judson Lord (8 July 1908), Robert W. McClaughry (27 January 1909), Thompson Ware McNeely (25 January 1909), John F. Mendonsa (2 July 1908), Addison G. Proctor (undated), John W. Proctor (1 July 1908), James P. Root (1 July 1908), Henry M. Russell (14 August 1908), John Q. Spears (18 and 22 June 1908), and J. F. Willson (15 January 1909).

Part 1

A Reporter's Lincoln

This notebook is dedicated to
CAPTAIN HENRY KING,
whose intimate knowledge of Lincoln
dated from the "Lost Speech;" whose youth
was passed among relatives of Lincoln;
whose appreciation of Lincoln was an
inspiration to the reporter for the
assembling of these recollections.[1]

They Knew Lincoln

These recollections of Lincoln were assembled in newspaper goings and comings. They are plain tales told by men and women "who knew Lincoln." In degree of acquaintance they range from a single, perhaps casual, meeting, to years of intimacy. In respect to time, they relate to Lincoln, the clerk at New Salem; to Lincoln, the president; and to Lincoln at stages of his career between the clerkship and the presidency.

New Salem, the settlement that was promising when Lincoln went there to begin his manhood life, passed away long ago.[1] When the site was visited by the reporter not a building was left. But living in and about Petersburg, the thrifty little city which succeeded New Salem, were men and women, advanced in years, who remembered "when nobody along the Sangamon could put Abe Lincoln on his back."[2] They told, from personal observation, how Lincoln took the death of Ann Rutledge.[3] They described the wrestling match between Lincoln and Jack Armstrong, the neighborhood champion.[4] They heard Lincoln read his argument about the Bible and saw his employer take the paper from him and burn it. They recalled how Lincoln saved Duff Armstrong with an almanac, in a murder trial, and Duff Armstrong, in the flesh, reformed and a church member, was there to stoutly assert that the almanac was not faked.[5]

After Lincoln the wrestler and clerk, Lincoln the surveyor and legislator, came Lincoln the lawyer and Lincoln the politician. Lincoln rode the eighth circuit.[6] Half a century afterwards his trail was followed by his lawsuits, his stories, his homely sayings. At the court towns on the circuit, people told of Lincoln from personal recollections.

Of Lincoln sitting on the log with the editors and framing the first platform of the Republican movement in Illinois; of Lincoln going fishing with a carryall full of boys; of Lincoln dropping from the statehouse window in Vandalia to break a quorum,—of such were the recollections. The Bloomington speech was "lost," but perhaps more vivid than the forgotten words were the impressions which listeners received and which they described.

Robert R. Hitt, many years Member of Congress from the Freeport, Ill., district, took the speeches of the Douglas-Lincoln joint debate for the *Chicago Tribune*.[7] During a mid-winter recess of Congress, Joseph B. McCullagh, editor of the *Globe-Democrat*, sent his Washington correspondent

[Walter B. Stevens] to Mr. Hitt for an interview on the joint debates.[8] Mr. Hitt was not willing to be quoted in direct narration. He had preserved much that was printed at the time of the debates. This material he supplemented with his recollection of many incidents connected with the historic meetings. The narrative was long. After it was written from the notes taken at the talk, another visit was made to Mr. Hitt's library overlooking McPherson Square.[9] The narrative was read at length. Mr. Hitt made some further suggestions which were noted. In this form, approved by Mr. Hitt, the story of the debates is given.

There were grayheads in Alton who saw Lincoln and Shields arrive from Springfield, who marveled as the long, clattering sabres were lifted down from the top of the stagecoach, who watched the two boatloads of solemn looking men cross to Lincoln-Shields island near the Missouri shore, and who told how Lincoln practiced lopping off the willow twigs while the seconds measured the ground and arranged preliminaries for a duel.[10]

These narratives include incidents which seemed trivial at the time of occurrence, but which, later, had important bearing on the great career. Going to see how his son Robert was getting on at Exeter, in preparation for Harvard, Lincoln made speeches in New England.[11] The next year [actually later in the same year] the eastern delegates who turned earliest from their first choices to Lincoln, in the nominating convention at Chicago, were from the New England localities where Lincoln had spoken.

Reminiscences of the family life, given by a favorite nephew [Albert Stevenson Edwards] who spent much time in the Lincoln home at Springfield are more satisfying than much that has been given by the biographers.

From the unpublished store of Lincoln manuscripts possessed by William K. Bixby have been drawn many revelations.[12]

With no purpose to prove or disprove anything about Lincoln, but with the sole intention to add to the popular comprehension of the Great American, these narratives have been reported.

W. B. S.

Growing Days at New Salem

New Salem, the town where Lincoln tended store and made his reputation as the champion jumper and wrestler, is a reminiscence. It was promising in 1833. Only the hill remains, from the summit of which there is a long stretch of the Sangamon bottom in view. Some years ago might have been seen the foundation timbers of the log house in which Bill Berry and Abe Lincoln kept the grocery.[1] But the old timbers have disappeared, gone to be manufactured into Lincoln souvenirs. The mill which stood on the river bank under the hill is gone. It was burned long ago. At this mill, according to Salem traditions, Lincoln played one of his practical jokes. He took advantage of the absence of the miller to prop up in the hopper a dead hog with an ear of corn in its mouth. All Salem, except the miller, laughed. The miller felt scandalized at the insinuation of excessive toll "as the wheel went around."

The everlasting hill, which was the site of New Salem, is there, but the road to the settlement, leading up a hollow, has been washed away. The abandoned town site is part of a pasture and the only way to reach it is roundabout, through gates and up a steep climb. From the height the visitor looks down the side of the hill almost as steep as the roof of a house. And that descent was the scene of another Lincoln joke, in which a boon companion, Jack Armstrong, aided and abetted. One day Lincoln and Armstrong, so the local tradition is told, put an old toper who was sleeping off his potations into a hogshead and started it rolling down the hill. About halfway the hogshead struck a stump, the head flew out, the hoops burst and the drunken man escaped with nothing worse than a bruise or two.[2]

These Salem traditions are entertaining, but in connection with them the fact should be kept in mind that when Abraham Lincoln came to the settlement to keep store he was only 22 years old. When he was past 25 he was elected to the Legislature, [and in 1837, at the age of 28] moved to Springfield and began to be a lawyer. A story of this New Salem period is that, having great difficulty in driving a drove of hogs across a bridge, Lincoln resorted to the expedient of sewing together the eyelids of several. He then started the blinded hogs ahead of those that could see and the drove passed over the bridge without any more trouble.[3] This is one of the stories of Lincoln's early manhood which has been questioned. It is still told and accepted in Petersburg, the Menard County town which grew as New Salem declined with the transition from river to rail. An old lady with an excellent memory laughed merrily as she declared her faith in the tradition about the hogs.

"I guess it is true," she said. "Perhaps Lincoln didn't really do the sewing, but only made the suggestion. You know, we hadn't many bridges in those days. We had to drive the hogs across the country to the Illinois River to ship them to market. Hogs weren't used to bridges and would refuse to cross. As I heard the story, Lincoln proposed the sewing and it was really done. Years after, when Mr. Lincoln had moved to Springfield, this story was told on him here. I think old Mr. Smoot started it as a reminiscence of Lincoln's early life in New Salem.[4] Some of Lincoln's Petersburg friends, who didn't know so much about the pioneer days, expressed disbelief in the story. They were indignant that such things should be said of Mr. Lincoln. One of them, a member of the Killian family, I think, went all of the way to Springfield to tell Mr. Lincoln what the Petersburg people were circulating on him and to get a contradiction.[5] Mr. Lincoln listened to him and said: 'Sh-sh—don't say another word about it. That thing was done right on old man Smoot's place.' So I judge it must have been a true story."

New Salem days made an important as well as an interesting period in the life of Abraham Lincoln. They transformed the lanky, fun-loving boy of 22 into the ambitious, studious man of 25. When Lincoln came to New Salem he was proud to win the jumping and wrestling matches. Before he went away he was writing his views upon religion. Development of the mind was rapid.

One community in the United States remembered the "ninety-ninth anniversary of the adoption of the constitution," and celebrated it in 1886. That place was Petersburg, the successor of New Salem. The scene of the celebration was the Menard County Fair Grounds, in the midst of fine Illinois farms, some of the lines of which were run by the great liberator fifty years before, when he changed his vocation from that of grocery clerk to country surveyor.

The celebration took the form of a fish-fry, a popular pastime of that period in that part of Illinois. Old residents could remember the fish-fry dating back to Lincoln's time. The fish-fry was to these people what the barbecue was to Kentucky. The master of the fish-fry at the Petersburg celebration came from "over on the Illinois river." He looked back upon twenty years of practice in the art. In a shed of the fair grounds he set up his rude furnace, simply two rows of bricks to keep the huge pans above fire. A wagon-load of cobs and pine wood was heaped at one end of the furnace. With a boy to feed the fire as he directed, the fish-frying chef was ready for his work. The fish, croppie and bass and those twin aboriginals of the Illinois, the cat and the buffalo, were cleaned, scraped and cut into quarter-pound sections. They were brought in bushel baskets and heaped on a large table in front of the master. Then the real expert work began. With a seemingly careless hand, the master poured out two bushels of meal on the table near the heap of fish. He emptied a sack of salt upon the meal. He spread two pounds of pepper over the meal and the salt. With arms bared to the elbow, he thoroughly mixed the mess, and stirred the pieces of fish. He continued to stir and stir until every piece of fish was well covered with meal and seasoning. In the long string of pans the lard was beginning to smoke when the master threw in the fish. With a long fork he moved from pan to pan, prodding and turning and at the same time giving sharp directions to the fireman.

The master turned off his first batch at ten o'clock. For eight hours he kept the pans hot. Every fifteen minutes the master delivered to the committee one hundred pounds of fish. Outside of the frying shed was stretched a rope, in a semi-circle. Over this rope were handed the loaves of bread and the hot fried fish in countless wooden plates, hour after hour. Before sundown over 3,000 pounds of fish had been served. This part of Illinois has been famous for the participation of the gentler sex in politics ever since Lincoln one day about 1833, told Mary Owens, as they were going up the hill west of town, his poor opinion of "a political woman."[6] Two hundred picnic parties spread their table cloths under the trees and furnished accompaniments to the fried fish. All Petersburg society was there. The wild and exuberant Rock Creek boys came in procession bearing a pole with a much embarrassed coon aloft and escorting a gaily decorated triumphal car filled to overflowing with lively girls.[7] Indian Creek, Athens and all of the other townships sent their delegations.

Out from the great throng a member of the committee led an old gentleman to a quiet spot where a wagon tongue offered seating accommodation and said, "Uncle Johnny, here's a reporter. He wants to see somebody who knew Mr. Lincoln when he lived here. You are just the one to talk to him."

And Uncle Johnny Potter, kindly-faced, with a twinkle in his eyes, a slight deafness, careful of his words, and with a recollection of detail that was marvelous, began to talk in 1886 of things that happened in 1831.[8]

"The first time I ever saw Abe Lincoln," he said, "was that summer. I was just starting in life myself, on my place below here and had a log cabin.

In front of the house was a tolerably low rail fence I had built, mebbe five rails high. We had done breakfast a few minutes, when two young men came walking along the road. One of them was Abe. A man named Offut [Offutt] was going to start a grocery at [New] Salem.⁹ That was the town then, just up the river a couple of miles above where Petersburg is now. Offut had engaged Abe to clerk for him, and Abe was walking up to go to work in the store. He had slept that night at Clary's Grove, and when he and the young man with him got along to my place they wanted to know if they could get a bite to eat.¹⁰ The old woman fixed them up something, the things were on the table, and they had their breakfast. When they got through they came out, and Abe straddled over that five-rail fence as if it wasn't in the way at all. I expect he would have gone over just as easy if it had been higher, for he had powerful long legs. When he got out to the road he turned and looked back at the table, and said: 'There's only one egg left; I believe I'd better make a clean thing of it.' So he straddled the fence again, got the egg and went off—laughing like a boy, shuffling the hot egg from one hand to the other and then peeling and eating it. That was the first time I saw Abe, but I saw a good deal of him afterwards, for Salem was where we all went to do our trading."

"Uncle Johnny, tell him about the wrestling match with father," said a sturdy, middle-aged man with a pleasant face. "You remember all about that."

The speaker was Jack Armstrong, the son of the famous Jack Armstrong, who was the champion in all athletic sports in this valley of the Sangamon fifty years before.

"I remember it," said Uncle Johnny. "Your father was considered the best man in all this country for a scuffle. In a wrestle, shoulder or back hold[s], there was only now and then a man he couldn't get away with. When Lincoln came into this country there was a crowd called the Clary Grove boys, who pretty much had their way, and Jack Armstrong was the leader among them.¹¹ Most every new man who came into the neighborhood had to be tried. Lincoln was pretty stout and the boys made it up to see what there was in him. They got him to talking about wrestling one day, and he said he could throw any man around there. Bill Clary kept at Lincoln until he got him into a bet of $5. Then he put Jack Armstrong against him. They were pretty well matched, but Abe was a good deal taller and could bend over Jack. They wrestled a good while, and I think Abe had thrown Jack two joints and was likely to get him down. Clary, I expect, thought he was in danger of losing his money for he called out: 'Throw him anyway, Jack.' At that Jack loosed his back hold and grabbed Abe by the thigh and threw him in a second. Abe got up pretty mad. He didn't say much, but he told somebody that if it ever came right, he would give Bill Clary a good licking. You see the hold Jack took was fair in a scuffle, but not in a wrestle, and they were wrestling. After that Abe was considered one of the Clary's Grove boys. I believe they called him president of their club. Abe and Jack got to be great friends and Abe used to stay at Jack's house."[12]

"Yes," said the Jack Armstrong of the later generation, "I've heard mother tell many times how she foxed Mr. Lincoln's pants when he got to be surveyor. You see the cloth wouldn't last no time out in the brush and grass and briars where surveyors had to tramp. So they used to sew a covering of buckskin on the outside of the legs. That was what was called foxing 'em."

"Abe," volunteered Riley Potter, one of the substantial farmers of Menard, "was mighty handy at frolics and parties. Most of the young people would sorter hang back, but Abe had a word for everybody, and especially for the smart girls. They couldn't any of them get the best of him. He was generally asked to help wait on the table and make folks feel sociable. One night Abe was helping the visitors and there was a girl there who thought herself pretty smart. When Abe got to her he asked her if he should help her. She said she'd take something. Abe, he filled up her plate pretty well, and when he passed it to her she says, quite pert and sharp, 'Well, Mr. Lincoln, I didn't want a cart-load.' Abe never let on that he heard her, but went on helping the others. By and by Liddy got through, and when Abe came around her way again she said she believed she'd take a little more. 'All right, Miss Liddy,' says Abe loud enough for the whole room to hear, 'back up your cart and I'll fill it again.' Of course there was a big laugh. Liddy felt awful bad about it. She went off by herself and cried the whole evening."

Uncle Johnny smiled and shook his head when he was asked if "Honest Abe" was the name given Mr. Lincoln in Salem days. "I think," he said, "the most of us had more confidence in Abe's smartness than in his honesty. When Abe ran for the Legislature, the time he was elected, Ned Potter and Hugh Armstrong had a pledge from him that he would try to get us cut off and made into a new county.[13] You know this used to be a part of Sangamon. The division was the big question. We elected Abe on the Whig ticket, although the Democrats had the majority. Well, he put our petition in his pocket and didn't do anything for us.[14] That is the way I recollect it. Afterward they cut us off and made this Menard County. Folks felt pretty sore about the way Lincoln did. He never came back here to live, but settled in Springfield and practiced law."

Lincoln could jump as well as wrestle. During the time that he clerked at the store in Salem, Lincoln made the acquaintance of the father of William B. Thompson of the St. Louis bar.[15] At Beardstown was located the house of Knapp, Pogue & Co., in those days the largest distributing store in that part of Illinois.[16] The stocks of goods were brought up the river by steamboat to Beardstown, and thence sent out to the small stores in the towns and neighborhoods of several counties. The clothing, the groceries and the other supplies reached the farmers by that method. A junior partner in the Beardstown house was [Nathaniel B. Thompson,] the father of Mr. Thompson. It was his business to visit the scattered stores in the interest of his firm. That the elder Thompson was a good deal of an athlete added to his prestige with the country people he met on his rounds. Coming to the New Salem store, Mr. Thompson met for the first time Abraham Lincoln. As he rode up, he noted the number of horses hitched to the rack, and saw that the farmers were engaged in the popular amusement of "three jumps." This was an athletic performance in which Mr. Thompson excelled. The young merchant from Beardstown lost no time getting into the game. He was astonished to see the new clerk, whom everybody called "Abe," toe the mark, swing forward in three standing jumps and pass his own scratch by some inches. As Mr. Thompson told the story afterward, this was the first time he had ever been beaten at "three jumps."

An acquaintance between the young merchant and the young clerk ripened into friendship. Mr. Lincoln confided to Mr. Thompson his ambition to do something more than to jump, and to be something more than a clerk in a country store. He said he had formed the purpose to study law and to be a lawyer. He asked Mr. Thompson to lend him books.[17] Returning home from New Salem the merchant told of this champion jumper who wanted to borrow books, and said to his friends that he had never met with any other man who was so anxious to read and to inform himself as was young Abe Lincoln. And after subsequent meetings, Mr. Thompson expressed to acquaintances his conviction that Mr. Lincoln would become one of the best self-educated men in the country. In after years Mr. Lincoln was often the guest at the house of Mr. Thompson in Virginia, Ill., when he was attending court at that town.

[Here Stevens quoted excerpts from the first debate between Lincoln and Stephen A. Douglas in 1858. Because they are given below in R. R. Hitt's account of the 1858 debates, they are deleted here.]

New Salem folks of Lincoln's time were not numerous in 1886. Mrs. Samuel Hill, who was the wife of the principal store-keeper, was one of the most interesting of the survivors.[18] Of the best Kentucky stock, she was a hale, vigorous old lady, and her memory of those days was still vivid. She lived in one of the pleasant residences of Petersburg, back on the bluff overlooking the valley.

Sitting before a wood fire in her comfortable parlor, Mrs. Hill let her memory go back fifty years and more to call up the appearance of Mr. Lincoln on the streets of Salem.

"He went about a good deal of the time without any hat," she said. "His hair was long. His yellow tow-linen pants he usually wore rolled up one leg and down the other. Many years afterward, when he was a candidate for the presidency, the recollection of how he looked in Salem would come up and make me laugh in spite of myself."

"I don't think Mr. Lincoln was overindustrious," Mrs. Hill continued. "My husband kept the principal store in Salem, and we lived in a little house close by. We had no cellar, and Mr. Hill cut a door in the rear so that I used the store cellar. The store was a great gathering place for all the neighborhood. When I would be in the cellar churning, or attending to some household matter, I could almost always hear Mr. Lincoln's voice and the crowd laughing. In front of the store was a kind of shed or porch where the people collected in warm weather. I could generally see Mr. Lincoln about when I looked out. He didn't do much. His living and his clothes cost little. He liked company, and would talk to everybody, and entertain them and himself."

The conversation turned upon Lincoln's early love affairs, and Mrs. Hill was asked about the story of Ann Rutledge, over whose death Lincoln's mind, it was claimed, became unhinged.

"Lincoln," said Mrs. Hill, "visited at the Rutledges, and he may have thought a good deal of Ann. She died of consumption, and after her death there was a long rainy spell. Some of Lincoln's friends at that time thought he was a little unbalanced, or at any rate they were afraid he would become so. I never thought he was so deeply interested in Ann Rutledge, for it wasn't very long after she died until he was courting Mary Owens. Mary came from Kentucky to visit her sister, Betsy Ables [Abell], who was Bennett Ables' wife.[19] They lived near Salem. Lincoln was at Bennett Ables' a good deal, and Betsy, who was a great talker, and sometimes said more than she ought, perhaps had told Lincoln she was going to bring her sister up from Kentucky to marry him. When Mary arrived Lincoln told some one he was intimate with that he supposed Mrs. Ables' sister had come up to catch him, but he'd show her a thing or two. This friend of Lincoln's was also a great friend of the Ables family, and it wasn't long until Mary heard just what Lincoln had said. Then she said she would teach him a lesson, and she did, too. I don't think they ever became really engaged, for Mary was a woman of too much character to go as far as that, and I don't think she ever got very much in earnest. She told me once that she didn't. But Mr. Lincoln thought a great deal of her, I expect. He used to write to her long after he went to Springfield. She finally moved to Weston, in Platte County, Mo., and became the wife of a Mr. Vineyard.[20] Mr. Ben Vineyard, the lawyer in St. Joseph, is a son of hers."[21]

Lincoln went to the Blackhawk war and became a captain of the volunteer company raised in the Salem neighborhood. In the four years after he came trudging into the Salem community, straddling the rail fence and making a "clean thing" of the breakfast at Uncle Johnny Potter's, he followed surveying, read law and was a successful candidate for the Legislature. Notwithstanding his sociability, the years from 22 to 25 had been improved. That first election to the Legislature, it is to be remembered, was on the Whig ticket in a district where the Democrats were in the majority. Lincoln was learning politics as well as a great deal else in the days at Salem.

J. F. Willson of Tallula, near Petersburg, recalled an incident of Lincoln's surveying. A line was being run not far from where the town of Tallula is now.

"It struck a sugar tree in the center," Mr. Willson said. "As was the custom with the surveyors of that time, the tree was marked with three hacks 'fore and aft,' as the description ran. Some one of the chain carriers bantered the party to show who could make the highest hack on the trunk of the tree. After the others had done their best, Lincoln took the ax handle by the end, and, reaching up, made a hack much higher than any other member of the party. The tree stood for more than thirty years afterwards, and was pointed out to visitors with Lincoln's high hack upon it. That tree fell soon after Lincoln was assassinated. I am not superstitious. I only mention the coincidence."

Papers which Lincoln made out while he was surveying were preserved for many years by the residents of Menard County, then Sangamon. The Lincoln souvenir collectors and the historical societies have gradually gathered most of these relics. The plat of the town of Bath was perhaps the most important of Lincoln's surveying jobs.[22]

Upon "Lincoln, the rail-splitter" the Douglas men rang the changes through the senatorial campaign of 1858. Two years later Republicans accepted the challenge and exploited "Lincoln, the rail-splitter," in convention and in campaign with speech and song and story and emblem.[23] Then the biographers, one after another, made much of "Lincoln, the rail-splitter." The winter he was 21 Abraham Lincoln did split rails on his Uncle Hank's farm, near Decatur.[24] He got 50 cents a hundred. Of that job he told when he was asked about his rail-splitting experiences. Coming back from a trip with a boat load of corn and pork to New Orleans, Lincoln entered upon his Salem days. Uncle Johnny Potter was for many years regarded as the best authority on traditions of Lincoln's life at Salem. He could not remember that there was much rail-splitting.

"Lincoln may have helped split rails when he was visiting some of the neighbors," Uncle Johnny would say, when asked, "but he didn't make his living by it, as they said afterwards, when he was running for president. I believe Abe and George Close took a job to cut 1000 rails for somebody over the river one time, but that is about the only time I remember of Lincoln's splitting rails."[25]

The traditions go to show that Lincoln did a variety of work while he lived among the Salem people, clerking in the stores, helping on the farms in the busy seasons and surveying as the country was settled and farmers wanted the lines run. And all of the time that he was living the life of the neighborhood he was reading, studying and thinking. This thinking was along original lines. It was speculative. It showed the mental activity of the young man. That is the most that should be said of it. As the result of his thinking Lincoln advanced views or suggestions which formed the basis for one of the Salem traditions that he was an infidel. He was a Bible student at the time. One day he startled the crowd gathered in the principal store of Salem by producing the manuscript and reading his argument that the Bible, as a whole, was not to be believed. He asked the advice of his listeners whether the paper should be printed. The keeper of the store, Mr. [Samuel] Hill, who had employed Lincoln as a clerk when he needed help, looked upon him as he might upon a younger brother. He very promptly replied to the argument by saying:

"Look here, Abe. The best thing you can do is to burn that and not tell anybody you ever wrote it."

With that Mr. Hill took the manuscript from Lincoln's hand and threw it into the fire.[26] It is not remembered that Lincoln was particularly disturbed by this summary disposition of his argument.[27] The traditions do not evidence that he had reached settled convictions on religion. He started discussion, however, in the little community, and that was what he liked very much to do. The wife of the man who had burned the argument asked

Lincoln, "Do you really believe there isn't any future state?" And Lincoln, so Mrs. Hill told, replied. "Mrs. Hill, I'm afraid there isn't. It isn't a pleasant thing to think that when we die that is the last of us." Mrs. Hill thought this unsettled view of religion underwent a change after Lincoln moved to Springfield. Upon such incidents as this in his Salem days the controversialists, after Lincoln died, built varying opinions as to what he thought about religion.

Giants in Those Days

Frederick W. Lehmann of St. Louis, one-time solicitor general of the United States,[1] said of the remarkable company of men that followed the procession of the courts in Illinois when Lincoln rode the circuit:

> There were no great corporation lawyers, there was not any great corporation business, but there was that which would tend to develop and tend to refine more than the exigencies of mere commerce would do, and that was the discussion of matters involving the human heart and human interests. A friend of mine speaking at a banquet in Chicago had been assigned to speak of the old bar of Illinois. His father had kept a hotel at Bloomington, and he took as the subject of his discourse a page of his father's hotel register on the opening day of a term of the court at Bloomington. There was nothing exceptional in the occasion; there were none present except those who followed the judges in their regular ride of the circuit. Among the not more than fifteen men upon the register of that day were James McDougall [McDougal], who became United States senator from California; James Shields, general in two wars and senator from three states; E. D. Baker, a major general in the Civil War and senator from Oregon; Lyman Trumbull, United States senator, and author of the amendment of the constitution abolishing slavery; David Davis, a United States senator and justice of the Supreme Court; O. H. Browning, who became a cabinet officer; Stephen A. Douglas, a United States senator, and later candidate for the presidency, and Abraham Lincoln.[2] Such men as these in that small and undistinguished group of country lawyers.

How He Broke the Quorum

The grievance of Vandalia against Abraham Lincoln has been ameliorated by time. It was acute seventy-five years ago. At that time the residents of the ancient capital of Illinois did not smile as they gazed at the windows of the room in which the representatives sat. One window in particular became historic. It is there to-day, the sill about 14 feet from the ground. Three generations of Vandalians and thousands of visitors have stood in the courthouse yard and along the street, imagining how Lincoln looked as he hung by his long arms from that window sill, and how far his long legs had to drop to reach the ground.

Vandalia was the capital of Illinois a score of years.[1] The seat of government was moved from Kaskaskia because immigration was settling the Wabash and the Sangamon regions.[2] Vandalia was chosen by a commission under an act which made the new location the capital for twenty years. At the expiration of that period the Legislature was required to determine whether Vandalia or some other place should be the capital for the next two decades.

The old Illinois Statehouse of 1830 became Vandalia's Courthouse. It stands in about the same form of architecture it did three-quarters of a century ago, with the massive columns and the spacious portico, which were considered indispensable in capitol buildings. Stone sills have been substituted for the wooden beneath the windows. The interior has undergone some subdivision and modernizing to make a convenient county courthouse. But the old residents can still show where the two branches of the Legislature met that memorable winter when Vandalia was trying to hold the capital, and when Springfield was trying to capture it.

There were giants in those days. Sangamon County had sent to the Legislature that session two state senators and seven representatives. Springfield had picked her best politicians for the supreme effort at capital moving. The combined stature of the Sangamon delegation was 55 feet. "The long nine" as they were called, stood for Springfield's hopes. Lincoln furnished 6 feet and 4 inches of the aggregate. He was about 25 years old, comparatively unknown to the Springfield people who had made up the delegation. His election seems to have been a result not contemplated in the capital-moving programme. It came about largely by reason of a local issue in Sangamon. The northwest part of Sangamon, where Lincoln had been living for years while he clerked and surveyed and helped on the farms and pursued his reading and studying, desired to be cut off from Sangamon, and to be made a separate county.[3] The movement was popular along the lower Sangamon. Water lines were trade routes. These neighbors of Lincoln looked to the Illinois river for their commercial relations with the rest of the world. They had little interest in Springfield. Hugh Armstrong and Ned Potter were political leaders in that part of Sangamon. They got up a petition to have what is now Menard County cut off, took from Lincoln a pledge that he would make it his business to obtain this legislation if it was possible, and then ran him as their candidate. The settlements along the Sangamon in that part of the county were strongly Democratic, but on the issue of separation Lincoln, although a Whig, was elected and became one of "the long nine." He was new in politics. Before the fight for the capital ended he was the leader of "the long nine." The service he rendered Springfield paved the way for his removal to the new state capital and gave him his start in the practice of law.

In that Legislature were four men who became United States senators. Two of the participants in the capital fight became nominees of their parties for the presidency, and one the nominee of his party for the vice-presidency. One of them was a general in the Mexican war, and three of them were generals in the civil war. The struggle was a long drawn-out game in parliamentary tactics. Lincoln's quick wit and physical agility played the winning move.

Vandalia secured the first advantage in the choice of the presiding officer.[4] Springfield carried on a campaign of education. The location of Vandalia, on the bluffs of the Okaw, is picturesque. The Springfield missionaries insisted that Vandalia was unhealthy and urged removal from the river to the prairie on sanitary grounds. There had occurred several deaths of members of the Legislature while the capital was at Vandalia. The Springfield argument attributed the mortality to the location of the capital. This aroused much indignation among the Vandalians. It was not mentioned by later generations without some feeling. An old resident remarking upon the iniquity of the charge against the climate of Vandalia, said:

"The trouble was busthead whiskey. I've heard them tell that at Ebenezer Capp's store, which was the general resort of the legislators of that time, a barrel of liquor was kept with the head knocked out and a dipper hanging on a nail so that thirsty members could help themselves.[5] I have seen some of the old accounts of Ebenezer showing a bill of $80 for the entertainment of members of the Legislature a single evening."

The session wore away without Lincoln being able to do anything with the petition to create a new county. All other business except the question of capital location was held back. Springfield continued working for votes. On one pretext and another the settlement was postponed. The removal sentiment seemed to be gaining. Vandalia people watched closely the attendance; the purpose being to force a vote when Springfield absentees might give the advantage. One morning the presiding officer suddenly laid before the members the question of capital location for the next twenty years. The Vandalia members to a man were in their seats. Several supporters of Springfield had gone to their homes, but had not returned. A hurried canvass showed the Springfield members their side was in the minority. There was only one way to beat Vandalia, and that was to break the quorum. The morning roll call had shown barely a sufficient number to do business. The Springfield men looked toward the door and saw what the plan was. There stood the sergeant-at-arms with a force which made exit impossible. Clearly the Vandalia people meant to hold the minority until the vote which would prevent removal of the capital could be passed. Lincoln was on the floor to delay action. It was evident that postponement of the vote would be only temporary, and that Vandalia controlled the situation. Lincoln nodded to his friends, turned and hurried to the window. A wooden sill at that time projected beyond the wall. Before his purpose was understood and before the officers of the House could reach him Lincoln stepped out on the sill, let himself down until he hung by his hands and dropped to the ground. Several other Springfield men followed. Those who remained in their seats raised the point of no quorum. That blocked the proceedings. The quorum remained broken until the supporters of Springfield reached the capital. Near the close of the session the issue was forced and the Legislature voted to remove the capital to Springfield. Such is the Vandalia story of "How Lincoln broke the quorum." When one of the old residents tells the story the others smile and say, "Yes, that was the way it was."[6]

The Duel He Didn't Fight

The old resident of Alton takes the visitor to the river bank in front of the City Hall and, pointing across the Mississippi to an island heavily wooded with willows, informs him that there is the "Lincoln-Shields Park." On the

22d of September, 1842, the stage coaches rattled down the long valley through the bluffs of Alton and unloaded an extraordinary passenger list at the Piasa Hotel. The people sitting and standing on the wide double galleries of the three-story, hipped roof, wooden hotel, looked and wondered as James Shields, the state auditor, accompanied by General Whitesides and several other well-known Springfield Democrats, stepped down from one coach and went into the hotel.[1] They were amazed when another vehicle delivered Abraham Lincoln, the lawyer; E. H. Berryman [Merryman] and William Butler.[2] About the same time Elijah Lott and J. J. Hardin and several others, well-known public men of Illinois, drove into town.[3] There was no hilarity as these groups arrived and entered the hotel. When a bundle of the great, clumsy cavalry sabres of that day was lifted carefully down from the coach and carried in, the lookers-on began to exchange excited comments. All over town went the rumor that a duel was coming off. Leaders of politics in Alton, Whigs and Democrats, were taken into confidence by their respective friends from the state capital. "Jim" Shields had challenged "Abe" Lincoln and they were going across the river to fight on Missouri soil with "broadswords," the regulation cavalry sabres of the United States Army. Those were the years of "dragoons" in this country.

The two parties did not waste time at the hotel. It became evident through hurried conferences that friends who had learned of the intended meeting had followed with the hope of preventing it. Hardin and Lott were two of the would-be pacificators. Lincoln and Shields, with their seconds and surgeons, and with an attendant carrying the bundle of sabers, left the hotel and walked down Piasa street to the river bank, where a ferry with paddle wheels which were driven by horses was tied. But expeditious as the movement was, the Altonians, old and young, had anticipated it, without any aid from the modern telephone. The hotel galleries were crowded, the street was full of people, hundreds stood on the river bank. There was difficulty in limiting the number of passengers on the ferry boat. The town constable was taken along. Friends who were trying to fix up the trouble pressed their way on board. Some prominent Altonians who could not well be refused were permitted to go. One newspaper man secured passage. He was "Bill" Souther, afterward better known to the history of Illinois as William G. Souther.

The Southers were of the earliest New England stock. Their ancestor was the first secretary of the Plymouth colony. They had moved to Alton shortly before this time and "Bill" Souther was a printer on the *Alton Telegraph and Democratic Review*.[4] He afterward became an editor at Springfield. Other members of the Souther family moved from Alton to St. Louis and established one of the great metal industries of that city. "Bill" Souther saw it all, but his paper printed not one word from him.[5] Traditions and some recollections written long afterward have preserved the facts of this, one of the most remarkable meetings under the code on American soil. Thomas M. Hope, Samuel W. Buckmaster and Dr. English were the Alton men who joined in the movement to avert bloodshed and to prevent political scandal.[6]

As soon as the ferry reached the island Mr. Lincoln was taken in one direction and Mr. Shields in the other. They were given seats on logs and left to themselves while seconds and peacemakers discussed the situation. In a short time a serious defect in the proceedings on the part of Shields came to light. The challenge had been sent prematurely. The mistake is explained quite clearly in the Alton traditions. Lincoln had amused himself and had entertained the Whigs by writing funny letters to a Springfield paper about the Democrats, and signing his epistles "Aunt Rebecca." Mary Todd, who afterwards became Mrs. Lincoln, and Julia Jayne conspired to add to the gayety of the community by getting up an "Aunt Rebecca" letter of their own composition and sending it to the paper along with some verses which they signed "Cathleen." The letter which the girls wrote went outside of politics and contained a burlesque proposal of marriage to Auditor Shields. Now, the auditor, afterward a United States senator from three states, and a brave general of two wars, was a fiery young man. While Springfield laughed, Shields began an investigation. He demanded of the editor the real name of "Aunt Rebecca." The girls became frightened. Bunn,[7] the banker, went over to Mr. Lincoln's office and said:

"We've got into an awful fix!"

"What's the matter?" asked Lincoln.

"The girls have written some poetry on Shields," said Bunn. "Didn't you see it in the paper? Well, Shields says he won't stand it. What shall we do about it?"

"You go back and when you meet Shields tell him I wrote it," said Lincoln.[8]

Shields accepted this without verification and sent the challenge. The peace-makers, hurrying to Alton, brought the true story of the authorship. The facts came out in the conference on the island. Mr. Hope went to Shields and told him he would bring disgrace on the Democratic party if he persisted in a meeting under such circumstances. The seconds began the interchange of notes. Shields saw the error of proceeding further when he learned that Lincoln was not the writer. For an hour or more the writing and exchanging of notes went on. Meantime the population of Alton stood in a dense mass on the river bank looking across the channel and having a good view of all of the movements. "Bill" Souther, good reporter that he was, kept his eyes on the principals. He told that for some time after the landing Lincoln and Shields sat quietly on their logs. Lincoln said nothing, and Souther thought he looked serious. After awhile something happened, and Souther said that when he saw it he "nearly blew up." The bundle of sabres had been laid down near the log where Lincoln was sitting. Lincoln reached out and took up one of the weapons. He drew the blade slowly from the scabbard, and Souther said "it looked as long as a fence rail." Holding the blade by the back, Lincoln looked closely at the edge, and then, after the manner of one who has been grinding a scythe or a corn knife, he began to feel gingerly the edge with the ball of his thumb. By this time "Bill" Souther was tremendously interested. Holding the sabre by the handle, Lincoln stood up and looked about him. He evidently saw what he was looking for in a willow tree several feet away. Raising the mighty weapon with his long arm, Lincoln reached and clipped one of the topmost twigs of the willow. When he had thoroughly satisfied himself as to the efficiency of the broadsword he sat down. A few minutes later the correspondence was closed on terms "honorable to both parties."

As the boat put back to Alton the spectators on the bank were horrified to see lying prone upon the deck a figure covered with blood, while a well-known Altonian leaned over the figure plying a fan vigorously. Not until the boat was close in shore was it seen that the figure was a log of wood and that the "bloody" covering was a red flannel shirt. Wentworth dropped the fan, stood up and grinned.

Lincoln was 6 feet and 4 inches, with an arm length in proportion. Shields was 5 feet and 6 inches, chunky and short-limbed. "Bill" Souther marveled much over the willow tree exhibition, and wondered how long Shields could have stood up against such odds.

A very sober second thought came to Alton after the first excitement over the Shields-Lincoln duel. Alton had one of the best weekly newspapers in the valley. The paper was large. It contained much interesting matter. It was called the *Alton Telegraph and Democratic Review.* The presidential campaign was two years in the future, but this paper carried at the top of the editorial page "For President, Henry Clay."

The paper came out as usual on the 24th of September, two days after the duel. Not one word of what "Bill" Souther saw on the island was printed. Not the slightest reference was made to the affair, which was the talk of the town. The next issue, on the 1st of October, contained an editorial beginning just below the announcement for Henry Clay. The caption of this leader was "Our City," and then followed the rest of the sentence and the editor's condemnation, in his severest style, of the disgraceful affair and his demand for indictment and punishment. This editorial was not the least interesting incident of the duel:

OUR CITY

Was the theatre of an unusual scene of excitement during the last week, arising from the visit of two distinguished gentlemen of the City of Springfield, who, it was understood, had come here with a view of crossing the river to answer the "requisitions of the code of honor" by brutally attempting to assassinate each other in cold blood.

We recur to this matter with pain and the deepest regret. Both are, and have been for a long time, our personal friends. Both we have ever esteemed in all the private relations of life, and consequently regret that we consider an imperative sense of duty we owe to the public compels us to recur to the disgraceful and unfortunate occurrence at all. We, however, consider that these gentlemen have both violated the laws of the country and insist that neither their influence, their respectability nor their private worth should save them from being made amenable to those laws they have violated. Both of them are lawyers; both have been legislators of the State and aided in the construction of laws for the protection of society; both exercised no small influence in the community—all of which, in our estimation, aggravates, instead of mitigates, their offense. Why, therefore, they should be permitted to escape punishment while a friendless, penniless and obscure person for a much less offense, is hurried to the cells of our County Jail, forced through a trial with scarcely the forms of law, and finally immured within the dreary walls of a penitentiary, we are at a loss to conjecture. It is a partial and disreputable administration of justice which, though in accordance with the spirit of the age, we most solemnly protest against. Wealth, influence and rank can trample upon the laws with impunity, while poverty, scarcely permitted to utter a word in its defense, is charged with crime in our miscalled temples of justice.

Among the catalogue of crimes that disgraces the land, we look upon none to be more aggravated and less excusable than that of dueling. It is the calmest, most deliberate and malicious species of murder—a relic of the most cruel barbarism that ever disgraced the darkest periods of the world—and one which every principle of religion, virtue and good order loudly demands should be put a stop to. This can be done only by a firm and unwavering enforcement of the law in regard to dueling toward all those who so far forget the obligations they are under to society and the laws which protect them as to violate its provisions. And until this is done, until the civil authorities have the moral courage to discharge their duty and enforce the law in this respect, we may frequently expect to witness the same disgraceful scenes that were acted in our city last week.

Upon a former occasion, when under somewhat similar circumstances our city was visited, we called upon the attorney general to enforce the law and bring the offenders to justice. Bills of indictment were preferred against the guilty, but there the matter was permitted to rest unnoticed and unexamined. The offenders, in this instance, as in the former, committed the violation of the law in Springfield, and we again call upon Mr. Attorney General Lamborn to exercise a little of that zeal which he is continually putting into requisition against the less favored but no less guilty offenders, and bring all who have been concerned in the late attempt at assassination to justice.[9] Unless he does it he will prove himself unworthy [of] the high trust that has been reposed in him.

How the affair finally terminated, not having taken the trouble to inquire, we are unable to say. The friends of Mr. Shields and Mr. Lincoln claim it to have been settled upon terms alike honorable to both, notwithstanding the hundred rumors, many of which border upon the ridiculous, that are in circulation. We are rejoiced that both were permitted to return to the bosom of their friends, and trust that they will now consider, if they did not do it before, that rushing unprepared upon the untried scenes of eternity is a step too fearful in its consequences to be undertaken without preparation.

We are astonished to hear that large numbers of our fellow-citizens crossed the river to witness a scene of cold-blooded assassination between two of their fellow-beings. It was no less disgraceful than the conduct of those who were to have been the actors in the drama. Hereafter we hope the citizens of Springfield will select some other point to make public their intentions of crossing the Mississippi to take each other's life than Alton. Such visits can not but be attended not only with regret, but with unwelcome feelings, and the fewer we have the better.

We should have alluded to this matter last week but for our absence in court.

The *Alton Telegraph and Democratic Review* was published by J. A. Bailhache & Co. The editor was George T. M. Davis, twice mayor of Alton, who afterwards was editor of the *New Era* in St. Louis.[10] Col. Davis served gallantly in the Mexican war and afterwards was prominent in public life at Washington. His grandsons became business men in St. Louis.

Duff Armstrong and the "Almanac"

At a political gathering in the little county of Menard a citizen said to the reporter:

"Do you want to see the man who was tried for murder and cleared by Abe Lincoln and an almanac?"

Thus came about an acquaintance with Duff Armstrong. Duff was a stocky little man with suspicious gray eyes, [and] a bristling reddish-brown mustache. He was standing on the edge of the crowd, listening with a look of patience rather than of interest to the orator, when he was called; and he walked away to a more retired spot without any apparent regret at leaving the speaking. Upon the pole of a wagon which had brought a load of farmers to hear the tariff expounded, Duff and the reporter found seats. Duff Armstrong was a reticent man, and almost under protest he told the story of the camp-meeting row, of his mother's appeal to Lincoln to come and defend him, of Mr. Lincoln's response, of the trial and of the introduction of the almanac.

The man for whose death Duff Armstrong was tried was Press Metzgar.[1] A campmeeting ground was the scene of the tragedy. Metzgar had a refreshment stand on the outskirts of the camp. There he sold whiskey as well as other things. Duff Armstrong, then a young man of eighteen or twenty years, had had something to drink at the place. A dispute arose over his demand for more. Metzgar refused to serve him unless he paid in advance. Young Armstrong took this as a reflection on his solvency. A fight followed as usual under such circumstances. Metzgar received wounds from which he died. There were others besides Armstrong in the fight but he was held as the principal responsible for the killing. It was not a shooting as the writer of an historical novel described it [Edward Eggleston in *The Graysons: A Story of Abraham Lincoln* (1887)] but the death wounds were given with a slung-shot. Witnesses of the fight made it appear that Armstrong was the aggressor, and that he beat Metzgar savagely, being assisted by a friend. These witnesses testified that they saw the fight from a little distance, and gave a minute account of it. They claimed that although the time was ten o'clock at night the moon was shining brightly, and it was possible to see the combatants almost as plainly as in the daytime.

"Armstrong," the reporter asked, "tell about the killing. Were you guilty?"

Duff looked down at the ground, stuck his knife in the sod two or three times and said with emphasis:

"No, I wasn't. Press pitched into me without any cause. I had had a drink or two but I knew what I was about. Press was getting the best of me when I gave it to him."

Then Duff told how Mr. Lincoln was brought into the case. His mother was known to the whole community as "Aunt Hannah."[2] She had been kind to Lincoln when he lived in the Salem neighborhood. Local sentiment about the Metzgar affair was against Duff. The man who was indicted as accessory to the killing [James H. Norris] had been given eight years in the penitentiary. In her distress, Aunt Hannah wrote to Mr. Lincoln who, at that time, had been living in Springfield a dozen or more years. Mr. Lincoln wrote back at once that he would defend Duff. He told the family to get a change of venue to Beardstown, on account of local prejudice. This was done. He told Aunt Hannah to rely upon him. Nobody knew what the defense was to be, Duff said. But when the case came to trial, Lincoln was there. He questioned the witnesses for the prosecution very closely. There were two men who testified to the details of the fight. Mr. Lincoln had them describe the positions of the combatants when the slung-shot was used; and they made the circumstances look bad for Duff. Then he pressed them to know how they could testify so accurately and led them into positive statements about the moonlight. They described the moon as being about the height of the sun at ten in the morning. Mr. Lincoln returned to this again and again, and asked the witnesses if they were sure they were not mistaken. As often as the question was put, so often they committed themselves. They insisted the moon shining down upon the combatants made every movement plain to them.

Then the almanac was produced. Duff said that Mr. Lincoln passed it to the jurors and asked them to see what kind of a night it was on which the fight took place and to judge of the accuracy of such testimony as they had heard. The almanac was examined. It showed that there was no moonlight such as the witnesses had sworn. Mr. Lincoln followed up this advantage with a speech in which he tore the testimony to pieces. He argued the theory that Armstrong had been attacked and that he had only exerted himself in self defense. He told the jurors how he had held "little Duff" in his arms many a time at the Armstrong cabin while Aunt Hannah cooked the meals and he described the character of the little chap, as he had seen it forming, in such a way it seemed impossible to imagine him as making the assault described by these witnesses who had sworn there was a high moon when there was not. Duff was acquitted.

"He told mother that he wouldn't charge a cent for defending me, and he never did," said Armstrong, as the narrative drew to a conclusion.

"But, Duff, what about that almanac?" was asked. "Where did Lincoln get it? Was it bogus?"

The gray eyes flashed. The jack-knife was plunged into the grass roots as Armstrong blurted out in an indignant tone:

It's all foolishness to talk about Lincoln having had that almanac fixed up for the trial. He didn't do anything of the kind. I recollect that after he had been asking the witnesses about the moonlight, he suddenly called for an almanac. There wasn't any in the courtroom of the year he wanted. So he sent my cousin Jake out to find one. Jake went out, and after awhile he came back with the almanac. Lincoln turned to the night of the fight at the camp-meeting and it showed there wasn't any moon at all that night. Then he showed it to the jury. That was all there was to the almanac story. The almanac was all right. I tell you he was a mighty smart man and a good one, too.

Duff Armstrong sold his trotting horse, joined the church and became a respected citizen of Menard County. He was always ready to defend Lincoln against the tradition of having palmed off on the jury a doctored almanac. But the tradition lived through two or three generations. Uncle Johnny Potter who was an intimate friend of the Armstrongs laughed and shook his head when the reporter asked him what the real facts were about the almanac. Some Petersburg people who were at the campmeeting insisted that there was nearly a full moon that night in spite of Mr. Lincoln's documentary evidence. Old almanacs were overhauled. A search was made for the almanac that Mr. Lincoln had used in the courtroom, but it could not be found, so the tradition ran.

Twenty years ago a wealthy collector of Lincolniana was offered what was claimed to be the almanac with which Lincoln cleared Duff Armstrong.[3] The trial at Beardstown took place in 1858, a year and a half after the affray. With the almanac was furnished a number of affidavits of its genuineness as the one used by Lincoln. The collector had no doubt that he was buying the real thing and paid a good price for it but nothing like the $1,000 at which the almanac was valued.

Then J. McCan Davis, a lawyer of Springfield, took up the investigation of the mystery.[4] He traced the almanac back through several successive owners, who had bought it at increasing prices. He talked with lawyers who were connected with the case. He hunted up the surviving jurors. Mr. Davis said he obtained cumulative testimony which entirely satisfied him Mr. Lincoln did not use the almanac sold to the Chicago collector. He traced this "Lincoln almanac" to a man who claimed to have been a deputy sheriff at the time of the Armstrong trial. This man's story was that he found the almanac in a book he bought at a sale of the effects of a somewhat noted Illinoisan named Shaw.[5] A prolonged deadlock occurred in the Illinois Legislature over the senatorship when John A. Logan and William R. Morrison were the rival candidates.[6] A vacancy occurred in one of the state senatorial districts where the Democrats had a normal majority. By a shrewdly managed still hunt, which is a chapter in Illinois political history, the Republicans elected Shaw to the Legislature and Logan was chosen senator by this narrow margin. Shaw died and when his library was sold this "Lincoln almanac" was discovered. The man who found it claimed that Shaw had been in some way connected with the Armstrong case. And thus the chain was begun. The collector who bought the almanac was a shrewd business man. He had no doubt of the genuineness of his relic. The almanac was of the issue of 1854. By skillful penwork the "4" was changed into a "7", making the almanac appear to have been issued in 1857, the year of the affray at the campmeeting.

But Mr. Davis did more than trace the almanac to its source. He went to the best astronomical records and learned that Mr. Lincoln had no need to take any other year in order to obtain almanac evidence to impeach the witnesses against Duff Armstrong. The genuine almanac for 1857 showed there was no full moon on the night of the affray. There was a new moon, Mr. Davis said, about two days old. Instead of being in the east where the sun would be at ten o'clock in the morning, as the witnesses testified, it was, at the hour of the fight, almost setting in the west.

Brand of Whiskey Grant Drank

A Lincoln story which will never die is the reply the president made to the criticism of Grant's habits. Lincoln said: "He wished he knew what brand of whiskey Grant drank, in order that he might send some to the other generals." The story survives and is oft told, but the circumstances which prompted Lincoln's remark are not so well remembered. A St. Louis man brought that story from Washington. He was Henry T. Blow.[1] His home was in Carondelet, now the southern part of the city, but then a separate municipality. Mr. Blow knew Gen. Grant when he was Capt. Grant. The Blows and Dents were acquainted, socially.[2] Although a Virginian, Mr. Blow had become first an emancipationist, then a Republican and at the outbreak of the war an ardent Union man. Mr. Blow was sent to Venezuela as United States minister. He did not like Caracas and came back to Missouri within the year to run for Congress. After entering upon this campaign, in which he was successful, Mr. Blow visited Washington and talked with the president on conditions in the West. The battle of Pittsburg Landing, or Shiloh, had been fought and almost lost.[3] Three months before the country had dubbed the victor of Fort Donelson "Unconditional Surrender" Grant and had made a hero of him.[4] Now, with the disputed responsibility for the Pittsburg Landing surprise, there arose a mighty clamor on the part of certain newspapers and politicians, that Grant be superseded. Mr. Blow talked freely with the president. He told him what he had known of Grant before the war and mentioned the fear entertained by some persons that Grant drank too much to be intrusted with high command. Mr. Blow was a smooth spoken man, with sharp black eyes, quick to appreciate humor. He had been a very successful business man for years before he became interested in politics. He was rather below the average height. President Lincoln listened thoughtfully until Mr. Blow had expressed himself, and then asked with apparent seriousness what brand of whiskey Grant drank. Explaining why he sought the information, he used the language about sending some to the other generals, which has become historic. Mr. Blow lost no time in starting the story on its rounds. The criticism of Grant's habits seemed to lose its force rapidly, as the story was spread.[5]

Captain Henry King's Experience

Who wrote Lincoln's speeches? That was a topic of discussion in the days before the country had come to know the man. Frederick W. Lehmann of St. Louis said:

Captain Henry King, for many years the well-known editor of the *Globe-Democrat*, a master in the use of language, had an experience which is enlightening. As a young newspaper man he had been assigned to report a speech of Mr. Lincoln. He had been greatly impressed with it, with its sentiment and expression. He made his report of it in the best style that he could command, using the words that he thought Mr. Lincoln ought to have used. He submitted the report to Mr. Lincoln, very proud of his accomplishment. Mr. Lincoln looked over it carefully and said, "Young man, you made a most excellent report of this but I think you did not quite get my language here and there." And he went through with it, changing back the words to the simple Saxon that he had himself used so well. Captain King said he was unable to recognize what he had written.

"There were men older than Captain King who tried to edit what Mr. Lincoln said," continued Mr. Lehmann, "Seward looked over the manuscript of the inaugural address, criticised it with some severity, and actually insisted on striking out the last clause as too sentimental for such an occasion. Mr. Lincoln always had faith in himself, where principle or sentiment was involved, and that clause often attributed to Mr. Seward, but which he did not write, but considered inappropriate remained, in which Mr. Lincoln made this appeal to his southern friends, 'We are friends, we are not enemies. We must not be enemies. Though passion may have strained, it must not break the bonds of our affection. The mystic chords of memory stretching from every patriotic grave and battlefield to every loving heart and hearthstone throughout this broad land, will yet swell the music of the Union when touched, as they surely will be, by the better angels of our nature.'"[1]

The "New Party" of the Fifties

Ira Haworth was one of the young men Lincoln selected to help him start the Republican party. The Haworths were pioneers in Illinois. One of them founded the City of Danville. Another member of the family started Georgetown. Ira Haworth grew up in Vermilion County, where as a boy he came to know and reverence Lincoln.

The Haworths were Quakers. When past eighty Ira Haworth had the placid look which made him the youngest-appearing octogenarian in Kansas. The Lincolns back several generations were Quakers. Between Abraham Lincoln and Ira Haworth's father in the forties there was correspondence on the iniquity of slavery.[1]

"I first met Mr. Lincoln at the boarding house of old Mrs. Carruthers in Danville, where he was stopping while attending court," Mr. Haworth said. "Mr. Lincoln didn't show at first all that was in him. He grew on you as you came to know him well. He was very tall, 6 feet and 4 inches in his bare feet. While he looked spare, he was muscular. He weighed 180 pounds. His hair was very dark brown and of coarse growth. His eyes were hazel, tending to a grayish hue in color, deep set, with a serious expression, which changed quickly to a twinkle at the prospective introduction of a joke or a story. Lincoln's nose was of more than medium size and of the Roman type. The mouth was large and lips firm, of medium thickness. The features were rather large to attract admiration. Lincoln's demeanor was that of extreme simplicity, with deliberate movements, and a mixture of cordiality and dignity."

Mr. Haworth said that Lincoln had no desire to go back to Congress after the term to which he was elected in 1846 by the Whigs; that he found the surroundings in Washington uncongenial.[2] He believed from his association with Lincoln that the latter began early the consideration of plans for the formation of the Republican party.

"The campaign of 1848 was closely contested," Mr. Haworth said, as he described this evolution of a new party in Mr. Lincoln's thoughts. "Lincoln took an active part that year, presenting the issues that were agitating the public mind. He achieved reputation not only in Illinois, but in neighboring States, through that campaign. The result of the campaign was the election of the Whig ticket, but within four years the Whig party had gone to pieces. Lincoln wrote to me to call a caucus in my county to consider the advisability of forming a new party.[3] I sent out a call and six of us met to talk over the proposition. We organized, elected officers, talked over the plan and adjourned with the understanding we would get a larger attendance for the next meeting. The work of starting the new party was arduous. The anti-slavery party discouraged the movement by urging those who were then without a party to join their ranks. The old Democratic party was in possession of the government, so well fortified that the leaders were defiant and uncompromising toward the slavery agitators. Those Whigs who were originally in favor of slavery extension joined the Democratic oligarchy, which received them joyfully."

Mr. Haworth described graphically the slow, discouraging progress made in the first few months with the organization of the Republican party in Illinois. Lincoln, as Mr. Haworth recalled those earliest efforts, was the head of the movement. To increase the interest the few original Republicans in each locality invited ladies to their meetings and endeavored to interest them. This was a decided novelty in politics. Lincoln carried on correspondence with his young acquaintances in the various counties, and pressed the organization by counties preparatory to a convention to form the state organization. Haworth was so active that he was afterwards given the title of "father of the Republican party" in his part of the state.

The biographers of Lincoln say that he gave little attention to politics in the early fifties. They seem to have derived this impression from the contemporaries of Lincoln who were themselves prominent in politics of those years.[4] But Lincoln, by the testimony of Haworth and others, who were young and scarcely known outside of their school districts in 1852–55, was very busy in politics. He was creating the Republican party of Illinois even before the name had been chosen. He was writing letters to young men who had just reached their majorities, or were about coming of age. He was going out from Springfield to little gatherings at schoolhouses and country stores, talking about the new party and outlining what principles it should build upon. He was scribbling tentative platforms. The old Whig leaders at the state capital and at the county seats were wondering what was going to happen, and waiting for some kind of a revelation of public drift. Lincoln, paying little heed to the leaders, was making sentiment with the people, organizing from the neighborhood and the school district upward. He was constructing the Republican party of Illinois. The man who was so handy with the manual tools that he could turn out cabinet work was putting together mentally the framework of a political organization, which, at the end of the decade, was to sweep the country. And he was doing it so quietly and with so little surface indication that the politicians did not appreciate what was going on; they thought "Abe Lincoln" had gone out of politics and was giving his whole attention to law business. They never did realize, as did Haworth and the other young unknowns to whom Lincoln had given the commissions of local organizers, the constructive work done by him long before the Bloomington convention was called [in 1856] to form the state organization.[5] Two new ideas Lincoln developed in this political creation. He converted and encouraged young men new in politics. His suggestion brought into the little meetings and gave prominence to women. The great moral issue appealed strongly to the feminine sympathy. Women turned out in numbers to these school district meetings of the new party. They entered upon the new party movement with enthusiasm. They had become a great political force in Illinois when the campaign of 1860 opened. They rode in the processions. They sang, they laughed and they cried for "Old Abe." And their interest dated back to those neighborhood gatherings which Lincoln had promoted in the counties of Central Illinois when the politicians thought he was giving all of his time and thought to the practice of the law. Thus Abraham Lincoln and the people created the Republican party in Illinois. The political leaders came in when the ground swell lifted them, and many of them never did quite realize how it all came about.

In the vault of one of the Kansas City, Kan., banks were long preserved as articles of great value a cane and a gavel, made of black walnut, handsomely turned by the lathe and adorned with metal bands. The cane was inscribed across the top, "Ira Haworth," and around the head, "Abraham Lincoln," with the word, "presented."

"When Lincoln's nomination was announced to the convention at Chicago," said Mr. Haworth, who was one of the Illinois delegates, "two stalwart ushers entered the door of the wigwam bearing on their shoulders a unique design. They carried two walnut fence rails, decorated with the national colors. Supported by the rails was an immense shield, and on the shield was a large picture of Lincoln. As the men slowly made their way up the densely packed aisle, with excitement already high, the audience went wild. Hats were thrown in the air; handkerchiefs were waved vigorously. The shouts made a deafening roar. The people arose to their feet and cheered the progress of the rails and the picture through the wigwam until the design was placed upon the platform."

"The rails used on that occasion," said Mr. Haworth, "were made by Mr. Lincoln in what was then Sangamon County, when he was 20 or 21 years old. They had been in use twenty years on the farm of John Hanks, who was Lincoln's uncle [cousin], until they were transported to Chicago, to be used if Lincoln was nominated. While John Hanks produced the rails and testified to their genuineness, the idea of using them in connection with the nomination was not his. Richard J. Oglesby and Richard Yates originated the plan."[6]

Mr. Lincoln, Mr. Haworth thought, had no part in the rail incident. He was in the Republican movement because of the principles it represented. But Lincoln was too good a politician to discourage the use of the rails when he saw how his rail-splitting record appealed to the every-day human interest.

"Mr. Lincoln," said Mr. Haworth, "obtained one of these rails of his own splitting and had made for me the cane and gavel which you see. The two were sent to me at Danville by express. The next time I met Mr. Lincoln, I thanked him for the remembrance. He said he had sent me the cane thinking I would have use for it when I became old. 'You know,' he added, 'the wicked generally do live to become old.' Referring to the gavel Mr. Lincoln said to me: 'I want you to arrange to go into the campaign for me.' I said: 'Mr. Lincoln, I always thought you a man of judgment.' He replied: 'Take these relics and go before the people explaining how you got them.' Well, the result was I arranged matters so as to leave the farm and went through the counties in my part of the State holding meetings at the schoolhouses. A man went ahead of me making appointments, I drove from schoolhouse to schoolhouse, holding three or four meetings a day, showing the gavel and the cane and telling the story about them. In thirty days, by the account I kept, I attended over 100 of these meetings. In the same time, according to a record made, there were at these meetings over 1000 changes of Democrats to become Republicans. That was the way we swept Illinois for Lincoln."

After that campaign his neighbors in Vermilion called Mr. Haworth "the father of the Republican party." When he moved away in 1870 to settle in Kansas, a farewell meeting was held and Mr. Haworth was given the title of "the grandfather of the Republican party" of Vermilion.

"I suppose that now I am entitled to be called one of the great-grandfathers of the Republican party," said Mr. Haworth, with a twinkle of the eyes.

"I never saw Mr. Lincoln drink liquor," said Mr. Haworth. "In 1847 he made an address in which he declared his fidelity to the cause of temperance.[7] He then pledged his assistance to its advancement in all future time. His assertions attracted me and made a profound impression on me, for I had been a total abstainer. Having found a public man thinking as I did about temperance, for that was unusual in those days, I became attached to him in no ordinary degree. The two great subjects of slavery and temperance led to an acquaintance with Mr. Lincoln by which I gained much as a young man. Lincoln was at heart a Christian. 'Whatever appears to be God's will, I will do it,' he said to a deputation representing different religious denominations which called upon him at the White House in September, 1862. That was his guiding principle all of the time I knew him. His influence over younger men who made his acquaintance was very strong and for much good. I have always felt that I was more indebted to him for my course in life than to any other person. Mr. Lincoln had wonderful self command. He told me on one occasion that he had never in his life been really angry.[8] His motives in the work he did to create the Republican party in Illinois were of the highest character. Previous to the meeting of the convention in Chicago, which nominated him in 1860, Mr. Lincoln was approached by persons who wished to be empowered to promise certain things in return for support. Mr. Lincoln replied, 'No, gentlemen. I have not sought the nomination. Neither will I attempt to buy it with pledges. If I shall receive the nomination and be elected, I shall not go into office as the tool of this or that man, or the property of any faction or clique. The people's choice will be my choice. I desire that the result shall be to keep the jewel of liberty in freedom's family.'"[9]

A Drink and a Sunrise

In 1859 B. F. Smith was a young brakeman on the Illinois Central railroad. Afterward he became one of the pioneers in the development of berry culture in Southern Illinois. He made Centralia famous and was known far and wide as "Strawberry" Smith.[1] Still later he moved to Kansas, helped to bring Lawrence into high repute as a fruit center, and published for many years a horticultural journal. Mr. Smith had these personal experiences with the two most talked of men in Illinois.

Senator Douglas rode with me in the brakeman's seat from Odin to Champaign one trip in 1859. He offered me a cigar, which I refused, saying that I had never learned to smoke. At Champaign he took a seat in the second-class car, next to the baggage car. Here he emptied a small bottle of liquor into his stomach, or nearly all of it. When I went through the car at Chicago, he roused up before his friends came to meet him and offered me a drink from his bottle, which I refused. It seemed strange to him for a railway brakeman to refuse to smoke or drink with him.

The other distinguished man who rode with me about that time was Abraham Lincoln. He sat in my seat on the run from Champaign to Tolono. It was about sunrise. There was only one farm then between those two stations, in 1859, all green prairie. A beautiful sun rising attracted Mr. Lincoln. He called my attention to it,—the sun just rising over those beautiful, undulating hills. He wanted me to share with him his admiration of the scene. I admitted that it was lovely. I had been seeing the sun rise every morning between those two stations, as we left Chicago at 9 P.M., and hadn't thought much about the beauty of it. Mr. Lincoln had been asleep until we reached Champaign. Well the moral of this is in the contrast of the two great men. One of them tempted me by offering a cigar at the beginning of the journey and at the end of it desired me to help him empty a bottle of whiskey. The other called my attention to that beautiful sunrise over the virgin prairies of Illinois and invited me to share with him the impression of it.

The Eighth Circuit

"The eighth circuit" and Mr. Lincoln's relation to it perhaps have had no counterpart in the history of the American bar. When this circuit was organized in 1847 it had fourteen counties, occupying the central part of Illinois, around Bloomington. As immigration from the North and South flowed in, the circuit was gradually reduced in area. But even after his own County of Sangamon was taken out Lincoln continued to practice and to be a strong personality in the eighth circuit. In each county of the circuit two terms of court were held yearly. Mr. Lincoln spent about half of the year attending these terms of court away from his home.[1] He continued to attend the eighth circuit terms after other lawyers had ceased to "ride the circuit." He was present at the spring terms of the circuit in 1860, a few weeks before his nomination to be president. And after his election it was necessary for him to visit Bloomington to make disposition of the cases in which he was retained. This peculiarly close relationship of Mr. Lincoln to the eighth circuit bore upon his political as well as upon his legal career. In the eighth circuit he won the reputation of being the best jury lawyer of Illinois. In the eighth circuit he organized the movement which led to the Republican party of Illinois. In the eighth circuit he won the influential and steadfast political friends who brought about his nomination for the presidency.

To Bloomington for the terms of court in the early days of the eighth circuit came with Lincoln Edwin [Edward] D. Baker, afterward a United States senator from Oregon; James A. McDougal, afterward United States senator from California; Stephen A. Douglas, United States senator from Illinois; Judge Stephen T. Logan of Springfield; Daniel W. Voorhees, afterward a United States senator from Indiana; Judge Usher, afterward secretary of the interior; Norman H. Purple of Peoria, and T. Lyle Dickey of Ottawa, both of them afterward judges of the Supreme Court.[2] David Davis was ten years judge of this circuit.

The late Ezra M. Prince of Bloomington, secretary of the local Historical Society, in a paper written some time before his death, described the customs and conditions which prevailed.[3]

"The relations between the court, lawyers, jurors, of the eighth circuit was peculiar, one that has long since passed away," Mr. Prince said.

The court was rather a big family consultation, presided over by the judge, than a modern court. Judge Davis personally knew a large portion of the people in the circuit. The jurors were then selected by the sheriff. In McLean, and probably in the other counties, substantially the same jurors appeared from term to term, personal friends of Judge Davis, men of intelligence, sound judgment and integrity, whose verdicts rarely had to be set aside. Court week was a holiday for the people of the county. Political years there was always speaking at the courthouse, the parties using it on alternate nights. The people attended court to get the news, hear the speeches, listen to the exciting trials and to do their trading. The lawyers and many of the jurors, witnesses and suitors stopped at the same tavern.

There was a singular comradeship of these attendants upon the court. Without the court at all losing its dignity, there was a freedom and familiarity as of old friends and acquaintances meeting upon a public occasion, rather than the formality and dignity associated with the idea of a modern court. Often the judge's room, which sometimes was the only decent one in the tavern, was used evenings by the lawyers in their consultations, without regard to the presence of the judge.

In several, perhaps all, of these counties, young lawyers who desired to avail themselves of Mr. Lincoln's popularity and who, perhaps, distrusted their own ability to prepare and try cases in the circuit court, arranged with Mr. Lincoln to allow them to advertise him as their partner. So there was Lincoln & Jones in this county and Lincoln & Smith in that; but the partnership was limited simply to Lincoln trying Smith's and Jones' cases, if they had any, and dividing fees with them. The only law partners, in the proper acceptance of the term, Mr. Lincoln ever had were his Springfield partners, Col. John T. Stuart early in his legal career, and later William H. Herndon.[4] Mr. Herndon never traveled the circuit. Mr. Lincoln was always a great favorite with the court, lawyers and all attendants upon the court. The young and inexperienced received from him wise and timely advice and aid in their cases.

The trial of cases was conducted almost entirely by these leaders of the circuit. Mr. Lincoln being on one side or the other of nearly every case tried. A crowd always gathered around him, whether in court or elsewhere, expecting the never-failing "story." The evenings were a contest of wits, for the pioneer lawyer always had a good story ready. These customs of the circuit made its leaders warm friends.

After most of the other lawyers had given up the practice of riding the circuit Leonard Swett continued it with Mr. Lincoln.[5] There developed between Mr. Lincoln and Mr. Swett a very close personal relationship. Mr. Swett, some time before his death, speaking of this friendship, said: "It seems to me I have tried a thousand lawsuits with or against Lincoln and I have known him as intimately as I have known any man in my life."

Letters of Lincoln to Swett are in the possession of Bloomington friends. Some of them indicate the confidential character of the relations between the two, especially during the presidential campaign of 1860.

With Mr. Lincoln's practice in the eighth circuit developed the acquaintance and grew the leadership which made him the master spirit in the formation of the new political party. No other location than Bloomington for the anti-Nebraska convention, not even Springfield, would have made easier Mr. Lincoln's guiding influence. From Bloomington, among the men who had known him most intimately in the years of the eighth circuit practice, started the movement to make Mr. Lincoln the nominee of the Republicans in 1860.

Jesse W. Fell of Bloomington began the detail work of organizing Illinois for Lincoln immediately after the defeat for the United States Senate in 1858.[6] He had been secretary of the Republican committee during that 1858 campaign. The first serious, active movement in Mr. Lincoln's candidacy was this effort of Mr. Fell. A better man for the undertaking there was not in Illinois. Mr. Fell had come to Bloomington in 1832 from his Quaker home in Pennsylvania. Giving up the law and going into [the] development business, he had founded the first newspaper of Bloomington, [and] had been instrumental in the establishment of the first library. He had planted 13,000 trees in the suburb of Normal before there was a house built. He had secured the Normal University. He was the pioneer horticulturist and arboriculturist of Illinois. He gave the names of trees to twenty streets. Consistently refusing office for himself, Mr. Fell became the devoted admirer and friend of Mr. Lincoln. There was no limit to Mr. Fell's industry when he set about the accomplishment of a purpose. In his avowed intention to make Mr. Lincoln the nominee for president he had the constant advice and aid of two other residents of Bloomington, both lawyers, who became of national prominence. One of them was Leonard Swett, a tall, dark, handsome man from Maine, whose magnetic presence and melodious eloquence had won for him the title of "the advocate of the West." The third member of this Bloomington triumvirate, determined to secure the nomination of Mr. Lincoln, was the heavy weight, the man of great mental strength whose sagacity the whole state of Illinois respected, David Davis. No man in politics ever had more loyal, more intelligent attention to his interests than these three Bloomington men gave to the candidacy of Mr. Lincoln. Their attachment to him was something phenomenal in politics. With his newspaper instincts and his inclination to promotion methods, Mr. Fell put in early operation at Bloomington a press bureau. At the instance of Mr. Fell, and as the result of not a little persuasion, Mr. Lincoln sat down to a table in the courtroom at Bloomington and wrote the autobiography of himself which is historic.[7] He did this in 1859. The first use Mr. Fell made of the sketch was to send a copy of it to a paper in Pennsylvania, his early home, with the information that this was the man whose joint debates with Douglas had aroused the whole country, and the man whose name Illinois would, in all probability, present to the Republican Convention of 1860.[8]

"Strikingly characteristic of Mr. Lincoln was the closing sentence of that autobiography," the former vice-president, Adlai E. Stevenson, said.[9] When Mr. Lincoln had completed the story of his life, he wrote, "No other marks or brands recollected." This was the usual form in which legal notices of animals "strayed or stolen" concluded in the northern states, while it was not infrequently employed in the South, especially Kentucky, for a notice of a "runaway slave." This sentence was the touch of humor which Mr. Lincoln added to an account of his life, straightforward, definite and concise. Mr. Lincoln, his Bloomington friends said, neither made capital of his self-made qualities, nor did he conceal the hardships of his early life. He drew often on his experiences with his wonderful memory to illustrate some point or thought he wished to convey. He did not talk of himself for his sake any more than he told stories because they were good stories. If Mr. Fell hadn't been the extraordinarily persevering man that he was, it is probable the story of Lincoln by Lincoln, would never have been written. To show what kind of a man Jesse W. Fell was, it is said of him in Bloomington that when he went into the office of Judge Davis one day, that sturdy "prairie farmer" called out loud enough for all in the room to hear: "Oh, here's Fell again. No, I can't do it. But it's no use to talk; you'll have me before you go away." Mr. Fell pressed Mr. Lincoln for this account of himself until he got him seated at a desk in the courthouse and saw the story put on paper. Mr. Lincoln wrote this, as he did his letters and his law papers, with very few changes and with seldom a pause to think. He wasted no words.

I was born February 12, 1809, in Hardin County, Ky. My parents were both born in Virginia, of undistinguished families—second families, perhaps I should say. My mother, who died in my 10th year, was of a family of the name of Hanks, some of whom now reside in Adams and others in Macon County, Ill. My paternal grandfather, Abraham Lincoln, emigrated from Rockingham County, Va., to Kentucky about 1781 or 1782, where a year or two later he was killed by the Indians, not in battle, but by stealth, when he was laboring to open a farm in the forest.[10] His ancestors, who were Quakers, went to Virginia from Berks County, Pa. An effort to identify them with the New England family of the same name ended in nothing more definite than a similarity of Christian names in both families, such as Enoch, Levi, Mordecai, Solomon, Abraham, and the like.

My father, at the death of his father, was but 6 years of age, and he grew up literally without education. He removed from Kentucky to what is now Spencer County, Ind., in my 8th year. We reached our new home about the time the state came into the Union. It was a wild region, with many bears and other wild animals still in the woods. There I grew up. There were some schools, so-called, but no qualification was ever required of a teacher beyond readin', writin' and cipherin' to the rule of three. If a straggler supposed to understand Latin happened to sojourn in the neighborhood he was looked upon as a wizard. There was absolutely nothing to incite ambition for education. Of course, when I came of age I did not know much. Still, somehow, I could read, write and cipher to the rule of three, but that was all. I have not been to school since. The little advance I now have upon this store of education I have picked up from time to time under the pressure of necessity.

I was raised to farm work, which I continued till I was 22. At 21 I came to Illinois, Macon County. Then I got to New Salem, at that time in Sangamon, now in Menard County, where I remained a year as a sort of clerk in a store.

Then came the Blackhawk war; and I was elected a captain of volunteers, a success which gave me more pleasure than any I have had since. I went the campaign, was elated, ran for the Legislature the same year (1832), and was beaten—the only time I ever have been beaten by the people. The next and three succeeding biennial elections I was elected to the Legislature. I was not a candidate afterward. During this legislative period I had studied law, and removed to Springfield to practice it. In 1846 I was once elected to the lower house of Congress. Was not a candidate for re-election. From 1849 to 1854, both inclusive, practiced law more assiduously than ever before. Always a Whig in politics, and generally on the Whig electoral tickets, making active canvasses. I was losing interest in politics when the repeal of the Missouri compromise aroused me again. What I have done since then is pretty well known.

If any personal description of me is thought desirable it may be said I am, in height, 6 feet 4 inches, nearly; lean in flesh, weighing on an average 180 pounds; dark complexion, with coarse black hair and gray eyes. No other marks or brands recollected.[11]

This, the only story of his life Lincoln wrote, he dated "Springfield, December 20, 1859," although the late Lawrence Weldon, Jesse W. Fell and the other Bloomington friends of Mr. Lincoln said it was written in the courthouse under the circumstances already given.[12] Mr. Lincoln signed the story, just as he always did his name, "A. Lincoln." Mr. Fell, with the wisdom of a newspaper man, preserved and published the story exactly as Mr. Lincoln wrote it.

The Bloomington Convention

The cradle of the Republican party of Illinois was Major's Hall, in Bloomington. It rocked May 29, 1856. The hand that rocked the cradle was Abraham Lincoln's.

The third story, which was the hall, was removed. There was apprehension about the strength of the walls after the place had served as the principal auditorium for two generations of Bloomingtonians. Major's Hall became Bloomington's historic landmark. The convention which created the Republican party of Illinois is Bloomington's political glory.

Painstakingly and intelligently Bloomington assembled, through an historical society of more than ordinary virility, the record and the recollections of that convention. More than the surface proceedings—more than the public events—have been sought. The hitherto unwritten history has been secured. And thus has come to be known the part that Abraham Lincoln performed in the planning for the convention, in the framing of the platform, in the selection of the candidates. Before they passed away the men who participated in the Bloomington convention and in the conferences and consultations preceding it gave to the Bloomington Historical Society their recollections. The results are revelations of Lincoln's active agency in the shaping of the Republican party movement in Illinois that add much to hitherto printed history.

The Bloomington convention grew directly out of a conference of fifteen editors and Abraham Lincoln at Decatur on Washington's birthday. Those who attended the conference called it the "Free State Editorial Convention." The call for the conference read:

"All editors in Illinois opposed to the Nebraska bill are requested to meet in convention at Decatur on the 22d of February next, for the purpose of making arrangements for the organization of the anti-Nebraska forces in this state for the coming contest."

The number of papers in Illinois which editorially indorsed the movement was twenty-five. The editors of this number of papers signed the call for the meeting. A heavy snowfall the night before cut down the attendance to fifteen. Mr. Lincoln arrived from Springfield. Paul Selby of the *Morgan Journal*,[1] who presided, was authority for this statement:

"The most important work of the convention was transacted through the medium of the committee on resolutions. Mr. Lincoln was in conference with the committee during the day, and there is reason to believe that the platform reported through Dr. Charles H. Ray of the *Chicago Tribune*, the chairman, adopted by the convention, bears the stamp of Mr. Lincoln's peculiar intellect."[2]

The editors recommended that a delegate convention be held at Bloomington on Thursday, the 29th day of May. They appointed a state central committee to make arrangements for the convention. Most of those named as the committee accepted the appointment. The committee met and issued the call, which announced:

"A state convention of the anti-Nebraska party in Illinois will be held in the City of Bloomington, on Thursday, the 29th day of May, 1856, for the purpose of choosing candidates for state officers, appointing delegates to the national convention, and transacting such other business as may properly come before the body."

Ten members of the committee which the fifteen editors had selected, signed this call. One of them was Mr. Lincoln's law partner. Another was Richard J. Oglesby, the young lawyer, who had presided at the banquet given to the editors at Decatur. Purposely the editors did not give a name to the new party. On the day that this conference was in progress at Decatur there was in session at Pittsburg a gathering of men from several states assembled "for the purpose of perfecting the national organization, and providing for a national delegate convention of the Republican party to nominate candidates for the presidency and vice-presidency." Not only did Illinois editors refrain from calling their movement "Republican," but the committee they appointed to bring into existence the Bloomington convention, did not make use of the word "Republican." Abraham Lincoln was a wise politician. The time had not come to name the child.

Mr. Lincoln did not participate openly in the proceedings of the editorial convention, but he was near at hand for consultation. In the evening a local committee of Decatur citizens—Isaac C. Pugh, who was afterwards colonel of the Forty-first Illinois; Dr. H. C. Johns, who died about fifteen years ago, and Maj. E. O. Smith—provided a banquet to the editors and several invited guests at the Cassell House.[3] Mr. Lincoln attended the banquet and made the principal address.[4] One of the editors, who preceded Mr. Lincoln on the list of speakers, suggested him as the most available man to be nominated for governor and to head the new party in Illinois. Mr. Lincoln, replying to the reference to himself, argued that it would be much better to nominate an anti-Nebraska Democrat for governor rather than an old-line Whig like himself, pointing out that it would be necessary for the new movement to draw from the Democrats and to widen the breach between the Douglas following and the Democrats who were opposed to Douglas in his Kansas-Nebraska policy. He concluded this argument with the opinion that William H. Bissell was the most available man for the nomination.[5] This advice the convention at Bloomington carried out, the successful result being just as Mr. Lincoln predicted to the editors at Decatur.

When Mr. Lincoln was presented by the toastmaster at the editors' banquet he began with an apology for his presence at a meeting of editors, speaking of himself as an interloper, and then he said he was reminded of an incident. He did not say that he was giving a personal experience of his own, but the editors surmised as much and were greatly amused. Mr. Lincoln said the man of whom he was speaking possessed features the ladies could not call handsome. This man, while riding through the woods, met a lady on horseback. He turned out of the path and waited for the lady to pass. The lady stopped and looked at the man a few moments and said:

"Well, for land sake, you are the homeliest man I ever saw."

"Yes, madam," the man replied; "but I can't help it."

"No, I suppose not," the lady said; "but you might stay at home."

Mr. Lincoln, when the editors stopped laughing, said that he felt on this occasion—a banquet to editors—with propriety he might have stayed at home.

The banquet address of Mr. Lincoln to the editors at Decatur was not the most important act of his in connection with the gathering. His influence and his suggestion carried the conference past a crisis of far[-]reaching consequence. In the conclusions at Decatur none contributed more to the success of the new party movement than the declaration against Knownothingism. The German immigration into Illinois had been large. A conspicuous figure in the Decatur conference was George Schneider, editor of the *Illinois Staats-Zeitung*.[6] He was put upon the committee on resolutions. Mr. Schneider considered it vital to have embodied in the resolutions a condemnation of the native American spirit. What occurred is given in his own words:

The revolution of 1848 and 1849 in Germany sent thousands of the best men of Germany—men of culture and strong will power—to this country, who were placed at the heads of many of the best newspapers printed in the German language. All of these papers opposed the extension of slavery in the new territories. Illinois was in advance of all of them, and nearly every paper published in the German language in the state opposed the Nebraska bill. But here appeared most suddenly a black cloud on the political horizon which seemed to assume such proportions and threatening form as to not only dampen the fire of the new movement against slavery, but to drive the Germans from the ranks of the party to be formed. I entered the Decatur conference with a resolution in opposition to this movement, and I had resolved to fight with all my might and win or go down, and with me, perhaps, the new party. My friend, Paul Selby, placed me on the committee on resolutions, and I helped to form a platform containing a paragraph against the proscriptive doctrine of the so-called American party. This portion of the platform raised a storm of opposition, and, in utter despair, I proposed submitting it to Mr. Lincoln and to abide by his decision. Mr. Lincoln, after carefully reading the paragraph, made the following comment:

"Gentlemen, the resolution introduced by Mr. Schneider is nothing new. It is already contained in the Declaration of Independence, and you can not form a new party on proscriptive principles.

This declaration of Mr. Lincoln's saved the resolution, and, in fact, helped to establish the new party on the most liberal democratic basis. It was adopted at the Bloomington convention and next at the great, and the first, national Republican convention at Philadelphia on the 18th of June, 1856.[7]

According to Mr. Schneider, the Illinois delegation performed an important part at Philadelphia in securing the proper committee on resolutions, and in obtaining the declaration which Mr. Lincoln saved at the Decatur conference.

"The great majority of the Germans in all the states of the North, and even in some portions of the South, entered the new party. The new light which appeared at Decatur and Bloomington spread its rays over the whole of the United States, and so the regeneration of the Union and the downfall of slavery dated from Bloomington."

Mr. Schneider, from his personal knowledge of the circumstances just given, and from his observation as a newspaper editor, always held that Lincoln had more to do with the creation and establishment of the Republican party on lines which insured its success than historians have credited to him.

Of Lincoln's activity in the organization of the new party movement before the convention of 1856 at Bloomington, J. O. Cunningham of Urbana was a witness.[8] Mr. Cunningham accompanied Mr. Lincoln to Bloomington. Mr. Lincoln had been engaged at the courts in Vermilion and Champaign counties before the convention. The way to reach Bloomington in those days was to take what is now the Wabash to Decatur and thence go by way of the Illinois Central to Bloomington. This was Mr. Cunningham's recollection of the journey:

A number of delegates and others from the eastern counties, mostly young men, happened on the train with Mr. Lincoln, and arrived at Decatur about the middle of the afternoon. No train going to Bloomington until the next morning made it necessary that we spend the afternoon and night at Decatur. The afternoon was spent by Mr. Lincoln in sauntering about the town and talking of his early experiences there twenty-five years before. After awhile he proposed going to the woods, then a little way south or southwest of the village, in the Sangamon bottoms. His proposition was assented to, and all went to the timber. A convenient log by the side of the road, in a patch of brush, afforded seats for the company, where the time was spent listening to the playful and familiar talks of Mr. Lincoln. We spent the night at the Cassell House, and early the next day a train took us to Bloomington. Mr. Lincoln was very solicitous to meet some of his old Whig friends from Southern Illinois, whom he hoped to enlist in the new political movement, and searched the train to find such. He was gratified in finding some one from the south, and it is believed that Jesse K. Dubois, afterward nominated at Bloomington as auditor of public accounts, was the man.[9]

Mr. Cunningham described the conditions in Bloomington when Mr. Lincoln and the delegates from the eastern counties arrived there in the morning:

> Many were awaiting the opening of the convention, largely from the northern counties. There existed a most intense feeling upon the situation in Kansas. Lawrence had been sacked but recently by the ruffianly pro-slavery men, and the greatest outrages perpetrated upon free-state settlers.[10] The evening previous to the convention Gov. Reeder arrived in town, having been driven a fugitive from the territory he had been commissioned to govern, and spoke to a large crowd of listeners in the street from an upper piazza.[11] He was moderate and not denunciatory in his address, only delineating the violence he had witnessed and suffered. Dispatches were received and often publicly read to the crowd at the hotels and on the streets, and excitement over the situation was intense. No convention in Illinois ever assembled under circumstances of greater excitement.[12]

The success of Mr. Lincoln's policy in the planning of the new party movement was seen when the convention assembled at Bloomington and it developed that the majority of the delegates present had voted four years previously for the Democratic nominee for president, Franklin Pierce. When the state ticket, which the convention nominated with a rush, was analyzed, it was found that the majority of the nominees had voted with the Democratic party four years previously. One of the nominees on the electoral ticket put forth at Bloomington, Mr. Ferry, had been on the Democratic electoral ticket in 1852.[13] Mr. Lincoln steadfastly refused to permit his name to be used for the head of the state ticket. When his nomination was suggested he met it with this opinion: "I wish to say why I should not be a candidate. If I should be chosen the Democrats would say, 'It was nothing more than an attempt to resurrect the dead body of the old Whig party.' I would secure the vote of that party and no more, and our defeat would follow as a matter of course. But I can suggest a name that will secure not only the old Whig vote, but enough anti-Nebraska Democrats to give us the victory. That name is Col. William H. Bissell." This suggestion was made to the editors at Decatur on the 22d of February. The editors went home and advocated the nomination of Bissell with such force that when the Bloomington convention met no other name was considered, and Bissell was nominated with a great demonstration. In fact, one enthusiastic delegate shouted that Bissell had already been nominated by the people of Illinois and the convention should only reaffirm.

The declaration which Mr. Lincoln's advice secured at Decatur, which was adopted at Bloomington and also in the Philadelphia convention with such tremendous influence upon the Germans was this:

"That the spirit of our institution[s], as well as the constitution of our country, guarantees the liberty of conscience as well as political freedom and that we will proscribe no one, by legislation or otherwise, on account of religious opinions, or in consequence of place of birth."

The call for the anti-Nebraska convention at Bloomington provided for 226 delegates. Some counties sent more than their apportionment, owing to the interest the people felt in the new party movement. Thirty counties, mostly in "Egypt," were wholly unrepresented.[14] The roll call contained 270 names. Bloomington was filled with excited people. The proceedings were regular, but there were no contests and no ballots. The business was transacted as rapidly as a mass meeting of one mind might have disposed of it. The programme had been arranged, and the master spirit in the arrangement was Abraham Lincoln. But Mr. Lincoln did not make himself conspicuous. He was on the committee which selected the ticket. He had already fixed the platform, practically, at a small conference held in Springfield between the Decatur editorial conference and the Bloomington convention. He followed the other speakers in a statement of the opportunity and of the demand for this new party movement. That statement or address was the keynote of the Republican campaign in Illinois that year. It was the historic "Lost Speech"—lost because no report was made of it. Two short sessions in one day comprised the whole of the convention of a party which was not at the time formally named. Yet that party in November following had grown to such proportions that it elected its entire state ticket with pluralities of from 3000 to 20,000. It polled 96,000 votes for the presidential electors, within 9000 of a plurality. Since that election in 1856 Illinois has had but two governors who were not Republicans. Before that election Illinois had been in the hands of the Democrats thirty years. Abraham Lincoln builded the new party well. In the Bloomington convention were Democrats, Whigs and Abolitionists. The idea which Mr. Lincoln had made dominant in the editors' platform at Decatur was opposition to extension of slavery into the new territories. Upon that platform all of these elements could and did stand. A lifelong Democrat, John M. Palmer, was elected president of the convention.[15] A Democrat and a hero of the Mexican war, Col. Bissell, was put at the head of the state ticket. Mr.

Lincoln planned and perfected this union of widely diverse elements as no other man could have done. His "Lost Speech" welded together these elements.[16]

The speaker who preceded Mr. Lincoln was John S. Emory [James S. Emery], the Kansas editor.[17] He was from Lawrence, the scene of the latest troubles. Years afterwards he wrote a graphic narrative of what he saw and heard in Bloomington that day. This account is preserved in the papers of the Historical Society of Bloomington.[18] It reads:

I got off the cars May 28 at Bloomington. I learned that the Missouri river was shut up to free-state men and that there was to be next day a big gathering of the friends of freedom from all parts of Illinois. I here met Gov. Reeder, who had got out of the territory in the disguise of an Irish hodcarrier. My own home city had been sacked and our newspaper office demolished, and the types and printing presses thrown into the raging Kaw. The morrow came in that Illinois town, May 29, 1856. It was full of excited men. The very air was surcharged with disturbing forces; men of all parties met face to face on the streets, in the overflowing hotels and about the depot platforms of the incoming trains. Anti-Nebraska Democrats, Free Soil Whigs and Abolitionists were all there. The large hall—Major's—was crowded almost to suffocation as I took my seat on one of the rear benches. [Orville Hickman] Browning was called for, and he enjoined upon us to "ever remember that slavery itself was one of the compromises of the constitution and was sacredly protected by the supreme law." After this—rather a cold dose to be administered just at that time—Owen Lovejoy appeared and carried the convention by a storm of eloquent invective and terrific oratory.[19] The committee on resolutions was named. While this was being done I felt a touch on my shoulder, when a young man said he was going to call me out to talk while the committee was out, adding that I must stop when I saw the committee come in, as it had been arranged to have "a fellow up here from Springfield, Abe Lincoln, make a speech. He is the best stump speaker in Sangamon County." This young man was Joseph Medill, a reporter for the *Chicago Tribune*, as I afterwards learned.[20]

I had no thought of anything of this kind, but of course I was prepared to tell the story of bleeding Kansas there in the house of her friends. But two things bothered me all of the time I was speaking. One was, I was trying to pick out Mr. Lincoln, who was to follow me, for he was "the best stump speaker in Sangamon County," as I had been told, and I had never heard his name before. Added to this was the watching I kept up at the hall door of the committee room to be sure to have a fitting end to my rather discursive talk on that now notable occasion, when the party standing for free Kansas was born in Illinois and when a great man appeared as the champion of the Kansas cause. As I stepped aside Mr. Lincoln was called for from all sides. I then for the first time, and the last, fixed my eyes on the great president. I thought he was not dressed very neatly and that his gait in walking up to the platform was sort of swinging. His hair was rather rough and the stoop of his shoulders was noticeable. But what took me most was his intense serious look. He at once held his big audience and handled it like the master he was before the people, pleading in a great and just cause. To-day that "Lost Speech" looks quite conservative. His chief contention all through it was that Kansas must come in free, not slave. He said he did not want to meddle with slavery where it existed and that he was in favor of a reasonable fugitive slave law. I do not now recall how long he spoke. None of us did, I judge. He was at his best, and the mad insolence of the slave power as at that time exhibited before the country furnished plenty of material for his unsparing logic to effectually deal with before a popular audience. Men that day were hardly able to take the true gauge of Mr. Lincoln. He had not yet been recognized as a great man, and so we were not a little puzzled to know where his power came from. He was not eloquent like Phillips,[21] nor could he electrify an audience like Lovejoy, but he could beat them both in the deep and lasting convictions he left on the minds of all who chanced, as I did, to listen to him in those dark days.

The impression the "Lost Speech" made upon J. O. Cunningham, who had accompanied Mr. Lincoln to Bloomington from Urbana, was expressed by him in these words:

During the absence of the committees many speeches were made. Lovejoy (and, by the way, Lovejoy was the greatest stump speaker I ever listened to), Browning, Cook, Williams, Arnold and among them one Emory, a free state refugee from Kansas, all made speeches.[22] Owing to the inflamed condition of public sentiment, the audience had become much wrought up in feeling when it came the turn of Mr. Lincoln to make his speech, the so-called "Lost Speech." I thought it then a great speech, and I now think it a great speech, one of the greatest and certainly one of the wisest ever delivered by him. Instead of adding, as he might have done, and as most speakers would have done, to the bitterness and exasperation his audience felt, as a manner of gaining control of the audience, he mildly and kindly reproved the appeal to warlike measures invoked by some who had spoken before him, and before entering upon the delivery of his great arraignment of the slavery question and of the opposing party, he said: "I'll tell you what we will do; we'll wait until November, and then shoot paper ballots at them." This expression, with his conciliatory and wise declarations, greatly quieted the convention and prepared the members for the well-considered platform which was afterward presented and adopted.

Gen. Thomas J. Henderson, close friend of Owen Lovejoy, long a member of Congress from Lovejoy's district,[23] said of the culminating scene of the convention: .

The great speech of the convention was the speech of Abraham Lincoln. His speech was of such wonderful eloquence and power that it fairly electrified the members of the convention and everybody who heard it. It was a great speech in what he said, in the burning eloquence of his words and in the manner in which he delivered it. If ever a speech was inspired in this world, it has always seemed to me that that speech of Mr. Lincoln's was. It aroused the convention and all who heard it and sympathized with the speaker to the highest pitch of enthusiasm. I have never heard any other speech that had such great power and influence over those to whom it was addressed. I have always believed it to have been the greatest speech Mr. Lincoln ever made and the greatest speech to which I ever listened. I can never forget that speech, and especially that part of it where, after repelling with great power and earnestness the charge of disunion made against the anti-Nebraska party, he stood as if on tiptoe, his tall form erect, his long arms extended, his face fairly radiant with the flush of excitement, and, as if addressing those preferring the charge of disunionism, he slowly, but earnestly and impressively, said:

"We do not intend to dissolve the Union, nor do we intend to let you dissolve it."

As he uttered these memorable and, I may say, prophetic words, the members of the convention and everybody present rose as one man to their feet and there was a universal burst of applause, repeated over and over again, so that it was some moments before Mr. Lincoln could proceed with his speech.

While the Bloomington convention refrained from the use of the name of the Republican party, it left no doubt as to the purposes of the party organization then formed. It did more than select a full delegation to the National Republican Convention, which was to meet in Philadelphia the following month. The Ohio Republican Convention was in session that 29th day of May, at Columbus. Judge Owen T. Reeves, a resident of Bloomington, was then a young lawyer recently from Ohio.[24] With Jesse W. Fell, Mr. Lincoln's zealous friend in Bloomington, Mr. Reeves prepared a telegram of greeting from the Bloomington convention to the Ohio Republican Convention, and John M. Palmer, the president of the Bloomington convention, signed it. This greeting breathed the spirit of Lincoln to combine all of the elements opposed to extension of slavery in the new party. It read:

"The delegates of the free men of Illinois in convention assembled send greetings to the free men of Ohio. William H. Bissell is nominated for governor with the enthusiastic acclaim of the most enthusiastic delegate convention ever assembled in Illinois. Gov. Reeder and Mrs. Robinson are here.[25] They have appeared before the public and have been greeted by the wildest applause. The excitement consequent upon the latest outrages at Lawrence, Kan., is sweeping like wildfire over the land."

The Ohio convention responded, addressing the telegram to "the Republican Convention of Illinois," and the telegram was read to the convention in Major's Hall, "amid great applause." Mrs. Robinson was the wife of the first governor, by election, of Kansas, "a most beautiful and interesting lady." She came to Bloomington on the train with the delegation from Springfield, having fled from Kansas to Illinois for protection. Her husband had been elected under the Free Soil constitution. He had been indicted on a charge of treason and had been imprisoned. Andrew W. Reeder was the first territorial governor. He had been elected to Congress by the Free Soil party, had been indicted with Gov. Robinson, but had escaped in disguise.

A committee of the Historical Society of Bloomington, headed by George Perrin Davis, son of Mr. Lincoln's long-time intimate friend Judge David Davis, made every effort that could be suggested to find the "Lost Speech."[26] John G. Nicolay, who was Lincoln's secretary and who, in collaboration with John Hay, wrote and compiled the standard history of Abraham Lincoln, was a delegate to the Bloomington convention.[27] At that time he was editor and proprietor of the *Pike County Free Press*, published at Pittsfield. He signed the call for the editors' conference at Decatur, his paper being one of the first to indorse the suggestion of Paul Selby's *Morgan Journal* of Jacksonville that such a conference should be held. Mr. Nicolay heard the "Lost Speech," but he took no notes of it. He wrote to the Bloomington committee that the address "held the audience in such rapt attention that the reporters dropped their pencils and forgot their work." Lincoln not only did not write out that speech, but he had no memoranda. So much the committee discovered. The conclusion of the committee was that "the speech is still lost."

Lawyer, Philosopher, Statesman

"There was this true of all of his law practice," said Judge Owen T. Reeves of Bloomington, who saw much of Mr. Lincoln in the courts for fifteen years preceding the election to the presidency.

He impressed court and jurymen with his absolute sincerity. Mr. Lincoln assisted the state's attorney in prosecuting a fellow [Isaac Wyant] who had killed somebody. Leonard Swett defended the man, and acquitted him on the ground of insanity. It was reported afterward that Mr. Lincoln said that was the last time he would ever assist in the prosecution of a man charged with murder. That was about 1857.[1] If Mr. Lincoln was employed in a case where the other side had little or nothing to it he would ridicule it out of court. I remember a man named Phil Miller brought a law suit to recover damages from a man named Jones in a neighborhood above here. The claim for damages was based on an alleged assault. Phil went on the stand and described the assault as having been a kind of running fight over a ten-acre field. Mr. Lincoln pressed the plaintiff on the cross-examination, bringing out fully all of the details of the affair, which had not resulted in serious injury. When the time came to argue the case to the jury Mr. Lincoln dwelt on the evidence and said: "I submit to you that for a fight which spread all over a ten-acre field this is about the smallest crop of a ten-acre fight you gentlemen ever saw."

"When Mr. Lincoln was busy preparing a plea or writing an instruction, nothing going on around him interested him or attracted his notice," Judge Reeves said.

This complete mental abstraction is described by others who knew Mr. Lincoln. J. H. Burnham of Bloomington, when he was editor of the *Pentagraph*, had a personal experience.[2] He sat in the courtroom one day waiting for Mr. Lincoln to make a speech.

"Whenever I looked toward him," said Mr. Burnham, "he was apparently gazing abstractedly into my own eyes. Again and again I felt his eyes upon me with an expression as if I reminded him of some one whom he had once known. Yet I really believed his mental abstraction was so great that he actually had no idea of my presence."

The reverse of this complete abstraction of mind was true of Mr. Lincoln. When Mr. Lincoln observed or directed his mind toward anybody or anything he received and retained impressions which were amazingly definite and lasting.

"Mr. Lincoln," Judge Reeves said, "had a faculty of asking questions of persons who had knowledge of any particular subject which would draw out all of the knowledge they possessed. He would sit in the hotel when not engaged in court and carry on conversations with various persons. He would describe the pioneer days and the pioneer practice with great detail. But I never knew him to tell a story unless it was in illustration of something else which had come up in the conversation. I never heard him tell a story which wasn't apposite and illustrative."

"The simplicity of Mr. Lincoln," Judge Reeves said, "was well illustrated by an incident which occurred, while he was addressing a jury in the old courthouse here. Mr. Lincoln had a way of getting close to the jurors and gesticulating with his long arms over their heads. On this occasion a button fastening his suspenders to the trousers gave way while Mr. Lincoln was in the midst of the argument. Mr. Lincoln stopped, looked down to see what had happened, and then said to the jury, 'Excuse me, gentlemen, for a moment while I fix my tackling.' He walked over to the woodbox by the stove—we burned wood in those days—picked up a splinter, took out his pocket knife and sharpened the splinter to a good point. He thrust the wooden pin through the cloth and fastened the suspenders over the ends. Returning to the jury, he said, 'Now, gentlemen, I am ready to go on.'"

An incident illustrative of Mr. Lincoln's philosophic observation, Judge Reeves told in these words:

> I remember one morning coming up town rather earlier than usual, and meeting Mr. Lincoln in front of the courthouse. Mr. Lincoln had his hands behind him, as usual. I greeted him and asked him if he had been taking a walk.
>
> "Yes," he said, "and I came past Gridley's new house and looked it over."
>
> Gen. Asahel Gridley was just finishing a handsome residence, much superior to other homes here.[3] I remarked that Gen. Gridley was going to have a fine house.
>
> "Yes, it is a fine house," Mr. Lincoln said, "but I was thinking it isn't the best thing for a man in a town like Bloomington to build a house so much better than his neighbors."[4]

"I think it was the most impressive speech I ever heard Lincoln make," Judge Reeves said, as he leaned back in his chair, recalling to memory Lincoln and the "Lost Speech." Judge Reeves was a young lawyer, recently from Ohio when the convention, which formed the Republican party of Illinois, filled Major's Hall to the doors in May, 1856. He helped Jesse W. Fell prepare the greeting to the Republican Convention of Ohio, which was meeting that day in Columbus to organize the new party in that state.

"Mr. Lincoln was wonderfully stirred," Judge Reeves continued. "Usually he was very calm and deliberate in his manner. That so-called 'Lost Speech' seemed to show that he had outlined in his mind the whole movement for a new party. He started out with a historical sketch of the legislation on the subject of slavery, beginning away back. He referred to the ordinance of 1787 when all of this northwest territory was dedicated to freedom.[5] Then he took up the Missouri compromise. Step by step he came down to the conditions then existing. My recollection is that the speech lasted about an hour. Lincoln's speech, as I remember, was the last one made. There were Whigs, Democrats and Abolitionists in the convention, which was the result of a conference of editors of anti-Nebraska bill papers held in Decatur the 22d of February, Washington's birthday. Paul Selby of Jacksonville was the leading spirit of that editorial conference. The Nebraska bill was, in effect, the repeal of the Missouri compromise of 1820, fixing the bounds of slavery.[6] General concessions were made to secure harmony in the Major's Hall convention. The main idea was opposition to extension of slavery into the new territories. There were nearly 300 delegates in the convention. They appointed a state delegation to represent Illinois in the Philadelphia Convention, which nominated Fremont and Dayton."[7]

"I first met Mr. Lincoln in March, 1855," Judge Reeves continued. "The impression Mr. Lincoln made upon me then was that he was a man out of the ordinary among men of distinction. I said to Judge David Davis, who took very kindly to young lawyers and was inclined to assist them,—I said to him the impression I had formed of Mr. Lincoln was that he was an extraordinary man.

"'H-m! h-m! That is a very correct impression you have obtained,' was the answer Judge Davis gave me to my comment. I think that Judge Davis understood Mr. Lincoln better than a great many did. I don't believe any man ever lived who had more perfect knowledge of human nature than had Mr. Lincoln. Mr. Lincoln knew the feelings, the prejudices, the motives of common humanity. He was a master of all that. No man had more sympathy for the common people than Mr. Lincoln had."

The judgment of his Bloomington friends Mr. Lincoln consulted, but he was not always guided by the advice he sought upon political matters.

Judge Reeves recalled the circumstances of a visit and a consultation Mr. Lincoln had at Bloomington in 1858.

"The first joint debate was at Ottawa," he said. "There Senator Douglas propounded certain questions to Mr. Lincoln to answer at the next debate at Freeport. Mr. Lincoln came to Bloomington to see Judge Davis. Norman B. Judd came down from Chicago for the conference.[8] There was a consultation on these questions offered by Senator Douglas. The answers to the questions were submitted by Mr. Lincoln and considered. Then Mr. Lincoln said, 'I'm going to propound certain questions to Douglas.' He told them the questions he intended to ask. They remonstrated and said that Douglas would answer Lincoln's questions in a certain manner and that the result would be the defeat of Lincoln for the Senate. Mr. Lincoln insisted that he would ask the questions, and said: 'If he answers as you say he will and it defeats me for the Senate, it will forever defeat him for the presidency.' And that was the result. Mr. Lincoln foresaw that if Douglas made the answers which Judge Davis, Mr. Judd and the others predicted Douglas would make, those answers would forever debar Douglas from getting the support of the Southern Democrats."

Wells H. Blodgett's Experience

Of Lincoln's friendliness toward younger men, there are many recollections. Wells H. Blodgett of St. Louis, had his experience.[1] He was reading law about 1859 in Mr. Judd's Chicago office where Mr. Lincoln visited whenever he came to the city. An acquaintance sprang up between them. Mr. Lincoln called the young student by his middle name "Howard" and gave him advice. Shortly before the nomination in 1860, Mr. Lincoln was in the office. As he passed out the door one of the law partners called after him:

"Are you coming up to the convention, Lincoln?"

Mr. Lincoln closed the door as if he had not heard or did not intend to answer. But he opened it again and, looking in, said:

"Well, I don't know. I am not quite enough of a candidate to stay away and too much of a candidate to come."

After the nomination Mr. Lincoln attended a public reception in Chicago. Among those who shook hands with the nominee, was Henry W. Blodgett, afterwards the judge.

"Where is Howard?" Mr. Lincoln asked.

The brother replied that he was at the office.

"Tell him to come over," said Mr. Lincoln.

Wells H. Blodgett went to the hotel. There stood Mr. Lincoln, a striking figure in his first swallow tail suit and with kid gloves, once white but now grimy from much hand shaking. Mr. Blodgett fell in line, when he had nearly reached Mr. Lincoln, the latter held up his hands and said with mock seriousness:

"Howard, look at this. Never go into politics."

Mr. Blodgett said that Lincoln never in his life wore a starched collar; that pictures depicting him wearing such a collar were untrue. Lincoln always wore a shirt with a loose collar, which turned outward from his neck, plainly showing a prominent Adam's apple.

The Rock Island Bridge, said Col. Blodgett, was the first built across the Mississippi river. Owners of river boats sued to have the draw bridge removed, as obstructing river navigation. Their contention was that a boat needed a space 150 feet wide in order to pass up and down the river. Lincoln, who was on the side of the owners of the bridge, argued that the interests of the people wishing to cross the river were equal to those of people going up or down the stream. He said Lincoln argued that at intersecting streets it was necessary for people going one way to wait until people going at right angles had passed, turn and turn about. Arguing along this line, Lincoln contended that boats and people crossing the river should take turns while the draw bridge closed and opened. He said the bridge offered ample space for boats to go up and down and that the river people were straining a point when they wanted space enough to turn about right at the bridge. Lincoln and his associate lawyers won the case and there is to-day a bridge across the river at Rock Island.[2]

A Land Case

Lincoln's popular fame as a lawyer rested largely upon his convincing power before juries. But Lincoln was more than a jury lawyer. He could untangle the knotty land cases in a way to make those who listened wonder why they had thought them difficult. J. H. Cheney of Bloomington went down to Springfield in August, 1853, to consult Lincoln about the title to a piece of land.[1]

"I took with me," he said, "a letter of introduction from Gen. Asahel Gridley of this place. Upon entering his office I found Lincoln in and presented my letter from Gen. Gridley. I stated my case. Lincoln gave close attention, asking a few questions as I proceeded. When I had finished he talked about the case, making every point clear, so clear, indeed, that I wondered why I had come. It seemed as if every one should have understood the case. Lincoln concluded by saying that I had a good title to the land, and then asked, 'What did old Grid. say about it?' I told him Gen. Gridley had said he thought my title a good one, but advised me to see him. Lincoln's comment was, 'Grid. is a good lawyer, and he knows.' I then asked him how much he charged for the advice. He said, 'I reckon if it is worth anything, it is worth $10,' which I paid."

Mr. Cheney had an experience with Mr. Lincoln later in which Mr. Lincoln was the seeker after information, and Mr. Cheney was the giver.

"It was in the spring of 1859," said Mr. Cheney, "when Mr. Lincoln was in Bloomington attending court. Mr. Lincoln was stopping at the Pike House. He was in the office reading what I took to be a comic almanac. He seemed to be very much amused and would frequently chuckle to himself. A gentleman and I were discussing difference in weights of cattle before and after being fed and watered. Mr. Lincoln addressed us and said: 'Gentlemen, I have been interested in your conversation. As a matter of information, I would like to know what the shrinkage would be.'"

The "Lost Speech"

Upon Judge Reuben M. Benjamin the "Lost Speech" of Mr. Lincoln made a peculiar impression.[1]

"It so happened," said Judge Benjamin, sitting at a table in the law library of Bloomington, "that I was in Washington when the anti-Nebraska [Kansas-Nebraska] bill passed the Senate in May, 1854. I had been principal of Hopkins Academy at Old Hadley in Massachusetts the winter before, and had gone down to Washington on a week's vacation. I went up to the capitol at 12 o'clock, midday, and I didn't leave until the bill passed at 1 o'clock in the morning. I heard Douglas, Lewis Cass, who was the only one to read what he had to say; Sumner, Gwinn [Gwin], Butler of South Carolina, Mason, Seward, Chase and Benjamin of Louisiana, speak upon the measure.[2] One thing impressed me so vividly that I can now see Sumner turning toward James Murray Mason and pointing to him, as he quoted what George Mason, his grandfather, had said about slavery when he refused to sign the constitution because it contained the clause deferring the abolition of the slave trade.[3] I came to Bloomington in April, 1856, and entered the law office of Asahel Gridley and John H. Wickhizer [Wickizer].[4] On the wall of the office I read in Mr. Wickhizer's handwriting: 'The repeal of the Missouri compromise will lead to civil war.' With the recollection of that debate in the Senate I listened to Mr. Lincoln as he made his speech in Major's Hall on May 29, 1856. The "Lost Speech" was not rhetorical, but it was logical. Every now and then Mr. Lincoln threw in some statement like a blow from a sledgehammer. Familiar as I felt that I was with the subject of extension of slavery in the territories, from having heard the leaders of both parties discuss it exhaustively at that session in the Senate, I was deeply moved by the manner in which Mr. Lincoln handled the subject."

"That Major's Hall convention," continued Judge Benjamin, "was made up of elements which differed widely, but which were agreed upon opposition to extension of slavery in the territories. And that was the issue to which Mr. Lincoln addressed himself as the one great question before the country. There were Democrats, like Palmer, who presided over the convention; Abolitionists, like Owen Lovejoy and John Wentworth, and Whigs, like David Davis and O. H. Browning.[5] The main thing in the resolutions, as in Mr. Lincoln's speech, was opposition to extension of slavery into the territories. The 'Lost Speech' of Mr. Lincoln at the Bloomington convention was very like what is known as the Peoria speech, delivered in 1854."

A few months after that Bloomington convention, Judge Benjamin had his first personal relationship with Mr. Lincoln. Judge Benjamin, after a study of the Illinois practice, felt prepared for admission to the bar. He made application. Mr. Lincoln was appointed by the court to examine him. He made some inquiries and wrote out the certificate. The part of the examination which left the strongest impression on the applicant's mind was that Mr. Lincoln omitted what was quite customary in those days with examining committees—extension of courtesy by the candidate at another kind of bar. There was no treating when Judge Benjamin was passed by Abraham Lincoln.

When He Was Just "Bob's Father"

"The only time I ever saw Abraham Lincoln was when I was a student at Exeter, N.H.," said Professor Marshall S. Snow when he was dean of Washington University.[1] "His son, Robert, was at Phillips-Exeter Academy, in the class above me.[2] Mr. Lincoln had been in New York the last of February, 1860, to make his famous Cooper Union speech against slavery.[3] He came up to Exeter to see 'Bob' for a day. I think, perhaps, he came to stay over Sunday. The national campaign was opening, but the presidential nominations had not been made. We had heard of Lincoln, had read his speeches, but I don't think any of us regarded him as likely to be the Republican nominee for president. We were for Seward, the New York candidate. As soon as it was known Mr. Lincoln was coming to Exeter, the Republican committee arranged for a meeting at the Town Hall, which would hold about 800 people. There were about ninety of us boys in the academy at that time. 'Bob' was a neat-looking boy, a favorite in the school and popular with the girls of Exeter. We turned out in full force for the meeting to see 'Bob's' father as well as to hear Mr. Lincoln speak. Prof. Wentworth presided."

The dean smiled, as he recalled the scene of forty-nine years before and described it.

Judge Underwood of Virginia had accompanied Mr. Lincoln to Exeter.[4] He was a short man. Mr. Lincoln was very tall. They came on the stage together. The contrast was striking. When they sat down Judge Underwood's feet did not reach the floor. Mr. Lincoln's legs were so long he had trouble in disposing of them and twisted them about under the chair to get them out of the way. One of the boys leaned over and whispered: "Look here! Don't you feel kind of sorry for Bob?" We didn't laugh. We were sympathetic for "Bob" because his father didn't make a better appearance. The girls whispered to each other, "Isn't it too bad Bob's got such a homely father."

The dean mused a few moments, calling back that impression of his student days, and went on:

Mr. Lincoln wore no beard at that time. His hair was mussed up. It stood in all directions. As he sat there in the chair he looked as if he was ready to fall to pieces and didn't care if he did. Judge Underwood spoke first, for about twenty minutes. We didn't pay much attention to him. We were looking at Mr. Lincoln. I remember I thought at the time he was the most melancholy man I had ever seen. When Mr. Lincoln was introduced he got up slowly until he stood there as straight as an arrow in that long black coat. He hadn't spoken ten minutes until everybody was carried away. We forgot all about his looks. Exeter was full of people of culture. It was a place to which people moved when they retired from active life. The audience was one of educated, cultivated people. I never heard such applause in that hall as Mr. Lincoln received that night. He spoke nearly an hour. There was no coarseness, no uncouthness of speech or manner. Every part fitted into the whole argument perfectly. As I recall it, the Exeter speech followed closely the lines of the Cooper Union address, which was on slavery. I suppose it had been carefully prepared. I know it captured all of us. When the meeting closed we went up to the platform and shook hands with Mr. Lincoln, telling him how proud we were to have the honor of meeting Bob's father. Mr. Lincoln has always been to me the man I saw and heard in that town hall at Exeter.

They Heard the Final Debate

Sixteen years and three weeks after he had shocked the dignity and aroused the resentment of that community by the farcical meeting with "Jim" Shields, Abraham Lincoln came to Alton to meet Stephen A. Douglas in the greatest debate duel in American history. A tablet in bronze on the front of the city hall records the date, October 15, 1858, and the site of the platform. This city hall had been built not long before. It presented the appearance of new brick walls then. Now it is smart looking under the latest of several coats of paint. The wooden platform built against the wall overlooked a large plaza. Two old residents of Alton who attended the meeting brought back vividly the scene of that October day. One of them, J. H. Yager [Yeager], stood well back in the throng, thrilled by the words of Lincoln and not missing the comments and the manner of those about him.[1] The other, Henry Guest McPike, was one of the twenty-five leaders of the two parties who sat on the platform.[2]

Better natural vantage for public speaking it would be difficult to find. To the eastward the surface rises like an amphitheater, but with easy slope. Southwestward the open space extended to the bank of the Mississippi.

From his seat on the platform, while waiting for Douglas to fill his time, Lincoln could look across to the island where he had sat on a log awaiting for seconds and peacemakers to determine whether the code required him to match broadswords with Shields. Quite possibly the funny duel never occurred to Lincoln, for this was the last of the seven joint debates, and, according to the local traditions, Lincoln spoke with a great deal of spirit. He drove home his points with more than his ordinary energy. He seemed to realize that this was his last chance at Douglas and that he was completing the record.

"We could almost feel the war coming," said Mr. Yager, as he recalled the degree in which Lincoln aroused the Republicans that day. The plaza is paved with brick now. It is the center from which the seven Altons radiate up the valleys and over the hills, occupying a considerable section of Illinois.

"There was no paving then," described Mr. Yager. "The surface was rougher than it is there. Over on that corner was the Presbyterian Church. Lincoln and Douglas were escorted from the hotel by committees made up of the principal men of the two parties in Alton. Douglas came down that street from the old Alton House on the arm of Judge H. W. Billings.[3] R. P. Tansey, who afterwards moved to St. Louis and became president of the Merchants' Exchange, was with them, and Thomas Dimmock, the editor.[4] Zephaniah B. Joab [Job] was another member of the Democratic committee that day.[5] Some of those who escorted Lincoln to the stand were Gov. Cyrus Edwards, Col. F. S. Rutherford, George T. Brown, Henry G. McPike and John M. Pearson of Godfrey."[6]

Mr. Yager and Mr. McPike agreed that, notwithstanding the immensity of the gathering, one of the greatest ever seen in Alton, the speakers could be heard distinctly. They recalled the not altogether encouraging figure Lincoln presented as he sat on the platform awaiting his turn to speak, and they also remembered that Lincoln filled the Republicans with enthusiasm before he had spoken half a dozen sentences. "We felt so good we didn't know what to do," said Mr. Yager.

"A house divided against itself can not stand. I believe this government can not endure permanently half slave and half free," was the declaration which Lincoln had made at the beginning of his campaign, and which he had reiterated at the several debates. Douglas had, as often, artfully interpreted this declaration to mean that Lincoln was for disunion.

"In other words," Douglas would say when his turn came, "Mr. Lincoln asserts as a fundamental principle of this government that there must be uniformity in the laws and domestic institutions of each and all the States of the Union; and he therefore invites all the nonslaveholding States to band together, organize as one body and make war upon slavery in Kentucky, upon slavery in Virginia, upon the Carolinas, upon slavery in all the slaveholding States in this Union, and to persevere in that war until it is exterminated."

The meeting at Alton was to close the joint debates. Douglas, by the terms of the agreement, had the advantage of closing at this final meeting. Standing where he looked over the heads of his hearers to valleys and hills of a slave State, Lincoln seemed to feel that he must make his position plain beyond all misinterpretation. He repeated to his Alton hearers his "A house divided against itself cannot stand." He quoted from Douglas the meaning attributed by the latter to the declaration, and then, raising his voice above the usual tone, and with impassioned manner, Lincoln exclaimed:

"He knows that is false!"

Recalling the words and the startling effect upon the listeners, Mr. Yager said the Republicans raised a mighty shout. The Democrats looked at one another in amazement. One of them, an eminently respectable citizen of Alton, who stood beside Mr. Yager, burst out with: "That is disgraceful. I won't stay here any longer." He made his way out of the crowd.

Three brothers, John Hitt, Emory Hitt and Robert R. Hitt, made hay one summer forenoon of the year 1856, on the farm near Mount Morris. They knocked off in time to reach Oregon, in Ogle County, for the speaking that afternoon.[7] Abraham Lincoln, John Wentworth and Martin P. Sweet addressed an audience of 3000 people.[8]

"Their object was to induce the people to vote for Fremont and Dayton," said John Hitt. "The people of Ogle County were convinced that day. I thought that Mr. Lincoln was an intellectual giant. From that day I trusted him. I never doubted that he was a safe leader."

Two years after that summer afternoon at Oregon, in Ogle County, Robert R. Hitt was the stenographer who traveled with Mr. Lincoln and made the reports of the joint debates between Lincoln and Douglas. John Hitt was present at the last of the debates which was held at Alton. He recalled an interesting incident of that day, which showed Robert R. Hitt to advantage as a diplomat, in which capacity he afterward obtained much distinction, before his district placed him in Congress for life.

"I was one of a party that dined with Mr. and Mrs. Lincoln that day," said John Hitt, "at the leading hotel in Alton. When the debate was over Judge Trumbull led the party to the table. He occupied a seat at the head of the table. To his right Mr. and Mrs. Lincoln were seated. Horace White, who accompanied Mr. Lincoln as the representative of the State Central Committee; Robert R. Hitt, my brother, who was shorthand reporter for the *Tribune*, and I, were seated opposite Mr. and Mrs. Lincoln.[9] Senator Trumbull conversed with Mr. Lincoln in an animated manner. In reply to the question of Mr. Lincoln whether any impression had been made upon the people, Mr. Trumbull said that public meetings in Madison County were usually undemonstrative, but he thought a favorable impression had been made. Mrs. Lincoln invited Mr. White and my brother Robert to go with Mr. Lincoln and herself to Springfield and rest for the coming week. My brother Robert thanked Mrs. Lincoln for her courtesy, and said, in declining, that he would never call at her house until she lived in the White House. She laughed at the suggestion, and said there was not much prospect of such a residence very soon."

[The account of Hitt's remarks in the *Globe-Democrat* for 31 January 1909 contained the following additional comments, which did not appear in Stevens's *A Reporter's Lincoln*: "I saw Mr. Lincoln very frequently in the United States courts in Chicago during the years of 1858 and 1859," Mr. Hitt continued. "I never lost an opportunity of listening to him when he tried cases. He was the most interesting man I ever saw. I saw him occasionally in the office of Scates, McAllister & Jewett, where I was a student. He would come in to settle a bill of exceptions. His good nature was a striking characteristic. He was extremely liberal to the opposing counsel."]

Impressions Made on J. S. Ewing

James S. Ewing of the Bloomington bar, boy and man, through a decade and a half saw much of Abraham Lincoln.[1] His father owned and conducted the National Hotel in Bloomington as early as 1844 and 1845. That was the only substantial tavern in town, the place where everybody came to talk politics. There Mr. Lincoln, John T. Stewart [Stuart] and the other lawyers stopped when they came to Bloomington to attend the terms of court twice a year. Judge Samuel H. Treat was the circuit judge at that early period.[2]

"Mr. Lincoln stayed at my father's house," Mr. Ewing said. "I was a boy of 9. I knew Mr. Lincoln as a boy of that age might. I was in the habit of going to the trials to hear the speeches. It was in the nature of a show. Of course I heard Mr. Lincoln try a great many cases. I knew him all through my boyhood and to the time I was admitted to the bar. One of the most interesting things I recall was a declaration I heard Mr. Lincoln make about temperance. I was present in a room in the National Hotel when Senator Stephen A. Douglas was in Bloomington in 1854 for the purpose of making a speech. Mr. Lincoln came in to call on Mr. Douglas. There was a bottle of whiskey on the sideboard or mantel. Mr. Douglas said, after the greetings:

"'Lincoln, won't you have something?'

"'No,' said Mr. Lincoln, 'I guess not.'

"'What,' said Mr. Douglas, 'do you belong to a temperance society?'

"'No,' replied Mr. Lincoln, 'I don't belong to any temperance society, but I am temperate in this that I don't drink anything.'"

"I believe," said Mr. Ewing, "that that was a statement of his exact position on the temperance question. He didn't drink anything himself, but he didn't try to dictate what any one else should do."

"Mr. Lincoln was fond of children. He took notice of boys, remembered them and spoke to them by name," Mr. Ewing said. "My father was a Democrat. He nicknamed one of my brothers 'Democrat' and he went by that name for years. Mr. Lincoln was a Whig; one day he commented on the nickname 'Democrat.' He said to my other brother, the one next to me, 'I'll call you Whig.' That was Judge W. G. Ewing of Chicago.[3] He never has gotten rid of the name Mr. Lincoln bestowed upon him. He has always been called by his friends, 'Whig Ewing,' instead of William Ewing. I only mention this to show the attention Mr. Lincoln paid to boys, even to the extent of knowing their names. Although Mr. Lincoln and my father differed in politics, they were great friends."

[The account of Ewing's remarks in the *Globe-Democrat* for 31 January 1909 contained the following additional comments, which did not appear in Stevens's *A Reporter's Lincoln*: "There are two things I want to say, in the way of correcting false impressions some people have about Mr. Lincoln," Mr. Ewing continued. "Mr. Lincoln wasn't a sloven and he wasn't a buffoon. People didn't call him 'Abe.' Nobody addressed him except as 'Mr. Lincoln.' Judge Davis, Leonard Swett, John T. Stuart, Judge Treat— all of those distinguished men invariably spoke to him and of him as 'Mr. Lincoln' long before he was nominated for president. People here would not have thought of calling Mr. Lincoln 'Abe' any more than they would have called Mr. Webster 'Dan' or Mr. Clay 'Harry.' It was 'Mr. Clay,' 'Mr. Lincoln.' There are some men who always command respect, and

Abraham Lincoln was one of them. Mr. Lincoln dressed as did the average lawyer in those days."

"Mr. Lincoln wasn't a story teller in the sense that people tell stories for the thing in the story," Mr. Ewing went on. "I doubt if he ever told a story just because it was a story. If he told an anecdote it was to illustrate or make more clear some point he wanted to impress. He had a marvelous aptitude for that—to illustrate the idea he wanted to convey. He was a wonderful observer, and he had rare ability to remember what he had seen and heard and read, so as to apply such information to the point of anything that struck him as ludicrous. But he never swapped stories. I never heard him tell a story or heard of him telling a story unless it was to illustrate something. He applied this wonderful gift of observation and appreciation of humor to a situation or to something which somebody had said."

"Mr. Lincoln," explained Mr. Ewing, "was a great orator in the best sense—in that he had something to say, said it well, and said it with great earnestness. His manner was very direct. Mr. Lincoln paid no attention to the manner. He was not a declaimer. [Owen] Lovejoy had the art of the declaimer; he was also a great orator. Mr. Lincoln's voice was not of much range; it would always command the attention of an audience or of a jury. Court was held here twice a year. The semiannual visits of the lawyers from Springfield, especially Mr. Lincoln's visits, were looked forward to by everybody with interest. 'Court week' was a great time. People came to town and attended the court trials. A lawyer trying cases, making speeches and telling stories was of very great interest. It was the custom during 'court week' to have at least one political speech from each party. Mr. Lincoln was always called upon to make the speech for the Whigs. There was never a 'court week' when he did not address the people of the county some night in the old brick Courthouse."

Mr. Ewing thinks it is a mistake to hold that Mr. Lincoln became great after he was elected to the presidency. In other words, the greatness of Mr. Lincoln did not depend upon the official honor with which he was clothed.

"Mr. Lincoln was always a great man in this," said Mr. Ewing, "that he was equipped by nature and education to meet great obligations and to conduct great enterprises. He was always the talker, always the man to whom other men listened, and at the time of which I am speaking there were other great men who attended court here who afterward became governors, senators and judges and acquired national fame."

Vividly the recollection of the last time he saw Mr. Lincoln comes back to Mr. Ewing:

"There were a number of years," he said, "when I was at college, and afterwards at law school in Philadelphia, when I did not see Mr. Lincoln. In the fall or early winter of 1860, Mr. Lincoln having been elected to the presidency, came to Bloomington to dispose of some law business before going to Washington. I met him on the sidewalk in front of the old brick Courthouse, and after I shook hands with him he said, 'Well, you have gotten to be a lawyer; let me give you some advice: Be a lawyer and keep out of politics.' I said: 'Mr. President, your example is more fascinating than your precept.' He said: 'Oh, that is an accident.' He went into the Courthouse, and that was the last time I ever saw Mr. Lincoln."]

How Jesse W. Fell Started the Debaters

As early as September, 1854, the suggestion of a joint debate between Lincoln and Douglas was made. It came from that indefatigable and zealous friend of Mr. Lincoln, the pioneer who made Bloomington "the Evergreen City," Jesse W. Fell. The circumstances of Mr. Fell's first effort to bring the two great speakers together on the same platform are recalled by James S. Ewing of Bloomington. The occasion was a call which Mr. Lincoln made upon Mr. Douglas at the hotel in Bloomington. Douglas was there to make a political address in vindication of his course on the Nebraska bill. Lincoln was attending court. Mr. Ewing remembers that just after Mr. Lincoln had greeted Senator Douglas and had declined to take a drink from the bottle on the mantel or sideboard, Jesse W. Fell came into the room:

"After some conversation," Mr. Ewing said, "Mr. Fell remarked to Senator Douglas:

"'A great many of the friends of Mr. Lincoln would be gratified to hear a discussion between you and him on these issues which are interesting the people.'

"'I will not do it,' replied Senator Douglas. 'The meeting [was] gotten up for me by my friends. I desire to explain my position. It will take all of the time I have. It is not fair. To what party does Mr. Lincoln belong now?'

"'To the Whig party, of course,' said Mr. Fell.

"'Not of course,' Senator Douglas said. 'In this day of fanaticism and disturbance he might belong to some other party. I find on coming back to Illinois a very strange condition. In the north part of the state I am assailed by an Old Line Abolitionist. Here, in the central part, I am beset by an Old Line Whig. In the southern part, I presume, I shall have to encounter an anti-Nebraska Democrat. I can't hold the Abolitionist responsible for what the Whig says. I can't hold any one of them accountable for what the others say. This looks to me like dogging a man all over the state. If Mr. Lincoln wants to make a speech he must get his own crowd. The people have come to hear me. I, therefore, decline to have a debate as you propose.'

"Lawrence Weldon of Clinton, who was present, said to Senator Douglas, 'Judge, I think you are right.'

"'Well, perhaps you are,' Mr. Fell said, "still I think that some other time it may be appropriate.'

"Mr. Lincoln made a speech a few days after Mr. Douglas' speech, in the old Courthouse in this town. I was present and heard it. In my judgment it was the most remarkable speech I ever heard. The statement of the facts leading up to the enactment of the Missouri compromise, the conditions which brought about the compromise of 1850, the things that the North got and the things that the South got by that omnibus bill, which was called the compromise bill of 1850—all of that was so clearly and so logically put by Mr. Lincoln that I could almost state it now as he stated it them. The chief characteristic of Mr. Lincoln's mind was that wonderful clearness of statement. In all the many lawsuits I heard him try, it was that kind of ability of Mr. Lincoln which always impressed me. When he had stated his case for plaintiff or defendant it was always a matter of astonishment to me that the lawyer on the other side would bring such a suit or defend such a suit, so clearly wrong or so clearly right. It was the same way in Mr. Lincoln's political arguments. I was present at the convention which met in Major's Hall in 1856 and created the Republican party in Illinois, at which Mr. Lincoln made what is called the 'lost speech.' I heard the speech, but I can't say that it made a particular impression upon me at the time. There were distinguished men present and great speeches made.

"Mr. Fell," continued Mr. Ewing, "never gave up the idea of having a joint debate between Lincoln and Douglas. He continued to agitate it until four years afterward it occurred in the contest for the senatorship. I think Mr. Fell, more than anybody else, is entitled to the credit of bringing about the seven joint debates in 1858.

"At that meeting of Mr. Lincoln and Mr. Douglas in the room of the latter," Mr. Ewing recalled, "Mr. Lincoln made the acquaintance of Lawrence Weldon, who afterward became one of his strongest supporters in this part of the state. Mr. Weldon was in the room when Mr. Lincoln entered. Senator Douglas introduced Mr. Weldon and said, 'Mr. Lincoln, Mr. Weldon is a young lawyer who has just settled in Clinton to practice there.' Mr. Lincoln shook hands and said: 'I am glad to get acquainted, Mr. Weldon. I practice in Clinton sometimes.' Four years later I was present in Senator Douglas' room in the Pike House, when Mr. Lincoln came in with Mr. Weldon, who had become his very warm friend. On that occasion Mr. Lincoln introduced Mr. Weldon to Senator Douglas. It so happened, rather curiously, that I was present at the introduction of Weldon to Mr. Lincoln by Senator Douglas, and, as you might say, vice versa."

How the News Came

At the close of election day, 1860, Lyman Trumbull and Henry Guest McPike, descendant of the old revolutionary hero, took the train at Alton for Springfield. The issues were too exciting to rest until morning without knowing the result. Trumbull was close to Lincoln. McPike, younger than either Lincoln or Trumbull, had been much in their company. It was late at night when the Alton train reached Springfield. Out in front of the old State capitol local orators were addressing the people, and from time to time returns were read out. Trumbull led the way to the telegraph office. Upstairs in a room were found Mr. Lincoln, Jesse K. DuBois and Edward Baker.

"Lincoln was sitting on a kind of sofa," said Mr. McPike, "DuBois, who was a stout man, was seated. Ed Baker was looking over the dispatches as they came in and trying to figure out something conclusive from them. After greetings all around Trumbull wanted to know how it looked. Mr. Lincoln was very quiet, less excited than anybody else in the party.

"'We are working now on New York State,' Baker said, in reply to Judge Trumbull's question. 'We have just had something from New York City that looks very well.'

"'Well,' said Judge Trumbull, 'if we get New York that settles it.'

"'Yes,' said Baker, 'that will settle it.'

"We sat there, nobody else saying much, but all listening to Baker as he looked over the dispatches and commented on them. I don't know what time it was, but it must have been very late, when Ed Baker got a dispatch and began to tell what was in it. He was so excited he did not read clearly.

"'How is that?' shouted old Jesse, sitting up. He had been half asleep for some time.

"Baker began again and read out the announcement that Lincoln had carried New York.

"Du Bois jumped to his feet. 'Hey!' he shouted, and then began singing as loud as he could a campaign song, 'Ain't You Glad You Jined the Republicans?'

"Lincoln got up and Trumbull and the rest of us. We were all excited. There were hurried congratulations. Suddenly old Jesse grabbed the dispatch which settled it out of Ed Baker's hands and started on a run for the door. We followed, Baker after DuBois, I was next, and then came Trumbull, with Lincoln last. The staircase was narrow and steep. We went down it, still on the run. DuBois rushed across the street toward the meeting so out of breath he couldn't speak plain. All he could say was 'Spatch! spatch!' He was going over with the news to the meeting. Ed Baker followed him. Lincoln and Trumbull stopped on the sidewalk.

"'Well, I guess I'll go over to the speaking,' said Trumbull.

"'Well, judge, good night. I guess I'll go down and tell Mary about it,' said Lincoln, still perfectly cool, the coolest man in the party. Across the street 10,000 crazy people were shouting, throwing up their hats, slapping and kicking one another. They had just heard the dispatch that old Jesse had grabbed from Ed Baker. You never saw such a sight. And down the street walked Lincoln, without a sign of anything unusual."

The Lincoln Scrapbooks

The most popular form which interest in Lincolniana takes is the scrapbook. Thousands of people keep Lincoln scrapbooks. They clip and paste the stories and reminiscences of Lincoln that appear in the newspapers and magazines. Some of them exercise selection. Others take everything they find about Lincoln, making book after book. Library shelves are occupied with long rows of Lincoln scrapbooks. Instead of the interest decreasing, there are to-day more of these Lincoln scrapbooks being filled than ever before.

The first Lincoln scrapbook was made by Lincoln himself. It was about four inches long and three inches wide—a memorandum book, in which

Mr. Lincoln pasted clippings from newspapers. He wrote on the first leaf of the book:

"The following extracts are taken from various speeches of mine, delivered at various times and places, and I believe they contain the substance of all I have said about 'negro equality.' The first three are from my answer to Judge Douglas October 16, 1854, at Peoria."

Among his old Whig friends, many of them from Kentucky, who were numerous in the central part of Illinois, Mr. Lincoln had a good deal of trouble to meet the artful argument of the Douglas men that the new Republican party in 1856 and 1858 meant "negro equality." A prominent man among these Kentucky Whigs was Capt. James N. Brown, who called himself a "Lincoln Republican." He had been in the Legislature.[1] He was a man of much popularity in Sangamon County. Capt. Brown was willing to identify himself with Lincoln's new party, but he shied at the proposition to be a standard bearer by taking the Republican nomination for the Legislature in 1858, although Lincoln was to be the candidate for United States senator. Mr. Lincoln urged; Capt. Brown consented. But when the captain got into the campaign he was met everywhere with the inquiry how he, a Kentuckian, could stand for a man who said the negro was as good as a white man.

Capt. Brown went to Lincoln and said he must have something that would plainly define Lincoln's position, so that he could meet the charge that the Republicans were black abolitionists. The captain said he understood the situation very well, but he couldn't state it satisfactorily; he wanted an answer he could read. Mr. Lincoln prepared the little scrapbook. He added to the clippings a letter addressed to Capt. Brown.[2] The candidate carried the scrapbook through the remainder of the campaign of 1858, reading from it to confound the Douglas men. Whenever, either on the stump or on the street or in private conversation, Capt. Brown heard the charge of "negro equality" made against Mr. Lincoln, he drew forth the book and read "Lincoln's own words."

The second Lincoln scrapbook was made in 1858 by Robert R. Hitt. Mr. Hitt not only reported the joint debates; he preserved the current newspaper accounts, not excepting the efforts of the Douglas organs to throw discredit by ridicule upon Mr. Lincoln.

[At this point in *A Reporter's Lincoln*, Stevens reproduced excerpts from a long article he had published in 1892.[3] That article is given here in its entirety.]

When Mr. Lincoln, of Springfield, challenged Senator Douglas, of Illinois, to a series of joint debates, there was derision among the Democrats. The challenge was treated as a bluff. The friends of the Little Giant professed to believe that Mr. Lincoln was not in earnest. And when the Senator accepted the challenge it was common Democratic sentiment that the challenger would look around for some hole by which to crawl out. Senator Douglas' organ, the *Chicago Times,* said:

> If the Republican "champion" does not effect a timely retreat there will be music at the times and places designated in Senator Douglas' reply to Mr. Lincoln. But will Mr. Lincoln meet our Senator? We should like to know. It is evident from the tone of the Republican papers that he and his friends have determined that he shall not acquiesce in the very fair arrangement proposed. It is even evident, we think, to all men cognizant of the facts that had Mr. Lincoln or any of his friends had any idea that his challenge would be accepted, it never would have been sent. They waited until it seemed impossible for Senator Douglas to accept their proffer before opening correspondence with him, and now that he had signified his willingness to meet Mr. Lincoln in debate before the people at one central point in each congressional district, the Republicans and their candidate are fearing and trembling and soon will be begging. Lincoln will not meet Douglas; this is what we think will come of the challenge.

This sounds queerly. In 1892 they are spoken of as the great debates of Lincoln and Douglas. In 1858 they were the debates of Douglas and Lincoln. Douglas was the man of established national reputation. Lincoln was the ambitious local leader. Douglas had been United States Senator for twelve years. Lincoln had been indorsed by his party, the minority party, as its candidate for the Senate in the event of the Legislature being carried by the Republicans. Douglas had not only been a Senator two terms, but he had become a national leader. He was at the head of a strong element of his party in the Senate. He was the representative of the majority of the Democratic party of the whole country, as subsequent events showed. And he was an acknowledged candidate for the Presidency. Lincoln had had some service in the Legislature; ten years afterward one term in Congress, which, from the Democratic point of view, had been disastrous to him; and then twelve years of obscurity. Under such conditions the two men came before the people of Illinois for the joint debates.

The coloring which has been given in late years to these debates has been that which takes into account Lincoln's subsequently achieved greatness. It has been a coloring which dwarfs Douglas and magnifies Lincoln as regards the public estimates of them when they met in these debates. It reverses the relations in which the two men stood before the people of Illinois and of the country at that time. These accounts of the debate, written long afterward, are very different from what they might have been had Lincoln been defeated and Douglas elected to the Presidency in 1860.

Lincoln, to be sure, felt strong in the soundness of his convictions. He believed he had both logic and justice on his side. But this did not blind him to the different relations in which Douglas and he stood before the public. About the time Lincoln entered upon these joint debates he wrote the following, which was made public many years afterward:

> Twenty-two years ago Judge Douglas and I first became acquainted. We were both young men then—he a trifle younger than I. Even then we were both ambitious—I perhaps quite as much so as he. With me the race of ambition has been a failure—a flat failure; with him, it has been one of splendid success. His name fills the nation and is not unknown even in foreign lands. I affect no contempt for the high eminence he has reached—so reached that the oppressed of my species might have shared with me in the elevation; I would rather stand on that eminence than wear the richest crown that ever pressed a monarch's brow.

Douglas, careful as he was to save every point favorable to him, and shrewd as he was in all his manner, could not but patronize Lincoln a little in his speeches. He felt his superior success and popularity. He probably meant to be magnanimous, and in trying to be so he said some things which seem in this day ridiculously condescending toward his antagonist. At the Ottawa debate, in the course of his opening speech, Mr. Douglas said of Lincoln:

> I mean nothing personally disrespectful or unkind to that gentleman. I have known him for nearly twenty-five years. There were many points of sympathy between us when we first got acquainted. We were both comparatively boys and both struggling with poverty in a strange land. I was a school teacher in the town of Winchester and he a flourishing grocery-keeper in the town of Salem. {Applause and laughter.} He was more successful in his occupation than I was in mine, and hence more fortunate in this world's goods. Lincoln is one of those peculiar men who perform with admirable skill everything which they undertake. I made as good a school teacher as I could, and when a cabinet-maker I made a good bedstead and table, although my old boss said I succeeded better with bureaus and secretaries than anything else {cheers}; but I believe that Lincoln was always more successful in business than I, for his business enabled him to get in the Legislature. I met him there, however, and had a sympathy with him because of the up-hill struggle we

both had in life. He was then just as good at telling an anecdote as now. He could beat any of the boys wrestling or running a foot race, in pitching quoits or tossing a copper; could ruin more liquor than all the boys in town together {uproarious laughter}, and the dignity and impartiality with which he presided at a horse race or fist fight excited the admiration and won the praise of everybody that was present and participated. I sympathized with him because he was struggling with difficulties and so was I. Mr. Lincoln served with me in the Legislature in 1836, when we both retired, and he subsided or became submerged, and he was lost sight of as a public man for some years. In 1846, when Wilmot introduced his celebrated proviso, and the abolition tornado swept over the country, Lincoln again turned up as a member of Congress from the Sangamon District. I was then in the Senate of the United States, and was glad to welcome my old friend and companion. Whilst in Congress he distinguished himself by his opposition to the Mexican war, taking the side of the common enemy against his own country (that's true), and when he returned home he found that the indignation of the people followed him everywhere, and he was again submerged or obliged to return into private life, forgotten by his former friends (and will be again). He came up again in 1854, just in time to make this Abolition or Black Republican platform in company with Giddings, Lovejoy, Chase and Fred Douglass for the Republican party to stand upon."[4] {Laughter. "Hit him again," etc.}

Lincoln, when his turn came, made but brief reference to this biographical sketch of himself by his antagonist. He contented himself with saying:

"The Judge is woefully at fault again about his early friend being a grocery keeper. I don't know that it would be a great sin if I had, but he is mistaken. Lincoln never kept a grocery in his life. It is true that Lincoln did work the latter part of one winter at a little still house up at the head of the hollow."

But at another time Lincoln turned the disparity in their public positions to good account in the following:

Senator Douglas is of world-wide renown. All of the anxious politicians of his party, or who have been of his party for years past, have been looking upon him as certainly, at no distant day, to be the President of the United States. They have seen, in his jolly, fruitful face, post offices, land offices, marshalships and cabinet appointments, chargeships and foreign missions, bursting and sprouting forth in wonderful exuberance, ready to be laid hold of by their greedy hands. On the contrary, nobody has ever expected me to be President. In my poor, lean, lank face nobody has ever seen that any cabbages were sprouting out.

The comparison is not overdrawn. Douglas had a run of luck almost without parallel in politics. "Twenty-five years ago," he said in his speech at Winchester during this very campaign, "I entered this town on foot with my coat over my arm." At the age of 21 he had walked to Illinois with a trade and a head full of brains. Yet in the twenty-five years that had elapsed he had been the State's Attorney for the Morgan Circuit, in 1835; a member of the lower branch of the Illinois General Assembly, in 1836; Register of the Land Office by appointment, in 1837; Secretary of State of Illinois, by appointment; Judge on the Supreme Bench of Illinois, by election; a representative, elected to the Twenty-eighth, Twenty-ninth and Thirtieth Congresses; twelve years a United States Senator. With that record behind him he was, at the age of 45, before the people of Illinois for a third term in the United States Senate and before the people of the whole country for the presidency in 1860. But one time in the twenty-five years of residence in Illinois had Douglas been defeated in any of his political aspirations. He had run for Congress in 1840, when he had been in the State only seven years, and had been defeated by the close vote of 18,405 to 18,337. Is there anything in American politics that surpasses this almost unbroken chain of successes? With such prestige Douglas entered upon the joint debates.

Lincoln's public career began with a short service in the Legislature. Then occurred a long hiatus. He applied for the land commissionership and was refused. He had one term in Congress and failed of re-election, and here he was the indorsed senatorial candidate of a party of rather incongruous elements, which hardly knew just what it believed.

Immediately after the first debate at Ottawa there broke out a fierce newspaper controversy. The issue was the integrity of the stenographic report of Lincoln's speech in the Douglas organ. Two papers printed what purported to be verbatim reports of the debate. They were the *Press and Tribune*, of Chicago, and the *Chicago Times*. But between the two reports, so far as Lincoln was concerned, there was very great difference. Mr. Lincoln's Ottawa speech, as it appeared in the *Chicago Times*, was a horrible mess. It abounded in ungrammatical expressions. Sentences were run together in such a way as to make no sense. Punctuation marks were either entirely omitted or misplaced. The friends of Mr. Lincoln immediately charged the Democrats with the despicable trick of misrepresenting him. They even went so far as to suggest that Douglas himself had access to the manuscript of the stenographer, and that he distorted Lincoln's speech so as to make his antagonist appear ridiculous. To this charge the Democrats replied that Lincoln had been reported exactly as he spoke, and that his speech had been printed as delivered. They made the counter charge that Lincoln's speech was taken by a self-appointed committee of Republicans and fixed up previous to publication. An extract from a venerable scrapbook is peculiarly interesting. The *Chicago Times*, in conducting its side of the controversy, said:

> Any person who heard at Ottawa the speech of Abraham, alias Old Abe, alias Abe, alias "Spot" Lincoln, must have been astonished at the report of that speech as it appeared in the *Press and Tribune* of this city. Our version of it was literal. No man who heard it delivered could fail to recognize and acknowledge the fidelity of our reporters. We did not attempt, much, to "fix up" the bungling effort; that was not our business. Lincoln should have learned before this to "rake after" himself. Or, rather, to supersede the necessity of "raking after," by taking heed to his own thoughts and experiences. If he ever gets into the United States Senate, of which there is no earthly probability, he will have to do that. In the congressional arena the words of debaters are snatched from their lips, as it were, and immediately enter into and become a part of the literature of the country. But it seems, from the difference between the two versions of Lincoln's speech, that the Republicans have a candidate for the Senate of whose bad rhetoric and horrible jargon they are ashamed, upon which, before they would publish it, they called a council of "literary" men, to discuss, reconstruct and rewrite; they dare not allow Lincoln to go in print in his own dress; and abuse us, the *Times*, for reporting him literally.

This controversy over the Democratic reports of Lincoln's speech was waged with great bitterness until long after the seven debates were finished. Republicans were very sore about it. They held Douglas in a large degree responsible for the unjust treatment. There was something in it which created great sympathy for Lincoln. The American sense of fair play was outraged. Minor matters which appeal to sentiment often go a long way in politics. There is scarcely any doubt that this misrepresentation of Lincoln cost Douglas many votes, both in the senatorial campaign and in the presidential campaign which followed two years later. Republicans did not forgive and forget the apparently shabby treatment of their candidate until the war came on, and Douglas, with all his might, espoused the Union cause, and came to the support of President Lincoln. That was the atonement.

Both sides were probably wrong to some extent in this controversy. It is doubtful if Douglas personally had anything to do in the first place with the misreporting of Lincoln. On the other hand, there is no doubt that the organ of Douglas treated Lincoln in a way of which no self-respecting newspaper would be guilty at this day. The accident of circumstances combined with the purpose of partisanship to make Lincoln ridiculous. Some facts, which have not hitherto been printed, may be told about the newspaper work on these debates.

Shorthand men who could follow political speakers of all kinds were not numerous in those days. Douglas brought with him to Illinois for that campaign a Philadelphia phonographer—a Mr. Sheridan.[5] The reports of Douglas' speeches which appeared in the *Times* were the work of Mr. Sheridan. Mr. Sheridan did not report Mr. Lincoln for the *Times*. There was the greatest possible difference in the two speakers. "There is no orator in America more correct in rhetoric, more clear in ideas, more direct in purpose, in all his public addresses than Stephen A. Douglas," his organ said in the course of the controversy. This was but slightly exaggerated truth. People of this generation who read the beautifully rounded periods and clean-cut sentences of Douglas may imagine the words pouring forth in a rapid, unbroken stream. But Douglas was one of the most measured of American orators. If he was in public life to-day he would be the delight of beginners in stenography. He was strongly regular; he was distinct; he paused between sentences; he used short sentences; he rarely exceeded 120 words a minute. Every one at all versed in short-hand work will appreciate what that is. It means a speed which the ordinary stenographic secretary of to-day can easily follow. It was no trouble to report Douglas. "The Little Giant," as he was usually called by his admirers, had a deep bass voice. No bass voice can go fast. His sonorous tones filled out the time so that he did not seem to be speaking slowly. Even-paced is probably a better expression than deliberate to describe his manner. That Douglas uttered not nearly so many words as Lincoln in a given period is apparent in the reports of the debates. Each had the same time. But Lincoln's speeches occupy more space than Douglas'.[6]

Lincoln was altogether different. His voice was clear, almost shrill. Every syllable was distinct. But his delivery was puzzling to stenographers. He would speak several words with great rapidity, come to the word or phrase he wished to emphasize and let his voice linger and bear hard on that; and then he would rush to the end of the sentence like lightning. To impress the idea on the minds of his hearers was his aim; not to charm the ear with smooth, flowing words. It was very easy to understand Lincoln; he spoke with great clearness. But his delivery was very irregular. He would devote as much time to the word or two which he wished to emphasize as he did to half a dozen less important words following it. This peculiarity of Lincoln's delivery helped the Democrats in carrying out a plan to belittle him. The Democratic organ, the *Chicago Times*, called Lincoln's speech, "weak, faltering, childish twaddle," and endeavored to make it appear so. At Ottawa, on the occasion of the opening debate, Douglas spoke an hour. Lincoln followed with an hour and a half. Douglas closed in a half hour. The reporting of Lincoln for the Democratic paper was done by an English stenographer, who had the old style.[7] His notes were almost unintelligible to the American phonographers. But there was no doubt about the Englishman's ability to follow Lincoln. The notes were written out, and the editor of the *Times*, Mr. Sheehan [Sheahan], afterwards boasted editorially, "Lincoln's speech was printed verbatim, just as it came from the reporter."[8] A single sentence taken from the scrap-book copy of the *Times'* report will serve to show how Lincoln was treated:

> I will remind him also of a piece of Illinois of the time, when the respected party to which the Judge belongs was displeased with a decision of the Supreme Court of Illinois, because they had decided that the Governor could not remove a Secretary of State, and he will not deny that he went in for overslaughing that court, by appointing five new judges, and it ended in his getting the name of Judge in that very way, thus breaking down the Supreme Court, and when he tells me about how a man who shall be appointed on such a principle, by being questioned, I say Judge, you know you have tried it, and when he seeks that the court will be prostituted below contempt.

This was very small business. The newspaper which would instruct its telegraph editor and proof-reader to follow an unrevised shorthand report with that kind of fidelity in this day and generation would hurt itself more than the orator it aimed to disgrace. But this was the way Lincoln was reported at Ottawa, and the Douglas organ glorified in the showing. The *Times* continued to print full reports, and continued to claim that it printed them just as they came from the reporter. It is noticeable, however, that the report of Lincoln's speech at Freeport, the second debate, was somewhat better. This may be accounted for by the discovery on the part of the Douglas organ that it had made a mistake in its treatment of his antagonist. After the Freeport report, the *Times*, acknowledging the improvement in the reading of the Lincoln speech, said:

"The debate at Freeport was remarkable, first for the immense ability displayed by Douglas, second for the weakness of Lincoln. We grant that he (Lincoln) spoke with rather more conspicuous fluency than is usual for him; but he failed utterly of coming up to the mark."

It is an interesting fact that while the Republicans, from one end of the State to the other, denounced the *Times'* report of Lincoln's speeches, Senator Douglas took occasion to seek out the phonographer for the *Press and Tribune* and to thank him for the faithful accuracy with which he had been reported in the Republican newspaper. The young man who reported the debates for the Republicans was the present Congressman, Robert R. Hitt, representing the Freeport district. Mr. Hitt was then a law reporter, having a short time previously completed his education at Asbury University. In the light of this explanation, and the foregoing statement of the controversy over the newspaper treatment of Lincoln, the following, with which the *Chicago Times'* report of the Freeport debate opened, will be found entertaining:

Mr. Lincoln. Fellow-citizens, ladies and gentlemen—

Deacon Bross.[9] Hold on, Lincoln, you can't speak yet. Hitt ain't here, and there is no use of your speaking unless the *Press and Tribune* had a report.

Mr. Lincoln. Ain't Hitt here? Where is he?

A Voice. Perhaps he is in the crowd.

Deacon Bross, after adjusting the green shawl around his classic shoulders after the manner of McVicker in [the role of] Brutus,[10] advanced to the front of the stand and spoke: If Hitt is in the crowd he will please to come forward. Is Hitt in the crowd? If he is, tell him Mr. Bross, of the *Chicago Press and Tribune*, wants him to come up here on the stand to make a verbatim report for the only paper in the Northwest that has enterprise enough to publish speeches in full.

Joe Medill. That's the talk.

Herr Kriesman [Kreismann] here wiped his spectacles and looked into the crowd to see if he could distinguish Hitt.[11]

A Voice. If Hitt isn't here, I know a young man from our town that can make nearly a verbatim report, I guess. Shall I call him?

Deacon Bross. Is he here?

A Voice. Yes, I see him; his name is Hitch.

Loud cries for "Hitch" were made and messengers ran wildly about inquiring "Where is Hitch? Where is Hitch?"

After a delay the moderators decided that the speaking must go on.

Deacon Bross. Well, wait (bringing a chair); I'll report the speech. Lincoln, you can now go on; I'll report you.

The idea of Deacon Bross making a verbatim report of Lincoln's speech was calculated to inspire hilarity. The Deacon had a bluff, hearty manner.

He talked loudly and often, but unlike some other men of such characteristics Deacon Bross had great ability and real nobility. He had unbounded faith in the future of Chicago. He never tired of glorifying the city, the *Tribune*'s enterprise and the Republican party's principles. A quill was the Deacon's idea of the best pen. Sitting in the editorial room of the *Tribune*, conversing with a room full of politicians the deacon would call out:

"Hold on. Give me [a] pen. I'll make a paragraph of that."

He would whirl around to the table, grasp the quill and scratch away, making a spluttering noise that could be heard above the hum of conversation. Then he would whirl back, hold up the paper and read aloud for comments, starting off like this:

"The Republican party—what's that next word? Oh, yes—," etc.

About the time of the Freeport meeting the *Times* had a grievance against the Deacon. At some gathering, so the story went, the Deacon had neglected to see that Matteson, of the *Times*, had a chair. For weeks and months afterwards the *Times* printed in its reports of various occurrences this single line:

"And Deacon Bross spoke."

Sandwiched between paragraphs of Lincoln's speech at Freeport; injected into proceedings of the School Board of Chicago; sown broadcast over the local page was the inevitable line: "And Deacon Bross spoke."

In its account of the closing of the Freeport meeting, the *Times* said:

"During the delivery of Douglas' speech Mr. Lincoln was very uneasy; he could not sit still nor would his limbs sustain him while standing. He was shivering, quaking, trembling, and his agony during the last fifteen minutes of Judge Douglas' speech was positively painful to the crowd who witnessed his behavior."

Then followed more and worse of this kind of abuse until the newspaper went beyond the border of decency. Injected into the *Times*' report of the Freeport debate was this:

"The reporter can not let this opportunity pass without returning his thanks to Parson Lovejoy for his very gentlemanly conduct in leaning over him during the latter part of Senator Douglas' speech and commanding, in a loud voice, Mr. Turner to announce to the people that he would address them after the adjournment of the meeting."

When the debate was over Lovejoy, who had been thoroughly aroused by Douglas' reference to "the nigger"—Douglas said "nigger" not "negro" as the *Times* reported him on that occasion—gathered the crowd in front of the Brewster House and made such an impassioned appeal as those who listened to it have never forgotten. Lovejoy was an artist who could paint word pictures, and a musician who could touch the human chords. He was a master at showing the emotions. He stood before that immense crowd that day and held up slavery in its worst possible light. He told the story of the slave girl's flight from her pursuers, and his hearers breathed so hard you could hear them, while their dilated eyes gleamed with passion. Republicans with the spell on them went from the Lovejoy meeting and said to the phonographer:

"Print Lovejoy's speech instead of Lincoln's."

Herr Kriesman, who is referred to in the opening of the Freeport meeting, was a local politician of note in those days. He was afterwards made Secretary of Legation at Berlin, and still later Consul General. He is to-day living in Berlin, wealthy and respected.

Douglas and Lincoln did not travel together during the campaign. They saw very little of each other until they met upon the platforms at the appointed places. The first debate, at Ottawa, was on the 21st of August. The seventh was at Alton, on the 15th of October. The others were scattered along between these dates. The candidates had other engagements which kept them apart. They were moving nearly all of the time. Lincoln made over sixty speeches and Douglas made even more. The newspapers were well satisfied to give the verbatim reports of the joint debates. That was enterprise enough for those days. The newspapers did not attempt to give full reports of more than two or three of the other speeches.

The way in which the reporting and the publishing of the debates was done was very different from the methods of to-day. Two phonographers did the actual reporting—Mr. Hitt for the Republicans and Mr. Sheridan for the Democrats, Mr. Lincoln being taken for the *Times* by the Englishman. The wires were not used. An attempt to telegraph one of those joint debates would have paralyzed the telegraph company of that period, and would have bankrupted the newspaper. As soon as a debate was finished the reporters took the first train they could get and traveled to Chicago. En route, and after their arrival, they wrote out the speeches, which were published the second day after the debate took place. The reports appeared simultaneously. Each paper seemed to be satisfied not to be behind the other. No heroic effort was made by one to beat the other. But to accomplish publication by the second day after the debate was a feat which strained the resources of the two offices. On more than one of the seven occasions the newspapers contained apologies to their readers for being late in the morning because of the extra effort to get in the Lincoln and Douglas speeches in full.

One particularly smart thing was done in connection with the Quincy debate. A train for Chicago departed while the speaking was in progress. The assistant of Mr. Hitt, a bright young man, picked up the note book containing the report up to a few minutes before train time, ran to the train and started for Chicago. Mr. Hitt followed with the remainder of the notes on the next train after the debate closed. When he reached Chicago he found that his assistant had transcribed the greater part of the earlier portion of the debate and the matter was already in type. It several times happened that Mr. Hitt did not see considerable portions of the notes after taking them until the matter appeared in the paper; the transcribing was done by the assistant, and the copy was rushed to the printers. The charge made by the Democrats was that "Mr. Judd, Judge Logan, Judge Davis, or some one else of great and conceded abilities," went over Lincoln's speeches and fixed them up before publication. It is answered by the story of the way in which the reporting and publishing was done. So also is answered the Republican accusation that Douglas had access to the transcribed notes of Lincoln's speeches, and mutilated them before they appeared in the Democratic paper. There was no time for revision or for putting up jobs with the manuscript by the principals in the debates. The misrepresentation of Lincoln in the *Times* was in accordance with the purpose to make him appear ignorant and uncouth in language beside Douglas. Among the reporters it was well understood that the report of Lincoln for the *Times* was to be done in a slovenly manner, to carry out the Democratic estimate of Lincoln. Sheridan, who reported Douglas for the *Times*, did not take Lincoln. He was above lending himself to such a dishonorable practice. He frequently talked privately about this treatment of Lincoln, but did not go further than to express his confidential opinion of it. With never-failing nerve the *Times* insisted to the end that its reports of Lincoln were verbatim and that the speeches were printed just as delivered. In American political history there is no other controversy quite like this. After the sixth debate—the one at Quincy—the *Times*, still carrying on the discussion, said:

"No man can be expert enough to caricature a speaker while speaking, or if that could be done once it would be impossible to repeat the operation and not expose the caricaturist. This we think must strike all judgments as it does ours. Again, we have urged the high characters for truth of our reporters of these debates, whose reputations are worth more to them than any wages for present services, in defense of ourselves from the slanderous charges of the zealots who alter Lincoln's speeches and then attempt to cast the guilt upon us."

The *Times*, with magnificent bluff, challenged the *Press and Tribune* to publish an affidavit from its phonographer, Mr. Hitt, that Lincoln's speeches were not "fixed up" before they were published. It alleged at one time that Mr. Ray, of the *Press and Tribune*, revised the "copy" of Lincoln's speeches before publication, and at other times it charged this work upon other prominent Republicans.

One of the tricks of the Democratic report of Lincoln was to insert a note at the end of his part of the debate to the effect that Lincoln "having run down, did not occupy all of his allotted time" by so many minutes. The fact was that both debaters took all of their time. On one occasion Lincoln stopped sixty seconds ahead of his limit and said: "I find I have just one minute left, and I will give that to Judge Douglas to see if he can't make a better answer to my question."

The whole three hours' debate ran between six and eight columns— long, closely printed columns—of the four-page sheets of those days. There was another striking difference between the two orators, and it was a difference which impressed itself upon the reporters. Douglas had one great finished speech. He made it seven times. Of course, he varied some- what in his introductions and in his specific replies to Lincoln's points. But his argument, in defense of his general position on the slavery question, was much the same each time. There were whole paragraphs which he re- peated each time. Lincoln made seven speeches, like so many chapters in a book, or distinct divisions of an argument. He did not repeat himself. Douglas' speech was a carefully prepared effort. He ignored interruptions. Lincoln spoke extemporaneously, having only the outline of his argument in mind, answering suggestions from the audience and replying to every new point advanced by Douglas.

The phonographers soon discovered that the Senator was repeating himself largely. Mr. Hitt carried with him copies of previous speeches, and when he came to these repetitions he cut them out and pasted them in his report, thereby saving himself so much work of transcribing. Sheridan, looking on at this saving of labor by means of a convenient bottle of mu- cilage, had his joke on more than one occasion. "Hitt," he was wont to say, "mucilates Douglas for the *Press and Tribune*, while" (mentioning the name of the English stenographer) "mutilates Lincoln for the *Times*."

The debate which seemed to afford Douglas the most satisfaction was the first—the one at Ottawa. There Douglas had the opening hour and the closing half hour. He put to Lincoln seven questions, and insisted on seven direct answers.

"He goes for uniformity in our domestic institutions," Douglas said, "for a war of sections until one or the other shall have been subdued. I go for the great principle of the Kansas-Nebraska bill, the right of the people to decide for themselves."

The seven questions were artfully framed. They were aimed to put Lincoln in the position of the most radical of the Republicans or to make him adopt the conservative side of the slavery question in such a way as to cause division and dissatisfaction in the newly organized Republican party. The Democrats were in high glee over the Ottawa meeting. Their organ, the *Chicago Times*, headlined the debate in this way:

LINCOLN BREAKS DOWN!

LINCOLN'S HEART FAILS HIM!

LINCOLN'S LEGS FAIL HIM!

LINCOLN'S TONGUE FAILS HIM!

LINCOLN'S ARMS FAIL HIM!

LINCOLN FAILS ALL OVER!

THE PEOPLE REFUSE TO SUPPORT HIM!

THE PEOPLE LAUGH AT HIM!

It was at Ottawa that Douglas undertook to hold Lincoln and his party responsible for a series of anti-slavery resolutions which he said had been adopted by the Illinois Republicans four years previously. For the most part both debaters preserved their tempers, but on this occasion Lincoln was not a little indignant. It turned out afterward that Lincoln had good reason for his anger. After referring to the Republican State convention held in 1854, Senator Douglas said:

"I have the resolutions of their State Convention then held, which was the first mass Convention ever held in Illinois by the black Republican party; and I now hold them in my hands, and will read a part of them and cause the others of them to be printed."

Douglas then read from a little memorandum book, which he took from his pocket, some very radical declarations on the slavery questions. When Lincoln rose to reply he accepted the resolutions as genuine, but denied that he was present or had any part in the adoption of such resolutions. When Douglas came forward for the closing half hour he reverted at once to the alleged platform and proceeded to "rub it in." He said:

"The fact that it was the platform of the Republican party is not denied, but Mr. Lincoln now says that although his name was on the committee which reported it, he does not think he was there, but thinks he was in Tazewell holding court."

Douglas pressed the advantage which he had gained. He tried to make it appear that Lincoln was present at the adoption of the platform. As he proceeded there was great excitement and much interruption. The Democratic version of what occurred is as follows:

Mr. Douglas. The point I am going to remind Mr. Lincoln of is this. That after I had made my speech in 1854, during the fair, he gave me notice that he was going to reply to me the next day. I was sick at the time, but I staid over in Springfield to hear his reply and to reply to him. On that day this very Convention which adopted the resolutions I have read was to meet in the Senate chamber. He spoke in the hall of the House, and when he got through his speech—my recollection is distinct, and I shall not forget it—Mr. Codding walked in as I took the stand to reply and gave notice that the Republican State Convention would meet instantly in the Senate chamber, and called upon the Republicans to retire there and go into this Convention instead of remaining and listening to me.[12] (Three cheers for Douglas).

Mr. Lincoln (interrupting excitedly and angrily). Judge, add that I went along with them. (This interruption was made in a fitful, mean, sneaking way, as Lincoln floundered around the stand.)

Mr. Douglas. Gentlemen, Mr. Lincoln tells me to add that he went along with them to the Senate Chamber. I will not add that because I do not know whether he did or not.

Mr. Lincoln (again interrupting). I know he did not. (One of the Republican committee here seized Mr. Lincoln and by a sudden jerk caused him to disappear from the front of the stand, one of them saying quite audibly: "What are you making such a fuss for? Douglas didn't interrupt you, and can't you see that the people don't like it?"

The temporary advantage was with Douglas, but it was only temporary. Two or three days later the whole State was agog with the exposure. How the discovery of the fraud came about is an interesting story. There is also in it a triumph for the science of phonography. The debate had been in progress nearly an hour when Douglas produced what he claimed was the first platform of the Republican party in Illinois, adopted four years before. Hearing Douglas refer to the platform and announce his intention of reading it, Phonographer Hitt dropped his pen for a moment's rest, thinking that he could easily get the platform after the debate and insert it. He looked up and saw that Douglas was reading from his memorandum book. It instantly occurred to him that he might have difficulty in getting the book to copy from. Picking up his pen he took down the rest of the resolutions as Douglas read them. At the time no question of the accuracy of the resolutions entered the mind of Mr. Lincoln. Nor did any one in the crowd detect fraud. Mr. Hitt, as soon as the debate was over, took a train to Chicago, and hurried into the *Press and Tribune* office. Then began the great and unusual work of turning out the "copy" of the debate. To facilitate the work two or three of the *Press and Tribune* men undertook to help. Coming to the reading of the alleged platform, in order to supply the few words he had missed, Hitt called to one of the *Press and Tribune* men:

"Hunt up the resolutions adopted by our State Convention at Springfield in 1854."

The file was brought out and the resolutions were found. Mr. Scripps, one of the editorial writers, began to read the platform.[13]

"Hold on!" exclaimed Hitt. "That's not it at all."

A little further reading showed that Douglas had put off on the Ottawa meeting an entirely different series of resolutions from that which had been adopted at Springfield. Then followed a long search of the files to discover the origin of the bogus platform. The resolutions had a familiar sound, but nobody could at once place them. At length they were found. They had been adopted at a meeting of radical anti-slavery men in Aurora. Scripps, who was a pungent writer, sat down and composed a stinging editorial on the trick. He headed it "The Little Dodger Cornered and Caught." This discovery was a terrible blow to Douglas, coming as it did in the very first debate. But his art helped him out. He at once owned up that he had made a mistake; he laid the blunder on a newspaper from which he had clipped the supposed platform. Nobody ever knew whether it was an honest error.

The debate which gave Lincoln the most satisfaction was the second—the one at Freeport. There he took up the seven questions Douglas had propounded at Ottawa, and answered them one by one. When he had done so he said he would now put certain questions to Senator Douglas. To make the questions more impressive he drew from his pocket a single slip of paper and read the four questions slowly. The purpose of Lincoln's questions was to make Douglas follow his great and fascinating doctrine of popular sovereignty to its logical conclusion, or else confess himself a demagogue. Three of the questions led up to the one which was the crucial test, in this form:

Can the people of a Territory of the United States in any lawful way, against the wishes of any citizen of the United States, exclude slavery from its limits prior to the formation of a State Constitution?

If Douglas said "Yes" to this he parted company with the South, which was insisting on the right, according to the Dred Scott decision, to take slaves into the Territories prior to the formation of a constitution. If Douglas said "No" he confessed that the great political dogma on which he had a personal patent—popular sovereignty, alias squatter sovereignty—was a delusion.

Douglas, when his turn came to speak, took up the slip of paper, Lincoln having laid it down before him where he could not but take notice of it. He took it up, read the questions one by one and answered them. When he came to the all-important question he read it and threw down the slip of paper as if he was disposing of a most trifling matter. He was a great actor. He could simulate passion; he could assume wild rage and defiance. He would shake his head with its mass of hair like a wild bull, and his admirers would cheer and cheer. But it was all acting. Douglas was a veteran of debate. On this occasion, when he read the question on which everything turned, he treated it as trifling, and after casting it aside he said:

"I answer, emphatically, as Mr. Lincoln has heard me answer a hundred times, from every stump in Illinois, that in my opinion the people of a Territory can, by lawful means, exclude slavery from their limits prior to the formation of a State Constitution."

And a little further on he assumed to explain that the people of a Territory could control slavery, "because it can not exist unless supported by police regulations. Those regulations can only be established by the local Legislature, and if the people are opposed to slavery they will elect representatives to that body who will, by unfriendly legislation, effectually prevent the introduction of it into their midst."

The full realization of what Douglas had done did not come to most of those who listened to him until afterwards. His manner was well calculated to deceive. He answered this question on which his future turned as if it was of the slightest consequence. Lincoln undoubtedly knew what he was about, but the stories which have been circulated in later years concerning the four questions are for the most part apocryphal. Lincoln prepared the questions. He based them on a report of a speech Douglas had made a few days before at Bloomington. A copy of the Bloomington speech was before him, and after examining it carefully he wrote the questions, believing that Douglas must answer just as he did. The questions were no surprise to Douglas. They simply forced him to emphasize what he had said to his followers at Bloomington. They drew him out, however, very clearly on an occasion when all he said was sure to get into print, under the fierce light of the debates, and to reach the whole country. The *New York Tribune* and other Eastern papers were reprinting the debates in full or nearly so. Some of Lincoln's friends claim to have advised him strongly not to present the questions, telling him that Douglas was sure to stick to his popular sovereignty idea and that, if he did, he would certainly be elected Senator. But Lincoln went ahead. Years afterwards, in the light of events which followed, some of these friends concluded that Lincoln had the gift of foreknowledge and, in 1858, was building for 1860 and the presidency. A story which fits in here may be told. The evening after the debate closed the two champions were accompanied by their respective friends to the depot to take the train. It was not long after the railroad had reached Freeport. Douglas was surrounded by a throng of enthusiastic and noisy admirers. Lincoln, as was usually the case, had with him a smaller and quieter escort. Lincoln had little to say. While waiting for the train he walked to the end of the platform and stood looking seriously towards the west where the sun had just set. Some one asked him:

"Mr. Lincoln, how are you satisfied with the debate so far?"

"Douglas may have beaten me to-day for the Senate," was the reply, "but I have stopped him from being President."

This story may [be] true. The fact is, however, it did not begin to have circulation until four years after the Freeport meeting, when Lincoln was in the White House and the popular demand for Lincoln stories had developed.

At the third debate, held at Jonesboro, a strongly Democratic locality, where only about 2000 people were present, Lincoln pressed Douglas hard on the answer to the Freeport question. He insisted that Douglas must explain how in the light of the Dred Scott decision the people of a Territory could control the introduction of slavery. Douglas' reply was ingenious, but it was not satisfactory. It turned the South against him. Six weeks afterwards Douglas was burned in effigy at Norfolk, Va., and when Congress reassembled, Senator Benjamin, of Louisiana, arraigned the Little Giant upon the floor of the Senate for the Freeport and Jonesboro speeches, declaring that Mr. Douglas had dodged the real issue and that his views were unsatisfactory to the South.[14]

The joint debates were very serious—intense both as to the speakers and to the listening crowds. Douglas was most of the time very earnest.

Lincoln, with all his humor, was never more solemnly urgent in his appeals to deep passions and lofty principles; especially so at Alton. The discussion was on a high plane. It was devoted mainly to the abstract, the legal, the constitutional phases of the slavery question. The orators talked about the Dred Scott decision and the Lecompton constitution and other judicial and legislative issues. On two occasions, however, they got right down to the homely question: "Is a nigger as good as a white man?"

The Senator made the first crack of this kind, and appealed to prejudice in a most remarkable passage at Freeport, in the second of the debates. He had just finished answering Mr. Lincoln's four questions, when he said:

I trust now that Mr. Lincoln will deem himself answered on his four points. He racked his brains so much in devising these four questions that he exhausted himself and had not strength enough to invent the others. {Laughter.} As soon as he is able to hold a council with his advisers, Lovejoy, Farnsworth and Fred Douglass, he will frame and propound others.[15] {"Good! good!" etc. Renewed laughter, in which Mr. Lincoln feebly joined, saying he hoped with their aid to get seven questions, the number asked him by Judge Douglas, and so make conclusions even.} You black Republicans who say "good" have no doubt that they are good men. {"White!" "White!"} I have reason to recollect that some people in this country think Fred Douglass is a very good man. The last time I was here to make a speech, while talking from the stand to you, people of Freeport, as I am doing to-day, I saw a carriage, and a magnificent one it was, draw up and take a position on the outside of the crowd; a beautiful young lady was sitting on the box seat, whilst Fred Douglass and her mother reclined inside, and the owner of the carriage acted as driver. {Laughter, cheers, cries of "Right!" "What have you to say against it?" etc.} I saw this in your own town. {"What of it?"} All I have to say of it is this, that if you black Republicans think that a negro ought to be on a social equality with your wives and daughters, and ride in a carriage with your wife while you drive the team, you have a perfect right to do so. {"Good!" "Good!" and cheers mingled with howling and cries of "White!" "White!"} I am told that one of Fred Douglass' kinsmen, another rich black negro, is now traveling in this part of the State making speeches for his friend Lincoln, the champion of black men. {"White men!" "White men!" "What have you got to say against it?" "That's right, etc."} All I have to say on that subject is that those of you who believe that the negro is your equal and ought to be on an equality with you socially and politically and legally have a right to entertain those opinions, and of course will vote for Mr. Lincoln. {"Down with the negro! No! No!"}

Senator Douglas said "nigger." His organ printed it "negro."

The crowd at Freeport was overwhelmingly Republican. Lincoln let the impression Douglas had by this appeal to race prejudice pass without reply. But when he got down to Charleston, in Coles County, a Democratic stronghold, for the fourth debate, he, too, got at the race question from a very concrete point of view. He met the great Democrat argument, "How would you like to have your sister marry a negro?" at the very beginning of his Charleston speech. Mr. Lincoln said, according to the Democratic report of his speech:

> While I was up at the hotel to-day an elderly gentleman called upon me to know whether I was really in favor of producing a perfect equality between the negroes and the white people. While I had not proposed to myself upon this occasion to say much upon that subject, as that question was asked me, I thought I would occupy perhaps five minutes in saying something in regard to it.
>
> I will say then that I am not, nor ever have been, in favor of bringing about in any way the social and political equality of the white and black races; that I am not, nor ever have been, in favor of making voters of the negroes or jurors or qualifying them to hold office, or having them marry white people. I will say in addition that there is a physical difference between the white and black races which, I suppose, will forever forbid the two races living together upon terms of social and political equality, and inasmuch as they can not so live, that while they do remain together, there must be the position of superior and inferior; that I as much as any other man am in favor of the superior position being assigned to the white man. I say, in this connection, that I do not perceive, however, that because the white man is to have the superior position, that it requires that the negro should be denied everything. I do not perceive because I do not want a negro woman for a slave that I must necessarily want her for a wife. My understanding is that I can just leave her alone. I am now in my 50th year, and certainly never had a black woman, either as a slave or as a wife, so that it seems to me it is quite possible for us to get along without making either slaves or wives of negroes.
>
> I will add that I have never seen, to my knowledge, a man, woman or child that was in favor of producing a perfect equality, socially and politically, between the negro and white people, and I recollect of but one distinguished instance that I have heard of a great deal, so as to be entirely confident of it, and that is the case of my friend Douglas' old friend, Col. Richard M. Johnston [Johnson].[16] {Laughter and cries of "Hurrah for Lincoln," and "Hurrah for Douglas!"}

Douglas did not let the opportunity slip. When his time came he insisted there was one point Mr. Lincoln had not made clear. That was whether he was in favor of negro citizenship. Lincoln had the closing half hour and in it he further defined his position to this effect.

> Judge Douglas has said to you, I believe, that he has not been able to get from me an answer to the question as to whether I am in favor of negro citizenship. So far as I know, the Judge never asked me that question before. And he will have no occasion to ever ask it again, for I tell him very frankly that I am [not] in favor of it. . . . Now, my opinion is that the different States have the power to make a negro a citizen under the Constitution of the United States if they choose. The Dred Scott decision decides that they have not. If the State of Illinois had that power I should be against the exercise of it. That is all there is of that. That is the whole thing.

These Charleston declarations of Lincoln made a great rumpus in the Republican ranks. The Abolitionists were loud in their denunciations. The *Congregational Herald*, a church paper, edited by Rev. W. A. Nichols, Rev. Wm. A. Pattin [Patton], Rev. S. C. Bartlett and Rev. J. E. Roy, came out with the most severe comments.[17] It said:

"Mr. Lincoln deliberately and with repetition declared himself to be opposed to placing colored men on a political equality with white men. He made color and race the ground of political proscription. He forsook principle and planted himself on low prejudice."

For these declarations at Charleston Wendell Phillips, in Boston, bestowed upon Lincoln the name of "the slave hound of Illinois."

There was not much of unpleasant personality in the debates. But Lincoln had one grievance of this kind. He did not succeed in getting much satisfaction for it. The story is interesting, because it illustrates the ingenuity of Douglas in turning small matters to his own account. At the close of the first debate at Ottawa the partisans of each orator gathered around and made much of him. Some of the overzealous friends of Lincoln picked him up and carried him off on their shoulders to the place where he was stopping. In the Democratic report of the Ottawa debate this version of the carrying scene was given.

> During Douglas' last speech Lincoln had suffered severely, alternately burning with fever and then suddenly chilled with shame; his respiratory organs had become obstructed, his limbs got cold, and he was unable to walk. In this extremity the Republican Marshal called half a dozen men, who, lifting Lincoln in their arms, carried him along. By some mismanagement, the men selected for the office happened to be very short in stature, and the conse-

quence was that, while Lincoln's head and shoulders towered above theirs, his feet dragged on the ground. Such an exhibition as the toting of Lincoln, from the square to his lodgings, was never seen at Ottawa before. It was one of the richest farces we have ever witnessed, and provoked the laughter of all Democrats and Republicans who happened to see it.

If Douglas did not suggest this version of the carrying, he promptly made it his own. A few days later, at Joliet, he described Lincoln as having trembled and as having been so overcome at Ottawa that he had to be carried from the platform. He also charged that Lincoln had been unable to answer the seven questions which he put to him at the first debate, and also that Lincoln had taken seven days to think over the answers, because the specific replies were not made until the second debate at Freeport.

At the third debate—that held at Jonesboro—Lincoln denounced this story of the Ottawa affair as false, and said that Douglas must be crazy to make such a statement. Then the following occurred:

A voice. Did they not carry you?

Mr. Lincoln. Yes, sir. Now that shows the character of this man Douglas. He smiles now, and says, "Did they not carry you?" You have said that I had to be carried. He sought to teach this country that I was broken down—that I could not get away, and now he seeks to dodge it. Why did you not tell the truth?

The above is, of course, the Democratic report, as is the following from Douglas:

Mr. Douglas. I will commence where Mr. Lincoln left off, and make a remark upon this serious complaint of his about my speech at Joliet. I did say there, in a playful manner, that when I put these questions to Mr. Lincoln at Ottawa he failed to answer, and that he trembled and had to be carried off the stand, and required seven days to get up his reply. {Laughter.} That he did not walk off from that stand he will not deny. That when the crowd went away from the stand with me a few persons carried him home on their shoulders and laid him down, he will admit. {Shouts of laughter.} I wish to say to you that whenever I degrade my friends and myself by allowing them to carry me on their backs along the public streets when I am able to walk, I am willing to be deemed crazy. {"All right, Douglas!" laughter and applause; Lincoln chewing his nails in a rage in a back corner.}

The seven meetings were scattered. By the terms of the challenge and acceptance, one meeting was held in each Congressional district. The series began at Ottawa, and was continued at Freeport. At both of these meetings the Republicans were in the large majority. But the third meeting was "down in Egypt," at Jonesboro. The Republicans were not numerous, and when somebody called out, upon the appearance of the Republican champion, "three cheers for Lincoln", the latter said: "I hope you won't make fun of the few friends I have here. That is all I ask."

The meetings were managed by joint committees. Banners and transparencies which might provoke friction were not allowed. There was no limitation on cheering. But interruptions of Douglas by Republicans or of Lincoln by Democrats were forbidden. There were occasional infractions of the rule. At Galesburg, on the occasion of the fifth debate, it was necessary to appeal to Republicans to give Douglas a fair hearing. At Quincy, enthusiastic Democrats interrupted Douglas with such encouragement as "Hit him on the woolly side!" At Alton, the last debate, the opening on Mr. Lincoln's part was as follows, according to the *Times*:

> *Mr. Lincoln.* Ladies and Gentlemen.
>
> *A Voice.* There are no ladies here.
>
> *Mr. Lincoln.* You are mistaken about that. There is a fine chance of them back here.

The Alton debate was characterized by two incidents. Lincoln was accused of violating the rules of debate. The accusation as set forth in the Democratic account of the meeting was this:

"Lincoln's conduct at the last debate was most improper and ungentlemanly. After he concluded his hour-and-a-half speech and Senator Douglas was to reply he seated himself where his motions could not be observed by the Senator, and, whenever a point was made against him, would shake his head at the crowd, intimating that it was not true and that they should put no reliance on what was said. This course was in direct violation of the rules of the debate, and was a mean trick beneath the dignity of a man of honor."

The other incident was occasioned by the attempt of one Dr. Hoke to make a little speech. Dr. Hoke was "a Danite."

"The Danites" in that great campaign of 1858 were the Buchanan Democrats, who were chiefly the Federal office-holders of Illinois. Douglas had broken with Buchanan. He was for the Dred Scott decision, but he was against the Lecompton Constitution. The whole power of the Administration was enlisted for the defeat of Douglas, and every Federal office-holder in his State was supposed to be knifing him. Many of these office-holders worked openly, fighting Douglas in every way. Early in the fight they were given the name of "Danites", and Douglas, in every one of his hundred speeches, denounced this action of Buchanan's administration. Lincoln rarely referred to the course of the Federal office-holders further than to insist that Mr. Douglas' quarrel with the Democratic administration was something that did not concern the Republican party. The fact was, as stated by one who went through the campaign, the Republicans lost rather than gained by "The Danites." "For every Federal office-holder who fought him, Douglas gained at least five votes", is the way he puts it. The possession of patronage was an element of party weakness rather than of strength even in those days. Douglas was wont to express himself to this effect:

"Whenever you recognize the right of a President to say to a member of Congress, 'Vote as I tell you or I will bring a power to bear against you at home that will crush you,' you destroy the independence of the representative and convert him into a tool of executive power. I resisted this invasion of the constitutional rights of a Senator, and I intend to resist as long as I have a voice to speak or a vote to give. Yet Mr. Buchanan can not provoke me to abandon one iota of Democratic principles out of revenge or hostility to his course."

Again he said: "The legislative department is independent of the President. In matters of legislation the President has a veto on the Senate. He has no more right to tell me how I shall vote on his appointees than I have to tell him whether he shall veto or approve a bill that the Senate has passed. Whenever you recognize the right of the Executive to say to a Senator, 'do this, or I will take off the heads of your friends' you convert this Government from a republic into a despotism."

Lincoln's Alton speech was the greatest of the seven. In that he reviewed the whole argument. Two short passages are the most notable. They contain the summary of the review. Lincoln uttered them with great impressiveness. He said:

The real issue of this controversy, I think, springs from a sentiment in the mind, and that sentiment is this: On the one part it looks upon the institution of slavery as being wrong, and on the part of another class it does not look upon it as wrong. The sentiment that contemplates the institution of slavery as being wrong, is the sentiment of the Republican party. It is the sentiment around which all their actions and all their arguments circle, from which all their propositions radiate.

And a little further on he said:

That is the real cause!—an issue that will continue in this country when these poor tongues of Douglas and mine shall be silent. These are the two principles that make the eternal struggle between right and wrong; they are the two principles that have stood face to face, one of them asserting the divine right of kings; the same principle that says you work, you toil, you earn bread, and I will eat it. It is the same old sentiment, whether it comes from the mouth of a king who seeks to bestride the people of his nation and to live upon the fat of his neighbor, or whether it comes from one race of men as an apology for the enslaving of another race of men.

President McKinley's Lincoln Story

Washington is an interesting center for news and gossip, but it is the worst place in the country for the formation of judgment on public sentiment. It is historically uncertain in that respect. A Washington correspondent wrote to his editor that public sentiment in Washington indicated something. The editor wrote back that public sentiment in Washington meant nothing. President McKinley in crises never made the mistake of some of his predecessors,—that sentiment in Washington was a safe guide as to conditions of sentiment in the country at large. He, personally, went through many letters that came to the White House. He did more of this than most presidents have done. He had a selected list of newspapers representing all parts of the country and all shades of politics. He read these, not trusting to any private secretary to cull for him. One day a public man called at the White House and undertook to tell Mr. McKinley what the sentiment in Washington was upon a pending question. Mr. McKinley checked the visitor and asked him if he had ever heard the story of President Lincoln and Leonard Swett. Mr. Swett had come to Washington at a critical period and called at the White House. President Lincoln asked him when he had arrived in the capital. Swett replied in a general way. Mr. Lincoln repeated the inquiry in such form as to bring from Mr. Swett the information that he had come in by the latest train, about an hour previous "Oh!" said Mr. Lincoln, "all right. How are things? If you had been in Washington all day, I wouldn't ask you. You would have heard so much your opinion wouldn't be worth anything."

"The national capital, or a state capital, is a bad place to form proper estimates of public sentiment. You can hear too much," was President McKinley's moral drawn from this Lincoln story.

How He Studied German

Of Lincoln getting up early and using the circuit clerk's office for study of the German language, Luman Burr had a definite recollection. Mr. Burr was the deputy clerk of McLean County, of which Bloomington is the seat.[1] His service extended from 1857 to 1862. During the early part of it Mr. Burr formed the acquaintance of Mr. Lincoln.

"I was only a boy of 20 years, and just from the East," he said.[2] "As the deputy clerk, I came to know Mr. Lincoln, but not in an intimate way. I came to know him so well, however, that the caricature of him in a book called 'The Crisis,' by a man named Churchill, fills me with wrath.[3]

"In the old Courthouse at Bloomington," continued Mr. Burr, "Judge Davis had his desk in the same office with William McCullough [McCullogh], the clerk of the Circuit Court.[4] Mr. Lincoln was a great friend of both of them. There was a large, round table in the clerk's office, and in the winter time there was a good fire in a big box stove. Mr. Lincoln had a habit of coming there mornings before court to read or study. Other lawyers would drop in. Leonard Swett, William H. Hanna, Asahel Gridley, John M. Scott, Ward H. Lamon and others were often there.[5] The conversation of such men to a young man just from a New England farm was a revelation. I have heard Mr. Lincoln talk, tell stories, try lawsuits and lecture. One morning, I recollect in particular, he was in the clerk's office studying German. He looked up and said: 'Here is a curious thing: the Germans have no word for thimble; they call it a finger hat (*fingerhut*). And they have no word for glove; they call it a hand shoe (*handschuh*). And then came one of Mr. Lincoln's inimitable laughs.'"

He Established Standard Gauge

President Lincoln, said L. D. Yager, the Alton (Ill.) attorney, is to be credited with the establishment of what is known as standard gauge in railroad construction. This Lincoln story is not only interesting in itself, but it is illustrative of the faculty for settling controversies which Mr. Lincoln possessed. Mr. Lincoln was the personification of fairness. If such a result had been within human agency, President Lincoln would have averted the civil war by a settlement which would have preserved the Union and gradually abolished slavery. Standard gauge is 4 feet 8 ½ inches between rails. Many people have wondered about that half inch.

"When the Union Pacific, the first transcontinental railroad project, reached the stage of legislation there was necessary, of course, an enabling act," said Mr. Yager. "One branch of Congress insisted that the rails should be 4 feet and 10 inches apart. The other body wanted a gauge of 4 feet and 7 inches. On an issue, apparently so trivial, the Senate and House took opposing sides. The question was taken to the White House by interested parties. President Lincoln was asked to express his opinion as to the proper width for a transcontinental railroad track. He took 1 ½ inches from the wider gauge and added it to the narrower gauge, making the width 4 feet 8 ½ inches. In other words, he split the difference. The compromise was accepted by the law-makers and standard gauge was fixed thereby. Other railroads conformed to this government gauge, one after another, until it became the almost universal width between rails."

The Bowl of Custard

When Lincoln "rode the circuit" Bloomington was a literary and social center. Springfield might claim political pre-eminence, as the state capital, but Bloomington performed the rites of hospitality in a way which charmed her guests. The visiting lawyers were entertained during court weeks. Little parties were given in their honor. And Lincoln was the life of these social gatherings.

"I was acquainted with Mr. Lincoln from 1845 to his election as president," said Mrs. Judith A. Bradner, when she was 95 years old.[1] "I am happy to say that I have entertained him in my house often when our city was but a village. The lawyers [from Springfield] would come to Bloomington twice a year to attend court for two weeks. During court weeks here five of us ladies would entertain the lawyers with parties. All of them seemed to enjoy these gatherings. When the two weeks of court were up, Mr. Lincoln would say regretfully, 'Well, our parties are through until fall.' The last time Mr. Lincoln visited us he was in fine spirits. The ceilings in our house were not as high as they are nowadays. Mr. Lincoln struck his head against the chandelier and then apologized, saying, 'We haven't got these things at our house.' At another time he remarked, 'Ladies, excuse me, but this is the nicest party we have had, and we did not have any custard, either.'"

The reference to the custard Mrs. Bradner explained. One of the stopping places on the circuit was Barnett's tavern at Clinton.

"Mrs. Barnett," Mrs. Bradner said, "always made a large bowl of custard for the visiting lawyers. One time when the lawyers arrived at Barnett's and came to the table Mr. Lincoln pointed to the usual bowl of custard and said to Judge Davis. 'Did you ever see anything keep like that custard? It looks as it did when we left it last fall.' The old lady made no more custard for the lawyers."

Neither card playing nor dancing entered into the social entertainments which the ladies of Bloomington provided for the lawyers during court week, as Mrs. Bradner remembers. There was conversation and Mr. Lincoln was the leading personality in the gathering. Occasionally there was singing. Mrs. Bradner remembers that Mrs. David Davis stood by a chair and sang some of the songs of that day. The words of one of these songs of the fifties Mrs. Bradner repeated without any hesitation:

So Miss Myrtle is going to marry?
What a number of hearts she will break!
There's Tom Brown, Lord George and Sir Harry,
All dying of love for her sake.
'Tis the match we all must approve,
Let the gossips say what they can,
For she's really a charming woman,
And he's a most fortunate man.
Chorus—'Tis a match that we all must approve,

Let the gossips say what they can,
Yes, she's really a charming woman,
And he's a most fortunate man.
She's studied both Latin and Greek,
And I'm told that she solved a problem
In Euclid before she could speak.
And the old lady spoke then;
"Had she been but a daughter of mine

I'd taught her to knit and to sew,
But her mother, a charming woman,
Couldn't think of such trifles, you know."
Chorus—'Tis a match that we all must approve, etc.

"Mr. Lincoln never seemed to me to look awkward or to be careless about his appearance but once, that I can remember," Mrs. Bradner said. "Mr. Douglas came to Bloomington to make a speech and I went to hear him. As we got near to the crowd I saw a man sitting on a log, stooping over with his hat on the ground in front of him. I didn't recognize the man, but thought to myself he looked rather careless. Once in a while the man would reach down, pick up some paper, write on it, and throw it in his hat. When I came nearer I saw it was Mr. Lincoln. I realized then that he was sitting back there taking notes of what Mr. Douglas was saying.

"The time that Mr. Lincoln attended the party at our house and struck his head against the chandelier, he passed it off so nicely it did not seem awkwardness on his part. In fact, he hit the chandelier twice with his head. The second time he said, 'Well, that was an awkward piece of business. You know we haven't got those things at our house.'"

"Mr. Lincoln was a kindly, patient man," said Mrs. Bradner. "I visited in Springfield and knew of his home life. Mrs. Capt. Bradford was a neighbor of the Lincolns.[2] She told me that Mrs. Lincoln would put the baby in the carriage and that Mr. Lincoln would wheel it up and down the street after the other men had gone down to the business of their offices. Mrs. Bradford said to Mr. Lincoln one day, 'I think that is pretty business for you to be engaged in, when you ought to be down to your law office.' Mr. Lincoln looked at her and said slowly, 'I promised.' And then he went on with the baby carriage."

"Mr. Lincoln was not so careless about how his clothes looked as some people say," continued Mrs. Bradner. "I recollect one afternoon he was called on to go to tea at somebody's house in Tremont. He had been lying on the grass reading. He said he couldn't go and as a reason showed a hole in the elbow of his coat. The excuse wasn't accepted. Mr. Lincoln yielded and went to the tea, but he sat through it with one hand over that hole in the elbow."

Mrs. Bradner told of a visit she made to Mr. and Mrs. Lincoln at their Springfield home.

"At the time Mr. Lincoln was elected," she said, "I was in Springfield with my sister, Mrs. [John] Albert Jones.[3] We went to the Lincolns the next day to offer our congratulations. Mr. Lincoln was in fine spirits. He told us he thought he had a good joke on his wife. Pointing to Mrs. Lincoln he said, 'She locked me out.' Mrs. Lincoln said to him: '[Shut your mouth.] Don't ever tell that again.'⁴ But Mr. Lincoln laughed and went on with the story. He said Mrs. Lincoln had said when he went downtown in the evening to hear the returns that if he wasn't at home by 10 o'clock she would lock him out. And she did so. But, Mr. Lincoln said that when she heard the music coming to serenade them she turned the key in a hurry."

Albert Blair's Three Vivid Impressions

Three vivid impressions Albert Blair of St. Louis received of Lincoln.¹ He was a native of Pike County, Illinois, a strongly Democratic section of the state, a section where Douglas was a political idol.

"The Senator," said Mr. Blair, "opened his campaign in 1858, early in August, by a speech at Pittsfield, the county town. His devoted constituents were present in great numbers, and to my young eyes he seemed to be the greatest personage in the nation—dignified, eloquent and masterful. The idea that Abe Lincoln, the story-telling rail splitter, should presume to meet him in debate seemed ridiculous. In October following I was present at Quincy, Ill., where a joint debate between the champions occurred. I was surprised at the very large number of Republicans present, and their enthusiasm. The 'Little Giant' in appearance and behavior that day disappointed me. His face was red, his voice husky, and his temper irritable. Mr. Lincoln was treble-toned, buoyant and aggressive. The manner in which at times he would tax 'my friend Judge Douglas,' with a troublesome question, or answer him humorously with 'that reminds me of a story,' or with some other form of telling repartee, all resulting in tremendous laughter and applause, however it may have affected Mr. Douglas certainly worried me very much, and, although I was too young to appreciate the arguments of the respective disputants, I went away with an improved opinion of the strength of the Republican party and of the capabilities of Abraham Lincoln.

"In 1858 and 1860 I was a student at Phillips-Exeter Academy, fitting for Harvard College. Robert Lincoln was there at the same time as a student. My interest in politics was strong, and I was still hoping that the great Illinois Senator might gain the presidency. Early in 1860 Mr. Lincoln made a trip to New York and New England. His speech at Cooper Institute, New York, attracted great attention, and brought him prominently forward as a possible nominee of the Republican party for the presidency. Naturally, his visit to Exeter to see his son was a notable event in the annals of that old academic town. On Saturday night of his stay he made a political speech in the town hall. The audience was large, and composed of the best people. Hon. Amos Tuck presided.[2]

"By this time, as an Illinoisan, I was sensible with pride of the increasing fame of Mr. Lincoln, and hoped he might make a good impression. With one of Exeter's charming daughters I sat in the front row of seats, where I had the best opportunity to hear and observe the speaker. We could not help noticing his lankness of stature, and an occasional uncouth posture or gesture. Some of his Western sayings must have sounded very odd to the precise easterlings. The attitude of the pro-slavery leaders toward Mr. Douglas, he said, reminded him of a story of a farmer out West who had a troublesome dog, and wished to get rid of him. One bitter cold night the farmer decided to freeze the dog by shutting him out in the cold; but somehow the dog would always find an opportunity to get back within doors. Finally the farmer, in greater determination, undertook personally to hold the dog on the north side of the house until the poor creature should succumb. But the dog was the better stayer of the two, and the farmer concluded to adjourn the killing until a more favorable season.

"During his speech Mr. Lincoln would occasionally put a question to the audience and pause for a reply. In one instance he looked about from side to side with an eager, expectant look; no reply coming, he good humoredly said, 'You people here don't jaw back at a fellow as they do out West.'

"These peculiarities did not detract from the general effect. Above the grotesque and the humorous a lofty feeling was dominant. Whether in boldly meeting the imperious legalism of the South, or in laying bare the equivocations of the Douglas doctrine, or in discussing generally the great issues before the nation, there was ever the clear, earnest call to reason in behalf of human rights which did not fail to impress every hearer.

"The month of February, 1865, shortly before the close of the war, and the death of Mr. Lincoln, I spent in Washington. On one occasion I attended a reception at the White House. It was a general reception, open to everybody. The procession of visitors included soldiers and civilians of every rank. Mr. Lincoln was stationed in one of the smaller rooms, and was attended by Judge David Davis. In the same room were a number of handsomely dressed ladies, including Mrs. Lincoln. The visitor was directed by officers first to enter the ante-room, where he gave his name to a lieutenant, and was by the lieutenant conducted and introduced to Judge Davis, and by Judge Davis to the president. A handshake and a word was all that could be practically extended, and the visitor was expected to move along to the larger East room. After my presentation and handshake I, in company with a friend, who was familiar with the etiquette of the White House, stepped aside from the line of exit and took my station for a few moments near the group of ladies, in order that I might have an opportunity to observe the president. I stood near enough to hear Mr. Lincoln in conversation with Judge Davis, which necessarily was quite desultory. The interruptions were incessant. Now it was 'How do you do, Colonel?' or 'My brave boy.' 'I am glad to see you,' or some other word of cordial recognition. There was no official starchiness or affectation. I was, in fact, impressed with the lack of conventional tone and bearing. I heard Mr. Lincoln, in a most unaffected way, and in a tone, if not loud, certainly not confined to the judge's hearing, exclaim to Judge Davis, 'Judge, I never knew until the other day how to spell the word "maintenance."' Then occurred a handshake, or howdy do with some visitor. 'I always thought it was "m-a-i-n, main, t-a-i-n, tain, a-n-c-e, ance—maintainance," but I find that it is "m-a-i-n, main, t-e te, n-a-n-c-e, nance—maintenance."' This was a spectacle! The President of a great nation at a formal reception, surrounded by many eminent people, statesmen, ministers, scholars, critics and ultrafashionable people—by all sorts—who honestly and unconcernedly, in the most unconventional way, speaks before all as it were, of a personal thing illustrative of his own deficiency.

"Whether on the platform in a Western town, or before a cultivated audience in New England, or at the very seat of authority of a great nation, he was ever the same, unaffectedly honest and open to every observer."

The Friend of the Boys

When William B. Thompson of the St. Louis bar was a boy he went fishing with Abraham Lincoln. That was before Mr. Lincoln was a candidate for president; earlier even than the historic Lincoln-Douglas debates. It was when Mr. Lincoln was practicing law in Springfield and wanted a day off.

Then he would put the neighbors' boys into the family carryall, as many as could be crowded in, and drive away to the banks of the Sangamon. The Lincoln whom William B. Thompson remembered best was not the lawyer, the orator, the candidate, the president, but the friend and associate of every boy on the street where he lived in Springfield.

"I lived half a block from Mr. Lincoln's," said Mr. Thompson, "and visited at the house, but more frequently I met Mr. Lincoln on the street as I went to and from school. Mr. Lincoln was not an observant man on the street; in fact, he hardly ever saw us unless we spoke to him. He walked along with his hands behind him, gazing upward and noticing nobody. But it was usual for all of the boys in the neighborhood to speak to him as we met him. He had endeared himself to all of us by reason of the interest he took in us. When one of us spoke to him as he was walking along in his absorbed manner he would stop and acknowledge the greeting pleasantly. If the boy was small Mr. Lincoln would often take him up in his arms and talk to him. If the boy was larger Mr. Lincoln would shake hands and talk with him. If he didn't recall the face, he would ask the name, and if he recognized it he would say, 'Oh, yes; I remember you.' If the boy was a comparative stranger Mr. Lincoln would treat him so pleasantly that the boy always wanted to speak to Mr. Lincoln after that whenever he met him.

"But besides showing interest in us, Mr. Lincoln was exceedingly popular with the boys in the neighborhood because of the fishing trips of the Sangamon river he took with us. He owned a bay horse, which was called a 'shaved-tail' horse. He had a 'calash,' as the roomy vehicle was known. Into the calash Mr. Lincoln would put all of the boys of the neighborhood who could crowd in, and drive out to the Sangamon. We carried our lunches and spent the whole day. After we were pretty well tired tramping about we spread out the lunches. Mr. Lincoln sat down with us. When we had eaten he told us stories and entertained us with his funny comments. No boy who had accompanied Mr. Lincoln on one of these fishing trips willingly missed another. Johnny Spriggs was one of those boys. He lived in our block. His mother was a widow. John Spriggs was hardly grown when four or five years afterward he went into the Union Army. He became an officer of distinction. For a long time he was connected with the Rice-Stix dry goods house in St. Louis. As long as he lived John Spriggs remembered and told those stories he heard from Lincoln on our fishing trips. One of the neighbors was Jesse K. Du Bois, who had two boys, one of whom became a United States senator from Idaho.[1] John G. Ives had three sons. Mr. Lincoln's boys were Robert and Tad. The neighborhood was well built up and nearly every family had boys. We went to a school which we called "the college."[2] One of the principal teachers was Dr. Reynolds, father of Judge George D. Reynolds of St. Louis, of the St. Louis Court of Appeals.[3] George attended the school. Boys came from the counties around Springfield to prepare for college."

"A case that Mr. Lincoln had in court at Springfield about 1857 won him great admiration from the boys," Mr. Thompson recalled. "Quinn Harrison was charged with murder.[4] Lincoln defended him. Harrison and Crafton, who was killed, were young fellows. They lived at Pleasant Plains, in Sangamon County. Harrison was a grandson of Peter Cartwright, the famous pioneer preacher and circuit rider.[5] Crafton was killed as the result of a quarrel. The feeling was quite strong between the friends of the two young men. Harrison was prosecuted by some of the ablest talent at the Springfield bar. My recollection is that James A. Matheney, who was considered one of the strongest lawyers there at the time, was the prosecuting attorney.[6] Mr. Lincoln saved Quinn Harrison, but it was a very hard fight. We boys followed it throughout. All of us who were able climbed to the windows. The others hung around the doors of the old courthouse. We listened with most careful attention to everything Lincoln said. His argument to the jury for Quinn Harrison made a lasting impression upon us. At that time Lincoln had not become famous as a debater. Harrison was acquitted. We boys agreed that Lincoln's speech and earnest manner did it, rather than the evidence.

"I think, perhaps, the Springfield boys recognized the power of Lincoln's eloquence earlier than did some of their elders," continued Mr. Thompson, thoughtfully. "Springfield in that day had a number of lawyers who had won fame at the bar. Milton Hay, the brother [uncle] of John Hay, had come up from Belleville with a great reputation as a lawyer.[7] John A. McClernand was known in all that part of Illinois as the 'Grecian orator' because of the many quotations from the classics he put into his speeches.[8] McClernand was called the most scholarly man at the Springfield bar.

"It was said that he had studied with the view of entering the priesthood, but had taken up the law instead. Logan, Stuart, Edwards, Matheney and Conkling were considered eminent lawyers.[9] Some of them stood so high that they did not have to go 'on the circuit.' Business came to them in Springfield. But with the acquittal of Quinn Harrison all of the boys agreed that Mr. Lincoln was their ideal. We took every opportunity to hear Lincoln speak. The campaign of 1858 was notable for the number of boys who attended whenever Lincoln spoke. We talked politics. We knew all about the 'Kansas-Nebraska bill.' Stephen A. Douglas was a favorite orator when the campaign opened. He was very widely known. He had practiced law in Jacksonville, Beardstown and Springfield and was personally acquainted with every man of prominence. Lincoln was not so well known. Some of the politicians belittled Lincoln. They did not think he was up to the standard of Douglas, who had been quite a figure in the Senate. But the Springfield boys followed the debate with great confidence in Mr. Lincoln. They never forgot the Quinn Harrison speech. It wasn't long after the speaking opened in the campaign before public sentiment as to the relative strength of Lincoln and Douglas in debate began to change. The older people began to see Lincoln in the estimate the boys had put upon him. While Lincoln did not succeed in winning the senatorship from Douglas, the feeling grew that his position was the stronger. Lincoln's speeches in that campaign of 1858 made a very strong impression.

"The day Mr. Lincoln left Springfield in 1861 to go to Washington for the inauguration was the last time I saw him. All of the boys were at the station, and the most enthusiastic cheering came from them. Some of the older people looked very serious; they were predicting that Mr. Lincoln would not be allowed to reach Washington; that he would be stopped if he tried to pass through Maryland. Many believed there would be interference. I remember that I went up to John Hay, who was going with Mr. Lincoln, and asked him if he had any doubt about getting through. As we young fellows shouted our farewell to Mr. Lincoln that day we felt as if we were parting from a personal friend to whom we were deeply attached."

"Mr. Lincoln was liked by young and old because he liked both young and old," George Perrin Davis of Bloomington said. He treasured an autograph album in which distinguished men, who were the guests or friends of his father, Mr. Justice David Davis, wrote their sentiments and names at his youthful requests. Before Mr. Lincoln was nominated for president— indeed, just after Mr. Lincoln had been beaten for the senatorship by Mr. Douglas—George Perrin Davis selected him for first place in the autograph album. And Mr. Lincoln wrote:

> My young friend, George Perrin Davis, has allowed me the honor of being
> the first to write his name in this book.
>
> A. LINCOLN.
>
> Bloomington, December 21, 1858.

Abraham Lincoln and George Perrin Davis, with a third of a century between their ages, were friends. Mr. Lincoln was a visitor at the Davis home from the earliest time that George Perrin Davis could remember. One year

George Perrin Davis "rode the circuit" day after day, week after week, the boy companion of Mr. Lincoln.

"The eighth circuit," he said, "as established in 1847, extended on the north from Woodford to the Indiana state line, south as far as Shelby and the western counties were Sangamon, Logan and Tazewell. It had nearly 11,000 square miles, about one-fifth of the whole state. There were no mail roads for many years and but few bridges over the rivers. Courts were held in the various counties twice a year, lasting from two or three days to a week. After court had adjourned in one county, the judge rode to the next county seat, and was followed by the state's attorney, whose authority extended over the whole circuit, and by some of the lawyers to a few of the counties near their homes. Mr. Lincoln, however, rode the entire circuit to all of the courts, which lasted about three months in the spring and three in the fall. Most of the lawyers rode horseback. After a few years my father, who was the circuit judge, and Mr. Lincoln were able to afford a buggy. My father, who was a very heavy man, used two horses. Mr. Lincoln had a one-horse open buggy and drove his horse, 'Old Buck,' as I remember his name. In the fall of 1850, when I was 8 years old, my mother went around the circuit with my father and Mr. Lincoln took me in his buggy. I have a distinct recollection of Mr. Lincoln, the horse and the buggy, but can not remember much of what Mr. Lincoln said."[10]

Boylike, Mr. Davis received some impressions on that trip which he recalled fifty years later. At Danville he saw his first coal fire, except in a forge, and amused himself heating and bending the poker. At Springfield the state attorney, Mr. Campbell, delighted the boy with the gift of some percussion caps which Master George proceeded to explode upon the wheels of Mr. Lincoln's buggy, getting some of the copper into his face.[11] One incident was very characteristic of the age of Mr. Lincoln's associate on the memorable trip. The boy wished to know from his own observation how tall Mr. Lincoln was. And the lawyer was obliging.

"Mr. Lincoln," said Mr. Davis, "was very tall, 6 feet 4 ½ inches, as I measured him although he gives it himself in his autobiography, addressed to Jesse W. Fell, at 6 feet 4 inches nearly; but when he became much interested in his speech he looked as if he was 8 feet high."

At the home of his friend, Judge Davis, Mr. Lincoln spent considerable time in 1858, "while he was writing some of his debates with Mr. Douglas," George Perrin Davis recalled. Most of Mr. Lincoln's speeches were not written out in advance of delivery. Those for the joint debates were prepared with extraordinary care.

"Mr. Lincoln," said Mr. Davis, "did not care much about dress, though he was always clean. I thought his clothes were too short for him, especially his coat. For a necktie he wore an old-fashioned stiff stock, which clasped around his neck. When he got interested in his speech he would take it off and unbutton his shirt and give room for his Adam's apple to play up and down. He had a clear voice that could be heard a great distance, every word of a sentence equally clear, a great contrast to Mr. Douglas, who failed sometimes to send every word the same distance. Mr. Lincoln was clean shaven until he was elected president."

The historical society at Bloomington preserves as one of its most valued records the tribute paid by Senator Daniel W. Voorhees of Indiana, who as a young lawyer practiced in the courts of Illinois along the Indiana line and met Mr. Lincoln and Judge Davis frequently. Of Lincoln and Douglas, Senator Voorhees wrote:

"They made such an impression on me as no two other men whom I have met in the tide of time or of whom I have read in the realm of history."

George T. M. Davis, the Alton editor, twenty-five years the friend of Lincoln, left his family an unpublished autobiography. A limited number of copies was printed and given to personal friends. In this way has been preserved the narrative of an incident revealing Lincoln, the father. Affection for his sons was a marked trait of Mr. Lincoln. There are many stories illustrative of that. But the methods Mr. Lincoln employed to instill into the minds of his boys the cardinal virtues have received little attention from the biographers. Mr. Davis told what he witnessed on one occasion:

I made a visit on business one summer to Springfield, where Mr. Lincoln resided. While I was standing on the sidewalk, on the shady side of the hotel where I was stopping, Mr. Lincoln came along with his youngest pet boy, Tad, who was holding on to the tip of the tail of father's frock coat. We drew up chairs in the shade and at once engaged in talking politics. Tad changed his position by taking refuge between his father's knees, and remained there a silent listener during our conversation. In a short time Bob, who was considerably older than Tad, came along, and, noticing us, also stopped and joined our circle. In a side conversation that ensued between the two brothers, the purport of which I had not noticed, something was said that induced their father to pause for a moment in his talk with me, and, turning to the boys, he exclaimed:

"Tad, show Mr. Davis the knife I bought you yesterday," and, turning to me, he added, "It's the first knife Tad ever had, and it's a big thing for him."

Tad hesitating and making no reply, his father asked, "You haven't lost your knife, have you?"

"No, but I ain't got any," the boy said.

"What has become of it?" inquired Mr. Lincoln in his quizzical and usual smiling, pleasant way. There was another momentary pause on the part of Tad, when he replied to his father, in the fullness of his childish simplicity, and the truthfulness which was a prominent element of his birthright:

"Bob told me if he was me, he'd swap my knife for candy."

At this Mr. Lincoln gave one of his good-natured laughs, and turning to Bob—who by this time bore somewhat the semblance of slight embarrassment—but without the slightest change in either his merry tone or manner, asked:

"Bob, how much did you pay for that candy?"

Bob naming the price, his father said to him, "Why, Tad's knife cost three bits (37 ½ cents); do you think you made a fair trade with Tad?"

Bob, in a prompt and manly tone, which I shall never forget, answered his father, "No, sir," and taking the knife out of his pocket, said "Here, Tad, is your knife," which Tad, with evident delight, took back, but without a word of comment. Their father, however, said to the eldest:

"I guess, Bob, that's about right on your part, and now, Tad, as you've got your knife, you must give back to Bob the candy he gave you for the knife."

Tad exclaimed, "I can't, 'cause I ate up all the candy Bob give me, and I ain't got no money to buy it."

"Oh!" said Mr. Lincoln, "what will you do then? Bob must have his candy back to make things square between you."

Tad was evidently in a quandary, and was at a loss how to get out of it, but his father, after waiting a few moments, and without making the slightest comment, handed Tad a bit (12 ½ cents). Tad looked at it with a good deal of satisfaction and shrieked out in his boyish glee:

"Come on, Bob, I'll get your candy back for you."

Both the father and I joined in a hearty laugh, and as the boys started off Mr. Lincoln called out to them:

"Boys, I reckon that's about right between you. Bob, do you take Tad right home as soon as he has paid you the candy."

Such was the sense and conviction of duty, justice, honor, integrity and truthfulness of Abraham Lincoln.

Mr. Lincoln did not hesitate to tell the same story more than once, or to vary it to make the application fit. He also modified or amended those apt sayings, which will never die, in order that they might suit different occasions. Maj. William K. Patrick of St. Louis recalled the story about the brand of whiskey which Grant drank, but he obtained it from another source than the late Henry T. Blow, and in somewhat different form from the version which William Hyde used to tell.[12] Mr. Hyde, afterwards editor, was a reporter on the *Missouri Republican* when Mr. Blow brought the story to St. Louis from Washington, during the war, and gave it local currency.

"The story as I heard it," said Maj. Patrick, "was that President Lincoln made use of the inquiry in conversation with Capt. W. J. [William W.] Kountz. Capt. Kountz, a wealthy steamboatman from Pittsburg, had obtained from the secretary of the treasury, through his Pennsylvania friends, a permit to buy cotton outside the Union military lines and ship the same up North. Capt. Kountz presented the permit to Gen. Grant, who refused to allow the agents of the captain to go beyond the military lines around Memphis. The captain was very indignant at being turned down, and took himself back to Washington. Calling on Mr. Lincoln, he stated his case, and demanded that Gen. Grant be relieved as commander of the Department of the Tennessee. To make his case as strong as possible, he said that Gen. Grant was a hard drinker. Mr. Lincoln listened with his usual patience to the tirade and asked Capt. Kountz what brand of whiskey Gen. Grant used. The captain said he didn't know. Then Mr. Lincoln said: "Find out and let me know, so I can send a barrel to each of my generals."

Mr. Lincoln's different ways of telling the same story was illustrated in connection with the historic joint debates. At one of those meetings Mr. Douglas said something half-way complimentary to Mr. Lincoln. When Mr. Lincoln arose he acknowledged the consideration of Senator Douglas, and added he felt a good deal as did the Hoosier who said he liked gingerbread better than anybody on this earth, and got less of it than anybody on this earth. In as much as Senator Douglas had been anything but complimentary before that meeting, and in as much as Mr. Lincoln had been unmercifully abused and misrepresented by the opposition from the beginning of the debates up to that time, the Hoosier story caught the popular sense of humor and made a great hit. That was in 1858. Several years afterwards, while he was in the White House, President Lincoln made use of the same story, but amplified it, showing its origin. The application was as happy as that in response to Douglas' faint praise. A Southerner, who had not gone with the Confederacy, but who had remained in Washington and had gradually overcome his intense personal prejudices toward Mr. Lincoln after several interviews with him, said to the president one day that he had heard everything mean about him that could be said of a man except one failing; he had never heard that Mr. Lincoln was too fond of the pleasures of life. Mr. Lincoln looked thoughtful at his rather meager, if not be-grudged, tribute, and after a little hesitation said he was reminded of what a boy had said to him when he was quite small.

"Once in awhile my mother used to get some sorghum and ginger and make some gingerbread," was the way Mr. Lincoln told it.

It wasn't often, and it was our biggest treat. One day I smelled the gin-gerbread and came into the house to get my share while it was hot. My mother had baked me three gingerbread men. I took them out under a hick-ory tree to eat them. There was a family near us that was a little poorer than we were, and their boy came along as I sat down.

"Abe," he said, "gimme a man?"

I gave him one. He crammed it into his mouth in two bites and looked at me while I was biting the legs from my first one.

"Abe," he said, "gimme that other'n."

I wanted it myself, but I gave it to him, and as it followed the first I said to him, "You seem to like gingerbread?"

"Abe," he said, "I don't suppose there's anybody on this earth likes gin-gerbread better'n I do." He drew a long breath before he added, "and I don't suppose there's anybody on this earth gets less'n I do."

The old Southerner who told this remarked that when Mr. Lincoln had finished the story there didn't seem to be anything more to be said.

The Bixby Collection

Abraham Lincoln stands at the head of the class of American presidents in penmanship, in spelling, in punctuation and in grammatical construction. "Awkward," "uncouth," "ungainly" are some of the adjectives used to de-scribe him physically. And yet when Mr. Lincoln took pen in hand he wrote "like copperplate." The letters were distinct. The words were com-plete. The writing was as easily read as print. There was mechanical finish and perfection about a specimen of Mr. Lincoln's writing, whether he used the old quill, the pencil or the pen. Eugene Field, the poet, wrote a style that was very like that of Mr. Lincoln.[1] At the age of 23 Mr. Lincoln could have qualified for teacher of penmanship in a commercial college. At the age of 50, with the crowded law practice and with the rush of political correspon-dence upon him, he did not do as fine pen work as in his younger days.

When he began law practice he had time to carry out his liking for a beautifully written page. Some of the legal papers prepared in that period of his career are marvelously well done. The lines are written as regularly as if the paper was ruled. Every "t" is crossed. Every comma requisite is in place. Not a misspelled word can be found. Seldom a correction was made after the first draft. As a rule interlineations in anything written by Mr. Lincoln—legal document, letter or speech—were rare, even in the later days, when the exercise of care in the writing is not so evident.

Mr. Lincoln was not at all boastful of his superiority as a writer. The biographers record that when, just old enough to vote, he was asked at the polling place in New Salem if he could write, he replied, "A little bit. I can make a few rabbit tracks." This sounds like Mr. Lincoln, and yet it was strange that a young man who wrote such an unusual hand as he did should have been asked that question by one of his neighbors.

To write was a family characteristic of the Lincolns. The president had first cousins, sons of his father's brother, who wrote in plain legible style much better than the average person of their day.[2] None of them wrote as well as did Abraham Lincoln of Sangamon. Whence came this accomplishment? Lincoln had it from the time he was a very young man. He was self educated, but this gift of superior handwriting was an inheritance and it came with the steady nerves and the equable disposition on the Lincoln side of the house.

While Mr. Lincoln did not make boast of his skill with the pen, he indirectly let it be seen that he scrutinized the composition of the other fellow. In one case, the papers of which have been preserved in the county where the trial took place, Mr. Lincoln wrote that the indictment was bad, "in that it does not show with sufficient certainty whether the defendant was the murderer of the murdered man."

Painstaking is not the word that applies to Lincoln's writing. The pen or pencil moved over the page easily, naturally, readily. That is apparent from the style of writing. Even stronger evidence is found in the volume of written matter which Mr. Lincoln turned out. From the beginning of his career as a lawyer down through the busiest days at the White House, Mr. Lincoln wrote and wrote. There are in existence letters and papers of his penmanship in greater number probably than any other president wrote. The letters number thousands. Many of them bear evidence that they were not answers and need not have been written and would not have been written by one to whom writing was irksome or in any sense a task. Lincoln liked to write so well that he very seldom dictated anything. When it was suggested to him, in 1858, during the campaign against Douglas for the senatorship that he avail himself of the assistance of a young newspaper man in the revision of his speeches for the press, Mr. Lincoln declined with a smile.

In the extensive and widely varied collection of Lincoln papers possessed by William K. Bixby of St. Louis are interesting revelations of this strong writing habit of Mr. Lincoln.[3] Whether in letter, law paper or state document, the composition was simple and closely condensed. But this did not mean that Mr. Lincoln wished to get through as quickly as possible. It indicated the habit of mind. There are very few letters of Mr. Lincoln which exceed a single page.

Prince L. Hudgins was a lawyer in St. Louis who was charged with conspiring against the government. In his letter to President Lincoln, Mr. Hudgins explained that the charge against him was based on a speech he had made in St. Joseph several months before the law under which he was being prosecuted was enacted.[4] Congressman King presented the petition and recommended the pardon.[5] The president wrote on the papers:

Attorney General: Please see Mr. King and make out the pardon he asks. Give this man a fair deal, if possible.[6]

And then, probably after a little further conversation with the Missourian, the president, in the kindness of his heart, added this to the indorsement:

Gov. King leaves Saturday evening and would want to have it with him to take along, if possible. Would wish it made out as soon as conveniently can be.

The attention which the president gave personally to even routine matters is shown by the instructions and comments written by him upon these many papers in the Bixby collection, the most of which have never been printed. Upon the application for a judgeship at Plattsmouth, Utah, appears this in the well-known hand:

I knew George May when a boy and young man, then a little inclined to be dissipated. If free from that now, he has intellect for almost any place. I suppose the within names ought to be a sufficient voucher as to that.

A. LINCOLN.[7]

"The within names" indorsing May are those of James Harlan, James F. Wilson and James W. Grimes of Iowa.[8] Harlan and Grimes were senators and Wilson was a representative in Congress from Iowa.

Upon the application of Judge S. P. McCurdy of Missouri for an appointment President Lincoln made an indorsement which reveals how well he remembered the sharp division between Missouri Republicans:

This is a good recommendation for a territorial judgeship, embracing both sides in Missouri and many other respectable gentlemen.

> A. L.[9]

Gov. Green Clay Smith of Kentucky presented in person, it appears from the papers in Mr. Bixby's collection, an application for a pardon in behalf of William Duke.[10] Col. Duke wrote that "in a state of excitement he had accepted a commission to raise a regiment" for the Confederate cause, but had reconsidered almost immediately, had taken the oath of allegiance and had given a bond of $5000 for his loyalty. Mr. Lincoln wrote upon the papers:

> William Duke is hereby pardoned for all offenses herein confessed by him up to the time of his taking the oath and giving bond.
>
> A. L.

Then he gave to Mr. Smith this note to the attorney general:

> "Please make out and send for my signature a formal pardon according to letter with my little indorsement which will be shown you by Gov. Green Clay Smith."[11]

Upon the papers accompanying an application for a justice of the peace appointment in Washington the president wrote:

> I do not recollect having acquaintance with Esquire Ferguson, but if the commissioner of public buildings inclines to appoint him to any place I have no objection.
>
> A. L.[12]

In forwarding the papers of Joseph M. Root of Ohio to the proper cabinet officer the president wrote upon the back:

> Of course it is not proper for me to indulge my personal feelings, but I am very partial to Mr. Root.[13]

The papers which Mr. Bixby has in his collection come down to the last days. There is the pardon of James McCan [James M. Campbell], granted on the 22d of March, 1865, with this indorsement:

> On the request of Vice-President Johnson it is ordered that a special pardon be made out in this case.
>
> A. LINCOLN.[14]

The kindly consideration for others which was shown by President Lincoln was marvelous. In the closing weeks of the war, with a multitude of matters pressing for attention, he went on examining and indorsing this endless mail conscientiously and thoughtfully. On the 9th of March, 1865, he sent an unsuccessful candidate's [John C. Grannis's] papers to the Department of Justice with this written by him on the back:

This came to me at half-past 3 p. m., after the nomination for district attorney had been sent in.

> A. L.[15]

Mr. Bixby has a letter written by Mr. Lincoln to O. H. Browning of Quincy, upon a professional matter, which illustrates the aptitude of the writer in coining phrases to express a great deal. The letter was sent in June, 1857:

> I learned that this note was given as a sort of "insolvent fix-up" with his creditors—a fact in his history I have not before learned of. Our interview ended in the assurance he will pay it middle of June.[16]

A copy of a telegram in his own hand-writing which Mr. Lincoln sent from the War Department to Mrs. Lincoln while she was in Boston the 9th of November, 1862, reads:

> Mrs. Cuthbert and Aunt Mary want to move to the White House because it has grown so cold at Soldiers' Home.[17] Shall they?

> A. LINCOLN.

Robert Lincoln in Two Crises

The visit to his son at the Exeter institution was to have important bearing upon Mr. Lincoln's political fortunes. At the time it was prompted probably with no other motive than a father's solicitude for his eldest son. Robert Todd Lincoln, in a reminiscent talk with Frederick W. Lehmann, told how unconsciously at the time, he had been associated with two crises in his father's life. The first was in the winter of 1859–60, a few months before the nomination. Mr. Lincoln very much desired that Robert should go to Harvard. Like many other men who had been denied advantages of higher education he was determined that his son should have the best that the time afforded. The son was not so strongly inclined toward Harvard. However, in accord with his father's wishes he went on from Springfield to Cambridge. He quickly discovered that he lacked the preparation for the high standards of the entrance examination. The Phillips-Exeter Academy was the leading preparatory school for college in those days. Thither Robert was sent, rather reluctantly on his own part, to be made ready for Harvard. Mr. Lincoln was so deeply interested in his plans for his son's education that one of the strong inducements to make the eastern trip and speak at Cooper Institute in New York City was his desire to see how Robert was progressing with his studies. From New York, Mr. Lincoln went to New Hampshire. On the way to and from Exeter he made several speeches in New England. Robert Lincoln said to Mr. Lehmann that the record of the balloting at the Chicago convention a few months later showed that the Eastern States which were the first to come over to the support of his father and insure the nomination were those where the speeches on the Exeter trip were made.

The other crisis, in which he unconsciously had a part, Robert Lincoln said to Mr. Lehmann was the night of the tragedy in Ford's Theater.

That day Robert Lincoln had come up to Washington from Virginia where he had been doing staff duty. He went to the White House and after the exchange of greetings was told of the plan to attend the theater that evening. The President said there would be room for him in the box and asked him to be one of the party. The son excused himself on the plea that he was tired and would prefer to rest. Robert Lincoln told Mr. Lehmann that he learned afterwards the one vacant seat in the box which he would have occupied was directly in front of the door by which Booth entered. He thought if he had gone to the theater and had taken that chair he might have been in a position to save his father's life.

The Courtship and Home Life

The true story of Abraham Lincoln's courtship, marriage and home life is not the story that has been oft told with variations. It differs in detailed circumstances and in general spirit from much that has been printed hitherto. The true story was told by Albert Stevenson Edwards.[1] There was, at the time, no one living so well qualified as Mr. Edwards to speak of Lincoln the lover, and of Lincoln, the husband. Albert Stevenson Edwards was the son of Ninian W. Edwards.[2] His grandfather was Ninian Edwards, the pioneer governor of Illinois, coming from Lexington, Ky.[3] Ninian W. Edwards was educated at the old Transylvania University in Lexington. There he courted and married Elizabeth, the oldest of a family of famous sisters.[4] Ninian W. Edwards early made his home in Springfield. Sisters of Mrs. Edwards came from Lexington to visit her until one after another, three of them, Frances, Mary and Ann Todd, were married and residing in Springfield.[5]

The third of these sisters became the wife of Abraham Lincoln. She wore to the end of her troubled days the plain gold band placed there by her husband, inscribed "Love is eternal." Town gossips dealt harshly and unjustly with Mrs. Lincoln in the Springfield years. Writers in Washington held this lady up to ridicule and adverse criticism. The makers of Lincoln literature have followed this lead of misjudgment and misrepresentation, even to the present. At the home of Ninian W. Edwards, Abraham Lincoln and Mary Todd first met. There the acquaintance grew quickly into stronger sentiment. There the courtship was seriously discouraged, but there, when family reasoning was unavailing, the wedding took place. And, finally, in that home Mrs. Lincoln found refuge and peace after all of her sorrows in the closing years of her life.

Albert Stevenson Edwards was a child witness of the marriage of his aunt to Mr. Lincoln. He became the favorite nephew of Mr. and Mrs. Lincoln. In his youth he spent many of his Saturdays and Sundays at the home of Mr. and Mrs. Lincoln. In later years he lived in that home, having been, most fittingly, given charge of it by the state. Sitting in the corner room of the home, with family reminders all about him, with original letters and records at hand, Mr. Edwards talked frankly about periods and events in the lives of Mr. and Mrs. Lincoln. He was a man of the even-balanced Edwards temperament, not inclined to make gossip and parade family history, and consenting only to the conversation because he felt it a duty to correct so much of misrepresentation which has been published.

"The acquaintance of my father with Mr. Lincoln," Mr. Edwards said, "began before Mr. Lincoln moved to Springfield. Dr. William Jayne's father and my father went out from Springfield to New Salem on some business matter and there saw Mr. Lincoln, then quite a young man, about 25 years old.[6] They were a good deal impressed with his brightness. Old Dr. Jayne said to my father, indicating Mr. Lincoln, 'That young man over there will be governor of Illinois some day.' The acquaintance was renewed and strengthened when Mr. Lincoln went to the Legislature in 1834. My father was attorney general of the state. To the next Legislature Sangamon County sent a delegation to work for the removal of the state capital from Vandalia to Springfield. That delegation was composed of two senators and seven representatives. Sangamon was a large county, much larger than it is now. The delegation was selected with care for what it was expected to accomplish. Mr. Lincoln and my father were two of the representatives. The other five were: William F. Elkins [Elkin], Dan Stone, John Dawson, Andrew McCormick, Robert L. Wilson.[7] The state senators were: Archer

G. Herndon and Job Fletcher.[8] This delegation was known as 'the long nine,' because the most of them were men of extraordinary stature. My father was a man 6 feet and 3 inches, only 1 inch shorter than Mr. Lincoln. McCormick was a very large man. Elkins was the smallest. Together those nine men measured 54 feet. The delegation was successful in what it undertook. On the 25th of February, 1837, the Legislature voted to remove the capital from Vandalia to Springfield. Three days later the account for the entertainment of the legislators was presented to the Sangamon delegation."

Mr. Edwards crossed the room and took from the wall this framed record of hospitality.

Vandalia, Ill., Feb. 28, 1837

Colonel Dawson to E. Capps, Dr.:

81 bottles of champagne at $2.00 each	$162.00
Drinks	6.00
32 pounds almonds	8.00
14 pounds raisins	10.00
Cigars	10.00
Oysters	10.00
Apples	3.00
Eatables	12.00
Breakage	2.00
Sundries	.50
Total	$223.50

Rec'd payment of N. W. Edwards, March 4th.

E. CAPPS.

"Ebenezer Capps," explained Mr. Edwards, as he restored the bill to its place among the relics of the Lincoln home, "was the principal storekeeper at Vandalia. It was about that time Mr. Lincoln moved from New Salem to Springfield. I have never heard why Mr. Lincoln made the change of residence. I suppose it was because Springfield was the larger place, with more future to it. My father from the beginning admired Mr. Lincoln and maintained friendship with him all of the time afterward. Mr. Lincoln's first call at my father's house was made in 1837. He was a frequent and welcome visitor there afterward, except during the period of the courtship between my aunt and Mr. Lincoln."

"There is no foundation for that statement," Mr. Edwards said, with emphasis, when reference was made to the story repeatedly published that the wedding of Mr. Lincoln was postponed because of his failure to appear at the appointed time.

"My father entertained a great deal," Mr. Edwards continued. "He kept open house, you might say, in those days, when the capital was being moved and established in Springfield. The governor received a very small salary, $1500 or $1800 a year. My father was looked upon as a man of considerable means. As a matter of public spirit, he undertook to supply the social courtesies deemed necessary at the new capital. He gave out that he would have four receptions during the session, inviting the members of the Legislature, the state officers and judges of the Supreme Court and leading lawyers, dividing them into four lists. He carried out the programme to the letter, entertaining that first winter the entire state government. There were many relatives of our family, young ladies. Father was a great hand to have the house full of company. In the Legislature of 1840 and 1842 were the young men who afterward became the most distinguished in the state. Lincoln was about 30, bright and jolly, and a great favorite with all of the young ladies at my father's. From 1837 to 1839 he was one of the most frequent visitors. There was nothing bashful about him. The ladies would urge him to call again. My father had a relative here from Alton, Matilda Edwards, daughter of Cyrus Edwards, a very bright girl.[9] The family thought that Lincoln was much taken with Matilda, but nothing came of it beyond story-telling and fun-making.[10] That first session of the Legislature at Springfield the House of Representatives met in the Second Presbyterian Church, the Senate in the First Methodist Church and the Supreme Court in the Episcopal Church. You see, Springfield had obtained the capital before provision had been made to take care of the Legislature. My father felt that it devolved upon him to provide hospitality, and so it was that his home became the social center. My mother's sisters came from Lexington to help do the entertaining. Frances was the second and Mary was the third of the family. Mr. Lincoln met Mary Todd soon after her arrival in 1839."

Mr. Edwards took up some family papers and showed this description of Mary Todd as a young lady, given by [to] one of her sisters:

She had a plump, round figure and was rather short of stature. Her features were not regularly beautiful, but she was certainly very pretty, with her lovely complexion, soft brown hair, and clear blue eyes and intelligent bright face. She was singularly sensitive. She was also impulsive, and made no attempt to conceal her feelings; indeed, it would have been an impossibility had she desired to do so, for her face was an index to every passing emotion.

Without desiring to wound, she occasionally indulged in sarcastic, witty remarks, that cut like a damascus blade, but there was no malice behind them. She was full of humor, but never unrefined. Perfectly frank and extremely spirited, her candor of speech and independence of thought often gave offense where none was meant, for a more affectionate heart never beat.[11]

If this is a true analysis of Mary Todd's character, and there is no reason to doubt the sister's estimate, writers on Lincoln have done his wife injustice. Mr. Lincoln's calls at the Edwards' home became more frequent after the arrival of Mary Todd. Other young lawyers flocked to the house, among them Stephen A. Douglas, who was very much smitten with the little Kentucky girl. But it was not many weeks before Mary Todd began to show decided preference for Abraham Lincoln.

"My mother and my father both liked Mr. Lincoln," Mr. Edwards said. "Up to the time of the courtship they had made Lincoln welcome and had encouraged his visits. A cousin of my mother, John Todd Stuart, was the law partner of Mr. Lincoln. But my mother and my father at that time didn't want Mary to marry Mr. Lincoln. There was no objection to the match on the ground of Mr. Lincoln's character or social standing. But Mr. Lincoln then hadn't $500 to his name. He was just getting started in the practice of his profession. My mother and my father felt that he could not support Mary as they thought she ought to be maintained, and for that reason only they opposed the engagement. Mary Todd might have married Douglas at any time. Shields paid her attention as did others. But Lincoln and Mary fell in love with each other almost at their first meeting in 1839. Mary was the belle of that period in the new capital. She was full of jokes. I have heard them tell of her pranks. One day she was down town with several other young ladies. Springfield had few sidewalks at that time. Mary and her companions took a dray, climbed on and rode home to escape walking through the mud. When my mother saw that things were becoming serious between Lincoln and Mary, she treated him rather coldly. The invitations to call were not pressed. This didn't have the effect my mother intended. During 1841 and 1842 my mother did what she could to break up the match."

Springfield people remember Mrs. Ninian W. Edwards, the eldest of the Todd sisters, as a lady of far more than ordinary attractiveness. Mrs. Edwards' traits especially fitted her to carry out her husband's spirit of hospitality. She was of gentle, winning disposition, a charming hostess; she is remembered to this day as having been the social leader at the new state capital. Mrs. Edwards did not resort to measures strenuous or extreme to prevent the marriage of her spirited sister, but she tried to avert it in her own way without hurting the feelings of Mr. Lincoln.

Lincoln was 30 and Mary Todd was nearly 20 when their acquaintance began. Lincoln's law practice was very small. He had been admitted to the bar only a short time before. He felt the weight of the seriousness of the objection which Mrs. Edwards raised. The girl was deeply in love with him. She was impulsive and strong-willed. It fell to Lincoln to do some hard thinking for both of them. That he had periods of depression and despondency, as he contemplated his unfortunate financial condition and realized what was expected of him, is not to be wondered. Mary Todd was highly educated for that day. Mr. Edwards preserved an account of her school days, written to a sister of Mrs. Lincoln by a schoolmate who remembered these facts:

> Mary was bright and talkative and warm-hearted. She was far advanced over girls of her age in education. She was a pupil of the celebrated Mr. Ward.[12] He was a splendid educator; his requirements and rules were very strict, and woe to her who did not conform to the letter. Mary accepted the condition of things and never came under his censure. We occupied the same room, and I can see her now as she sat on one side of a table, poring over her books, and I on the other, with a candle between. She was very studious, with a retentive memory and a mind that enabled her to grasp and thoroughly understand the lessons she was required to learn. Mr. Ward required his pupils to recite some of their lessons before breakfast. On a pleasant summer morning, nature would hardly rebel, but what an ordeal to rise in winter by candlelight and make the needful preparations to encounter the furious blasts! I have nothing but the most pleasant memories of her at that time. I never saw any display of temper, nor saw her reprimanded during the months I was an inmate of your father's house.

The education that Mary Todd received included the classics. She studied Latin and Greek. From Ward she went to a finishing school kept by Mrs. Montell [Victoire Charlotte Leclere Mentelle] for the favored daughters of the blue grass region. There she remained four years. Nothing but French was spoken at that school. All of her life Mrs. Lincoln was a thorough French scholar, speaking and reading the language. She read the best French authors. At this school of Mrs. Montell Mary Todd was taught, with other accomplishments, dancing. She came heart free to the new Illinois capital. One of her especial friends in Lexington had been Miss Margaret Wickliffe, who became the wife of Gen. William Preston.[13] The father of the Todd sisters was Robert Smith Todd, descended from an old colonial and revolutionary family.[14] He was a merchant in Lexington and for some years president of a bank. His first wife, the mother of Mrs. Lincoln, was a daughter of Maj. Robert Parker of Lexington.[15]

Mary Todd, of the best blood of Kentucky, fascinating in appearance and in manner, intellectual, educated with the best advantages that Lexington could give, quickly fell in love with Abraham Lincoln, the young lawyer just starting in his profession. Her bright sayings became the talk of the town. At least one of them was at the expense of Mr. Lincoln. It is told that at a social gathering Mr. Lincoln approached the young lady and said to her:

"Miss Mary, I want to dance with you the worst way."

The pressing request was complied with. A little later one of the other young ladies mischievously asked how Lincoln danced.

"The worst way," laconically replied Miss Mary.

She was Miss Mary, for there was between Mrs. Edwards and Mary Todd, another sister, Frances, who also spent much of her time in Springfield, a guest at the hospitable Edwards' home, and who married a Springfield resident, Dr. Wallace. The Wallace wedding was one of the grand affairs of its time. Curiously this marriage of the Wallaces has been described and pictured again and again, even down to the immediate present, as the wedding of Abraham Lincoln and Mary Todd, which was an altogether different kind of an affair. One of the earliest biographers of Lincoln led off with a description of this Wallace wedding, mistaking it for the Lincoln wedding, and other writers have fallen into the same error, making it contribute to the misrepresentation of Mrs. Lincoln and using it as evidence of excessive display and vanity on the part of one who was to marry a young man of no financial resources. The facts are that the marriage of Lincoln and Mary Todd was an unostentatious affair, taking place on short notice in the presence of a few relatives. The grand affair was the wedding of the sister which preceded it only a few weeks. The biographer Herndon made this mistake of confusing the Lincoln with the Wallace wedding.[16] Later writers have accepted his version.

"When Lincoln saw that his attentions to my aunt were looked upon coldly by my mother and father, his visits to our house became less frequent," Mr. Edwards said. "But that did not mean a suspension of the courtship. Lincoln and Mary arranged to meet at the houses of mutual friends. One of the houses where they were made welcome and where they met often was the residence of Simeon Francis, who was editor of the *Sangamo Journal,* as it was then called.[17] Afterward Sangamo, the Indian form, was changed to Sangamon. There was no break in the courtship and there was no setting of the date and then postponing the marriage. The courtship was a long one because Lincoln was in no condition to support a wife. The two remained loyal to each other, meeting from time to time and waiting for Mr. Lincoln's circumstances to justify marriage.[18] Very shortly after Frances Todd married Dr. Wallace, Mary told my mother that Mr. Lincoln and she were going to be married that night. At the same time Mr. Lincoln met my father on the street and said that they were going to be married that evening at the residence of Simeon Francis. My father said to Mr. Lincoln:

"'That will never do. Mary Todd is my ward. If the marriage is going to take place, it must be at my house.'

"There was an immediate change of plans. The arrangements were made for a quiet wedding that Sunday evening. Word was sent to the relatives in Springfield. The ceremony was performed in the presence of a few people thus hastily summoned."

The wedding took place on the 4th of November, 1842. Mr. Edwards was present, but a child. His statements as to the circumstances are borne out by the often-repeated recollections of Mrs. Lincoln's sisters. Mrs. Dr. Wallace said again and again that there was only one ceremony arranged for, and that there was absolutely no truth in the Herndon story that Lincoln disappeared and could not be found when the hour came.[19] Mrs. Wallace was as positive in her corrections of other misstatements made by Herndon and repeated by other writers that the wedding was a large one, that Mrs. Lincoln wore a white silk dress, and so on. The Lincoln marriage was a quiet one by the expressed preference of the bride. According to the very clear and definite statement of Mrs. Wallace, Mr. Lincoln and Mary Todd told Mrs. Edwards on a Sunday morning that they had decided to be married that evening. Mr. Lincoln went in search of Mr. Edwards and told him. Mrs. Wallace was sent for. The sisters hurried the preparations. They yielded their objections and determined that Mary should have a home wedding, instead of going to the home of Mr. Francis. Mrs. Wallace, in telling of the preparations, said she never worked harder in her life than she did that Sunday in November, getting things ready for the marriage. Only a few persons were present, as Mrs. Wallace clearly remembered. They were Mr. and Mrs. Benjamin Edwards, Maj. and Mrs. John Todd Stuart, Dr. John Todd and family, Dr. and Mrs. Wallace, and, of course, Mr. and Mrs. Ninian W. Edwards, and perhaps one or two others.[20] The bride, Mrs. Wallace said, wore a simple white muslin dress. The ceremony was performed by Rev. Mr. Dresser, who came up to Mr. Edwards' house following the evening service at his church.[21] After this quiet marriage Mr. and Mrs. Lincoln went to the tavern and boarded until they were able to furnish three or four rooms.[22] In a few years they were able to buy a story and a half house on South Eighth street, and that is the house, enlarged, now known as the Lincoln home.

Following the lead of Herndon, most writers have made the marriage appear unfortunate. They have represented Lincoln as unhappy in his home life. They have attributed to Mrs. Lincoln the character of a high-tempered, extravagant, ambitious, tormenting woman. They have assumed that Mr. Lincoln endured a living martyrdom.[23] Within the most recent revival of interest in all pertaining to Mr. Lincoln there has been cast reproach upon Mrs. Lincoln. A sister's testimony to the relations of Mr. and Mrs. Lincoln is far at variance with some of the printed statements.

"They understood each other thoroughly," is the language of one of Mrs. Lincoln's sisters: "and Mr. Lincoln looked beyond the impulsive words and manner and knew that his wife was devoted to him and to his interests. They lived in a quiet and unostentatious manner. Mrs. Lincoln was very fond of reading, and interested herself greatly in her husband's political views and aspirations. She was fond of home. She made nearly all her own and her children's clothes. She was a cheerful woman, a delightful conversationalist and well informed on the topics of the day."[24]

This is the recollection based upon the observation of Mr. and Mrs. Lincoln some part of every day for six months at a time. The sisters and other near relatives saw none of that unhappiness in the relations of Mr. and Mrs. Lincoln which is so often mentioned.[25]

The marriage ended all objection or antagonism toward Mr. Lincoln on the part of his wife's relatives. Mr. Edwards preserves the autograph letter which the father of Mrs. Lincoln wrote to Ninian W. Edwards in December, 1844, showing the estimate he had put upon Mr. Lincoln as a son-in-law at that early date. Mr. Todd wrote:

"I feel more than grateful that my daughters all have married gentlemen whom I respect and esteem, and I should be pleased if it could ever be in my power to give them a more substantial evidence of my feelings than in mere words or professions. Whether it will ever be in my power I can not say, and perhaps it matters little. I will be satisfied if they discharge all their duties and make as good wives as I think they have good husbands."

After the marriage Mr. Lincoln never showed any trace of resentment toward his wife's relatives for their opposition to the marriage. With Mrs. Lincoln it was different. She had said a little defiantly to her brother-in-law, Ninian W. Edwards, before the wedding, that she was going to marry a man who would one day be president of the United States. In the years afterward she would recall those long months of courtship without home sympathy and show that the memory of the family opposition to her choice still rankled.

"After the marriage," said Mr. Edwards, "Mr. and Mrs. Lincoln visited at our house. They were always invited there on social occasions. They went out in Springfield society. I can remember that when I was a boy the trouble Mr. Lincoln used to cause at social gatherings. He would get a crowd around him in the gentlemen's room and start a conversation, with the result that the ladies would be left alone downstairs, and would have to send some one to break up Mr. Lincoln's party, in order to get the gentlemen downstairs. Mr. Lincoln and my father were always very friendly. Mrs. Lincoln, I think, always was a little cool toward my mother for the course she had taken to discourage the engagement. But my mother and Mr. Lincoln were very friendly. At the first inauguration Mr. Lincoln insisted that my mother must come to Washington. At that time my mother was at Andover, where my brother and sister were going to school. When there was affliction, Mr. Lincoln always sent for my mother. He had her come to the White House and remain some time after Willie's death."

The best kind of a witness to the home life of Mr. and Mrs. Lincoln was Mr. Edwards.

"I used to come to their house Saturdays and Sundays almost every week," he said. "I never saw a more loving couple. I never heard a harsh word or anything out the way. Mrs. Lincoln always spoke of him as Mr. Lincoln. She was devoted to him. Mr. Lincoln was a home man. On Sundays he was to be found here. He would go downtown for his mail, stop in at the drug store for a few minutes, and then come home to stay."

Mr. and Mrs. Lincoln were very unlike physically and temperamentally. Mrs. Lincoln was a gentlewoman bred to all of the little niceties of life. Mr. Lincoln had grown to manhood with no thought of some of the customs which Mrs. Lincoln thought essential. Of several ways Mrs. Lincoln succeeded, after many trials in "breaking" Mr. Lincoln. But he would get up and open the front door when somebody knocked, instead of waiting for the girl to go. To one of her relatives [Emilie Todd Helm, her half-sister] Mrs. Lincoln complained of this habit of Mr. Lincoln as a great annoyance.

"Mary," said this young relative, "if I had a husband with a mind such as yours has, I wouldn't care what he did."

Mrs. Lincoln showed the pleasure this tribute to her husband gave her, as she replied, apologetically, "It is very foolish; it is a small matter to complain of."[26]

"Mrs. Lincoln," said Mr. Edwards, "had more to do with making Mr. Lincoln president than many people think."[27]

Part 2

Supplementary Material from the
St. Louis Globe-Democrat

William T. Baker

Lincoln as a Rail Splitter and Soldier

The men "who knew Lincoln" are coming, Father Abraham, in numbers to Springfield on the 12th of February [1909].[1] The Lincoln Centennial Association, with Judge J. Otis Humphrey at the head, is preparing for "the appropriate celebration of the 100th anniversary of Lincoln's birth."[2] What could be more appropriate for the centennial day than the assembling of the men "who knew Lincoln"—Lincoln, the rail splitter; Lincoln, the navigator of the Sangamon; Lincoln, the surveyor; Lincoln, "the best jury lawyer in the State of Illinois"; Lincoln, the legislator, who taught "Uncle Joe" Cannon parliamentary quirks;[3] Lincoln, who was in at the genesis of the Republican party more actively and effectively than most historians have told; Lincoln, the president and the emancipator?

A spry old gentleman walked into the office of the Lincoln Centennial Association the other day and told his personal recollections of "Honest Abe's" rail-splitting days. Incredible as it seemed, the story was true. William T. Baker was a boy when his father bought a saw and grist mill on the Sangamon River. People came twenty miles to get their grinding done. The boy ran the grist mill, which was the lighter work, and his father took care of the sawmill. That was over seventy years ago.

"My first acquaintance with Abe Lincoln," Mr. Baker said, "was when he came with a sack of corn on a horse to get it ground into meal to make hoe cake for himself and an uncle named [William] Hanks, west of Decatur, where they were splitting rails at 50 cents a hundred and cutting wood at 50 cents a cord."[4]

The Bakers were early settlers in Illinois. They came from Kentucky in 1828, making ten Baker families in one neighborhood. They were children of Isaac Baker, who, with his brothers, Abraham and Jacob, Virginia patriots, fought through the revolutionary war. James Baker, the father of William T. Baker, who came up from Christian County to tell the centennial association his recollections, was the messmate of Lincoln in the Black Hawk war.[5] The elder Baker's home was one of Lincoln's favorite visiting places. With Gen. Whitesides [Samuel Whiteside], who was an officer in the Black Hawk war, Lincoln passed many a night at James Baker's house, fighting the campaign over.

"There was great story telling," said Mr. Baker, "much talk that interested a young boy like me. They couldn't drive me to bed. I remember well they told that when they were in the Black Hawk War, trailing the Indians, they came to Rock Creek, which was narrow, but had a deep channel. The general ordered a tall, slick back walnut tree that stood near that bank to be cut so that it would fall across the creek, to be used as a foot bridge. He told my father to go down the creek with the wagon to find a fording place, saying they would camp in a little bottom below where they were. The troops were commanded to cross by way of the log. Several of the soldiers fell off the log into the creek. Among them was Lincoln. After supper the troops went to sleep in dog tents, which were sheets with four pegs. After they had lain down Lincoln said to my father, 'Major, I forgot my pistol when I fell in the creek and got it wet.' He crawled out from under the dog tent, pointed in the air and turned it loose. The pistol fired as clear and clean as if it had just been loaded fresh. My father said, 'Come in here, Abe, quick, or you will be in the guard house in five minutes.' Directly an orderly came riding up and asked, 'Major, where was the gun fired?' My father said, 'Just above here somewhere.' The orderly went further up the camp and made inquiry. Some told him it was 'down below.' The orderly came back and said to my father, 'Major, they say it was down this way.' My father replied, 'My head was on the ground and I might have been mistaken. It might have been above and it might have been below our tent.' And that was all the satisfaction the orderly got."

Whitesides lived seven miles east of James Baker's. If Lincoln could get the general and the major together for a night of reminiscences of [the] Black Hawk war he keenly enjoyed it.

"One morning," said Mr. Baker, "as they told the story, they came to where the Indians had camped. Whitesides showed his men how he knew the Indians had been there two nights before. He explained that the marks of the Indian moccasins in the ashes and dust showed that a dew had fallen upon their tracks and had made a little crust, which would not have formed if the Indians had been there the previous night. Whitesides and his men followed the trail until they came to where the Indians had camped the night before. There was no crust on the tracks. The general ordered the men to examine their flints and priming to see that the guns were in perfect order, as, he told them, they were liable to come upon the enemy any moment. He told his men to be careful to draw down, so as to shoot the Indians in the lower part of the body rather than to overshoot them. He gave orders that there must be no talking. The command moved on, but Abe Lincoln and some of the others kept talking and laughing to each other, to the great annoyance of Gen. Whitesides. The general halted the command and told the men to examine their flints and priming again. Then he told every man to take a bullet from the pouch and put it in his mouth, so that when he fired his gun he would have another bullet ready for instant use. Of course, that stopped the talking, and that night at our house Abe said: 'General, I never thought until now what your object was in having us put the bullets in our mouths. It worked like a charm.'"

When Lincoln Built His Boat

Lincoln was in his 20s when he became a navigator of the Sangamon.[6] William T. Baker of Bolivia, now well past four-score, an old fox hunter, whose greatest pleasure at that age, he says, "is to be in the saddle with a good-spirited horse under me," was the boy who helped Lincoln overcome his flatboat problem.

"Lincoln patronized our grist mill for nearly two years," Mr. Baker remembers, "up to the time he built the flatboat for navigating the Sangamon River. This flatboat he built at his cabin the second winter that he and John Hanks were partners in cutting cordwood and making rails. This boat was hewed out of native timber. It was about 30 feet long and about 12 feet wide. It was built of white oak and very heavy. It was launched and shortly afterwards loaded with bacon and shelled corn to be taken to New Orleans by way of the Sangamon, Illinois and Mississippi rivers. When Lincoln started from our mill he found that the river had fallen so much that the boat would not pass over the dam. The boat hung on the dam and the pressure of the water behind was so strong we could not move the boat back. Lincoln had a small dugout canoe and we had one at the mill. We used these two canoes to move the bacon and corn out on the bank. Then we got the boat over the dam and cabled it to a large walnut tree below the dam. We moved the cargo along the back to the boat and loaded it on again. This occupied about four days.[7]

"I did not see Lincoln again until he was a lawyer and came to my father's to attend to a suit for one of the neighbors. He spent the day and night, going after and bringing Gen. Whitesides, who commanded the force to which Lincoln and my father belonged in the Black Hawk war. The three had a warm visit. That night, as was generally the case when Lincoln came to our house, the house was full of company. Mother had to make a bed on the floor for us boys, but Lincoln slept on the floor with us, so that he could tell us some late stories before we went to sleep."

Plenty of Threshers

The 8th of August [1860] . . . the Republicans had a rally at Springfield.[8] Christian County sent up a delegation. William T. Baker, who, while a boy, had ground Lincoln's bags of corn for him during two years at the mill on the Sangamon in the rail-splitting days, was marshal of the delegation.

"We mustered 105 wagons, most of them having four or six horses, and loaded with Christian County Republicans," said Mr. Baker. "On the way up we camped over night on the Sangamon, near Rochester. When we came to Springfield we formed in line and passed down in front of Lincoln's home, where we halted. Lincoln was standing on the steps shaking hands with hundreds of people who had come in to attend the rally. As I rode up at the head of my delegation Lincoln left the steps, came out to us, took me by the hand, and said, 'How are you, Baker?' Then he looked down the long line of wagons and men and said, 'Baker, it must take a good many men to run a threshing machine in Christian County!'"[9]

Lincoln and the Temperance Question

Did Lincoln take a drink?[10] "Much can be said on both sides of that question," to use the words of the great man himself, employed in reference to another matter. The men "who knew Lincoln" offer rather conflicting testimony. When they come together on the 12th of February [1909], under the auspices of the Lincoln Centennial Association, they will disagree somewhat as to whether Lincoln was a total abstainer. But they will, doubtless, agree that they never saw Lincoln under the influence of liquor. William T. Baker of Christian County says:

> Mr. Lincoln was in all things a temperate man. I never knew nor heard of him being under the influence of liquor and I do not think he was ever the worse for it. During the past year there has been a great effort to prove that Mr. Lincoln was not only a temperate man, but that he was a teetotaler. In regard to

this I want to say that I have seen Mr. Lincoln take a drink many a time at my father's house, at Mount Pulaski; at Pottsville, in Logan County, and at other places. Mr. Lincoln was too liberal to have been a teetotaler.

Orville F. Berry

The Pedigree of President Lincoln

"President Abraham Lincoln," said Senator Orville F. Berry of Carthage, "was the flowering of generations of honorable, upright men."[1]

In the Military Tract of Illinois live descendants of the Prairie Fathers who do not accept the assertions and deductions of many writers on the origin of Mr. Lincoln.[2] They know better. There are families in Hancock County who [know] the Lincoln genealogy as well as their own. The Berry who was partner with Abraham Lincoln in the little store at New Salem [William Berry] was a relative of the Berrys of Carthage. The mother of President Lincoln lived in a family of Berrys, the Kentucky branch. Of good American stock, as good as there was, according to family history, came President Lincoln.

"His ancestors," said Senator Berry, who has given some careful investigation to the matter, "were men who for nearly 200 years before President Lincoln was born were active and well-to-do citizens of Massachusetts, New Jersey, Pennsylvania and Virginia. The Lincoln family, back to the Samuel Lincoln in Massachusetts of early colonial times, was endowed with the spirit of adventure, of daring, of patriotism and of thrift.[3] Among the descendants of Samuel Lincoln, including ancestors of President Lincoln, were many strong and prominent men. One of Samuel Lincoln's descendants was a member of the Boston Tea Party. One was a captain of artillery in the revolution. Three served on the brig *Hazard*.

"Levi Lincoln," continued Senator Berry, "born in 1749, graduated from Harvard, was a minute man in the revolution and was a delegate to the convention at Cambridge, which framed the constitution of Massachusetts in 1781. Declining a seat in the Continental Congress after election, this Levi Lincoln served in both branches of the Legislature of Massachusetts. He was appointed attorney general of the United States, and for a short time preceding Madison was secretary of state. In 1807 he became lieutenant governor of Massachusetts. He was appointed a justice of the Supreme Court of the United States, but declined. For a third of a century he was considered the head of the Massachusetts bar.[4] The eldest son of Levi Lincoln, in accordance with a common custom of the Lincoln family, was named after him. He was a graduate of Harvard, became governor of Massachusetts and was given the highest honorary degrees by both Harvard and Williams.[5] Enoch Lincoln was a member of Congress from 1818 to 1826, and governor of Massachusetts in 1827.[6] These Lincolns were of the same family as was President Lincoln. Closely related with the Massachusetts Lincolns was Mordecai Lincoln, from whom President Lincoln came by direct descent. This Mordecai Lincoln was the great-great-grandfather of President Lincoln and the ancestor as well of the Hancock County Lincolns.[7] He had important and extensive iron works in Massachusetts. The sons of this Mordecai Lincoln were named Mordecai and Abraham.[8] They moved to New Jersey and thence to Pennsylvania. Both of them were men of means and left large estates to their families. Abraham Lincoln settled in Berks County. He was a member of the Pennsylvania Legislature and of the Constitutional Convention of that state in 1790. Descendants of the Pennsylvania Lincolns moved to Virginia. One of them, a later Abraham Lincoln, sold his place in Virginia for $17,000 and moved to Kentucky and took up 1000 acres of land. He was the grandfather of President Lincoln [I] have described.[9] He [here a line of type seems to have been deleted; evidently it said something to the effect that Abraham Lincoln had two sons] Mordecai, named for the Massachusetts ancestor, and Thomas.[10] Mordecai was an Indian fighter and a famous narrator of stories.[11] Two of his sons he named Abraham and Mordecai; he moved with them to Hancock County, in the 30s.[12] Thomas Lincoln, the son of Abraham, the pioneer and the father of Abraham the president, was left an orphan at an early age and did not receive the advantages of his brother Mordecai. But he was not of the character which some of the biographers of President Lincoln have described.[13] He acquired a farm.[14] He was a good carpenter.[15] He was chosen road surveyor when care of the highways was a position of responsibility in Kentucky. He owned one of the most expensive Bibles in the neighborhood. He had credit at the store and was able to wear suspenders which cost $1.50. I heard an old horseman once say in reply to an expression of surprise at the speed of an animal:

"'Go? Of course he can go. Look at his pedigree. He's got a license to go.'

"President Abraham Lincoln had a license to be great."

Abraham Lincoln of Hancock County

Abraham Lincoln was indicted in Hancock County for riot.[16] Ten or twelve others were included in the bill. The time was back in the pioneer days when indictments were drawn at Carthage to read: "Not having the fear of God before their eyes, being moved and seduced by the instigation of the devil."

There was so much feeling in Hancock County over this case that Abraham Lincoln and his associates did not go to trial at Carthage. A change of venue to Quincy was taken. There the prosecution was postponed from time to time until public sentiment in Hancock cooled off. The prosecution was dropped.

The location of the trouble was the vicinity of Fountain Green. Jabez Beebe was one of the founders of the town of attractive name. He was from New York. Many of his neighbors were from Kentucky. Eastern and Southern ideas clashed. Looking to a quick regulation of their neighborhood affairs, Abraham Lincoln and his friends met Mr. Beebe out-of-doors and whipped him. One tradition is that they embraced the opportunity of a church gathering to administer the punishment. Sixty years after this occurred a Quincy newspaper man came upon the musty papers and started on the rounds of the newspapers of the country the story that Abraham Lincoln had once been indicted for riot. If he was better informed he neglected to say that the indicted Abraham Lincoln was not the one who became president. The assumption of the press generally was that this was "another Lincoln story." Thus labeled the story had wide circulation. The Abraham Lincoln indicted for riot was a first cousin of the president. He came to Hancock County about the time the great Abraham Lincoln came to Sangamon. He was the elder of the two Abraham Lincolns.

The whipping of Jabez Beebe was not an act of lawlessness in the view which the Fountain Green Lincolns took of law enforcement. While James Lincoln was justice of the peace he discouraged litigation.[17] If there was a neighborhood controversy, which promised to get into the courts, Justice Lincoln was accustomed to send for the parties and, acting as a volunteer arbitrator, try to bring about a compromise and reconciliation. Jabez Beebe was very fond of litigation. He wasn't a lawyer by profession, but he had picked up some knowledge of court procedure. He was quite a talker. He liked to act as attorney before a justice of the peace, and would take the case of anybody who wanted to sue. Litigation was encouraged by the course of Jabez Bebee. This amateur lawyer made a specialty of tax titles.

Occasionally, after a settler had obtained what he thought was a good title to his farm and had made improvements, a tax title would be presented, owned perhaps by some stranger. Suit would be entered, and Jabez Beebe would appear in the case on the side of the holder of the tax title. To Abraham Lincoln and his neighbors this conduct of Beebe gave great offense. A notice was posted ordering Beebe to leave the country. No attention was paid to this. Abraham Lincoln and the others who shared his opinion that a man who helped enforce tax titles was undesirable got together, supplied themselves with good-sized switches, met Beebe on the road, and whipped him rather severely. Beebe did not press the prosecutions for riot, and he ceased to be a ready promoter of litigation.

Abraham Lincoln of Hancock County had three sons and a daughter. The sons were Robert, Hezekiah and Nicholas.[18] The daughter was Amanda.[19] She died in the asylum at Jacksonville. Robert and Nicholas did not marry. Hezekiah married, but left no family.

Robert Lincoln lived many years in Carthage. He had those qualities of character which leave definite and lasting impressions of personality upon a community. The Carthage recollections of this Robert Lincoln are vivid, although he died forty years ago. Resemblance between Abraham Lincoln, the president, and Robert Lincoln of Carthage was notable. The two men were not only of the same physical appearance in form, but in facial features. Robert Lincoln had the Lincoln art of conversation. He illustrated what he had to tell with stories. Senator Orville F. Berry as a youth knew a great deal about Robert Lincoln.

"Bob," said the state senator, "was a man to attract attention anywhere. He dressed well. We boys looked up to him as a kind of beau ideal. While his appearance was very much like that of President Lincoln, Bob dressed so well and took such care of himself that we never thought of him as a homely man. I am not sure but that in the hands of a modern tailor and barber President Lincoln might have lost that reputation for homeliness of which the writers make so much. Bob Lincoln rode horseback a great deal. He had a riding costume which included patent leather boots, in which he made a striking appearance that excited the admiration of all the boys in Carthage. He never seemed to be posing, but he had that manner of the Lincolns about him which drew attention to him. He was a good talker and a pretty fair story teller. You never saw him at leisure that he didn't have a bunch of fellows around him listening to him. He was a candidate for the nomination of sheriff of Hancock County once, but was beaten in the convention. Like the rest of the Lincolns, Bob was a man of independent views. In politics he was a Democrat. After Abraham Lincoln was elected president Bob made a trip to Washington. Carthage people wondered whether 'Old Abe,' as they called the president, would give Bob an office. Some prophesied that Bob would not get anything if the president knew how he had talked about the Republicans. Bob came back after his visit without an office and lived here until he died."

One of the Lincoln stories told in Hancock County to this day has to do with the Mormons of 1844. At that time the Nauvoo saints were having most astonishing revelations. There was a settlement of Mormons called Ramus, near where some of the Lincolns lived, in the Fountain Green neighborhood. One of the Lincolns came out of the house in the morning to discover two Mormons loading a wagon with cabbages from his patch. He inquired what they meant. The Mormons said they had had a revelation to come to that place and get a load of cabbages. Lincoln turned and went into the house. In a few minutes he came out carrying a shotgun. He said to the Mormons:

"I've just had a revelation that if you don't unload those cabbages and get out of here in five minutes I am to blow the tops of your heads off."

The Mormons pitched out the cabbages and went away with their horses on the gallop.[20]

Francis E. Brownell

Lincoln and Ellsworth

In the home of Capt. Brownell on Q street [in Washington DC], there is a room set apart for Ellsworth relics.[1] In one corner stands the double-barreled shotgun with which Jackson shot Ellsworth.[2] President Lincoln in person presented the gun to "the avenger." In another corner is a Harper's Ferry rifle of ancient pattern and of enormous 58 caliber, surmounted by the broad saber-bladed bayonet. This is the identical weapon with which Ellsworth's death was so promptly and terribly avenged. There are medals and testimonials presented to Capt. Brownell by citizens and organizations shortly after the tragedy. But most interesting of all are the letters and papers which throw light upon the character and strangely romantic career of the boyish commander of the Fire Zouaves.[3] Over the mantel hangs a large picture of Ellsworth, and above it is a magnificent imitation of the little gold badge which he wore on his breast, and which was torn to pieces and carried into his body by the buckshot. This badge was presented to Ellsworth in Baltimore, when he was on his famous trip with the Chicago Zouaves.[4] It was the badge of the Baltimore City Guard, and arranged in a circle upon it were the letters: "*Non Solum Nobis, Sed Pro Patria.*" What significance!

To the request for something of Ellsworth's personal appearance, Capt. Brownell said:

> His person was strikingly prepossessing. His form, though slight, was exactly the Napoleonic height. He was very compactly built, and his head was finely poised, and crowned with luxurious curling, black hair. He had a hazel eye, a nose such as you see on old Roman medals. A light mustache just shaded lips that were continually shading into the sunniest smiles. His voice, deep and musical, once heard was never forgotten. He always dressed well, looked tidy and neat, and sometimes wore the military medals presented him by different organizations. He had great tact and executive ability. He was a good mathematician, possessed of a fine artistic eye, and sketched wonderfully well.
>
> I recollect one incident that illustrated his artistic ability. It was when the Fire Zouaves were being hurriedly uniformed. A New York hatter came in with the drawing of a cap and asked Ellsworth if that would do. "No," said Ellsworth. "See here," and taking a pencil he made half a dozen strokes like a flash and there was the pattern of the cap he wanted.
>
> His personal magnetism was wonderful. No one ever possessed greater power of enforcing the respect and of fastening the affections of men. Strangers soon recognized and acknowledged this power.
>
> It is said he could stand ten paces from a window and fire seven shots from his revolver and not shiver the glass beyond the circumference of a half dollar.

Much of his interesting information Capt. Brownell obtained from the parents of Ellsworth. One of the stories they told him was this: In the winter of 1858–9, after Elmer had met with his reverses in the West, he visited his parents in New York State.[5] His mother says that one day, while he was talking with her about his future, he told her he had worked hard and faithfully, but still had not succeeded. His mind had been so occupied with military ideas that it was impossible for him to concentrate it upon business matters with that force necessary to success. He felt that he was intended for the military profession, and henceforth he intended to make it the object of his life. His mother laughed and told him it was unfortunate for him he had not been born in Europe, where there was war nearly all the time, as there was no prospect of utilizing his talents in this country. He replied very earnestly that he was not so certain that there was so little danger of war. On the contrary, he felt that the great political struggle then agitating the country would eventually end in war, and that the North was wholly unprepared for such an event, and that he intended from that time forward to devote his whole energy, so far as possible, toward putting the militia of the North in such a condition that if such an emergency should arise it would be of some benefit. With that determination he went back to Chicago.

About this time the whole military world was attracted by the exploits of the famous French Zouaves in the Crimean war. Ellsworth became acquainted with a Dr. [Charles A.] de Villiers, who had been a surgeon in the original Zouave corps in Algiers. He practiced the manual of the rapier with him until he became perfect. He also invented a system of tactics based on this Zouave drill.

On the 2d of February, 1860, Ellsworth submitted a plan to the Zouave Cadets for a trip through the country. He thought the time had come to show what he had done. The Zouaves left Chicago on tickets furnished by a friendly railroad official to Detroit. There they gave their first exhibition, and the money thus received carried them to the next stopping place. The company drilled in all the principal cities of the North during the summer of 1860 and stirred up a military fever wherever they went. Immense crowds greeted them everywhere. The organization of military companies followed in their wake. The Wide-Awakes of the presidential campaign took up the Ellsworth drill, and all went to prepare the popular mind for the great struggle of the following year. Perhaps nothing in the way of military display ever excited more attention and emulation than this remarkable trip.

Ellsworth on his return to Chicago found himself the most talked-of military man in the country. He received requests from all points for information and instruction as to the new tactics. Zouave companies sprang up everywhere. His main object—to create a military enthusiasm—had succeeded.

Capt. Brownell has among his relics one of the pledges taken by the candidates for membership in the famous Zouave company. It is interesting. "The principal requirements of the regulations of this corps are," says the pledge, "abstinence from entering drinking saloons, houses of ill-fame, gambling halls and all disreputable places, under penalty of expulsion, publication in the city papers of the offender's name and forfeiture of uniform, etc., to the company. You will be required to treat all members of the company as brothers, and observe strictly the company regulations, obey the orders of your officers, and conduct yourself in all the relations of life in a manner that will reflect credit on the company."

Coming back to Chicago from the triumphal tour young Ellsworth received an invitation to go to California to teach the Zouave drill to a crack San Francisco corps. His fame had spread rapidly. He was wanted at Rockford and at Springfield to teach local companies. He consulted Col. Eaton who advised him to continue his connection with the Cadets. Col. Eaton introduced him to many people. The Adjutant General of Illinois pressed him to accept a position on his staff. Several other military honors were thrust upon him but nothing to eat.

Together with several officers, he attempted to secure the passage of a law for the complete reorganization of the militia system of Illinois. This was his pet idea. The project failed, though the system proposed by Ellsworth was considered the most perfect. The bill passed one house and fell.

Ellsworth's plan was complete in every detail, from the sword-drill of the officers, with accompanying sketches, to the fastening of the soldiers' shoes. It included every particular of uniform, with sketches and price, movements (from the French drill) of the company and battalion, with illustrations, and finally a code of moral law and discipline that presupposed the perfect human machine.

"About this time," said Capt. Brownell, "Ellsworth was introduced to Mr. Lincoln. The latter had been nominated for the Presidency. The young Zouave Captain tendered him a complimentary drill in the wigwam, the last appearance of the famous company. I believe Ellsworth was aware the strain could not be kept up. He had accomplished his purpose. The corps disbanded and a skeleton regiment was formed to extend the plan of organization.

"Mr. Lincoln made inquiries of friends about young Ellsworth, and offered him a place in his law office at Springfield. There Ellsworth went. He participated in the campaign, and, when the President elect started for Washington, Ellsworth went with him. A closer relationship had sprung up between the President and Ellsworth than is generally known."[6]

Capt. Brownell has among his papers the official order, worn and stained, which governed the movements of the presidential party at stopping places between Springfield and Washington. One paragraph shows how important was Ellsworth's position.

"The President elect will under no circumstances attempt to pass through any crowd until such arrangements are made as will meet the approval of Col. Ellsworth, who is charged with the responsibility of all matters of this character, and to facilitate this you will confer a favor by placing Col. Ellsworth in communication with the chief of your escort, immediately upon the arrival of the train."

Ellsworth wished a position in the War Department that would give him an opportunity to effect the reform he hoped for in the militia of the country, but the jealously of certain officials made his task hopeless, almost. An order was drafted organizing such a bureau and detailing him to take charge of it. He had been appointed a Lieutenant in the regular army with this end in view, and the following is an unsigned letter of President Lincoln's upon the subject:

EXECUTIVE MANSION, March, '61.—To the Secretary of War: You will favor me by issuing an order detailing Lieut. E. Ellsworth, of 1st Dragoons, for special duty as Adjutant and Inspector General of Militia Affairs for the United States, and in so far as existing laws will admit charge him with the transaction, under your direction, of all business pertaining to the militia, to be conducted as a separate bureau, of which Lieut. Ellsworth will be the chief, with instructions to take measures for promoting a uniform system of organization, drill and equipment of the United States militia, and to prepare a system of instruction for the militia to be distributed to the several States. You will please assign him suitable office rooms, furniture, etc., provide him with a clerk and messenger, and furnish him such facilities in the way of printing, stationery, and access to the records as he may desire.

Ellsworth's plan for organizing the militia of the country as set forth in a paper which Capt. Brownell has, was as follows:

1. The gradual concentration of all business pertaining to the militia now conducted by the several bureaus to this department.
2. The collection and systematizing of accurate information of the number, aim and condition of the militia of all classes of the several States, and the compilation of yearly reports of the same for the information of this department.
3. The compilation of a report of the actual condition of the militia and the working of the present systems of the General Government and the various States.

4. The publication and distribution of such information as is important to the militia and the conduct of all correspondence relating to militia affairs.

5. The compilation of a system of instruction for light troops for distribution to the several States, including everything pertaining to the instruction of the militia in the school of the soldier, company and battalion, skirmishing, bayonet and gymnastic drill, adapted for self-instruction.

6. The arrangement of a system of organization with a view to the establishment of a uniform system of drill discipline, equipment and dress throughout the United States.

It is interesting to know that twenty-seven years later the General Government is adopting Ellsworth's idea of establishing a closer relationship between the regular army and the militia of the States. The steps which he urged then are being taken now.

John Hay, who was at that time one of Mr. Lincoln's secretaries, and Ellsworth's most intimate friend, says: "One night we were talking of coming probabilities, and I spoke of the doubt so widely existing of the loyalty of the people. He earnestly replied: 'You know I have a great work to do, to which my life is pledged; that I am the only earthly support of my parents; that there is a young woman whose happiness I value as dearer than my own. Yet I could not ask a better death than to fall before Sumter next week. You will find that patriotism is not dead, even if it sleeps.'" Sumter fell, and the sleeping awoke. Ellsworth at once resigned his commission and left for the City of New York. On the 12th of April Sumter was fired on. Two days later the President issued his call for 75,000 volunteers, but before that call had gone over the wires Ellsworth was on his way to New York with a personal letter from the President to Mr. Greeley, indorsing him.

At the time Ellsworth had the conversation with Mr. Hay no overt act had been committed, and very few believed that rebellion would actually come. Ellsworth was one of the few. A short time before he had urged his views upon Mr. Lincoln, and declared that war was inevitable. The President merely smiled. And when he gave the young Captain his appointment as a Lieutenant of Dragoons he told him, laughingly, that he might at least drill.

Ellsworth arrived in New York Friday morning. He laid his plan to organize a regiment of Zouaves before the officials of the Fire Department and they approved them. Saturday notices of the intention were posted in the engine houses and published in the papers. [By] Sunday 2000 had enrolled. There were two Company As, two Company Bs and so on. Ellsworth took two companies at a time, arranged them facing each other and went down the line picking out the men he wanted. That night he had a regiment of 1100 men. Monday he laid the plans for uniforms and equipments before the Fire Department officials. They approved them and the tailors went to work on the gray flannel suits. Thursday, the seventh day after Ellsworth's arrival in New York, the regiment was ready to start for Washington, but there were no arms. Jealous influences were delaying the issue of the guns. Ellsworth appealed to his fire department friends. They went out into the street, raised the money and cleaned out the gun stores. There were twelve different patterns of rifles and carbines distributed. Each company had its own peculiar arm[s]. Monday Ellsworth started with his regiment, marching to the Astor House to receive a stand of colors. Three times that day he received orders from the Governor of New York not to leave with his regiment. The third message came just as the regiment reached Canal street. To return east meant to go back to the barracks, to turn west was to go to the *Baltic*, lying ready to convey the troops. At the corner of Canal stood Gen. Wool, then in command of that department.[7] Ellsworth showed him the message of the Governor, and asked what he should do.

"Go on," said Wool, "it don't make any difference if you've got 11,000 men." Ellsworth went on. Shortly afterwards Gen. Wool was relieved, and it was said he was not in harmony with the Governor of New York. The steamer conveyed the zouaves to Annapolis, and thence they went to Washington.

"The regiment," said Capt. Brownell, "was the first of the United States volunteers to arrive in Washington. There were militia here, but this was the first regiment under the call. The Fire Zouaves were quartered in the House of Representatives. There were some pretty hard characters among the men. It was not more than a day or two before some acts of lawlessness raised a storm of indignation in the city and created a prejudice against the whole regiment. Ellsworth privately ascertained the amount of the damages and paid it out of his own pocket. From that time it was easy to charge every act of lawlessness upon the zouaves. I do not wish to be understood as trying to convey the idea that the regiment was any better than the rest, but it was not much worse. Ellsworth's soul revolted at this disorder, and he procured an order changing our quarters from the Capitol to the eastern shore of the Potomac, near the Insane Asylum and afterwards to what is known as Glesboro point.

"But the day before the change took place a big fire broke out on the 9th of May in the Owen House, adjoining the Willard.[8] The zouaves were at home at a fire, and their conduct there, which saved the block, excited great admiration. A purse of $500 was raised and presented to them. I remember that fire well. I was corporal of the guard and had just then been out on some duty when I saw the light. I stood for a moment debating in my mind what I should do, and then shoved my gun under some boxes and started. When I reached the old Franklin engine house some of the boys were already there, and they needed just one more hand. We soon had that engine out and at work. An order was sent up for 200 of our command to come down, but the whole regiment responded, took possession of the apparatus, and put out the fire. The boys played all the old tricks of the New York firemen—stood on each other's shoulders, held one another by the heels over the cornices and enjoyed themselves. The Washington firemen stood by and looked on. One hook and ladder company turned back sooner than let the apparatus fall into the hands of the zouaves."

Martin L. Bundy

Martin L. Bundy has written from New Castle, Ind., to the Lincoln Centennial Association, contributing to the information about Lincoln's earliest relations with the formation of the Republican party.[1]

"The Whig National Convention of 1848," Mr. Bundy writes, "was completely under the control of Toombs and Stephens of Georgia.[2] They had decided that Gen. [Zachary] Taylor should be nominated on no platform but his record as a soldier and slaveholder. Greeley was there from New York offering to guarantee that that state would cast its electoral vote for [Henry] Clay if the convention would nominate him, but the Taylor managers would listen to no such proposition, no doubt for the reason that Clay's record as a slaveholder was not satisfactory. Lincoln and Greeley both agreed after the informal ballot that it was useless to press the name of Clay any longer, as the nomination of Taylor was a foregone conclusion, and it so turned out. In the convention of 1856, when Fremont was nominated, the name of Lincoln was suggested for vice president, but the leaders deemed it wise to give the place to William M. Dayton of New Jersey, and it was, perhaps, fortunate for Lincoln that the convention did so."

The growth of the Republican party in the campaign of 1860 was marvelously rapid throughout Illinois. It confounded the Democrats. Soon after the nominations for president were made, the Douglas men believed they were in the overwhelming majority. They ridiculed the Republican claims. There was no mid-summer dullness in the politics of that year. On the 20th of July the Douglas men had a large meeting at Springfield. Judge Horatio Vanderveer, [Vandeveer] father of William T. Vanderveer of Taylorville, was one of the speakers.[3] He had come up with an imposing delegation of Douglas men from Christian County. There were shouts of laughter and mighty cheering when Judge Vanderveer said to the audience:

"When we left Christian County, gentlemen, they had to stop the threshing machines. There are not enough Republicans in Christian County to run a threshing machine."

Stephen R. Capps

Lincoln's View of His Sense of Humor

Lincoln realized the sense of humor which was his by natural inheritance.[1] He also knew that in the estimation of the world generally the man who took life and himself seriously had the chances of success in his favor. He saw that what enabled him to get great enjoyment out of living was likely to be regarded by his fellow-men as a handicap, but he never made any effort or showed any desire to change himself. In fact, he made a joke of the handicap. About 1859, when he had failed of the senatorship, and when the presidency was apparently in the remote future, Lincoln lectured before the Phi Alpha Society of Illinois College at Jacksonville.[2]

"The lecture," said Stephen R. Capps, "was delivered in the old Congregational Church, a two-story frame building on the east side of the square. The subject was inventions. I remember that Mr. Lincoln read from Horace Greeley that a great man was one who, by reason of the responsibility of his position, was serious and not given to levity. Greeley argued that such a man had no time for frivolity and that pressure of pubic duties would, in a measure, weigh upon him, causing him to be sober-minded. With an amused expression, Mr. Lincoln, after he had concluded the quotation from Greeley, commented: 'If Mr. Greeley's definition of a great man is correct, then farewell, a long farewell to all my hopes of greatness.'"

John Carmody

One Who Played Ball with Lincoln

On the vacant lot adjoining John Carmody's, on the east side of Sixth street, in Springfield, Lincoln played ball.[1] John Carmody was one of the players, and he remembers there were many games in which Lincoln participated.

"An incident took place, during one of those games," Mr. Carmody said, "which I have retained clearly in my memory. I had a nephew named Patrick Johnson who was very expert in the game. He struck the ball in such a manner that it hit Mr. Lincoln in the ear. I ran to sympathize with him and asked if he was hurt. He said he was not, and as he said it he reached both of his hands toward the sky. Straining my neck to look up into his face, for he was several inches taller than I was, I said to him, 'Lincoln, if you are going to heaven, take us both.'"

Mr. Carmody remembers that this ball game occurred only one or two days before the nomination of Mr. Lincoln to be president. He was one who saw Mr. Lincoln just after the news from Chicago was received. He recalls that he met Mr. Lincoln coming out of the *Journal* office, and that the conversation between them ran in this way:

"Good morning, John," said Mr. Lincoln.

"Good morning, Mr. Lincoln. How is your ear?" said Mr. Carmody.

"All right, John. I have got the nomination," replied Mr. Lincoln.

"For what, Lincoln?" asked Mr. Carmody.

"For president of the United States," said Mr. Lincoln.

"Ah! Friend Lincoln, I wish you had. I seem to think Mr. Seward has had that bonus in his pocket for the past six months," Mr. Carmody said.

"No, I have got it," repeated Mr. Lincoln, producing a paper.

There were business dealings between Mr. Lincoln and Mr. Carmody. The impression that these transactions left upon Mr. Carmody was that he had dealt with one who was more than ordinarily fair-minded.

"I had relations with Mr. Lincoln growing out of purchase of real estate," Mr. Carmody said. "At the time Mr. Lincoln had charge of the sale of property owned, I think, by parties of the name of Bullock, in Massachusetts. The purchasers, under the terms, were bound to pay a certain amount down at the time of sale. Some of these purchasers could not pay the amount required by the terms. I assumed the responsibility for a short time, promising Mr. Lincoln that I would pay compound interest on the amounts which should have been paid at time of sale. When I went to make settlement with him he said: 'John, it is enough for them to get one interest.' I have always held Mr. Lincoln, as a business man, in the highest estimation."

Coming in his youth from another country, Mr. Carmody was greatly impressed with the character of the men in Springfield who were contemporaneous with Lincoln. He found a community of which he thinks too much in praise can not be said.

"Mr. Lincoln was a real type of an American gentleman. Like him the leading citizens of Springfield showed toward each other respect and kindness and friendship to such a degree in their daily intercourse that this 'stranger in a strange land' remembers to the present day the honor he felt it to be to have the acquaintance of such men."

Mr. Carmody speaks of Jesse K. Dubious, John T. Stewart [Stuart], J. C. Conkling, J. H. Robinson, Judge Broadwell, John A. McClernand, Judge [Milton] Hay, Christopher Brown, Judge [Stephen T.] Logan and William H. Herndon as the men he felt gave character to the community in which Abraham Lincoln had developed as its greatest man.[2]

"Others I do not forget," said Mr. Carmody, "including James L. Lamb, who proved himself the worthy associate of these great men.[3] With John M. Palmer I had business relations, and I found him to be always ready to be merciful toward those so unfortunate as to violate the laws of the state.[4] Gov. Richard Yates, the senior, the war governor, I remember as a man who never refused to assist those in need who appealed to him. Gov. Edwards and his brother Benjamin were worthy to be fellow-citizens of Lincoln."[5]

Augustus H. Chapman

Mr. A. H. Chapman,[1] a step-nephew by marriage of Mr. Lincoln, has this to say of him as to why he was called "Honest Abe":

In his law practice on the Wabash Circuit he was noted for his unswerving honesty. People learned to love him ardently, devotedly, and juries listened intently, earnestly, receptively to the sad-faced, earnest man. He was never blamed for bribery; nothing could move him when once his resolutions were formed. There was nothing scholarly in his speeches, and he always rested his case on its merits, only asking for simple Western justice, and the texture of the man was such that his very ungainliness was in his favor before a pioneer jury. His face always wore a sweetened and kindly expression, never sour, and burning to win them, his tall frame swaying as a pine, made him a resistless pleader. I remember one case of his decided honest trait of character. It was a case in which he was for the defendant. Satisfied of his client's innocence, it depended mainly on one witness. That witness told on the stand under oath what Abe knew to be a lie, and no one else knew. When he arose to plead the case, he said:

"Gentlemen, I depended on this witness to clear my client. He has lied. I ask that no attention be paid to his testimony. Let his words be stricken out, if my case fails. I do not wish to win in this way."

His scorn of a lie touched the jury; he laid his case before them magnificently, skillfully, masterly, and won in spite of the lie against him. From such work came his "Honest Abe." I never knew Abe to have a coat to fit him, all were ill-fitting, but underneath was a big, hot heart that could adjust itself to all humanity. He had at his tongue's end the little items that make up the humble world of the pioneer farmer. Once at a hotel, in the evening during court, a lawyer said:

"Our case is gone; when Lincoln quit he was crying, the jury were crying, the Judge was crying, and I was a little damp about the lashes myself. We might as well give the case up."

Jonathan H. Cheney

Lincoln's Farewell Speech at Springfield

Lincoln's speeches have suffered in the reporting.[1] As they have been collected from various sources, they show marked differences. The speeches which Mr. Lincoln wrote in advance were not many. The speeches which were taken down by a competent stenographer, like those delivered in the joint debates, are, of course, authentic. But many short speeches were written out from memory or from longhand notes, and varying versions of them appear in the later histories and collections. One of the most notable of Lincoln's impromptu short addresses was that which is called his farewell at Springfield, when he started for Washington. There are several versions of this speech. J. H. Cheney of Bloomington was one of the crowd "of not more that 150," he says, who went to the Great Western Depot and heard the farewell address. "This speech," Cheney thinks, "has seldom, if ever, been correctly quoted in the histories of Lincoln. Nicolay and Hay, who of all men you would look to for a correct version, fail to give it as it was spoken."

Mr. Cheney took the copy, which is here reproduced, from the *Chicago Tribune*, the morning after Lincoln's departure, and has kept it until now as the correct version. He thinks any one who will take the trouble to compare this with the version in the later histories will agree with him that it is the better speech.

My Friends—No one not in my situation can appreciate my feelings of sadness at this parting. To this place and the kindness of this people I owe everything. Here I have lived a quarter of a century, and have passed from a young to an old man. Here my children were born and one lies buried.

I now leave, not knowing when or whether ever I may return, with a task before me greater than that which rested on the shoulders of Washington.

Without the aid of that Divine Being who ever aided him, who controls mine and all destinies, I can not succeed. With that assistance I can not fail.

Trusting in him who can go with me and remain with you and be everywhere for good, let us confidently hope that all will be well.

To his care commending you, as I hope in your prayers you will commend me, I bid you, friends and neighbors, an affectionate farewell.[2]

Enos Clarke

Lincoln and the Radical Union Men of Missouri

At 9 o'clock in the morning of the last day of September, 1863, President Lincoln accompanied by one of his secretaries, came into the great east room of the White House and sat down.[1]

"He bore the appearance of being much depressed, as if the whole matter at issue in the conference which was impending was of great anxiety and trouble to him," says one of the Missourians who sat awaiting the president's coming.

There were seventy "Radical Union men of Missouri"; they had accepted that designation. They had been chosen at mass convention in Jefferson City—"the largest mass convention ever held in the state," their credentials said. That convention had unqualifiedly indorsed the emancipation proclamation and the employment of negro troops. It had declared its loyalty to the general government. It had appointed these seventy Missourians, from fifty-seven counties, to proceed to Washington and "to procure a change in the governmental policy in reference to Missouri."

This action by Missouri meant more than a local movement. It was the precipitation of a crisis at Washington. It was the voice of the radical antislavery element of the whole country speaking through Missouri, demanding that the government commit itself to the policy of the abolition of slavery and to the policy of the use of negro troops against the Confederate armies. It was the uprising of the element which thought the administration at Washington had been too mild. President Lincoln understood that the coming of the Missourians meant more than their local appeal. The Missourians understood, too, the importance of their mission. On the way to Washington the seventy had stopped in city after city, had been given enthusiastic reception by the antislavery leaders; they had been encouraged to make their appeal for a new policy in Missouri insistent and to stand on the platform that the border states must now wipe out slavery of loyal owners.

Hence it was that immediately upon their arrival in Washington the seventy Missourians coming from a slave state put into their address to the president such an avowal as this:

> We rejoice that in your proclamation of January 1, 1863, you laid the mighty hand of the nation upon that gigantic enemy of American liberty and we and our constituents honor you for that wise and noble act. We and they hold that that proclamation did, in law, by its own force, liberate every slave in the region it covered; that it is irrevocable, and that from the moment of its issue the American people stood in an impregnable position before the world and the rebellion received its death blow. If you, Mr. President, felt that duty to your country demanded that you should unshackle the slaves of the rebel states in an hour, we see no earthly reason why the people of Missouri should not, from the same sense of duty, strike down with equal suddenness the traitorous and parricidal institution in their midst.

Here was the essence of the Missouri movement which gave it national interest, which prompted the grand chorus of approval, which led to the series of indorsing ovations concluding with the mighty demonstration over the seventy Radical Union men in Cooper Institute, New York City, with William Cullen Bryant presiding.[2] President Lincoln, pursuing the course which seemed to him necessary to keep the united North with him felt fully the critical character of the issue which the Missourians were raising.

Conditions and events wholly apart from what was going on in their states added to the significance and importance of this conference between President Lincoln and the radical Union men of Missouri. The week before the seventy started from St. Louis for Washington that bloodiest battle of the war, Chickamauga, had been fought, and the whole North was depressed by the narrow escape of Rosecrans' army.[3] When the Missourians arrived in Washington Hooker's army was marching all night long over the Long Bridge out of Virginia and into Washington to take trains for the roundabout journey to Chattanooga to re-enforce the penned-up troops, that they might not be forced north of the Tennessee by Bragg.[4] Meade's failure to follow up the success at Gettysburg in July previous had given great dissatisfaction.[5] In the cabinet there was division over administration policies. The presidential campaign was coming on in a few months. Perhaps at no other time since the beginning of the war had President Lincoln faced more discouraging criticism and more hostile opinion in the North.

The address reviewed the origin and the development of antagonism between the Gamble administration and the radical Union men.[6] It charged Gamble with the intention to preserve slavery in Missouri, and asserted "the radicals of Missouri desired and demanded the election of a new convention for the purpose of ridding the state of slavery immediately." It dwelt at length upon the "proslavery character" of "Gov. Gamble's policy and acts."

"From the antagonisms of the radicals to such a policy," the address proceeded, "have arisen the conflicts which you, Mr. President, have been pleased heretofore to term a 'factional quarrel.' With all respect we deny that the radicals of Missouri have been or are, in any sense, a party to any such quarrel. We are no factionists; but men earnestly intent upon doing our part toward rescuing this great nation from the assaults which slavery is aiming at its life."

With the Missourians affirming such a position, it is not difficult to understand the wave of sympathy from the antislavery element which spread over the country, taking the form of indorsements by newspapers, speeches by leaders of the antislavery people and enthusiastic public attentions to the delegation.

The climax of the address of the seventy radical Union men was the prayer that Ben Butler be sent to succeed Schofield to restore peace and order in Missouri.[7]

> We ask further, Mr. President, that in the place of Gen. Schofield a department commander be assigned to the Department of Missouri whose sympathies will be with Missouri's loyal and suffering people, and not with slavery and proslavery men. Gen. Schofield has disappointed our just expectations by identifying himself with our state administration, and his policy as department commander has been, as we believe, shaped to conform to Gov. Gamble's proslavery and conservative views. He has subordinated federal authority in Missouri to state rule. He has become a party to the enforcement of conscription into the state service. He has countenanced, if not sustained, the orders issued from the state headquarters, prohibiting enlistments from the enrolled militia into the volunteer service of the United States. Officers acting under him have arbitrarily arrested and imprisoned loyal citizens, without assigned cause, or for daring to censure Gov. Gamble's policy and acts. Other such officers have ordered loyal men to be disarmed, and in some instances the order has been executed, while under the pretense of preventing an invasion of Missouri from Kansas, notorious and avowed disloyaltists have been armed. He has issued a military order prohibiting the liberty of speech and of the press. An officer in charge of negro recruits that had been enlisted under lawful authority, as we are informed and believe, was on the 20th inst. arrested in Missouri by Brig. Gen. Guitar, acting under Gen. Schofield's orders, his commission, side-arms and recruits taken from him, and he imprisoned and sent out of the state.[8] And, finally, we declare to you, Mr. President, that from the day of Gen. Schofield's accession to the command of that department, matters have grown worse and worse in Missouri, till now they are in a more terrible condition than they have been at any time since the outbreak of the rebellion. This could not be if Gen. Schofield had administered the affairs of that department with proper vigor and with a resolute purpose to sustain loyalty and suppress disloyalty. We, therefore, respectfully pray you to send another general to command that department; and, if we do not overstep the bounds of propriety, we ask that the commander sent there be Maj. Gen. Benjamin F. Butler. We believe that his presence there would restore order and peace to Missouri in less than sixty days.

The closing paragraph of the address was well calculated to impress Mr. Lincoln with the intensity of feeling inspiring the delegation. Perhaps in the history of White House conferences such strong language was never before used by a delegation in declaring the personal responsibility of the chief executive. The conclusion was in these words:

Whether the loyal hearts of Missouri shall be crushed is for you to say. If you refuse our requests, we return to our homes only to witness, in consequence of that refusal, a more active and relentless persecution of Union men, and to feel that while Maryland can rejoice in the protection of the government of the Union, Missouri is still to be the victim of a proslavery conservatism, which blasts wherever it reigns. Does Missouri deserve such a fate? What border slave state confronted the rebellion in its first spring as she did? Remember, we pray you, who it was that in May, 1861, captured Camp Jackson and saved the arsenal at St. Louis from the hands of traitors, and the Union cause in the Valley of the Mississippi from incalculable disaster. Remember the home guards, who sprung to arms in Missouri when the government was without troops or means to defend itself there. Remember the more than 50,000 volunteers that Missouri has sent forth to battle for the Union. Remember that, although always a slave state, her unconditional loyalty to the Union shines lustrously before the whole nation. Recall to memory these things, Mr. President, and let them exert their just influence upon your mind. We ask only justice and protection to our suffering people. If they are to suffer hereafter, as now, and in time past, the world will remember that they are not responsible for the gloomy page in Missouri's history, which may have to record the independent efforts of her harassed but still loyal men to defend themselves, their families and their homes against their disloyal and murderous assailants.

The names of the seventy radical Union men of Missouri were signed to this remarkable document. The signature of Charles D. Drake, afterwards senator from Missouri, and still later chief justice of the Court of Claims at Washington, came first as chairman.[9] Two Missouri congressmen, Ben Loan and J. W. McClurg, the latter afterwards governor, signed as vice chairmen of the delegation.[10] One of the secretaries was the late Emil Preetorius of the *Westliche Post*.[11] Three of the seventy signers are living and well known in St. Louis—Enos Clarke, Charles P. Johnson and David Murphy.[12] They were among the youngest members of the delegation. One of them, Charles P. Johnson, was chosen to speak at the Cooper Institute demonstration given to indorse this Missouri movement for universal emancipation, and was introduced to the great audience by the poet and editor, William Cullen Bryant. The forty-five years gone by have not dimmed the recollection of that journey to Washington and of the scene in the east room of the White House by these three participants, although time long ago tempered the sentiment and dissipated the bitterness.

"The feeling over our grievances as radicals had become intense," Mr. Enos Clarke said, as with some reluctance he consented to talk about the visit to President Lincoln, explaining that it would be difficult for those who had not lived through these years in Missouri to comprehend the situation. We represented the extreme antislavery sentiment. We were the Republicans who had been in accord with Fremont's position. Both sides to the controversy in Missouri had repeatedly presented their views to President Lincoln, but this delegation of seventy was the most imposing and most formal protest which had been made to the Gamble state administration and the national administration's policy in Missouri. The attention of the whole country, it seemed, had been drawn to Missouri. Our delegation met with a series of ovations. When we reached Washington we were informed that Secretary Chase proposed to tender us a reception. We were entertained by him the evening of the day we were received at the White House.

Who was the author of the address, Mr. Clarke?

The address was the result of several meetings we held after we reached Washington. We were there nearly a week. Arriving on Saturday, we did not have our conference at the White House until Wednesday. Every day we met in Willard's Hall, on F street, and considered the address. Mr. Drake would read over a few paragraphs, and we would discuss them. At the close of the meeting Mr. Drake would say, "I will call you together to-morrow to further consider this matter." In that way the address progressed to the finish.

How did the president receive you?

There was no special greeting. We went to the White House a few minutes before 9, in accordance with the appointment which had been made, and took seats in the east room. Promptly at 9 the president came in, unattended save by one of his secretaries. He did not shake hands, but sat down in such a position that he faced us. He seemed a great, ungainly, almost uncouth man. He walked with a kind of ambling gait. His face bore the look of depression, of deep anxiety. Mr. Drake stepped forward as soon as the president had taken his seat and began to read the address. He had a deep, sonorous voice and he read slowly and in a most impressive manner. The reading occupied half an hour. At the conclusion Mr. Drake said this statement of our grievances had been prepared and signed by all of those present.

Did the president seem to be much affected by the reading?

No. And at the conclusion he began to discuss the address in a manner that was very disappointing to us.[13] He took up one phase after another and talked about them without showing much interest. In fact, he seemed inclined to treat many of the matters contained in the paper as of little importance. The things which we had felt to be so serious Mr. Lincoln treated as really unworthy of much consideration. That was the tone in which he talked at first. He minimized what seemed to us most important.

Did he indulge in any story telling or humorous comment?

No. There was nothing that seemed like levity at that stage of the conference. On the contrary, the president was almost impatient, as if he wished to get through with something disagreeable. When he had expressed the opinion that things were not so serious as we thought he began to ask questions, many of them. He elicited answers from different members of the delegation. He started argument, parrying some of the opinions expressed by us and advancing opinions contrary to the conclusions of the Committee of Seventy. This treatment of our grievances was carried so far that most of us felt a sense of deep chagrin. But after continuing in this line for some time the president's whole manner underwent change. It seemed as if he had been intent upon drawing us out. When satisfied that he fully understood us and had measured the strength of our purpose, the depth of our feeling, he took up the address as if anew. He handled the various grievances in a most serious manner. He gave us the impression, that he was disposed to regard them with as much concern as we did. After a while the conversation became colloquial between the president and the members of the delegation—more informal and more sympathetic. The change of tone made us feel that we were going to get consideration.

What inspired that assertion in the address that the president had spoken of the trouble in Missouri as a "factional quarrel"?

It was based on a letter President Lincoln had written to Gen. Schofield some time previously. A copy of that letter was before us when we drew up the address. Apparently, for the purpose of informing Gen. Schofield of his view of affairs in Missouri, Mr. Lincoln had written to him in this way: "I did not relieve Gen. Curtis because of my full conviction that he had done wrong by commission or omission.[14] I did it because of a conviction in my mind that the Union men of Missouri, constituting, when united, a vast majority of the whole people, have entered into a pestilent factional quarrel among themselves. Gen. Curtis, perhaps not of choice, being the head of one faction and Gov. Gamble that of the other. After months of labor to reconcile the difficulty, it seemed to grow worse and worse until I felt it my duty to break it up somehow, and, as I could not remove Gov. Gamble, I had to remove Gen. Curtis." This letter had found its way to the public and was made the basis of what our address said by way of vindication of the Radical Union men.

Did the president make any reference to that part of the address about the "factional quarrel"?

Yes, he did. And it was about the only thing he said that had a touch of humor in that long conversation. In the course of his reply to us he took up that grievance. "Why," he said, "you are a long way behind the times in complaining of what I said upon that point. Gov. Gamble was ahead of you. There came to me some time ago a letter complaining because I had said that he was a party to a factional quarrel, and I answered that letter without reading it."[15] The features of the president took on a whimsical look as he continued: "Maybe you would like to know how I could answer it without reading it. Well, I'll tell you. My private secretary told me such a letter had been received and I sat down and wrote to Gov. Gamble in about these words: I understand that a letter has been received from you complaining that I said you were a party to a factional quarrel in Missouri. I have not read that letter, and, what is more, I never will." With that Mr. Lincoln dismissed our grievance about having been called parties to a factional quarrel. He left us to draw our own inference from what he said, as he had left Gov. Gamble to construe the letter without help.

Did the conference progress to satisfactory conclusions after the president's manner changed?

We did not receive specific promises, but I think we felt much better toward the close than we had felt in the first hour. The president spoke generally of his purposes rather than with reference to conditions in Missouri. Toward the close of the conference he went on to speak of his great office, of its burdens, of its responsibilities and duties. Among other things he said that in the administration of the government he wanted to be the president of the whole people and of no section. He thought we, possibly, failed to comprehend the enormous stress that rested upon him. "It is my ambition and desire," he said with considerable feeling, "to so administer the affairs of the government while I remain president that if at the end I shall have lost every other friend on earth I shall at least have one friend remaining and that one shall be down inside of me."

How long did the conference continue?

Three hours. It was nearing noon when the president said what I have just quoted. That seemed to be the signal to end the conference. Mr. Drake stepped forward and, addressing the president, who was standing, said, with deliberation and emphasis: "The hour has come when we can no longer trespass upon your attention. Having submitted to you in a formal way a statement of our grievances, we will take leave of you, asking the privilege that each member of the delegation may take you by the hand. But, in taking leave of you, Mr. President, let me say to you many of these gentlemen return to a border state filled with disloyal sentiment. If upon their return there the military policies of your administration shall subject them to risk of life in the defense of the government and their blood shall be shed—let me tell you, Mr. President, that their blood shall be upon your garments and not upon ours."

How did the president receive that?

With great emotion. Tears trickled down his face, as we filed by shaking his hand.

James D. Conner

A member of the committee of the Indiana Legislature which escorted Mr. Lincoln through that state when he was on his way to Washington in 1861 resides at Wabash.[1] He is Mr. James D. Conner.[2] In 1861 he was a state senator.

"A short time before Mr. Lincoln left home," said Mr. Conner, in recalling the incidents of the journey, "the Legislature adopted a resolution authorizing Gov. Morton to appoint a committee of five, two of the Senate and three of the House, to correspond with Mr. Lincoln and to request him to come by way of Indianapolis on his way.[3] If he consented, the committee was to meet him at the state line and to escort him to Indianapolis. Gen. Stead [Steele] and I were appointed on behalf of the Senate.[4] Mr. Lincoln decided to accept the invitation. We met him at the state line. Mr. Lincoln was traveling on a special train. In the car he occupied there were only two or three people besides the committee. This afforded us quite an opportunity to get acquainted with the president elect. Large numbers of people assembled at every station, and at every station the train made a stop. Mr. Lincoln never failed, when the car stopped, to go out on the platform and make a brief speech. The promptness, the high order, the adaptability of these short speeches—and there were many of them—astonished me. Mr. Lincoln seemed to be cheerful and composed. He talked very freely and entertainingly to the committee, interspersing his remarks with anecdotes. Several times when we were approaching a station Mr. Lincoln would be in the midst of conversation, perhaps engaged in telling a story. He would stop without finishing, go to the platform and make a short talk. As soon as the train was under way Mr. Lincoln would resume the seat and go on with the conversation or story just as if there had been no interruption. At one very small station the address was so brief that I can recollect every word of it. As he came out on the platform and greeted the crowd he said simply this: 'Many people are asking what shall we do? Stand still and see the salvation of the Lord.'"

Shelby M. Cullom

The public career of one man spans the period between the Lincoln administration and the Lincoln centennial.[1] Shelby M. Cullom was in politics at Springfield before Lincoln had his joint debates with Douglas in 1858. He had been prosecuting attorney and member of the Legislature. Senator Cullom was speaker of the Illinois House of Representatives when Lincoln was elected president of the United States.[2] The campaign of 1860 brought wise men from afar to see the new head of the young Republican party. Visitors, from all manner of motives, flocked in throngs to the political Bethlehem. Some one had to take charge of a situation wholly novel to Springfield. Cullom had tact beyond his years. He liked the atmosphere. Upon him devolved for some time, until organization was effected, the duty of making the strangers feel comfortable and of arranging receptions.

"I remember," Senator Cullom said some time ago, recalling this experience, "when the first arrivals came and the House was crowded, looking at Lincoln's high stature—he was 6 feet 4 inches—and his countenance was really noble, I thought, making him look like the choice of a nation for their chief magistrate. He conducted himself with dignity. Any idea we might have had as townsmen that he would fall below the mark disappeared from that first day."

After Lincoln was inaugurated Cullom went on to Washington to see about the local patronage. His activity in politics, his leadership of the younger element in the party, his official position, he felt, naturally entitled him to consideration. Cullom desired to suggest the appointments of postmaster and collector at Springfield. Progress with President Lincoln was rather slow.

"I waited around some time and did not get his promise," said the senator. "Finally I went to him and said: 'I am going home. Why can't you give me those two offices?' 'Now,' said the president, 'you can have the collectorship, but the Post Office I have promised to old Mrs. [Seymour] Moody for her husband. I can't let you have that Post Office, Cullom; take the collectorship.' 'Now, Mr. President,' said I, 'why can't you be liberal, and let me have both?' 'Mrs. Moody would get down on me,' Mr. Lincoln replied."[3]

Mr. Cullom had another White House experience with Mr. Lincoln, which is firmly impressed upon his memory. He was relieved of a temporary embarrassment by that instantaneous exercise of pleasant tact with which the president so often relieved disagreeable situations.

"It was just after I was elected to Congress from the Springfield district and before I had taken my seat," is the way Senator Cullom tells the story. "I knew the secretaries of President Lincoln very well. Both Hay and Nicolay had gone to Washington from Springfield.[4] I was accustomed to go without ceremony to see them at the White House. At this time I came to the door of the room through which I was to pass to reach Mr. Nicolay's office, and without knocking I opened it and went in, to find myself in the presence of President Lincoln and the cabinet. Seward, Chase and Stanton were there. I colored to the roots of my hair, begged pardon for the intrusion and started to go out. President Lincoln arose from his chair at the head of the table and called me by name. He came over to me, got hold of my hand and pulled me into the group of cabinet members. As he did so he said to the secretary of state, 'Seward, I want you to know this boy. You remember the old congressman from Springfield named Stewart [John Todd Stuart]? I want to introduce to you the boy who beat him. This is the boy.' He thereupon presented me to the different secretaries. I shook hands with them and backed my way out just as soon as I could. That was in 1864. The next year I took my seat in Congress for the first time."

The interest of Lincoln's in Cullom dated back to a period earlier than the political friendship. The Culloms were from Kentucky. Shelby M. Cullom's father moved to Illinois because he didn't like slavery and settled in Tazewell County, which was in the circuit Lincoln as a lawyer rode.

"My father," said Senator Cullom, "was a Whig and went to the Illinois Legislature. He sat beside Mr. Lincoln. He was not a speaker. Lincoln voiced my father's political sentiments. Lincoln was one of nine men chosen as a delegation to get the capital away from Vandalia for Springfield. Those nine men put together measured 54 feet. They were called 'the long nine.' When Mr. Lincoln was nominated for Congress in 1846 he had to run in my father's county. My father took him in his carriage all over the county to his meetings. I can remember hearing Mr. Lincoln speak in that campaign. I was about 17 years old. Mr. Lincoln would say, 'Fellow citizens: Maj. Cullom has been everywhere with me, and has heard this speech time and again. The only way I can deceive him with it is to go down to the other end and give it to him backward.' With that he made one of those curious jerks with his long arms which we remember as so characteristic of him. He had a reaching voice, not very deep."

In 1853 young Cullom had been to Mount Morris College and was ready for a profession. He talked it over with his father. The law was chosen. To the elder Cullom, Abraham Lincoln was the ideal lawyer of that day. Even before Lincoln became so well known at the Illinois bar the elder Cullom had great confidence in his professional ability.

"My father," Senator Cullom recalls, "when asked to advise as to a lawyer for any person would say, 'Get Judge [Stephen T.] Logan if you can, but if you can't, there is a young man in his office by the name of Lincoln who will do just as well.'"

It was natural, then, when the legal profession had been selected for young Cullom, that the father should wish to have him trained by Lincoln.

"My father," said Senator Cullom, "took me to Mr. Lincoln at Springfield to have me study law with him. Mr. Lincoln told my father that he could not give me the attention I ought to have, the catechising and directing of my studies, as he was then much engaged and a good deal absent. He advised that I be turned over to a firm of lawyers, one of whom was a connection of Mr. Lincoln—Mr. Edwards. With them I studied law. I saw Mr. Lincoln constantly and he was my friend. I have been in his law office when he returned from riding the circuit. Mr. Lincoln kept no account books to speak of. He practiced at the courts of all the counties around Springfield. After trying a case he would take the fee that he received from his client, wrap it up in a piece of paper, write on the back of the paper the name of the case and the amount—ten, fifteen or twenty-five dollars, whatever it might be—and put the paper in his pocket. When Mr. Lincoln came home he would take these papers out of his pockets, one at a time, and divide the amounts with his partner, Herndon. Theoretically, Mr. Lincoln was strong on financial questions. On political economy he was great. Practically, he knew little about money and took no care of it. As a lawyer in practice, he was very strong before both court and jury. He had a great deal of personal magnetism and his honest, plain way captured the jurors. Mr. Lincoln would lean over the jury, gesturing with his long arms and holding the jurors fascinated with his homely eloquence."

Great [was the] influence Mr. Lincoln exercised over his young protege. Probably that influence had more to do with the almost unparalleled success of Cullom in public life than the senator realizes. Approaching four score, Senator Cullom looks back upon official service, beginning as city attorney at Springfield in the '50s, immediately after he was licensed to practice law. He was a presidential elector as early as 1856. He served four terms in the Illinois Legislature, two of them as speaker. He was six years in Congress and was twice elected governor of Illinois. He has been a United States senator twenty-five years and has more years to come. As a representative in Congress, Mr. Cullom was one of the half a dozen who met at a dinner, selected James G. Blaine as their candidate for speaker, started the campaign and pushed it to success.[5] A part of the incentive which moved Mr. Cullom to activity was what President Lincoln had said to him about Blaine years before.

"President Lincoln called my attention to Blaine," said Senator Cullom. "Somebody in Congress had assailed the president in an exasperating manner. Blaine replied to the attack. President Lincoln said to me, 'There is a young fellow up there from Maine, by the name of Blaine, who has plenty of ability, and I think is going to cut a big figure in this country.' I don't recollect what speech of Blaine's President Lincoln had in mind when he spoke about Blaine in that way, but I remember that in assisting to elect Blaine speaker I recalled how he had been praised by Mr. Lincoln."

It came in the way of the senator to show in a practical way some return for the friendship of Lincoln. When Mr. Cullom was governor of Illinois he went to Mentor [Ohio] to urge upon President-elect Garfield the appointment of Robert T. Lincoln, son of Abraham Lincoln, as a member of the new cabinet.[6] Mr. Lincoln was made secretary of war. He was a guest at Gov. Cullom's home when the letter came tendering the place in the cabinet. Cullom had just been elected governor when the attempt was made to steal the remains of Abraham Lincoln.

"It was in 1876, the night of the election," the senator remembers. "A set of whelps had conspired together to steal the body of Lincoln and hold it for ransom. Their plans were carefully laid and they would have succeeded had they not been betrayed by one of their number. The monument was built over a great vault, in which were two rooms. One of these rooms contained the relics of Lincoln and memorials of various kinds. The other room held the body of Lincoln in a zinc casket, which was inclosed in a marble sarcophagus, as was thought, securely sealed. As soon as the information of the plot was received a party of citizens of Springfield hid themselves in the memorial chamber and waited for the attempt. At midnight the ghouls came, broke open the marble sarcophagus and had pulled the zinc casket about one-third of the way out, when the watchers tried to capture them. The ghouls got away, but two of them were afterward caught and went to the Penitentiary. After that a tomb was excavated in the masonry under the obelisk. In that the body was placed and the casket was imbedded in hydraulic cement, so that it can not be reached."

Very frank were some of the communications of President Lincoln to Mr. Cullom. When the second inauguration was coming on Andrew Johnson sent word from his home in Tennessee to Mr. Lincoln that he did not think it necessary to come to Washington for the inauguration.[7] Mr. Lincoln showed that message to Mr. Cullom and commented upon it, 'This Johnson is a queer man.'"

George T. M. Davis

A Lincoln Letter Written in 1860

In the autobiography which Col. George T. M. Davis, the Alton and St. Louis editor, left to his family is a Lincoln letter of historical interest.[1] A close personal friend of Lincoln, Davis, after his service in the Mexican war, and after some years in official life at Washington, went to New York and engaged in railroad business. He was there when the campaign of 1860 was on. There was so much timidity of business interests in the East over the possibility of Lincoln's election, that Davis thought some expression from the candidate just at the close of the campaign might help the situation. He wrote to Lincoln suggesting the expediency of the issue of a quieting statement that nothing radical was contemplated. He received a reply, dated at Springfield the 27th of October, 1860. The letter, like nearly all of Lincoln's letters, and even state papers, is brief, but it is evidence of Lincoln's perfect comprehension of his relation to the great moral movement which was sweeping on without regard to threats of politicians in the South or timidity of business interests in the North. Lincoln wrote:

> What is it I could say that would quiet alarm? Is it that no interference by the government with slaves or slavery, within the states, is intended?
>
> I have said this so often already that a repetition of it is but mockery, bearing an appearance of weakness and cowardice which, perhaps, should be avoided.
>
> Why do not uneasy men read what I have already said? And what our platform says?
>
> If they will not read or heed them, would they heed a repetition of them?
>
> Of course the declaration that there is no intention to interfere with slaves or slavery in the states, with all that is fairly implied in such declaration, is true, and I should have no objection to make and repeat the declaration a thousand times if there was no danger of encouraging bold, bad men to believe they are dealing with one who can be scared into anything."[2]

Lincoln's Sense of Honor in Politics

Lincoln refused the governorship of Oregon.[3] He did it under circumstances showing a sense of honor not common in political life. Simeon Francis was the editor of the *Sangamon Journal*.[4] He had been for several years. While the relatives of Mary Todd were trying to discourage the courtship and while Mr. Lincoln was being made to feel he was not welcome at the Edwards home, where Miss Todd was living with her sister, the residence of Simeon Francis was the meeting place of Mr. Lincoln and Miss Todd.[5] It was at the house of Mr. Francis that Mr. Lincoln and Miss Todd were to be married until the relatives, yielding to the inevitable, insisted on a home wedding. The personal friendship between Mr. Lincoln and Mr. Francis continued very close for years. All that the *Journal* could do to advance the political interests of Mr. Lincoln it did.[6] In 1849 Oregon had advanced in population and in organization to the status of a territory. Friends of Mr. Lincoln, notably George T. M. Davis, who had been the editor of the *Alton Telegraph* and a staff officer in the Mexican war and had become an official in Washington, proposed Abraham Lincoln for the appointment of governor of Oregon. In a little autobiography which Col. Davis wrote and left to his family, the facts about the tender of the governorship and about the refusal of it are told. This incident in the life of Lincoln is one that has escaped most of the biographers. Col. Davis wrote:

> John Addison of the City of Washington, with myself and a few other strong

political and personal friends of Mr. Lincoln, then at the seat of our national government, united in an effort to have him appointed governor of the territory of Oregon.[7] Those efforts were so far crowned with success as to be dependent only upon the willingness of Mr. Lincoln to accept the position to secure his appointment. Mr. Addison was delegated to correspond with Mr. Lincoln, to inform him of the assurances given that his appointment would follow if he would accept it, and to urge him to do so. The letter was written, and in due course of time Mr. Lincoln's reply thereto was received, which, much to our discomfiture and disappointment, was as follows:

John Addison, Esq.—My Dear Sir: Your letter received. I can not but be grateful to you and all other friends who have interested themselves in having the governorship of Oregon offered to me, but, on as much reflection as I have had time to give the subject, I can not consent to accept it.

I have an ever-abiding wish to serve you, but as to the secretaryship I have already recommended our friend, Simeon Francis of the Journal. Please present my respects to G. T. M. Davis, generally, and my thanks, especially, for his kindness in the Oregon matter. Yours as ever,

A. LINCOLN.

"The motives," continues Col. Davis, "influencing Mr. Lincoln in declining the public honor which was held in abeyance for him were these: His friend and neighbor, Simeon Francis, who was the proprietor and editor of the *Sangamon Journal* of Springfield, and at the time the leading and most influential Whig paper in the state, was an applicant for the office of secretary of the Territory of Oregon. Mr. Lincoln had not only strongly recommended Francis to the president, but, upon both personal and political grounds, felt the deepest interest in his success. Of course, Mr. Lincoln was well aware that the president would not, for a moment, entertain the idea of making both appointments from the same state. And as soon as he received the letter from Mr. Addison, without hesitation and with his proverbial magnanimity and high sense of honor, wrote the letter in which he said: 'I can not accept it.' This disinterestedness became the more conspicuous, as Mr. Lincoln had been advised by us that for political reasons the president had determined against the appointment of Mr. Francis during his administration. Mr. Francis never did receive the appointment, but a short time previous to the election of Mr. Lincoln to the presidency he removed with his wife to Oregon, on account of his health, and Mr. Lincoln subsequently appointed Mr. Francis paymaster, with the rank of major, in the United States Army, which he held till his death."

Thomas Dowling

"Can I tell you anything of Abe Lincoln? I reckon I can," said Mr. Thomas Dowling, of this city [Charleston, Illinois], a gentleman 79 years old.[1]
I ought to know something. Abe used to make my home his stopping place when he came to Charleston. I could tell him as far as I could see him by his walk: his head would be going back and forth as though on a pivot. One little circumstance I distinctly remember to show how he appreciated a joke. At one time he and Congressman Bromwell were to make speeches in Charleston on a certain great occasion, political, of course, and early in the morning they both came to my house.[2] It was before daylight, and Abe said to me and my wife:

'We have been riding all night and are tired, and must sleep. Don't wake us up until dinner time, and don't tell anybody we are in town—not a soul.'

I went to my work as usual, but was bothered every little while by people coming and inquiring for Abe. He wasn't to be found, and there was no train now for him to come on. I never saw such a crowd of people before. I told them I would guarantee Lincoln would be on time. But it was all I could do to keep his presence unknown. After dinner Abe made his appearance and their cry hushed. No doubt he had been awake and laughing in his sleeve, for he was aware of the crowd's disappointment.

Lincoln was always of even temperament, never showing anger.[3] While he was speaking in a grove north of this city one time, a Dr. Banks, who lived here, in order to bother him, yelled out at the top of his voice:

'Mr. Lincoln, did you ever drive cattle through Charleston barefooted?'

'Yes,' answered Lincoln, instantly: 'and I can get twenty men in this town to prove it.'

It is needless for me to say he never did; but he was not interrupted again while speaking by Banks.

While Lincoln was still keeping store at [New] Salem, Ill., he formed the acquaintance of Lawyer Logan, of Springfield, who loaned him law books to read.[4] He has often walked from Salem to Springfield and return, carrying these books, and would read one or two while walking before reaching home, so eager was he for knowledge.

Mary [Lincoln] was a little high strung. She came of blue blood, blue grass Kentucky stock; and her tastes were somewhat different from Abe's, but, law, they got along well together. Mrs. Lincoln loved the dance, and often left her husband to take care of the children while she enjoyed the pleasures of the ballroom. To show you she was of a kindly disposition, however, and very womanly withal, when I came home from the Mexican war I stopped over night with Lincoln and his family, and when bedtime came she showed me to my sleeping apartment. I was very tired, and when I had retired she came in the room and carefully tucked the covers around me as though I were a child. The papers have said many things utterly untrue of Lincoln and his home life. After all, who of us is perfect? I think Lincoln was the best conversationalist of his time. We never retired when Lincoln stopped with my family until 11 or 12 at night, and only wished then time was not so rapid in its flight.

Mrs. Benjamin S. Edwards

Pilgrims to the Home of Lincoln

Lincoln was worth about $7000 when he was nominated for president.[1] He had to borrow money in anticipation of the presidential salary, when he went to Washington.[2] Pilgrims, in increasing numbers, visit Springfield to see where Lincoln lived and where he is buried. In one direction from the business center is the costly tomb, built originally from $270,000, offerings of soldiers in the field and people at home, but rebuilt by the State of Illinois.

In a direction almost opposite, about eight blocks from the Courthouse, is the "Lincoln home," as the modest sign says. This home was the chief asset of Lincoln's fortune. It was almost the only home he had. When he was married he went to live in a tavern, and later kept house in a few rooms. Most of the pilgrims seem to find more satisfaction in the home than in the tomb. They seek to feel the life of Lincoln, rather than to mourn his tragic end. They linger in the rooms; they ask innumerable questions; they touch the furniture; they reveal a reverence for the personality that once dwelt there.

The State of Illinois did well in acquiring the Lincoln residence. The house remained the property of the president until his death. Then it passed to his son Robert. As interest grew the agent found difficulty in keeping tenants, because of the number of visitors. Public sentiment insisted that the house ought to be the property of the state and ought to be preserved for the association connected with it. Judge Ninian W. Edwards, who was Lincoln's brother-in-law, they having married sisters, the Misses Todd, advised his nephew to transfer the house to the state to preserve as a trust. The offer was accepted, and a custodian was put in charge to receive those who came to visit the home of Lincoln.

When he moved to the Lincoln home to take charge of it, Albert Stevenson Edwards brought with him furniture which was his father's and his mother's, and which is closely associated with the Lincolns. The old hair-cloth sofa, the identical upholstering on the back, is the one which was in the Edwards parlor when Lincoln, Douglas, Shields and other young, rising lawyers of Springfield came to call upon the vivacious Mary Todd in 1839–42. Upon the mantel are the old-fashioned astral lamps which shed the light the Sunday evening that Abraham Lincoln and Mary Todd were married. In one corner is the tall combination desk and bookcase which stood in Lincoln's law office. Judge Edwards took possession of this desk and case when Mr. Lincoln went away to Washington to be inaugurated.

When the Lincoln family went to Washington in 1861 much of the furniture in this Eighth street house was disposed of by sale. The Tiltons, who admired Mr. Lincoln very much and who were people of means, bought most of the articles that were for sale.[3] When the volunteers were received at Springfield and prepared for the front during the civil war many of them came to the house to "see where Uncle Abe lived." The Tiltons were patriotic: they permitted the soldier boys to sit down in the dining room and have a glass of milk off the table at which Mr. Lincoln had eaten so many years. The Tiltons moved to Chicago. They took with them the Lincoln furniture, prizing the articles more than ever after the president was killed. In the great Chicago fire of 1871 this furniture was burned. At the same time was destroyed the original draft of the emancipation proclamation, which had been taken to Chicago from Washington for an exhibition.

The exterior of the home is very like it was when Mr. Lincoln lived in Springfield. The addition of a kitchen is about the only change which has been made. When the place was bought by Mr. Lincoln the house was only a story and a half. Mrs. Lincoln inherited some money from the Todd estate in Kentucky. Mr. Lincoln advised her to invest it in land. Mrs. Lincoln wanted to improve the home. There was a compromise, as the result of which Mrs. Lincoln kept out some of the money when the investment was made. Waiting until Mr. Lincoln departed on the circuit and knowing that he would be away several weeks, Mrs. Lincoln put carpenters to work, had the roof raised and made a full second story. Mr. Lincoln did not get back until the work was finished. When he did return he looked at the place curiously, turned and went across to the house on the opposite corner and asked his neighbors if they could tell him what had become of his family. He said, with a serious air, he had left a wife and children living in a little one-story house when he went away and he could not find the place. He added that he did not care for the house, but would like to recover his family.

One of the fictions which the visitor hears in Springfield is that at this point in the story Mrs. Lincoln came to the door and called to Mr. Lincoln to "come in and not make a fool of himself." When this was repeated to Mrs. Edwards,[4] she quickly said:

> That isn't true. Mrs. Lincoln did not talk in that way. She was high spirited, but she has been much misrepresented. She would sometimes speak and act quickly and regret it the next moment, but she did not speak to Mr. Lincoln in that way. She was one of the kindest of mothers. I remember that a new clock was brought home. Mrs. Lincoln told the boys they must not touch it. A short time afterward she went into the room and found that two of them had taken the clock to pieces. She whipped them. Almost immediately afterward she felt so sorry for what she had done she told the boys to take the clock and do what they pleased with it.

Mrs. Edwards was a little girl living on the next corner when Mr. Lincoln practiced law in Springfield. She was almost a daily visitor at the Lincoln home until the family moved to Washington. She could always depend upon Mr. Lincoln to take her to the circus. Of Mrs. Lincoln she speaks from personal knowledge and the intimacy of a next-door neighbor. Her memory is overflowing with the reminiscences of close acquaintanceship which add much to the interest of a visit to the Lincoln home. There are days when the time of Mrs. Edwards and her daughter is occupied continuously in showing visitors through the home. Under ordinary conditions regular visiting hours are kept. But not long ago a minister came to the house at 11 o'clock at night and asked the privilege of seeing the place, explaining that circumstances made it impossible for him to remain over until the next day. A middle-aged man was being shown through the home by Mrs. Edwards some time ago. When he came to the upper room, which was Mr. Lincoln's bedchamber, upon the walls of which is still to be seen some of the paper which was there when Mr. Lincoln occupied it, the visitor stepped forward and kissed the paper.

"I can't help it," he said brokenly, as if by way of apology.

Not long after this occurrence Mrs. Edwards was showing an old man through the rooms, when he suddenly dropped into a chair and sobbed. With the tears rolling down his cheeks, he talked of Mr. Lincoln, whom he had known personally before the war. Many visitors linger long in the rooms. Incidents going to show the deepening veneration for all that pertains to Lincoln are of almost daily occurrence. On holidays the visitors include many mechanics and working people. There is yet to be noted at the Lincoln home a single act wanting in respect for the associations of the place.

"We have never had a rude, ill-bred word spoken here," Mrs. Edwards said. "We have never had anything stolen. Often the home is full of people. Respect to the memory of Lincoln is universal with visitors."

Orlando B. Ficklin

Hon. O. B. Ficklin, of this city [Charleston, Illinois], recently deceased, who was a member of Congress with Lincoln and an associate at the bar,[1] leaves this statement of the martyred President:

He was naturally despondent and sad, like many another who has made mirth for a merry company. He could tell a story to make a group roar with laughter, but when his face was unlit by pleasantry it was dark, gloomy and peculiar. The pictures we see of him only half represent him, as they can only show him in repose. Lincoln was a man of two distinct personages. He was a man of keen insight and absorbing meditation. His sudden changes from elated joy to silent brooding over the problems of life were noticeable to all his friends. One moment a boy exultant, sunny, cheery, the next a care-burdened man, deep in thought. His characteristics were honor, fidelity and transparent truth. Had Douglas had these qualities to as great degree he would have been a greater man than Abe Lincoln. I am a life-long Democrat, but I loved Lincoln. He was, I say, a greater man than Washington. He was a lover of music, flowers, birds, Burns' poetry, and could read Campbell's "Last Man" as no one else.[2] Abe was not what you would call eloquent in speaking; he was a strong, sensible speaker, of keen discernment, and was at his best before a jury. He could present his points in a stately array. He had a fashion of pointing at the jury with his long bony forefinger of his right hand. There seemed to be something magnetic always about that finger. He was elected to Congress in 1846 over Peter Cartwright, the great pioneer preacher of Illinois. I was elected, too, the same year, but had been before.

This was during the Mexican war. He opposed the war.[3] I indorsed it and advocated it. He was particularly bitter in his denunciations of [President James K.] Polk, and thereby called down on himself the wrath of the Democrats in Congress. The success of the war and the vast territory won by it somewhat overshadowed Lincoln, but while he won no great fame in Congress he learned there the lessons that afterward made him famous.[4] In those days we did not board at hotels while at Congress, but "messed" together in groups of ten or twelve. Up to that time I had not known him to favor abolition.[5] His views were the common nebulous whiggery of his party; but he was thrown in a "mess" with a set of Abolitionists, headed by Joshua R. Giddings. In this company his views chrystallized, and when he came out from them he was fixed in his ideas of the emancipation of the slaves. Thus unconsciously he was prepared for his part in the great drama of the civil war, and made ready for his eternal fame as the great American Liberator. He was an entire man. I have seen his rocky-featured face light up like a sea-fronting cliff bathed in dawn, while his dark eyes literally glowed as he asked for justice for his fellow-man. I have seen notable men in my day, but another like Lincoln I shall not see this side of the judgment.

William Fisher

Journey to a Henry Clay Convention

A Henry Clay convention was held in Peoria in 1844.[1] Springfield sent a delegation and Lincoln was a conspicuous member of it. One member of the party is living, perhaps the sole survivor. He is William Fisher of Springfield. His story of the trip is a revelation of pioneer transportation difficulties as well as evidence of the interest Lincoln took in politics when he was in his early manhood.

The Springfield band, of which I was an humble member, and a few citizens, of whom Mr. Lincoln was one, boarded a car on the Wabash Railroad for Meredosia on the Illinois River. The cars, at that time, were propelled by mule power. After we had proceeded about ten miles we met the freight coming east. There was no other way but to lift our car off the track and let the freight go by and then lift our car on again. Lincoln was one of the most active lifters. He would get his back to the car, let himself down to get a low hold and then lift his best. He gave all of us a good example. There was no shirking or feigning. We reached Meredosia and got through by boat on the Illinois River in time for the convention.

An Early Temperance Lecture

Early in his career, Lincoln lectured on temperance.[2] Mr. Fisher of Springfield remembers one of these occasions about 1842.

"Four or five of the people in our neighborhood were informed there would be a temperance meeting at the Dunlap Schoolhouse," he says. "We went to the meeting, which was some distance away, and when we got there we learned that former temperance lecturers at that place had been somewhat rough and unguarded in their presentation of the subject; they had given offense to some of the neighbors. Mr. Lincoln had been persuaded to speak and to throw oil upon the troubled waters. After so long a time I could not pretend to give an outline of his speech. I only know there was much in it that was convincing, sensible and soothing.[3] All of our little company that Sunday in the Dunlap Schoolhouse agreed that Mr. Lincoln was a wise and good man."

Mrs. Annie C. Fox

Greeting Lincoln Gave to Bride

Mrs. Annie C. Fox of Springfield remembers the greeting Mr. Lincoln gave to her as a bride more than half a century ago.[1]

"I came to Springfield in 1856," Mrs. Fox told. "My husband, Benjamin Fox, had been engaged in business here several years before that time. Mr. Lincoln and Mr. Fox were personal friends. They attended the same church, the First Presbyterian. The building now stands opposite the Chicago and Alton Railroad depot. Mr. Lincoln's pew was just across the aisle from Mr. Fox's. In honor of my coming Mr. Fox had fitted up his pew with new carpets and cushions. The first Sunday I attended church in Springfield Mr. Lincoln and I were introduced to each other. I remember Mr. Lincoln saying that he had wondered why Mr. Fox was fitting up his pew so fine, but he understood it now. Mrs. Lincoln, who was present, suggested that Mr. Lincoln himself might do a little fixing. It was not long after that before Mr. Lincoln's pew had a new carpet and new cushions."

Mrs. Fox recalls the interesting fact that "Mr. Lincoln was a regular attendant at church. He always paid close attention to the sermons and took an active part in the services."

An illustration of the extent to which political prejudices were carried, is afforded by one of Mrs. Fox's recollections of Mr. Lincoln.

"Mr. Fox," she said, "was born and grew up in Buffalo. He was thoroughly imbued with the doctrines of abolitionism. He subscribed for the *Washington Era* and newspapers edited by [William Lloyd] Garrison and other abolitionists.[2] Mr. Lincoln came regularly to Mr. Fox's store to read these newspapers. In the days of which I speak abolitionists were not thought of kindly, as a rule, by the people of Springfield. The postmaster was not in favor of distributing such newspapers through the mails. He at length refused to deliver the papers to Mr. Fox. One evening when Mr. Lincoln was in the store Mr. Fox told him about the action of the postmaster in withholding the newspapers and asked what he should do about it.

"Mr. Lincoln said he 'guessed the newspapers would be delivered.' After a conference between Mr. Lincoln and the postmaster the papers were again given the privilege of distribution at the Springfield office, but the postmaster, instead of giving Mr. Fox his mail in the usual manner, threw the papers over the transom of the door. The Post Office was located just south of Mr. Fox's store. When Mr. Lincoln learned about the throwing of the papers over the door, he remarked that he 'guessed from the manner in which the postmaster handled abolition doctrines he must be afraid of catching something.'"

Of Mr. Lincoln's manner and appearance, Mrs. Fox said: "He was always courteous and polite to the women. He was tall and rather awkward in his movements. His clothing did not fit him well, but the material was of the best. His linen was always fresh and clean."

Thomas Goodwin

Rev. Thomas Goodwin, an old gentleman of this city [Charleston, Illinois], 79 years of age, the pastor who preached the funeral sermon of Thomas Lincoln, was met on the street the other day.[1] He says:

> I was teaching at the time at Springtown five days in the week, and in the eight days preceding the funeral exercises [for Lincoln's father, Thomas Lin-

coln] rode seventy-two miles on horseback and preached seven times, Lincoln's funeral being the sixth meeting. It occurred on Saturday, January 8, 1851, and I remember the day well, as it was very cold and snow was on the ground. Services were held at his stepson's, John D. Johnson's [Johnston's] residence.[2] It is now known as Thomas Lincoln's homestead. The exercises commenced at 10 o'clock. The text I selected on the occasion was I. Corinthians, xv., 21–22: "For since by man came death, by man came also the resurrection of the dead. For as in Adam all die, even so in Christ shall all be made alive." In his case I could not say aught but good. He was buried in what is called Gordon's graveyard, Pleasant Grove Township, Coles County. He was a consistent member through life of the Church of my choice, the Christian Church, or Church of Christ, and was, as far as I know—and I was a very intimate friend—illiterate, yet always truthful, conscientious and religious. At his death he had reached the age of 78 years. He walked with the poor of this earth, wore homespun clothes and a coonskin cap, but I think, when the martyred President entered the gates of the city which stand ajar, that among the first to welcome him was Thomas Lincoln.

"Old Tommy used to delight in telling about Abe's uglier man than himself," continued Mr. Goodwin. "When Abe was about 18 years old he went out one day to look for game. Deer and turkey were at that time quite plenty. Going along he met coming towards him, two or three hundred yards away, a man. They kept coming nearer, and when about fifteen or twenty yards apart Abe stopped and drew up his gun as though in the act of shooting. The man halloed to him to stop, and Abe lowered his gun. Being asked the reason for such an act, Lincoln replied: 'I always said that if I ever met a man uglier than myself I would shoot him on the spot.' The man looked at Lincoln steadily for a moment, then he stepped out in the clearing and, drawing up his coat, said: 'Well, sir, if I am any uglier than you are, you can shoot.' It is needless to add that the shot was never fired."

Dennis Hanks

Your correspondent had the pleasure of an interview with Mr. Dennis Hanks, an own cousin of Nancy Hanks, the wife of Thomas Lincoln and the mother of Abraham.[1] Mr. Hanks is now 88 years of age, well preserved, and never tires of speaking of the many virtues and excellences of his relative.

When did you first see Abe?

About twenty-four hours after birth—hardly that—I rikkilect I run all the way, over two miles, to see Nancy Hanks' boy baby. " 'Twas common then to come together in them days to see new babies. Her name was Nancy Hanks before she married Lincoln. I held the wee one a minit. I was 10 years old, and it tickled me to hold the pulpy, red little thing. When Abe was about 9 [actually 7] years old his father moved to Indiana, Spencer County. We came out a year later, and he then had a cabin up, and he gave us the shanty. On this spot Abe grew to manhood. Our cabins were about fifteen rods apart. Abe killed a turkey the day we got there, and couldn't get through telling about it.

It is stated you taught him to read; is that so?

I reckon. I taught him to spell, read and cipher. He knew his letters pretty wellish; his mother taught him his letters. If there ever was a good woman, she were one, a true Christian of the Baptist Church, but she died soon after we arrived, and left him without a teacher. His father couldn't read a word. Abe went to school in all about a quarter; I then set up to help him; did the best I could. Webster's speller was his first favorite; a copy I had of the Indiana statutes came next. Then he happened on to a copy of the *'Rabian Nights*! Abe would lay on the floor with a chair under his head, and laugh over that book for hours. I told him they was likely lies from end to end, but he learned to read right well in them.

At that time he was not grown, only six feet two inches; he was six feet four and one-half inches when grown. Tall, lathy and gangling; not much appearance; not handsome; not ugly, but peculiarsome. This kind of a fellow: If a man rode up horseback, Abe would be the first out and on the fence to ask questions, till his father would give him a knock on the head; then he would throw at birds or something; but pondered all the while. He was very strong and active. I were ten year older, but I couldn't rassle him down; his legs were too long for me. Strong? My, how he could chop wood! His ax would flash and bite into a sugar tree or sycamore, and down it would come. If you heard him falling trees you would think there were three men in the woods cutting. But he never was sassy or quarrelsome. I have seen him walk in some crowd of rowin' rowdies and tell some droll yarn that would bust them all up. It was the same when he was a lawyer. There was a sumthin' perculiarsome about him. We then had no idea a' his future greatness. He was a bright lad, but the big world seemed ahead of him. We were all slow-going folks, though we never suspected it.

Did he take to books eagerly?

No; we had to hire him at first. But when he got a taste, it was the old story—we had to pull the sow's ears to get her to the trough, and then pull her tail to get her away. What church did Abe belong to? The Baptist Church. I will tell you a circumstance about him. He would come home from church, put a box in the middle of the cabin floor, and repeat the sermon from text to doxology. I've heard him do it often.

Did he get his sterling principles of character from one or both parents?

Both. His strong will from his father. His father used to swear a little. One day his little girl picked up a foul oath, and was bruising the bitter morsel in her sweet lips, when Nancy called "Thomas!" and said: "Listen, husband." He stopped that habit thar; never swore again. Abe's kindliness he got from his mother. His humor, love of humanity, hatred of slavery, all came from her. I am free to say Abe was a mother's boy.

About ten or fifteen years ago a story was put in circulation that President Lincoln was an illegitimate child. It was stated that his father's name was Abraham Inlow, and not Thomas Lincoln. A Mr. Christopher Graham, in 1882, of Louisville, Ky., aged 98 years, made a sworn statement about the marriage of Thomas Lincoln and Nancy Hanks, in many particulars correct, but not in all.[2] I am an own cousin of Nancy Hanks, the wife of Thomas Lincoln; we were both residents of Kentucky. Her parents resided in Mercer County, and I was a resident of Hardin County. My uncle, Joseph Hanks, was a resident of Elizabethtown, the county seat of Hardin County, and engaged for a time in cabinet making. It was at Uncle Joseph's house that Thos. Lincoln and Nancy Hanks first met each other. Thomas, at the time, was learning the cabinet-making trade with [my] uncle. Thomas and Nancy were lawfully married by Alex. McDougal, a Baptist preacher, in 1806; I can not recall the day or month of the year. The wedding took place at McDougal's house, which was eight or ten miles southeast of Elizabethtown, in Hardin, now La Rue County. At the time I was 7 years old and was living with my uncle, Thomas Sparrow, who had taken me to raise. The newly married couple staid all night at our house the day of their marriage. Thos. Lincoln gave a $40 bond before he got his marriage license, which he obtained at the county seat. The name of the Circuit Clerk from whom Lincoln received his license was Benjamin Helms. Thomas Lincoln was aged 27 years and Nancy Hanks was in her 25th year when they were married. Among those present at the ceremony was a daughter of McDougal's, to whom I wrote and got a statement at the time the report was circulated that Abe was an illegitimate child, in which she declares that Nancy Hanks and Thomas Lincoln were married according to law, on the south fork of Nolin Creek, Hardin County, Kentucky, in 1806. This statement I sent to Robert Lincoln, Abe's son. I can not now recall the lady's maiden name. Abe Lincoln was born on a small tributary of Rolling Fork River, called Knob Creek, the same county, in 1809, three years after Thomas and Nancy were married.

John B. Henderson

Emancipation: Mr. Lincoln's Connection with the Bill to Compensate Loyal Slaveholders

Gen. John B. Henderson, who was Chairman of the last National Republican Convention, entered the United States Senate in January, 1862.[1] He came first by appointment of the Governor of Missouri to take the place of Trusten Polk, who had resigned to join the Confederate service.[2] At the next session of the Legislature he was fully elected to fill out the unexpired term and was then re-elected for a full term, sitting until March, 1869.

Gen. Henderson was then but a few months past 35, and very youthful for a Senator, but he sprang at once into prominence. Before he had been a Senator three months his standing at the White House was generally known. Mr. Lincoln had a border State policy, and he settled upon the young and energetic Missourian as the one to represent it.

There was a great pressure being brought to bear upon the President by the anti-slavery people. One day a hundred clergymen came down in a body from New England to urge emancipation. Some of the leaders of the Republican party, notably Mr. Sumner, Ben Wade and Zach Chandler, made almost daily visits to the White House to tell the President what he ought to do.[3]

Mr. Lincoln hesitated, not because he hadn't made up his mind, but because he wanted to protect the loyal slaveholders of the border States as far as he could. His idea was that a plan to pay for these slaves could be put in operation, and then he would by proclamation strike off the shackles of all whose owners were engaged in rebellion. While he was trying to get this programme going he sent often for Gen. Henderson to come to the White House to discuss the details, and to urge more rapid action. It was on the occasion of one of these talks that Mr. Lincoln told the story which Gen. Henderson called to mind a few evenings since.

"As I went in," said the General, "I noticed that the President was looking troubled. He was sitting in one of his favorite attitudes—in a rocking chair, with one leg thrown over the arm. I knew that he suffered terribly from headaches, and I said to him:

"'Mr. President, you must have one of your headaches; you look gloomy.'

"'No,' said he, 'it isn't headache this time. Chandler has just been here to talk again about emancipation; and he came on the heels of Wade and Sumner, who were here on the same errand. I like those three men, but they bother me nearly to death. They put me in the situation of a boy I remember when I was going to school.'"

Gen. Henderson says the President's face brightened, and he knew a story was coming. Mr. Lincoln leaned forward and clasped his hands around the knee of leg resting on the arm of the chair. Then he proceeded with the story:

"'The text-book was the Old Bible,' Mr. Lincoln went on. 'There was a rather dull little fellow in the class who didn't know very much, and we were reading the account of the three Hebrews cast into the fiery furnace. The little fellow was called on to read, and he stumbled along until he came to the names of the three Hebrews—Shadrach, Meshach and Abednego. He couldn't do anything with them. The teacher pronounced them over slowly and told the boy to try. The boy tried and missed. This provoked the teacher, and he slapped the little fellow, who cried vigorously. Then he attempted again, but he couldn't get the names. 'Well,' said the teacher impatiently, 'never mind the names. Skip them and go on.' The poor boy drew his shirt sleeve across his eyes two or three times, snuffed his nose and started on to read. He went on bravely a little way and then he suddenly stopped, dropped the book in front of him, looked in despair at the teacher, and burst out crying. 'What's the matter now?' shouted the teacher, thoroughly out of patience. 'He——he——here's them same————three fellers agin,' sobbed the boy.[4]

"'That,' said Mr. Lincoln, 'is just my fix to-day, Henderson. Those same ————three fellows have been here again with their everlasting emancipation talk.'

"He stopped a few moments to enjoy the story, and then becoming serious, continued:

"'But Sumner and Wade and Chandler are right about it. I know it, and you know it too. I've got to do something, and it can't be put off much longer. We can't get through this terrible war with slavery existing. You've got sense enough to know that. Why can't you make the border State members see it? Why don't you turn in and take pay for your slaves from the Government? Then all your people can give their hearty support to the Union. We can go ahead with emancipation of slaves in the other States by proclamation and end the trouble.'"

Gen. Henderson says that as early as May, in 1862, Mr. Lincoln told him of his intention to issue the emancipation proclamation. The action was not taken until six months later, and then the proclamation was made to take effect January, 1863. The President held out as long as he could in the hope that he might be able to carry out his border States policy.

The introduction of the bill to pay for the slaves of loyal owners in Missouri was the result of Mr. Lincoln's earnest support of this plan. This was the first of the bills. It was followed by others for Kentucky, Maryland and other border States which had slaveholders.

"I do not remember," the General says, "whether Mr. Lincoln drafted the bill or whether I got it up, but the inspiration came from him. I did all in my power to press it. The proposition went through both House and Senate. But it was passed in somewhat different forms. The Senate increased the amount, and this difference had to be adjusted in conference. There was a good majority for the Missouri bill in both branches of Congress, and there was not much trouble about compromising the difference of opinion on the amount to be appropriated, but the session was almost at an end, and a small minority in the House was able by filibustering and obstructing to prevent the final action there. If the bill could have been got before the House in its finished form it would have passed as easily as it did in the Senate."

President Lincoln watched the progress of the legislation with a great deal of interest and did all he could to further it. He could not understand why the border State members should not be for it.

"And I could not either," says the General; "it was perfectly plain to me that slavery had got to go. Here was a voluntary offer on the part of the Government to compensate the loyal men in the border States for the loss of their property. I talked with the members from Missouri and from Kentucky and with the others who were most interested, but I couldn't make them see it as I did. They had exaggerated ideas of the results which would ensue from a free negro population. They took the position that slavery must not be touched, and it was their determined opposition to the end that defeated the bill to give the Missouri slaveholders $20,000,000 for their slaves. If the Missouri bill had gone through the others would have followed undoubtedly and the loyal slaveholders in all of the border States would have received pay for their slaves."

Gen. Henderson was asked if he remembered what the compensation would have amounted to in the case of the Missouri slaveholders.

"Yes," he replied, "I recollect quite distinctly the calculation I made at the time. I found that the amount which the Government would have turned over to Missouri under the terms of the bill finally agreed upon would have paid the loyal owners in my State $300 for each slave—man, woman or child. That I considered a pretty good price, for, while we were legislating, the emancipation proclamation had gone into effect, and it was very evident to my mind that slavery was doomed, even among those slaveholders who had remained loyal."

J. F. Humphreys

J. F. Humphreys of Riverside, Cal., heard the "lost speech."[1] He has written to Mr. Van Cleve of the Lincoln Centennial Association at Springfield:

I lived in Bloomington during the 50s and often met Mr. Lincoln when he "rode the circuit," attending the courts in Judge David Davis' judicial district. Many times have I listened to his keen arguments in cases which he was trying in our old Courthouse at Bloomington. It was also my privilege to listen to the great speech he made in Major's Hall in Bloomington when the convention was held to form the Republican party. This is called the "lost speech," there being no record of it made at the time, and it seems strange that no one who heard it has been able to remember but very little of it. It was so grand, surprising, sublime and inspiring that the audience was held spell-bound as though electrified. Could that speech be reproduced to-day, I have no doubt it would go into history as an equal to his famous Gettysburg oration.

"As I now recall the number of times it was my privilege to see and hear this man so truly great, I am deeply thankful," continues Mr. Humphreys. "I see Mr. Lincoln and Mr. David Davis, as it were but a day ago, passing my home on the way to Judge Davis' home for dinner, where Mr. Lincoln was often an invited guest. Lincoln, tall, gaunt, bowed shoulders, wearing seedy, old-style clothes, while the description of Judge Davis was in most respects directly the opposite."

Lincoln told his stories in such a manner that they made a different impression from the stories told by others, just as his speeches left a feeling of conviction that did not follow other speakers.

"For some part of the period mentioned, from 1850 to 1860," Mr. Humphreys writes, "I boarded at the old Eagle Hotel, in Bloomington, which Lincoln and his brother attorneys made their stopping place while attending court. They usually spent their evenings telling stories, Mr. Lincoln always being in the lead. As a boy I remembered many of these stories better than his great speeches. The wit was so keen and plain and the expression so clear that his stories assumed the realism of a picture at once comprehensive to the minds of his hearers."

Looking backward, this generation can not realize how much wider was the acquaintance and how much greater was the popularity of Stephen A. Douglas than of Lincoln before their debates in 1858.

"When Douglas returned to Illinois after his famous defense of his Nebraska bill," says Mr. Humphreys, "he stopped at Bloomington on his way to Springfield and made a speech. He defended his bill. Lincoln happened to be in Bloomington at the time, and on the day following he went on the same train with Douglas to Springfield. I was on the train, and shall never forget how the crowd at every station en route called for Douglas, while Lincoln sat in his seat unobserved and as demure as any private citizen. This, of course, was before the famous debates of Lincoln and Douglas, which brought the greatness of Lincoln not only before the people of the state, but of the nation."

Mr. Humphreys has a vivid recollection of the "Wideawakes" of 1860.

"My last meeting with Lincoln," he recalls, "was at a grand rally in Springfield, just before the election. The Wideawakes from all over the state turned out with their torches, making an immense procession. After the marching was over as many of us as could do so called upon Mr. Lincoln to give him a farewell handshake. He endured this ordeal as long as his arm could stand it, and then he called Mrs. Lincoln to take his place, which she did until she gave out."

James T. Jones

Lincoln's manner of telling stories is recalled by James T. Jones, who was a boy when the lawyers "rode the circuit" and stopped at his father's house in Pekin and in Tremont, Tazewell County.[1]

"The stories must have been amusing to Mr. Lincoln himself," Mr. Jones argued, "for he would begin laughing before he had said a word and continue laughing until the story ended, when everybody would be laughing, Mr. Lincoln as heartily as the rest. Mr. Lincoln repeated his stories to some who had heard them before. He seemed to be well aware of it. On one occasion at our house, he began by saying that the story he was about to tell he had already told to some who were present and they need not listen. I think, however, they all listened. The late Judge Samuel H. Treat, who was on the circuit bench, told me that he asked Lincoln if he had read Joe Miller's joke book. Lincoln replied that he had not. The judge loaned the book to Mr. Lincoln; he afterwards charged Lincoln with drawing on Joe Miller for some of his anecdotes. Mr. Lincoln's only answer was that he had the right to use a good story wherever he found it."

The "Economy of Space Man"

There are stories that Lincoln told about other people, from a fund inexhaustible; there are stories told about Lincoln, created by his word or deed, almost innumerable.[2] The story of "the economy of the space man," told in Pekin to this day, had its origin, according to James T. Jones, with Lincoln in this way:

"There was an eccentric man named John Wightman in Pekin. He had a peculiar habit in entering a door. He would open the door no wider than sufficient to admit his body, as if he was trying to keep some one else from coming in at the same time. Mr. Lincoln saw Wightman go through this act of squeezing through the door, opening only enough to get through. He remarked that Wightman's performance was an example of 'the economy of space.' Mr. Wightman was referred to afterward by his fellow-citizens of Pekin, in the language of Mr. Lincoln, as 'the economy of space man.'"

Mr. Jones tells of an instance illustrating Lincoln's ability for turning everything to account in his court practice.

"I remember Mr. Lincoln being alone in a case before the Pekin court in which there were two lawyers on the other side. Lincoln remarked to the jury that his client's adversary was able to employ two lawyers. He laughingly said he was afraid the interest of his client would suffer, as the two heads of the lawyers on the other side ought to be stronger than his head alone."

"As an example of the kindness of Lincoln's heart," said Mr. Jones, "I remember that I saw Mr. Lincoln, unsolicited, take on his knee my barefooted brother, not over 5 years old, and with a pen-knife open a painful bruise on the little boy's foot."

Lyman Lacey

The world has read "Lincoln stories" and enjoyed them.[1] The testimony of all who heard Lincoln tell his stories is that they sounded even better than they read. Lincoln, those who knew him well say, smiled and chuckled and laughed outright as he proceeded with his narrative. Sometimes he stopped and laughed aloud before he reached his climax. He gave localities and persons to his stories. He lived over the incidents he described, if they were personal reminiscences. He was not the professional entertainer. He enjoyed the story as much as the listener. He told the story to illustrate rather than for the mere sport of telling.

"Lincoln was a great joker and was always telling funny stories, making them apply to something that was said or done in his presence," is the way Lyman Lacey, Sr., of Havana puts it.[2] Mr. Lacey began to practice law in Havana in 1857. He was in partnership with William Walker, then the foremost lawyer of this country.[3] He met Lincoln at court in the litigation of that period.

"Lincoln was always being 'reminded of something,' as he would say, that had been said or done by some one. And he would name the person. Even when he lived in Menard County, as it is known now, he had his own peculiar way of telling his stories. When he came to the point where the merriment should come in Lincoln would laugh very heartily and then finish the story. The auditors would then laugh. By this habit he informed them where the laugh came in, if there was any doubt about it. Everyone liked 'Old Abe,' as they called him."

The Straight of the Bar Story

While there were only seven joint debates [in 1858] of formal character under the challenge, there were other occasions when Douglas and Lincoln filled appointments so close together as to afford the excitement of personal passages.[4] Lincoln was anxious to get before the Democratic supporters of Douglas. He did not shun, but rather sought opportunities to follow Douglas as closely as he could. At Havana Douglas and Lincoln spoke the same day, in 1858. This was not one of the joint debates, but Lincoln in the afternoon answered what Douglas had said in the forenoon. Lyman Lacey, Sr., describes the two meetings. Lincoln avoided being present at the meetings of Douglas. He arrived in Havana just before his afternoon appointment, but there were friends who outlined to him the speech of Douglas in the forenoon.

"Douglas," said Mr. Lacey, "tried to kill Lincoln with faint praise. Referring to his opponent at the morning meeting, Douglas said: 'Mr. Lincoln is a very nice man, very sociable and entertaining. He makes a very pleasant companion. I used to know him when he lived at Old Salem in Menard County, when he kept store and sold whisky to his customers.' Douglas never referred to Lincoln as a great lawyer or a man of ability. At the afternoon meeting Lincoln spoke of Mr. Douglas personally and said he had been informed of the tribute of praise Mr. Douglas had bestowed upon him. 'Mr. Douglas,' he said, 'has seen fit to give me praise in his speech, for which I am thankful. I am like the Hoosier with the gingerbread, who said he liked it better than any other man did, but got less of it. As to what Mr. Douglas said about his acquaintance with me in Old Salem, that I kept store, attended bar and sold whisky, all I have to say is that while I practiced at the bar on the inside, Judge Douglas practiced on the outside of the bar.' This created great applause from Mr. Lincoln's audience. I have always remembered this debate. A few days ago I had a conversation with Kay Watkins of Menard County, who knew Lincoln in those days, and was at the speeches I have referred to; he remembered it as I have stated."[5]

Edward F. Leonard

The journey to Washington in 1861 was made by Mr. Lincoln in very different style from that in which a president elect is conveyed in these days to his inauguration.[1] E. F. Leonard, who now lives in Amherst, Mass., was on the train which took the Lincoln party from Springfield on the 11th of February.[2]

"Early in January," Mr. Leonard said, "W. S. Wood of New York came to Springfield bearing a letter of introduction to Mr. Lincoln from Mr. Seward.[3] Mr. Seward stated that Mr. Wood had had great experience in railroad transportation, and especially in organizing excursion trips over long distances. Mr. Wood, Mr. Seward said, was well acquainted with railroad officials. He suggested that the matter of arranging and conducting the trip to Washington be placed in Mr. Wood's hands. This suggestion was accepted by Mr. Lincoln, and Mr. Wood took charge of the whole matter of transportation. I refer to this in detail because it is a matter of interest showing the great changes which have taken place in railroad business and facilities. In 1861 the shortest and most direct route from Springfield to Cincinnati was by Lafayette, Ind., involving the use of four distinct railroads, each of which had to be consulted in making the schedule for the journey; and so on through Ohio and Pennsylvania. Mr. Wood also arranged the hotel accommodations for the party, which traveled only by day. In the details of the work Mr. Wood was greatly assisted by Col. Francis W. Bowen, general superintendent of the Great Western Railroad of Illinois, a line from Naples, on the Illinois River, to the border of Indiana, now a part of the Wabash system.[4]

"Mr. Lincoln," Mr. Leonard explained, "had the rear car. The special train leaving Springfield consisted of three ordinary day coaches and the baggage car, all heated by coal stoves. No person went into the rear car except on Mr. Lincoln's summons. The entire morning [of February 11] Mr. Lincoln was busy writing. It was understood that he was preparing for a speech in Indianapolis that evening. He wrote with a pencil on a large pad, and as he turned off the sheets his secretaries took them and made copies of them. There was a change of cars at State Line and again at Lafayette Junction, where dinner was ready in the eating house on the arrival of the train. A considerable number of prominent people of Indiana joined the party for Indianapolis, and Mr. Lincoln spent the afternoon more sociably than he had the morning. Late in the afternoon, on reaching Indianapolis, the whole party went to the Bates House, then the largest hotel in the city. From the balcony Mr. Lincoln addressed a large number of people who had come to see and to hear him.[5] Early in the forenoon next day the special train was made up for Cincinnati. Mrs. Lincoln came from St. Louis on a night train and joined the party at the Indianapolis depot. On her arrival the train started. The Springfield party started back by way of Lafayette, arriving home that evening."

Thomas J. Lincoln

Cousins of Abraham Lincoln, in many degrees, lived in and around the quaintest of Illinois towns, Fountain Green.[1] The first of these Hancock County Lincolns settled in Illinois about the time "Cousin Abe" was splitting rails and making a log cabin home for his stepmother on ten acres of the Hanks farm in Sangamon County. There are more relatives of the martyred president in Hancock County than anywhere else. These cousins have the Lincoln forehead, the Lincoln high cheek bones, the Lincoln nose. Among the men is found, here and there, a resemblance to the Abraham Lincoln of history, so striking as to startle. These Lincolns of Hancock County are self-reliant, self-contained people. They have not exploited their relationship to the former president of the United States. But they have preserved the family traditions as handed down through the generations and they give in their quiet, unostentatious way much information about the Lincoln family which the biographers and historians of President Lincoln have missed. This does not seem quite so strange when it is discovered that Fountain Green is at the end of a long drive from the nearest railroad point. Seventy-five years ago Fountain Green was laid out. From Kentucky migrated the Duffs and Goughs, and John Day and James Broomfield [Bradford] Lincoln with their families making a frontier community of enduring character.[2] A year or two later Jabez A. Beebe and Stephen G. Ferris settled in the neighborhood. The pioneers felt strong enough to start a town. They came together and created Fountain Green. There were springs of clear, cold water, bursting from the limestone. There was a charming natural lawn of closely rooted, short grass on the edge of a prairie where the tall, coarse grass grew as high as the backs of the horses. Hence came the selection of Fountain Green, with only one other town of that name in the United States in the 30s, and that in Maryland. From back home the kinsfolk addressed their letters to these pioneer founders of Fountain Green in "Illinois, Hancock County, at the Head of the Rapids."

Fountain Green was laid out around a park. Two blocks in the center of the townsite were set apart for the "green." If there is another park in the state three-quarters of a century old, history fails to record the fact. Government was established at Fountain Green. The first "squire" was this James B. Lincoln. Through four generations of Fountain Green people have come the recollections of the wise and efficient manner in which Squire Lincoln administered law and order on the frontier. So long as he lived this first cousin of Abraham Lincoln held the office of chief responsibility in Fountain Green and the adjacent country. At that time young Abraham Lincoln was tending store for [William] Berry at New Salem, three counties away, and was borrowing law books to read when trade was slow.

The Lincolns were of good stock. They were not rich, but they held property. They were educated. They corresponded. They kept books. And

Abraham Lincoln, the president, was a Lincoln. As he became famous he was called upon for biographical data, but could tell little respecting his family. The Lincolns of Fountain Green have preserved the family history in more detail. The first Abraham Lincoln, of English Quaker descent, lived in Pennsylvania at the time of the revolution.[3] It is tradition that he fought in the patriot army. Going by way of Virginia, Abraham Lincoln reached Kentucky and took a piece of land to clear as a farm near the Hay-craft fort in what is now Hardin County.[4] He had two sons, Mordecai and Thomas Lincoln, the former several years the oldest. When Abraham Lincoln went out from the protection of the fort to work on his farm he took the boys with him and put them in a tree to watch for Indians. About 1784 [1786] Abraham Lincoln was shot and killed while at work on his flax crop. Mordecai and Thomas heard the gun and saw their father fall. They had failed to detect the Indian in ambush and to give the alarm. The brothers grew to manhood, married, and settled in the adjoining counties of Grayson and Hardin, Ky. Mordecai Lincoln was the father of the Lincolns of Fountain Green in Illinois. Thomas Lincoln was the father of President Lincoln. Each of these brothers named a son Abraham after their father. Not many months ago an Abraham Lincoln story went the rounds of the newspapers, it being assumed that the incident had occurred in the life of the late President Lincoln. The truth was the Abraham Lincoln of that particular story was the Abraham Lincoln of Hancock County, the cousin of President Lincoln. And the Fountain Green Lincolns are still smiling over the mistake. Each of these Abraham Lincolns named a son Robert Lincoln. The son of President Lincoln is the head of the Pullman Company. The [other] Robert Lincoln, son of the other Abraham Lincoln, died some years ago [1868] at Carthage in Hancock County.

Strong physical resemblance is not all that goes with the kinship between President Lincoln and the Fountain Green cousins. The knack of handling tools and making things was a Lincoln inheritance. Thomas Lincoln, the father of President Lincoln, was known as one of the best carpenters of the locality where he lived. Abraham Lincoln, as a youth, not only built a house and flatboats, but he did cabinet work. He made furniture. There are in existence several articles, the handiwork of Abraham Lincoln, showing an aptitude toward mechanical work quite unusual. One of these was a small bureau or cabinet made of black walnut, put together without a single nail. It is said to have been made by Lincoln when he was a boy, the tree being cut and the boards sawed and planed by him. After he became a lawyer at Springfield, Mr. Lincoln had furniture made under his specific directions. He knew just what he wanted.

The same natural skill with tools was possessed by the Lincolns of Fountain Green. These cousins of Abraham Lincoln have been noted for dexterity in woodworking. They had farms, but they built houses, made furniture, repaired vehicles, turned out farming implements and used the lathe.

"They could make anything," say the old settlers.

The mechanical turn had its bearing of considerable influence upon the families of Mordecai and Thomas Lincoln before they left Kentucky. Hardin County is down the Ohio, the third county south of Louisville. Grayson is beyond, to the southward. The "obscurity" of Abraham Lincoln's birth, as the early biographers have it, disappears in the light on the family history preserved by the Lincolns of Fountain Green. "The humble origin" takes on different meaning from that to be inferred from some of the books written about the president. The Lincolns acquired farms, but they did not follow farming exclusively. Mordecai Lincoln brought up his sons and daughters in or near Leitchfield, the county seat of Grayson.[5] He was a man of some means and he gave his children what a century ago in Kentucky was much better than the average education. Mordecai Lincoln's family grew to maturity in Grayson County. Thomas Lincoln did not settle in life so early as did Mordecai. He remained in Hardin County following the trade of carpenter. For some years he was in and out of Elizabethtown, the county seat of Hardin, about thirty miles from his brother Mordecai's home. A single man until he was 28, Thomas Lincoln didn't develop a saving disposition. Those who were more thrifty called Thomas "shiftless." Going where the carpenter work took him, Thomas Lincoln acquired the "rolling stone" habit. It is tradition that he was not as well educated as the other Lincolns. But he wasn't worthless. He was industrious. If he spent his money as fast as he made it he did no differently from many Americans. When he courted Nancy Hanks, who was the daughter [niece] of his employer [Joseph Hanks], Thomas Lincoln, although verging upon 30, began to feel the propriety of looking to the future. Some of the writers upon Abraham Lincoln have treated this as a "lowly" marriage. Nancy Hanks had been to school in Virginia. She was considered better educated than most of the girls of that part of Hardin. The family tradition is that she was tall, dark haired, and attractive. Thomas Lincoln could hardly have been what some biographers have described him for Nancy Hanks, fully matured, 23 years old, strong of mind and dignified, accepted him, bore him children and lived with him as long as she was on earth.

Thomas Lincoln continued to make his home in Elizabethtown, the county seat, for a year or two after the marriage in 1806. Then, with a view of improving the family circumstances, encouraged by the ambition of his wife, he moved fifteen miles south into what is Larue County and took a piece of land, 160 acres, about three miles from Hodgensville. He built a house 50 yards from a fine spring, which welled up under an overhanging ledge of rock. There Abraham Lincoln was born February 12, 1809. He was given the name of the grandfather who had been killed by the Indians. About the same time, or a little earlier, a son was born to Mordecai Lincoln, near Leitchfield, about thirty-five miles distant and he, too, was given the name of his grandfather Abraham.[6]

Many of the Kentucky neighbors of Mordecai and Thomas Lincoln had a curious pronunciation of the family name. They called it as if spelled "Lincorn." And after the migration to Illinois the Fountain Green Lincolns say they were so addressed frequently by the Hancock County pioneers.

If there was such dire poverty in the Thomas Lincoln family as several of the biographers of the president have told, the Mordecai Lincoln family has not preserved any tradition of it.[7] The Lincolns lived in a log house. So did most of the Kentuckians of Hardin and Larue and Grayson and other counties a century ago. More than half of the homes of St. Louis were built of logs in that period. The probability is, the Lincolns of Fountain Green believe, that Thomas Lincoln, by reason of his skill as a carpenter, had a better built and better furnished cabin home than the neighbors. They do not take seriously the "shack" shown of late years as the one in which President Lincoln was born. The Lincolns attended religious services in the Little Mound [Mount] Church at Hodgensville, three miles from their home. Little "Abe" was taught to read by his mother. He was the brightest 5-year-old in the neighborhood. The first day he went to Knob Creek School he spelled his way to the head of the class.

The wanderlust came back to Thomas Lincoln. The family made two or three moves while the father of it resumed his trade as a carpenter and cabinet maker. A year or two was passed in Elizabethtown, the Lincolns occupying a house on the bank of Valley Creek, perhaps 150 yards from the Courthouse square. That temporary home of the Lincolns stood a short distance from the present railroad depot.

Residence in Elizabethtown gave the boy his first taste of town life. Ben Helm kept the principal store, "a general store," it was called in those days.[8] When he was 6 or 7 years old, "Abe" Lincoln was taken to this store. He never forgot the impression it made upon him. Along one side of the long storeroom ran the counter with goods piled on the shelves behind.

Along the opposite wall was a row of kegs, holding nails of different sizes. Above the nail kegs were shelves on which was displayed the stock of dishes and earthenware. Mrs. Lincoln put "Abe" on one of the kegs and told him to sit there until she made her purchases. The chief clerk of the store was John B. Helm, the nephew of the proprietor.[9] He broke off a piece of maple sugar, and with a smile gave it to "Abe." Thirty-five years afterwards, John B. Helm was living in Hannibal, Mo. He was known as Judge Helm. Abraham Lincoln was passing through from Springfield. The time was before the presidential election of 1840. Mr. Lincoln called upon Judge Helm. He introduced himself and then presented two or three friends who were with him.

"Gentlemen," said Mr. Lincoln, in the mixture of humor and pathos which was characteristic of him, "this is the first man I ever saw who wore store clothes Sunday and every day, too." And then he described his boyhood visit to the Helm store in Elizabethtown, his seat on the nail keg, the good clothes which the clerk wore, and the present of the piece of sugar by John B. Helm.

"I have never forgotten him for that little kindness to me," said Mr. Lincoln as he concluded his true story.[10]

The Lincolns and the Helms were pioneers together in the same locality of Kentucky. Thomas Helm built a fort for protection against the Indians near where the first Abraham Lincoln was killed by an Indian.[11] He had two sons. One of them, Ben, at whose store "Little Abe" Lincoln had his interesting experience, walked barefooted from Louisville, forty-five miles, while snow was on the ground, carrying a bag of meal for the family, when he was 16 years old. A descendant of Thomas Helm was twice elected governor of Kentucky.[12] Years afterwards Abraham Lincoln and Ben Hardin Helm married sisters.[13] Ben Hardin Helm went into the Confederate Army, became a general and fell in battle. His widow, the sister of Mrs. Abraham Lincoln, was given the Post Office at Elizabethtown. The "obscurity" of the Kentucky Lincolns seems to be an historical myth.

One more incident strangely links the histories of the Lincoln and Helm families. When Abraham Lincoln was 8 years old, and while the family home was still in Elizabethtown, Thomas Lincoln caught the Western "free state" fever. The time was 1817 [1816]. Leaving the family, he crossed the Ohio River into Indiana and sought a location. All through that part of Kentucky the talk was of moving west. A migration which was to obtain great proportion had begun. Thomas Lincoln did not go so far as many other Kentuckians. He sold his Larue County place and selected a new quarter section in what is now Spencer County, Indiana. A station called

Lincoln on the railroad between St. Louis and Louisville indicates the near-by location of the farm which Thomas Lincoln opened and upon which Abraham Lincoln grew to young manhood.

Thomas Lincoln was the first of the Lincolns to leave Kentucky. Mordecai Lincoln's sons did not begin to move to the "free states" until about ten years later. The house which Thomas Lincoln built upon his Indiana farm was of logs, but larger and better finished than the average farmhouse of that day. Abraham Lincoln remembered and told long afterwards that there were neighbors poorer than the Lincolns. In the autumn after the first winter in Indiana, Thomas Lincoln lost his wife. Nancy Hanks Lincoln died on the 5th of October, 1818. Abraham Lincoln was 9 years old. He wrote a letter to a minister the family had known in Kentucky asking him to come and preach the funeral sermon. The minister complied, but he did not get there until after the father had made the coffin and the burial had taken place. He preached the funeral sermon.[14]

"All that I am and all that I hope to be I owe to my angel mother," was the tribute Abraham Lincoln paid to her memory when he had grown up and had achieved some measure of success in life.[15]

About a year after his wife's death Thomas Lincoln made a visit to his relatives and friends in Kentucky. There lived in Elizabethtown a hard-working, good woman, Mrs. Sarah Bush Johns[t]on, who was known as "the widow Bush."[16] She had three children.[17] Thomas Lincoln called upon the widow, told her that his first wife was dead and that he had come to Kentucky to find some one who would be "a mother to Sarah and Abe." Mrs. Johns[t]on was at the wash tub when she received Thomas Lincoln's proposal. She told him she would think about it. He said that wouldn't do; he wanted to settle the matter and get back to his place. She said there was some business she must attend to, some bills she must settle. Thomas Lincoln said he would attend to all of that. The widow consented to the hasty courtship. Thomas Lincoln went about Elizabethtown that day and paid all that the widow owed. Ben Helm was county clerk as well as storekeeper. Thomas Lincoln went after the license. Friends facilitated matters. The marriage took place that evening and Thomas took the new family to the home on Pigeon Creek, in Indiana. And yet history describes Thomas Lincoln as "shiftless."

From Indiana and from Kentucky the movement of the Lincolns to Illinois was almost in the same year. Thomas Lincoln's family left Pigeon Creek for the new home in Sangamon County, just west of Decatur, Abraham Lincoln, who had come of age, driving the ox team. James Bloomfield

[Bradford] Lincoln, the son of Mordecai Lincoln, rode through from Leitchfield, Ky., to Hancock County, about the same time, 1829–30. One after another the members of Mordecai Lincoln's family followed James B. Lincoln until all of them were living in the vicinity of Fountain Green. Thomas Lincoln, the father of President Lincoln, died and was buried in Coles County. Mordecai Lincoln, the uncle of President Lincoln, died at Fountain Green and was buried in the old cemetery near the town.

Two miles out of Fountain Green, on the edge of the early settlement of Ramus, or Macedonia, as it was called in the days of the Mormons, but now known to rural free delivery as Webster, lives Thos. Lincoln, just past 86.[18] "Uncle Tommy" he is to the whole countryside.

"Maybe he'll talk to you; and then maybe he won't," said one of the Lincoln cousins in Fountain Green. "It all depends on how you find him. Sometimes he's just as sociable as can be. And then again, he walks about in the woods and you can't hardly get him to talk at all."

That sounded like the descriptions of Lincoln, the immortal, as he was in the days before the responsibility for the nation's life rested on his shoulders and monopolized his mental faculty. Sure enough, the Lincolns of Hancock County are known to their neighbors as men who at times communed with themselves, absorbed in their own thoughts.

With gentle dignity, wearing his four score and six years easily, Thomas Lincoln arose to shake hands with his visitor and then, without the slightest hesitation, entered upon a long and free conversation about the Lincolns.

"My father, James B. Lincoln, was the first of the family to come here," said Uncle Tommy. "That was before Fountain Green was named. I was very small. I should say it was just before 1830. Next came my grandfather, who was Mordecai Lincoln. He rode horseback all of the way from Kentucky, leaving my grandmother there to come out later with my uncle. I have heard grandfather tell many times the story of my great-grandfather, Abraham Lincoln, being shot by the Indians when they were out in the field, my grandfather and his brother Thomas up in the tree to give warning if they saw the Indians. Some time after grandfather came from Kentucky Uncle Abraham brought grandmother to Hancock County. Grandfather did not live many years after coming to Illinois. When he died there was no way to get a coffin. The neighbors cut down a linn tree, hewed out puncheons and made a coffin of them. Grandfather is buried just a little ways over yonder," and Uncle Tommy inclined his head toward the southeast.

"You knew Abraham Lincoln, who became the president?"

"Yes," replied the old man, in the same simple, unemotional manner that he had told of the burial arrangements of the grandfather. "I saw Abe several times. Once I went to Springfield and visited him. I was there a week."

"Was that the first time you had met him?"

"No; I was only a boy the first time, but I remember it very well. A man named Frame was on trial for murder. Abe Lincoln was defending him.[19] The trial had been moved from place to place and finally it came off at Carthage, in our county. I was about 13 years old. One of the Fountain Green men, Mr. Renshaw, took me down to Carthage and introduced me to Abe. That must have been in 1836 or 1838. Abe was very pleasant with me, and asked about the family. I didn't have much talk with him."

"You spoke of making a visit to Mr. Lincoln at Springfield?"

"Yes. That was in 1846. I stayed about a week. Abe beat any man for reading at that time I ever saw. If he wasn't talking he would have something in his hand, a book or a paper or an almanac. He was reading all of the time that he wasn't saying something. I went about with him. Whenever Abe had anything to say everybody else kept still."

"There seems to be quite a strong family resemblance in the Lincolns. Of all of the relatives, who looked most like the president, Mr. Lincoln?"

"I think Robert, my cousin, looked most like President Lincoln. There was a very strong likeness about the forehead, the nose and the figure generally."

"Robert Lincoln was the son of your father's brother, Abraham?"

"Yes. That is it. My father had two brothers, Abraham and Mordecai, the last named after my grandfather. Uncle Abe named a son Robert just as Cousin Abe named his son Robert. President Lincoln had a son, Thomas, you remember, who died, named after his father, Thomas Lincoln. In my family we have a Thomas Lincoln, named after President Lincoln's father. He has always gone by the name of 'Tad' Lincoln. You remember that President Lincoln called his son 'Tad.' Our Thomas Lincoln lives in Clinton, Mo."

The Hancock county cousins of Abraham Lincoln were not unanimous in the campaign of 1860. Two or three of them were Democrats. But Fountain Green was enthusiastic for "Cousin Abe." At Keokuk was held one of the greatest rallies of the Northwest.[20] Wideawakes marched in from many miles around. A portrait in oil of Abraham Lincoln, life size, was offered for the largest delegation of Wideawakes attending the rally. Fountain Green, although off the railroad, sent overland the delegation of Wideawakes which captured the prize. Conspicuous in the company was Thomas Lincoln, "Uncle Tommy," namesake of Abraham Lincoln's father, to-day the patriarch of the Hancock County Lincolns. The portrait was carried back to Fountain Green and placed in the care of the widow of James B. Lincoln, the first Lincoln of the neighborhood. It was held a treasured relic of Fountain Green until a few years ago. One day the portrait was taken out and, with Thomas Lincoln and his maiden sister, Emily Lincoln, standing beside it, was photographed.[21] A few years ago Thomas Lincoln took the interesting relic to Springfield and placed it in the Lincoln memorial collection.

To the inquiry if the portrait was a good one, as he remembered his cousin, Uncle Tommy replied: "It was as natural a picture as you ever saw."

The last time Thomas Lincoln saw his cousin was at the Lincoln-Douglas joint debate in Quincy.

"That was in 1858," Uncle Tommy said. "I went to Quincy early in the morning of the day of the speaking. As soon as I got in I began to look for Abe. I went to all of the taverns and public places, one after another, but couldn't find him. Nobody could tell me where he was. Along about noon I came across Douglas at the Quincy House. I was acquainted with him. As soon as I spoke to him he said, 'Abe is at [Orville] Browning's.' It was too late then to go up to Browning's house. I went to the speaking without having a chance to talk with Abe. As soon as the speaking was over I hurried down to the station to get the train home."

Abraham Lincoln reminded him, Uncle Tommy Lincoln said, of his father and uncles very much except in one respect.

"My father and my uncles, Mordecai and Abraham, were not talkers like Abe," he explained.

These Lincolns of Hancock County had the straightforward, sincere manner of President Lincoln. They were honest men in their dealings. They were independent. Thomas Lincoln says that not one of the cousins, so far as he can recollect, held an office by appointment of President Lincoln.

Mrs. James Judson Lord

Newcomers were not long resident of Springfield before they learned something of the position Mr. Lincoln occupied in the community.[1] James Judson Lord came to the state capital to live in 1852.[2] Mrs. Lord tells of her husband's earliest knowledge of Abraham Lincoln as a fellow citizen:

"Mr. Lord knew nothing of Mr. Lincoln until one day passing through the Statehouse grounds he observed a group watching a tall man swinging a scythe in a graceful and an efficient way, while one member of the group held his hat and coat. 'Who is that tall man mowing?' Mr. Lord asked. 'That is Abe Lincoln,' said the man, laughing, 'he is showing some of his fellow-townsmen the proper way to mow.'

"That was Mr. Lord's first glimpse of Mr. Lincoln, for whom in after years he came to have the highest regard and greatest friendship." Mrs. Lord continued. "Standing near Mr. Lincoln at the time of his nomination, Mr. Lord said to him, 'Mr. Lincoln, you will be our president.' Mr. Lincoln smiled a little and said, in his slow, impressive way, 'Well, things do seem to point that way.'"

The ethics of his profession, as Mr. Lincoln construed them, are illuminated by an incident which Mrs. Lord tells:

"Mr. Lord, going into Mr. Lincoln's office one day, saw Mr. Lincoln talking earnestly to a young man, who stood, hat in hand, looking down rather dejectedly. Mr. Lord heard Mr. Lincoln say: 'Yes, I can gain your case for you. I can take the money from the widow and her six children for you, but, young man, I would advise you to make that amount of money some other way.'"

Robert W. McClaughry

From boyhood to early manhood Robert W. McClaughry, warden of the Government Penitentiary at Leavenworth, knew, as near-by neighbors, the Lincolns of Hancock County.[1] Col. McClaughry was "born and raised" at Fountain Green. The first Lincolns settled there about 1830. Others, of the near relatives of President Abraham Lincoln, migrated from the old home in Kentucky to the vicinity of Fountain Green. Among them, Col. McClaughry mentions James, Abraham and Mordecai Lincoln, first cousins of the president, sons of his father's oldest brother.

"President Lincoln," Col. McClaughry said, "took great interest in these relatives, though he seldom visited them. I remember him coming to our place during my boyhood, when legal business had called him to the county seat. He then made a short visit to Mordecai Lincoln and some of the other cousins. It must have been in the year 1852 that my father took me with him to hear Mr. Lincoln make a speech for the Whig ticket upon which Gen. Scott was a candidate for president. At that time I shook hands with the future President Lincoln, and I remember hearing him inquire of my father concerning his cousin Mordecai. Six years later, in 1858, when Mr. Lincoln spoke in Monmouth [on October 11], he sent for me to come to the hotel where he stopped and made inquiries concerning his Hancock County relatives, again manifesting his interest in his cousin Mordecai, to whom he seemed quite attached."

There was a good deal of the Lincoln originality, sense of justice and sturdy integrity in the Hancock County branch of the family as Col. McClaughry describes the relatives.

"James B. Lincoln," he said, "was a justice of the peace in Fountain Green from 1832 to 1836. It is one of the traditions of that neighborhood that he never had a lawsuit come to trial before him. In every case where complaint was made by one neighbor against another, he sent for both parties, and heard their statements, made his own investigations, and decided what ought to be done by each, without entering the case on his docket. It was further the tradition that no man who failed to comply with James Lincoln's decision could continue to live in that community."

Even differences between husband and wife were not beyond the jurisdiction and adjudication of this pioneer justice.

"In a certain case," Col. McClaughry recalled, "where Justice James Lincoln had married a couple, he learned that the husband and wife were living unhappily. He went to see them, heard their statements and concluded that they were about equally to blame. He settled the case by threatening to 'unmarry' them if there was any more trouble. The tradition of Fountain Green has it that the couple, as the novels say, 'lived happily ever afterward.'"

James Lincoln died early, but the other two first cousins of President Lincoln lived in Hancock County for many years.

"Abraham Lincoln, the brother of James," said Col. McClaughry, "was also a justice of the peace for several years. He was noted for his great knowledge of human nature and his sound common sense, through which he served the community better than he could have done by any technical acquaintance with the statutes. Mordecai Lincoln, the third cousin, was a cabinet maker, a very intelligent, well-read man. He was something of a misanthrope, because of a disappointment in a love affair of his early years, which he always charged to the Jesuit fathers who taught the school in Kentucky which he attended. While Mordecai and the other Hancock County Lincolns were faithful Catholics Mordecai was always bitter against the order of Jesuits, and did not hesitate to denounce them on all occasions. I remember making frequent visits to his shop with neighbor boys and hearing him talk about the Jesuits."

Most Pathetic Sight at Lincoln's Funeral

"The most pathetic sight" at the obsequies of Abraham Lincoln is described in graphic language by Col. Robert W. McClaughry, the superintendent of the United States Penitentiary at Leavenworth.[2] Col. McClaughry was on military duty at Springfield when the body of the martyred president was brought there for burial. He was one of the officers of the immense procession which escorted the body from the State House to the cemetery.

"The most pathetic sight to me," Col. McClaughry said recently, "was the intense grief manifested by the colored people, thousands of whom had journeyed for days in order to be in Springfield at the funeral. In addition to their section in the procession they were assigned a place extending from the city limits toward the cemetery, and there thousands of them massed. Every one of them, it seemed, had possessed himself or herself of some badge or token which would indicate their grief. Sometimes it was a simple piece of black cloth or crepe not larger than a man's hand. Others had secured black handkerchiefs. All who could afford it had clothed themselves entirely in black, and, as the bier passed, almost every one of them knelt or prostrated himself or herself upon the ground and gave way to touching demonstrations of grief. They well knew that their greatest friend was passing to his rest and the future seemed dark to their vision."[3]

Thompson Ware McNeely

Message Denton Offut Sent to Lincoln

The traditions of New Salem, the vanished town of great expectations, are well preserved at Petersburg.[1] A well-known resident of Petersburg is Judge T. W. McNeely.[2] While teaching school near Woodville, Miss., in 1857, Judge McNeely met and talked with Denton Offut [Offutt] about Abraham Lincoln. Offut was the queer genius who gave Mr. Lincoln his start in the world. He told Judge McNeely the story of his first acquaintance and his growing confidence in the young man. Offut was the man of affairs at

New Salem. He had established a store and a mill on the Sangamon. He was enterprising, but not stable. Lincoln had just passed 22 when, in March, 1831, Offut sent for him and employed him to go with a flatboat loaded with pork and corn and other products of the Sangamon farms to New Orleans. It was on this trip, while in New Orleans, that Lincoln is said to have made the often-quoted remark about slavery—that if ever he got a chance he would hit that institution and hit it hard.[3] Coming back up the river by slow stages, Lincoln reached New Salem and was put in charge of the store by Offut. The merchant had concluded to make a change. While he looked about he employed Lincoln to sell the stock of goods. Offut disappeared from New Salem [in 1832]. He had been lost to the New Salem folks, who had become Petersburg folks, a quarter of a century when Judge McNeely, by chance, met him in Mississippi. Offut was then in the business of traveling through the Southern States, taming horses. Judge McNeely recognized the name and made himself known to the horse tamer.

"When I told Offut," said Judge McNeely, a few days ago, "that I resided at Petersburg, Ill., on the very edge of New Salem, and had frequently seen Mr. Lincoln, he lost his interest in his crowd and the horses. We had a long talk about Mr. Lincoln and the old settlers, but Mr. Lincoln was the center of Offut's thought and conversation. Offut had not seen any one who knew Mr. Lincoln for about twenty-four years. He had heard something of Mr. Lincoln in politics during the Fremont campaign of the preceding year. He said that after leaving Lincoln at New Salem he had gone South and taken up the business of treating wild and fractious horses and had followed it. The crowd with horses to be tamed became impatient and broke in on the conversation with calls for Offut. As we separated I told him I was going back to Illinois in May. Offut's parting request was: 'Go and see Mr. Lincoln and tell him about me and give him my best wishes. Tell him for me to quit his damned politics and go into some honest business like taming horses.'"

Judge McNeely delivered the message, and the manner in which it was received is an interesting illustration of Mr. Lincoln's character. Much sympathy has been invoked by writers for Mr. Lincoln because of the hardships of the early part of his career. There is nothing to show that Mr. Lincoln pitied himself for what he went through, or that he considered himself in any sense an object for sympathetic regard from others. Judge McNeely's recollection coincides with that of others, that Mr. Lincoln rather enjoyed recalling his New Salem days and was wholly forgetful of those terrible fits of depression and gloom which some of his biographers have emphasized as clouding the life of his early manhood.[4]

"In August following," Judge McNeely said, "while I was in Springfield to obtain license to practice law, I told of this meeting with Denton Offut. William Turney, clerk of the Supreme Court, suggested that we go to see Mr. Lincoln at his law office. It will be remembered that this was not only before Mr. Lincoln's candidacy for president, but was in the year before his joint debate with Douglas. We found Mr. Lincoln in. I told of meeting Offut, but did not give the message. It seemed to give Lincoln great pleasure to hear of Offut. It revived memories of his life at New Salem, where although only 22 years old, he was trusted by Offut with the management of the store and mill. It reminded him of the time when he saw his first English grammar and entered upon what might be called the higher educational field for him. It carried him back to the times when he was postmaster, deputy surveyor of Sangamon County, captain of a company in the Blackhawk war, candidate for the Legislature and member of that body. Mr. Lincoln talked freely of those days. Being young and meeting Mr. Lincoln for the first time, I hesitated to deliver the latter part of Denton Offut's message until Mr. Turney, who was well acquainted with Mr. Lincoln, said, 'Give him all of Offut's message.' Then I repeated Offut's advice to quit his darned politics and go into some honest business like taming horses. Mr. Lincoln laughed heartily. He laid aside the book which he had been reading when we went in, and which he had continued to hold in his hand, got up from his chair, walked across the room and said, 'That sounds like Offut.' He wanted to know if I could tell him where Offut lived or what had become of him. I had not asked Offut as to his home, and could not tell Mr. Lincoln where he could reach his old employer. On subsequent occasions when I met Mr. Lincoln he referred to what I had told him of my meeting with Offut in Mississippi, and of the message Offut had sent to him, seeming to find keen enjoyment in the recollection."

Henry Guest McPike

The Father and Tad

Lincoln was not troubled with an excess of dignity during his Springfield days.[1] He did not always permit the dignity of others to restrain him when he felt like boyish sport. In the presence of one small person, he unbent to the limit of romping. That person was "Tad," the beloved son who died after the family went to the White House. [Tad died in 1872; his older brother Willie died in the White House in 1862.]

"I remember one day I went up to Springfield in company with Mr. Trumbull," said Henry Guest McPike of Alton. "We had political business at Mr. Lincoln's office. Trumbull was a very dignified man. We were sitting in the office talking to Mr. Lincoln, when the door opened and a boy dashed in, running as hard as he could. He was Tad. His father stood up and opened wide his arms. Tad came running. When he was about 6 feet away he jumped and caught his father around the neck. Lincoln wrapped his arms around the boy and spanked him good, both of them laughing and carrying on as if there was nobody looking at them."

What Judge Trumbull thought of the interruption he did not say. He sat there observing the frolic without a sign to indicate that to him this was a novel interlude in the midst of a grave discussion on affairs of national concern.

John F. Mendonsa

"My father," said Mr. Mendonza [Mendonsa], "used to work for Mr. Lincoln, tending his garden and sawing wood.[1] This was from the year 1858 up to his election to the presidency. At the time Mr. Lincoln had his office on the northwest corner of the square over the Stebbins' hardware store. I often went to the office with father to get the pay for the work done. Father could not talk English. I went to interpret for him. I hardly ever went there that Mr. Lincoln did not make me a present of a piece of money and pat me on the face and say: 'Now, you must be a good boy. Come again.'"

"Mr. Lincoln was a great friend to the poor man and a great lover of little children," said Mr. Mendonza, with a world of feeling in his tone and manner. "The last time we saw him, father and I, was after his election. It was that sad morning at the old Great Western Depot, when he bid all farewell from the rear platform of the last car. He saw father standing by, and reached his hand down and shook father by the hand and bade him goodby. It was the last time we saw him alive."

And then Mr. Mendonza told, in his own way, a story of Lincoln, homely, trivial in incident, but full of the nature which made him great.

"One day, the latter part of July, 1859," he said, "my father and brother-in-law and I went after blackberries five miles out of the city. We started at 4 o'clock in the morning. The day was very hot. We hunted for blackberries all morning, for at that time they were getting scarce. We were gone until 11:30 in the forenoon, and all father got was 3 pints. He took them to Mrs. Lincoln, but when she saw them she complained because they were so small. Father told me to tell Mrs. Lincoln these were the last picking; they were smaller than the last, but no more were to be found. He had been all morning since 4 o'clock finding these. Mrs. Lincoln wanted to know what father asked for these. I told her 15 cents. She refused to pay more than 10 cents. Father said he could not afford to sell for that. So just as we were about to start away, Mr. Lincoln came around the house from the front. He greeted father and asked me why we did not sell the berries to Mrs. Lincoln. I told him that we had only 3 pints; that father had been out ever since 4 o'clock gathering the 3 pints, and that Mrs. Lincoln wanted to give father only 10 cents for them. Mr. Lincoln put 15 cents in my hand and told Mrs. Lincoln to take them and put them away. Mrs. Lincoln did not like that. Mr. Lincoln spoke up and told me to tell father it was cheap enough; that he had every cent and more, too. Mr. Lincoln was a very kindhearted man."[2]

Joseph B. Messick

Lincoln's Favorite Chair at Carthage

There were houses where Mr. Lincoln felt very much at home and where he established intimate friendships, as he went the round of the county seats of Illinois.[1] One of these was Alexander Sympson's at Carthage.[2] With few exceptions, Mr. Lincoln, while upon his frequent visits to Carthage, was the guest of Mr. Sympson. The county seat of Hancock is now a college town. It has more than the normal quota of fine homes. But half a century ago, the Sympson home was one of the show places. It is quaint indeed compared with the smart architecture of today.

Mr. Lincoln was very comfortable at the Sympson home. He found there a chair that just suited him. He occupied it so regularly and with such evident satisfaction that it is known to the present generation in Carthage as "the Lincoln chair." Mr. Lincoln was very fond of a lounging attitude. Those long legs were not at ease always when their owner was sitting. Only when he stood up did Mr. Lincoln tower above other men. His excess of stature was in his legs. Hence when Mr. Lincoln found [a] chair or settee so constructed as to meet his odd proportions he enjoyed it thoroughly. When Joseph B. Messick of East St. Louis was a very small boy, on the farm, in Macoupin County, his father took him on the horse behind him and they rode into Carlinville. After the trading the father said:

"Now before we start home I want to go to Mr. Palmer's office and see Mr. Lincoln."

As they went into the law office of John M. Palmer, the vision which came to little Joe was of a very long man stretched out on a very long sofa on one side of the room. The long man raised himself slowly, as if it required some effort to get up, and called out to Mr. Messick:

"Hello, Joe!"

That is Joseph B. Messick's recollection of Abraham Lincoln. The Lincoln chair at Carthage, when tilted back on the rockers, made it possible for Mr. Lincoln to stretch his legs in a comfortable position, and he manifested his liking by occupying it whenever he was at Mr. Sympson's.

Ezra M. Prince

Ezra M. Prince, the secretary of the Historical Society of Bloomington, who died a few weeks ago, left the recollection of a day and a night with Abraham Lincoln.[1] The time was October, 1856, near the close of the "Fremont and Freedom" campaign. Mr. Lincoln came to Bloomington and took a horse and buggy to drive across the country to Tremont. Mr. Prince went with him.

"It was one of the most beautiful of our Indian summer days," Mr. Prince wrote. "The 'Peoria road,' then the great emigrant trail from the East to the West, passed through luxuriant prairies and noble groves. The time was in the height of the Kansas excitement, and the road was lined with emigrant wagons, the destination of which was indicated by the legend, 'Kansas or Bust' rudely painted on their sides. As we passed them the men sang out their presidential preferences. Nine-tenths were Fremont, with an occasional Buchanan. Did Mr. Lincoln have any idea then that in four years the people would be singing his name as loudly? If he had he gave no intimation of it. About dusk we reached a house in the edge of Stout's Grove, where we stayed all night, getting supper, lodging and breakfast. Mr. Lincoln and I slept together in an unfurnished attic. The bill for ourselves and horse was 75 cents. As we were driving away in the morning, Mr. Lincoln said to me: 'Seventy-five cents, pretty cheap, but perhaps all it was worth considering what we got.' Judge Davis said that on the circuit Mr. Lincoln never complained of the food, even when there was nothing but boiled cabbage, which one could eat."

Where Mr. Lincoln and Mr. Prince stopped was a favorite camping place with the emigrants, affording wood and water. Mr. Prince remembered that in the evening Mr. Lincoln "went down to the camp and talked with the men and women about the long tramp they had undertaken and the political campaign that was just closing." Mr. Lincoln was so kindly on that drive that Mr. Prince asked him about his early life.

"I remember," Mr. Prince said, "of his saying that the only schooling he had was six weeks; that his father intended to give him a 'thorough education,' by which he meant that young Abraham should learn to cipher through the rule of three, or proportions, as I believe it is now called, but after six weeks the boy was taken out of school to help pay a debt his father had incurred by signing a note of security for a friend. The rest of his education he had obtained by his own efforts. He read all the books he could obtain, and fortunately these were the very best. The Bible, Shakespeare, Burns, 'Aesops Fables,' 'Pilgrim's Progress,' and a history of the United States—these he read and reread until they became a part of his mental being."

Addison G. Proctor

How Lincoln Got the Kansas Delegates

The youngest delegate to the convention which nominated Lincoln for President at Chicago in 1860 was A. G. Proctor.[1] He was a member of the Kansas delegation, but is now a resident of Michigan. Quite recently the

Lincoln Centennial Association at Springfield obtained from Mr. Proctor his personal recollections, not of the convention, but of the influences and arguments brought to bear upon the delegates of Kansas and other states in favor of the nomination of Mr. Lincoln. The narrative of Mr. Proctor has been made a part of the Lincoln collection in the Illinois Historical Society.

"There probably never came to a national convention a more confident body of men than the Seward delegation to the convention of 1860," Mr. Proctor writes.

And they had reason for their confidence. They had in their candidate a great party leader, a statesman of national reputation, of large public experience, popular with his party, a great orator, a finished scholar, and a trained diplomat. In control of the Seward delegation were men known as most adroit party managers, with abundant means to carry on a successful campaign. Thurlow Weed, the manager of the Seward forces, was an able manipulator. He had been a Warwick in New York politics for years. He had a broad acquaintance with party leaders all over the country, was a man of wonderful tact, a diplomat. With this man to do the manipulating, and with John C. Heenan, the champion pugilist, as standard bearer to attract the "boys," the great Seward excursion party, with rockets, red fire and martial music, poured out on Michigan avenue that evening in May, setting the whole front, from the station to Twelfth Street, aglow with fireworks, and with cheers and yells giving notice that they had come to town to show ordinary politicians how to do business.[2]

Against this exultant, compact organization of veterans there seemed to be no really organized sentiment in opposition. Chicago crowds were shouting "Lincoln," but this was looked upon merely as a local influence and did not carry much weight with outside delegates. The Ohio crowd, in a kind of hesitating way, flung out a Chase banner; the Pennsylvania crowd one for Cameron, Vermont one for [Jacob] Collamer, and New Jersey one for [William L.] Dayton.[3] Missouri spit tobacco juice and talked [Edward] Bates.[4] But all of them were waiting for something to turn up. There was nothing aggressive in the opposition to Seward except the constant yelling on the streets for "Lincoln." And yet out of a mass of disorganized elements was forged a movement which overwhelmed all of the old party leaders and gave us a new leader whose wisdom was to give character, victory and endurance to the new party for the coming fifty years.

The two most active and conspicuous leaders of the conflicting forces were Thurlow Weed and Horace Greeley. Mr. Weed sent his card to our dele-

gation the very day we reached Chicago, asking us to meet him for a conference in his parlor in the Richmond Hotel. He was certainly a most agreeable
and adroit diplomat. I recall that as we sat there in earnest conversation he
addressed each of us by name, a thing I have not seen done successfully since
except by James G. Blaine and William Alden Smith.

"We have come here," Mr. Weed said to our Kansas delegation, "to nominate Mr. Seward. He is our representative man. A party that has not the courage of its political convictions and is afraid to avow its principles by placing
its leader in nomination does not deserve to succeed."

He spoke of the Philadelphia convention four years before nominating a
most unfit man, or "boy," as he called him [John C. Fremont], for expediency, as a cowardly policy deserving defeat. He said that the nomination of
Fremont was the most unfit nomination ever made by any responsible party,
that Fremont had not one single qualification for the office, and that it was
unwise and impolitic to make any more nominations of untrained men, as
the country was in no mood to consider such a policy.

"What the country demands now," Mr. Weed said, "is that a great party
shall put forward its representative man—a man who represents its highest
ideals. The country will be satisfied with nothing short of this. We are drifting into perilous times. We need the very highest order of statesmanship and
political experience as we never needed them before." Mr. Weed spoke with
great deliberation, and impressed all of us by his earnest and sincere manner.

We had hardly returned to our hotel from this session with Mr. Weed
when Horace Greeley was announced. Greeley was at his best, fairly aglow
with enthusiasm, as active as a boy. He was determined to defeat the nomination of Seward for reasons personal to himself, and he was leaving nothing
undone to accomplish his purpose. He seemed at home with us, addressing
us as "boys," entering into the discussion with much earnestness and ad-
monishing us against committing ourselves too early in the contest. He said:
"Boys, I can satisfy every one of you that Seward can not be elected, if nominated. There are states he can not carry. I can bring leading men from those
states, whose judgment you can not question, to verify what I say." And that
he did, bringing and introducing Gov. Curtin of Pennsylvania, Henry Lane
of Indiana, and Gov. Kirkwood of Iowa, each of whom stated that the nomination of Mr. Seward would be most discouraging to his state.[5]

"Whom do you want, Mr. Greeley?" asked one of our Kansas delegates.

"I am not fully satisfied myself at this time just who will be our most available man to name," said Mr. Greeley. "I think well of Judge Bates. Mr. Lin-

coln may be found most available. I am for a Western man, whom we may be reasonably sure of electing. Whom that man may be we must determine later. Just now I am undecided." And this was from the leader of the opposition to Mr. Seward only about thirty hours before the nomination.

The two elements that seemed to form the opposing camps and to be about equally divided were:

The element represented largely by the Eastern people who were of that great moral upheaval against slavery as an institution, who hated it for its hateful self.

The element willing to tolerate slavery within limits where it existed and seemed to belong, but determined to prevent its extension into the free Northwest at every hazard, even to the invoking of civil war.

The first element wanted Seward. The second element was looking for a leader. At this juncture there came to the front, from sources not before taken into consideration, a movement led by the men of the border states. This body of resolute men from Maryland, from the mountains of Virginia, from Eastern Tennessee, from Kentucky and from all over Missouri had organized and selected Cassius M. Clay as leader and spokesman. They were a group of men as earnest as I have ever met. They asked for a conference with us, which we arranged without delay. The Kansas delegation was the first to receive them. It may have occurred to them that Kansas was awake to what was coming, and would more likely appreciate the full force of their logic. The company completely filled our room. There was something about the atmosphere of that meeting that seemed to mean business. Mr. Clay was a man of strong personality. He had all of the mannerisms of a real Kentucky "colonel"—very courtly, very earnest, very eloquent in address.

"Gentlemen," he said, in beginning, "we are on the verge of a great civil war."

One of our Kansas delegates said: "Mr. Clay, we have heard that before."

Clay straightened himself and, with a real oratorical pose, exclaimed: "Sir, you undoubtedly have heard that before. But, sir, you will soon have it flashed to you in a tone that will certainly carry conviction." He went on: "We are from the South. We know our people well. I say to you the South is getting ready for war. In that great strip of border land, reaching from the eastern shore of Maryland to the western border of Missouri, stands a body of resolute men, determined that this Union shall not be destroyed without resistance. We are not pro-slavery men, not antislavery men, but Union Republicans, ready and willing to take up arms for the defense of the border.

We are intensely in earnest. It means very much—what you do here—to you and to us. Our homes and all we possess are in peril. We want to hold this Union strength for a Union army. We want to work with you for a nomination which will give us courage and confidence. We want you to nominate Abraham Lincoln. Mr. Lincoln was born among us, and we believe in him. Give us Lincoln for a leader and I promise you that we will push back the disloyal hordes of secession and transfer the line of border warfare from the Ohio to the regions beyond the Tennessee, where it belongs. We will make war on the enemies of our country at home and join you in driving secession to its lair. Do this for us, and let us go home and prepare for the conflict."

No one could give a satisfactory report of that appeal. It was the most impressive talk that I had ever listened to. That delegation of border men, headed by Mr. Clay, made this appeal to most of the delegations of the different states. The effect was instantly felt. There was getting together of those who felt the Lincoln sentiment, all along the line. This movement formed the group around which the earnest Lincoln men rallied and organized their forces. I honestly believe that this was the movement that gave to Lincoln his nomination. It was the turning point. It awoke all to a realization of what was before us and compelled recognition of a new element on which might rest great results for good or evil. In short, this action of the border men set us all thinking.

The only argument used most effectively against Mr. Lincoln was his inexperience in national affairs. It was the one thing that made us pause, for we all came to realize that we were fast drifting toward a terrible struggle that would demand the highest order of leadership. We realized that not only our home affairs would need the most able statesman that we could find, but that the complications in our foreign affairs demanded the very highest order of diplomatic genius. Mr. Lincoln, although admitted by all to be a most adroit politician and wonderful in debate, had never been called upon to show that he possessed a single one of the qualities at that time most in demand. Though the point was pressed that Mr. Lincoln could be elected, there were some who felt that we could not afford to take the chances of placing a man without experience at the head of public affairs at such a time. This conflict seemed more and more to impress us with the responsibility resting upon us. We simply put our trust in God, and he gave us—Abraham Lincoln. We were all building better than we knew. Most of us remember the effort that was required to assure the country that we had made no mistake. The people were slow to realize. They thought we had taken a desperate hazard; but when, at last, during the summer, Mr. Seward announced that he was ready to take the field for Lincoln, and when he came forward with an eloquence and an earnestness that surprised us all, urging his countrymen to make sure of the election of Lincoln if they would save the country, the whole North responded with a wide-awake campaign, and every Northern state swung into line. And when through the succeeding four years of trial Mr. Lincoln so happily displayed his great ability and complete fitness, we of the convention rested and still rest in the assurance that our work was well done.

John W. Proctor

"I have passed my 80th year, and thank the dear Lord of Glory that I knew Abraham Lincoln, and had the privilege of laboring for his election to the presidency," is the way John W. Proctor prefaced a narrative of his recollections.[1]

My father moved to Illinois, settling in St. Clair County, across the river from St. Louis, in 1813 [1818]. When the Winnebago [Indian] war closed, and all that great Sangamon country was opened for settlement, he moved [in February 1820] to Fancy Creek in Sangamon County, ten miles north of Springfield. Ten years later he moved to Fulton County, [and died in Lewistown in 1879]. We knew Lincoln as a rising young lawyer and legislator. I was not personally intimate with him until the campaign of 1858, when I was chairman of the delegation from Fulton County to the State Convention, which brought Mr. Lincoln out for the Senate against Senator Douglas. As Mr. Douglas was to be in our county Monday, the 15th [16th] of August of that year, I wrote Mr. Lincoln suggesting that he come over on Saturday and remain over Monday to speak to our people the day after Douglas. I have his reply, in which he says in his terse way: "I don't think Mr. Douglas would like me for an auditor, but I will be with you on the 17th, if you think you can give me a good audience."

It is history that Mr. Lincoln followed Douglas throughout that campaign, "camping on his trail," but it is not so well known that Mr. Lincoln was thoughtful of the proprieties and careful to do nothing which Mr. Douglas might think discourteous.

"Mr. Lincoln came, was my guest, and delighted a fine audience with a speech that was an excellent forerunner of the great debates later," said Mr. Proctor. "Late in that wonderful political year, at my request, he came once more into our county and spoke at Vermont, October 31.[2] It was a cool day. The rain fell steadily. But he spoke from under an umbrella for more than an hour to over a thousand people."

Mr. Proctor's recollection dates back to college days in 1844 at Jacksonville.

"I was a student at Illinois College that year," he said. "In June word came to the college that there would be political speaking at the Courthouse Monday evening. There were no daily papers at that time in our section, and the people were glad to get their news at these political gatherings. Nearly a hundred of us went down on that occasion. We were addressed, as I now recall, by a Mr. L. C. Woodson for the Democrats. During his speech he made an attack upon the character of John Quincy Adams, who had been president of the United States. At the close of the speech a tall, dark man in a corner of the courtroom arose and said: 'Now, ladies and gentlemen, if you will come out tomorrow evening, I will try to reply to the very able address of this evening.' So we all went down from College Hill, and, with the citizens from the town, we filled the courtroom. Mr. Lincoln, in reply to Mr. Woodson, said he had been very much interested in Mr. Woodson's address, for it reminded him of an incident which occurred when his mother and he (Lincoln) removed to Illinois.

"He said: 'We had all our effects in one wagon and had one yoke of oxen for a team. We camped by the way. One night, after we entered Illinois, we were so fortunate as to find a deserted cabin in which to camp. I made a good fire in the wide fireplace and carried in such of our effects as mother needed for our comfort while waiting for supper. I noticed at one end of the cabin a sort of shelf, and there was something that looked like a newspaper on it. A newspaper was a rarity in those days, worth a dollar apiece, even at a time when a man would work all day for 25 cents in silver. I found the paper to be one published at Vandalia, then the capital of Illinois. I found in it a speech made before the Legislature by my friend Woodson here, then a member of the Legislature, in which was a very warm defense of the character of John Quincy Adams.' Then Mr. Lincoln proceeded to quote from the speech whole paragraphs, until it brought Mr. Woodson to his feet, saying: 'Abe, stop. I was a Whig then, but am a Democrat now.'"

"Of course," said Mr. Proctor, "the laugh was on Woodson, but all was in good humor. The incident serves to illustrate Mr. Lincoln's wonderful memory and tact in political debate. The speeches of Woodson and Lincoln opened the campaign of 1844 in that part of the state. Lincoln was then 35 years old."

Owen T. Reeves

Lincoln's Prediction of Ingalls' Future

"Mr. Lincoln went out to Leavenworth to deliver an address," said Judge Owen T. Reeves of Bloomington.[1] "I can remember something he said when he came back which illustrated what an accurate observer he was. The office of our circuit clerk was a large one. In one end of it Judge Davis had a stove and a desk. As I went in one day Mr. Lincoln, who had just returned, was talking with the judge. Judge Davis was asking Mr. Lincoln whom he met in Kansas. Mr. Lincoln told him and in the course of the conversation said: 'I met two young men who struck me as being men of great promise.' Judge Davis asked for their names. 'One was named Ewing—Thomas Ewing,' Mr. Lincoln said.[2] 'The other was a young man by the name of Ingalls.'[3] 'Which did you think was the brightest?' asked Judge Davis. 'That young man Ingalls struck me as having one of the brightest minds I ever saw,' replied Mr. Lincoln. Ewing afterward became governor of Ohio. Ingalls was the brilliant senator from Kansas. 'I predict for that young man Ingalls a great future,' was the way Mr. Lincoln concluded his description of the two young men to Judge Davis."

How Lincoln Got His Largest Fee

The story of Mr. Lincoln's $5000 fee is history, but there are some facts about it, as told by Judge Owen T. Reeves of Bloomington, that the Lincoln biographies do not contain.[4]

"The Illinois Central Railroad was built under a state charter, which was thought to cover all taxation," Judge Reeves said. "Bloomington authorities believed that the railroad property within the county was subject to their local assessment. They levied a tax. The railroad people employed Mr. Lincoln to defend the company on the ground that the charter provision requiring payment of 7 percent of the revenue to the state was in lieu of all taxation. Mr. Lincoln filed a bill to enjoin the Bloomington authorities from the collection of their tax. He won the case in the lower court and also in the Supreme Court, to which it was appealed. The decision was that the railroad was exempted from local taxation under its charter. Mr. Lincoln rendered a bill for the service, and the railroad people objected to the amount. Mr. Lincoln brought suit in the Bloomington Court for $5000. He took depositions of eminent lawyers—Judge Purple of Peoria, O. H. Browning of Quincy and several others. The case was set for trial in the Circuit Court. When the day came the lawyer for the Illinois Central didn't appear. A jury was impaneled, Mr. Lincoln presented his case, including the depositions. Some of the lawyers stated in their depositions that they considered the fee ridiculously low. A verdict for the full amount was rendered. In the afternoon the railroad's lawyer, John C. Douglas, arrived from Chicago. He went into court and was informed of the judgment. Before Mr. Douglas could take action, Mr. Lincoln stated to the court that it was not necessary for the counsel for the defense to move to set aside the judgment and reopen the case; that he would consent to such a course without motion. The judgment was set aside and the case was reopened and retried. The result of the afternoon trial was the same as that at the morning session."

James P. Root

A Good One on Stephen A. Douglas

"I do not think too much can be said or written to perpetuate the memory of one of the greatest men who have lived," James P. Root of Chicago said recently.[1] Mr. Root believes it is a duty as well as a privilege of the men "who knew Lincoln" to give their recollections of him. The Briggs House was a favorite stopping place with the lawyers who came from down the state to attend the terms of the United States Court fifty years ago. At such times the hotel included among its guests such men as Lincoln, Browning, Purple and Manning.

"I was boarding at the Briggs House in 1858," Mr. Root said. "The Illinois Central had retained Mr. Lincoln to recover ground south of the river and along the lake shore. This was the historic case in which Lincoln showed so much modesty about the size of his fee. It was tried before Associate Justice McLean and Judge Drummond.[2] Negotiations were then pending for the debate between Lincoln and Douglas, but had not been brought to a conclusion. Douglas was opening his campaign in Chicago with a speech from the north balcony of the Tremont House. I walked with Mr. Lincoln over to the Tremont. Lincoln remarked just before we started, 'I guess we had better go over and hear what Douglas has to say.' Lincoln was invited to a seat on the balcony and I trailed out with him. The crowd in the street was immense. During his speech Douglas, to illustrate a point, said: 'Your great lawyer, Justice Butterfield, once said the constitution of Illinois would be greatly improved if it contained an appeal from the Supreme Court to a justice of the peace.'[3] Lincoln sang out in a clear voice, audible to all, 'Judge, that was when you were one of the judges of the Supreme Court.' Mr. Douglas took it good-naturedly, turning to Lincoln as if he would say, 'That is a good one on me.' Of course, we Republicans had the innings for a couple of minutes."

Of Lincoln as a story-teller, Mr. Root received this impression: "During the evenings I spent with him under the awning of the Briggs House many stories were told. I do not think he told stories for the sake of the stories, but rather to illustrate something. His sense of humor and appreciation of fine wit did much to keep him up during the dark hours of the rebellion. Other men, as Mr. Beecher wrote home, would have gone into a cave of gloom."

Henry M. Russell

Lincoln's First Game of Billiards

Lincoln played his first game of billiards at Urbana.[1] He liked out-of-door sports, especially ball playing, up to the time he was elected president. Indoors his preferred recreation was reading or conversation. Games of cards had little attraction for him. This first game of billiards at Urbana was an hilarious affair for the spectators. H. M. Russell, who came to Urbana in 1847, remembered well the game and described the entertainment it afforded.[2]

"An uncle of mine, James S. Gore [Gere], was keeping the old Champaign House, then the stage house, and was local agent for the stage lines," Mr. Russell said.

"In May, 1848, Judge Samuel H. Treat, Abraham Lincoln and David Davis came to hold the term of the Champaign County Circuit Court and stopped at the hotel. I was working for my uncle, looking after the wants of the judge and of the attorneys, attending the fires in their rooms, carrying water and cigars as needed. I also assisted in waiting on the table. I at once took a liking to Mr. Lincoln, because of his gentleness and friendliness so different from most of the other attorneys. Mr. Lincoln was always pleasant in asking for things he wished and in thanking for them when they were brought to him. The rooms occupied by the lawyers were good-sized, containing usually three beds in the same room. Two of the members of the bar slept in the same bed, except the judge, and two or three others who had single rooms. The evenings were spent in the large rooms, where there were fireplaces and comfortable fires. At a later date Leonard Swett and Gen. Gridley of Bloomington traveled the circuit.

"The traveling bar came from Monticello to Urbana and went from Urbana to Danville and thence to Paris, Charleston and other court towns."

"In the rooms of evenings," said Mr. Russell, introducing his recollection of the recreation of the legal minds sixty years ago, "there were jolly times. There was some drinking. There was some card playing for small stakes, with grains of corn or coffee for the chips at 5 or 10 cents a kernel. I am glad to state that I never saw or heard of Mr. Lincoln touching the whisky or playing cards. I often heard of him telling stories to the other lawyers. He would occasionally tell a story on some unfortunate drinker or card player. His stories were always interesting with a point to them. I saw Mr. Lincoln play his first game of billiards. I heard him say that was the first game of billiards he had ever played. A billiard hall had been opened, the first in Urbana. In some way there was started a bantering conversation among the lawyers about the game. Visiting lawyers and citizens of Urbana were discussing the fine points. Mr. Lincoln remarked that he had never played. J. C. Sheldon, a young attorney, also said that he had never played.[3] The lawyers and the citizens bantered Mr. Lincoln and Mr. Sheldon to play their first game against each other, telling them they were behind the times. They took the jollying good-naturedly and the match was made, the visiting lawyers urging on Mr. Lincoln and the Urbana people encouraging Mr. Sheldon. Mr. Lincoln and Mr. Sheldon, with their friends, started for the billiard hall.

"The news spread, and in a short time the hall was full of citizens to see the match between two lawyers who had never before had cues in their hands. I have always felt sure that both of them told the truth, for the game

was the most awkward and the most amusing billiard game I ever witnessed or heard of, even among amateurs. Mr. Lincoln was tall and angu-
lar, Mr. Sheldon was short and stocky. They formed a contrast that was
laughable from the start. Before they made many shots the whole crowd
was shouting with laughter. No matter where the balls lay, Mr. Lincoln
would lean his whole body over the rail and with his long arms reach anywhere on the table. Mr. Sheldon's large prominence came in contact with
the rail for nearly every shot; he could not lean over, but would try to lie on
the table with his feet off the floor. That position was prohibited. So Mr.
Sheldon would have to resort almost every shot to the bridge. Whether Mr.
Lincoln or Mr. Sheldon was playing the movements were very funny. The
game was 100 points. It lasted far into the night. I do not remember who
won the game, and I do not think anybody cared. We were too much
amused with the performance to think of the score."

Mr. Russell was an active Lincoln man in the campaign of 1860. He re-
paid the kind words which had been given to him in the days when he was
helper in the Stage House. Going to Decatur as the head of the delegation
of his county, he helped make the Lincoln delegation to the National Convention at Chicago which nominated Mr. Lincoln.

"I went to Chicago with the delegates," Mr. Russell said, "and was in
the confidence of David Davis, O. H. Browning, Leonard Swett and the
other friends of Mr. Lincoln. I had the honor of securing the two votes for
Mr. Lincoln in the Pennsylvania delegation on the first ballot. I also helped
to organize the coup which got about 300 Illinois rooters into the wigwam
on 75 or 100 visitors' tickets, and surely kept out fully 300 New York-
ers when they came. I got our hooters in while the New York folks were
parading."

Benjamin F. Shaw

Benjamin F. Shaw, for half a century proprietor of the *Dixon Telegraph*,
was one of the fifteen editors who attended the Decatur conference and afterward the Bloomington convention, which organized the Republican
party of Illinois in 1856.[1] He had a newspaper man's experience with Mr.
Lincoln. He had gone with some other Dixon people to call upon Mr. Lincoln at his home in Springfield a few weeks before the inauguration in

1861. His account of what occurred is given as the Historical Society at Bloomington has preserved it:

When we arrived we were ushered into the parlor, where we found several gentlemen from Arkansas, and, I believe, from other border states, as they were then called, who had come as a sort of committee to urge upon the president elect to issue some sort of manifesto assuring the people of the South that it was not his intention to liberate the slaves. The committee was very urgent in the matter and seemed to believe that such a precaution was necessary to prevent insurrection among the slaves, who were impatient regarding their anticipated freedom. It was urged by the gentlemen from the South that the slaves believed that Mr. Lincoln's election meant their freedom. They had been told that they would be liberated. They heard the people of the South talk about it and were discontented. The committee understood very well that Mr. Lincoln did not intend to abolish slavery. But the negroes and the ignorant whites of the South did not so understand it.

The gentlemen believed that it was the duty of the president elect to undeceive them. Several members of that committee of safety earnestly urged the importance of some assurance from Lincoln to colored men and ignorant people of the South that an emancipation proclamation would not be among his first official acts. He listened respectfully, and after the importance of a proclamation was fully urged he made a reply that was so masterful in logic, so touching in kindness and yet so full of marvelous sarcasm, coupled with witticism, showing the absurdity of the proposition of the committee, that I shall never forget it. Mr. Lincoln opened in answer by stating that such a manifesto would indicate fear on his part and would be, by most of the citizens of the South, attributed to cowardice, a charge freely made against the people of the North generally. He believed that his inaugural address, which would, in a few days, be delivered from the steps of the national capital, would be in ample time to undeceive people having erroneous opinions upon matters which troubled them. To anticipate his inaugural address, as requested, would be unwise and lacking in dignity. He closed his remarks with much earnestness and no little emphasis. The words I remember quite well:

"In all my speeches," he said, "I have never uttered a word indicating intention to interfere with slavery where it exists in states. Republican speakers and newspapers not only never advocated abolition of slavery, but are constantly refuting the charge that they are radical abolitionists. Such utterance has been one of the principal contentions of the campaign just closed. So you see, gentlemen, if the colored people of the South have heard that I intended to abolish slavery they received the idea from the lips of your own people; from their masters at the dinner table, or heard it at your own political meetings, and not from any Republican source; therefore, it is your duty to rectify the mistake. It is certainly not incumbent upon me to correct at this time the falsehoods of our opponents."

As the people of the South were then threatening to destroy the government and civil war was inevitable, he remarked that the committee reminded him of the disadvantageous excitement of the man whose house was on fire, who, in his efforts to save the property, threw mirrors, pitchers and valuable vases out of the second-story window, and carried flatirons and bedding carefully downstairs in his arms. The committee retired with the firm impression that Lincoln had a mind of his own, as one of them was heard to remark. Meeting Mr. Lincoln the next day at the hotel, I requested permission to print that interview at his private residence in my paper. He replied: "I'd a heap rather you had done it without asking me." This was a characteristic precaution in Lincoln, that his indorsement should not even by inference appear to such an absurdity as the interview on the issuing of the manifesto. So I never printed it.

John Quincy Spears

A Prophecy of the Presidency

Twenty-four years before Lincoln started for Washington, one of the grand pioneer women of Illinois stood in the door of her farm home, where the town of Tallula now is, and followed with her vision the tall, awkward figure moving down the road.[1] She said:

"He is a very smart boy. I'll not be surprised if he is president sometime."

Many who "knew Lincoln" thought of him as a presidential possibility, it seems, long before he did. But the earliest prophetic utterance, probably, is the one just quoted, which J. Q. Spears of Tallula has sent to Mr. Van Cleave of the Lincoln Centennial Association at Springfield.[2] The grandmother of Mr. Spears looked forward to an event which she did not live to see.

"In 1837," Mr. Spears records, "when Mr. Lincoln was preparing to move to Springfield, he came to my father's one Saturday to visit my grandmother and remained until Monday morning. When he was going away my grandmother followed him to the door. He turned and took her hand between his long, lean hands and said: 'Grandmother, I am going to Springfield, and maybe I will never see you again. Good-by. God bless you.' She replied: 'Abraham, God bless you.' He started away in a rapid walk. She stood there for a minute, the tears trickling down her cheeks. Then she turned to me and said: 'He is a very smart boy; I'll not be surprised if he is president sometime.'"

"I met Mr. Lincoln while he was the nominee in 1860," continued Mr. Spears, adding the sequel to his grandmother's prophecy. "Mr. Lincoln asked me if my grandmother was still living. I said, 'No.' He spoke of that last meeting. What my grandmother said after he started away was related. The tears filled his eyes. Mr. Lincoln hesitated for some time and then said, 'She was a good guesser, wasn't she?'"

The Beginning of the Republican Party

Some men "who knew Lincoln" do not believe the political history which has been written credits him with his full part in the genesis of the Republican party.[3] They remember where Lincoln stood toward the last Whig conventions. They recall the movement to make him vice president on the ticket with Fremont in 1856, which, fortunately, was abandoned on grounds of expediency. And they mention political acts of Lincoln which possess not small significance when taken with subsequent events. John R. [Q.] Spears of Tallula knew Lincoln from 1833, when he was a surveyor. He was prominent in the politics of his day. He heard Lincoln speak in the Harrison convention of Illinois in 1840 and in support of the nomination of Clay before the Whig convention of Illinois in 1844, and on other occasions before the Republican party organized. Mr. Spears has this recollection of the beginning of the Republican movement:

> Lincoln called a meeting of a few friends at a country store where Tallula now is. He had been a surveyor when the county (now Menard) was part of Sangamon. He knew almost everybody. There were forty or fifty in the gathering at the store. Mr. Lincoln made a talk reviewing political conditions and offering suggestions as to the future. He called for some paper to write down what position he thought should be taken upon the questions of the day, es-

pecially upon slavery. There was no paper to be had. Lincoln drew a newspaper from his pocket, lay down on the cellar door and wrote on the margin
the essence of the principles which formed the Republican party. This, I believe, was the first meeting of the kind in the United States. This meeting at
the country store where Lincoln drafted a platform was more than [here a
line of type seems to have been inadvertently dropped] [Fre]mont, the first
presidential candidate of the Republican party. It was a year or more before
the convention at Bloomington, where the Republican party of Illinois was
started and where Lincoln made one of the best speeches of his life, which
was lost.

Mr. Spears does not recall the exact time of this meeting at which Lincoln wrote on the margin of a newspaper the first Republican platform. He
knows that the meeting was called by Lincoln two years or more before the
national convention nominated Fremont in 1856. He knows that this enun-
ciation of Republican principles was before the Bloomington convention.

Adlai E. Stevenson

"Bloomington is a good place to live," the former vice president of the
United States, Adlai E. Stevenson, said, sitting in his library, looking out on
the trees and lawns of Franklin Park.[1]

Bloomington is a good place to live. Here, still in the flesh, are the men
and women, cheerful in spirit, clear in memory, vigorous in health, who
give some of the most vivid personal recollections of Abraham Lincoln.
From sixty-five to fifty years ago, Mr. Lincoln walked these tree-lined
streets of Bloomington, sat through the semiannual terms of court, knew
everybody, and was as much at home here as in his own Springfield. Those
who never saw the face of the great president feel that they approach very
near his personality as they listen to the reminiscences of the Bloomington
people. The descriptions of appearance, of manner and of actions are wonderfully interesting. Bloomington knew and appreciated Mr. Lincoln intimately and intelligently during the years from 1845 to 1860.[2]

"I have never known a more powerful advocate," was tribute Mr. Stevenson paid to Mr. Lincoln. "I recall distinctly his speeches in the old courthouse of Bloomington in the years long gone. I was a student at the time,
and my acquaintance with Mr. Lincoln was only such as a boy interested in

public discussion would have with a man of his prominence. Mr. Lincoln took a deep interest in young men, and often spoke to them words of encouragement. He was ever the generous, kindly gentleman. He was always addressed and referred to in Bloomington as Mr. Lincoln. People did not call him 'Abe' Lincoln."

The joint debate was not new in political campaigns, and Mr. Lincoln had been tried in that way long before the meetings with Douglas, Mr. Stevenson recalled:

> Mr. Lincoln was a representative in Congress from the district of which this county, McLean, was a part. His competitor for that office [in 1846] was Peter Cartwright, the famous Methodist minister. It was said of Mr. Cartwright that he was of the "church military," as well as of the "church militant." During the campaign Mr. Lincoln and Mr. Cartwright had joint debates throughout the district, as was the time-honored custom here sixty years ago. Those debates, if they had been preserved, would be interesting reading at this day.[3]

Mr. Lincoln's readiness with argument and humor gave him an advantage in joint debate which few speakers possessed. He rather courted interruptions and questions from his hearers. Mr. Stevenson mentioned an occasion when Mr. Lincoln was frequently interrupted by a doctor in the audience who had a turn for politics and thought he could tangle the speaker.

"Mr. Lincoln," said Mr. Stevenson, "took the interruptions, which were rather impertinent and abusive, with entire good nature until he thought the time had come to put an end to them, and then, addressing the man in the crowd, said: 'Doctor, I'll take anything from you but your medicine.'[4]

The shouts of laughter from the crowd put the doctor out of political business for that meeting.[5]

"A struggle of giants" Mr. Stevenson called the joint debates between Mr. Lincoln and Mr. Douglas. "With the single exception of the earlier debate between [Massachusetts Senator Daniel] Webster and [South Carolina Senator Robert Y.] Hayne in the Senate, the country has known no such polemic struggle as that between Lincoln and Douglas. No one of the seven joint discussions occurred in Bloomington, but each candidate spoke here upon different occasions during that eventful contest.[6] I heard them both, and will remember to the last their masterful discussion of the great questions that then divided the country."

Speaking of the joint debates, Mr. Stevenson said:

> They were held in the open, and at each place immense crowds were in atten-

dance. The friends of Mr. Lincoln largely preponderated in the northern portion of the state; those of Mr. Douglas in the southern, while in the center the partisans of the respective candidates were apparently equal in numbers. The interest never flagged for a moment from the beginning to the close. The debate was upon a high plane, each candidate was enthusiastically applauded by his friends and respectfully heard by his opponents. The speakers were men of dignified presence, their bearing such as to challenge respect in any assemblage. There was nothing of the "grotesque" about the one, nothing of the "political juggler" about the other. Both were deeply impressed with the gravity of the questions at issue, and of what might prove their far-reaching consequence to the country. Kindly reference by each speaker to the other characterized the debates from the beginning. "My friend Lincoln" and "My friend the Judge" were expressions of constant occurrence during the debates. While each mercilessly attacked the political utterances of the other, good feeling in the main prevailed. Something being pardoned to the spirit of debates, the amenities were well preserved. They had been personally well known to each other for many years, had served together in the Legislature when the state capital was at Vandalia, and at a later date Lincoln had appeared before the Supreme Court when Douglas was one of the judges.

"Profound" was the word Mr. Stevenson used to define the quality of Mr. Lincoln's humor. The former vice president was known to all public men in Washington during his years of official life there as one of the most charming of speakers and conversationalists. His stories possessed the Lincoln character of application. His humor was always genial and happy. Peculiarly qualified, by his own faculty to express the opinion, Mr. Stevenson said:

Mr. Lincoln's profound humor never appeared to better advantage than during these debates. In criticizing Mr. Lincoln's attack upon Chief Justice Taney and his associates for the "Dred Scott" decision, Mr. Douglas declared it to be an attempt to secure a reversal of the high tribunal by an appeal to a town meeting. It reminded him of the saying of Col. Strode that the judicial system of Illinois was perfect except that "there should be an appeal allowed from the Supreme Court to two justices of the peace." Lincoln replied: "That was when you were on the bench, judge."

Referring to Douglas' allusion to him as a kind, amiable and intelligent gentleman, Mr. Lincoln said: "Then, as the judge has complimented me with these pleasant titles, I was a little taken back, for it came from a great man. I was not very much accustomed to flattery and it came the sweeter to me. I was like the hoosier with the gingerbread, when he said he reckoned he loved it better and got less of it than any other man."

Mr. Douglas, referring to the alliance between the Republicans and the federal officeholders said: "I shall deal with this allied army just as the Russians dealt with the allies at Sebastopol. The Russians when they fired a broadside did not stop to inquire whether it hit a Frenchman, an Englishman or a Turk. Nor will I stop to inquire whether my blows hit the Republicans' leaders or their allies, the federal officeholders." To which Lincoln replied: "I beg the judge will indulge us while we remind him that the allies took Sebastopol."

Comparing the mental habit and the action of the two men, Mr. Stevenson said of Douglas:

That he possessed rare power as a debater, all who heard him can bear witness. Douglas was imbued with little of mere sentiment. He gave little time to discussions belonging to the realm of the speculative or abstract. He was in no sense a dreamer. In phrase choosing the simple and most telling, he struck at once to the very core of the controversy. Probably no man ever was less inclined "to darken counsel with words without knowledge." Positive and aggressive to the last degree, he never sought "by indirections to find directions out." In statesmanship in all that pertained to human affairs, he was intensely practical.

Mr. Stevenson does not think the looking-backward views give the correct impressions of the joint debates.

"The name of Lincoln is now a household word," he said. "Nothing that can be uttered or withheld can add to or detract from his imperishable fame."

For the proper consideration of the joint debates it must be remembered, he argued, that Mr. Lincoln's great opportunity and fame came afterward. Mr. Lincoln was then "the country lawyer, the debater, the candidate of his party for political office." And also in the judgment of Mr. Douglas, Mr. Stevenson said, existing conditions of 1858 should be always borne in mind.

"The trend of thought," he said, "the unmeasured achievement of activities looking to human amelioration during the fifty intervening years must be taken into account before uncharitable judgment is passed upon what has been declared the indifference of Mr. Douglas to the question of abstract right involved in the memorable discussion. It must be remembered that the world has moved apace, and that a mighty gulf separates [us] from that eventful period in which practical statesmen were compelled to deal with institutions as then existing."

A Democrat all his life, Mr. Stevenson is the historian when he talks of the debates of 1858.

"It is a pleasure," he said, "to recall the two men as they shook hands upon the speakers' stand just before the opening of the debates that were to mark an epoch in American history. As they stood side by side and looked out upon 'the sea of upturned faces' it was a picture to live in the memory of all who witnessed it. The one stood for the 'the old ordering of things' in an emphatic sense for the government established by the fathers—with all its compromises. The other, recognizing—equally with his opponent—the binding force of constitutional obligation, yet looking away from present surroundings, 'felt the inspiration of the coming of the grander day.' Few survive of the vast assemblages which listened spellbound to the impassioned words of the masterful debaters. The conditions mentioned by Webster as essential to true eloquence had arisen—'the orator and the occasion had met.' The people of the entire state were aroused, the interest profound, the excitement at times intense. The occasion was worthy [of] the great orators; the orators worthy [of] the great occasion. Within less than two years from the first debate Lincoln and Douglas were opposing candidates for the presidency, and the area of the struggle was enlarged from the state to the nation."

As a companion scene to the picture of the opening of the joint debates, Mr. Stevenson recalled that other meeting of the two men at the inauguration in 1861, with Douglas holding the hat of Lincoln:

> Standing by the side of his successful rival, whose wondrous career was only opening, as his own was nearing its close, he bowed profound assent to the imperishable utterances of the inaugural address: "I am loath to close. We are not enemies but friends. Though passion may have strained, it must not break our bonds of affection. The mystic chords of memory, stretching from every battle field and patriot grave to every living heart and hearthstone all over this broad land, will yet swell the chorus of the union, when again touched, as surely they will be, by the better angels of our nature.

After the inauguration of Lincoln and the firing on Fort Sumter, Douglas went back to Illinois to say to the Legislature of his state: "I deprecate war, but if it must come, I am with my country, in every contingency and under all circumstances."

Mr. Stevenson likes to believe that if Douglas had lived, "he would, during the perilous years, have been the safe counselor, the rock, of the great president, in preserving the nation's life, and, later, 'in binding up the nation's wounds.'"

And of Lincoln he said: "His name and fame are the priceless heritage of all people."

J. G. Stewart

"The most patient man I ever saw," was the description of Mr. Lincoln that J. G. Stewart, one of the old-time photographers, gave.[1] Mr. Stewart made a great many photographs of Mr. Lincoln during the campaign of 1858. He lived in Springfield, knew the Lincoln family well, played chess with Robert Lincoln, the oldest son, when he was a boy.

"The second son, Willie," said Mr. Stewart, "was the brainiest boy I ever saw. His memory was so great that after he had heard a sermon he could repeat it almost word for word. Taddy was the youngest son, the baby boy."

Willie was the boy who died at the White House. This wonderful memory he inherited from his father. It is told of Mr. Lincoln that while a child in the Kentucky home he would climb on a bench or a chair and repeat portions of the sermon he had heard at the country schoolhouse. Mr. Stewart came to Springfield in 1855.

"The first time I saw Mr. Lincoln," he said, "I saw a tall, lank awkward man, who wore a tall hat, a short raglan coat, short top boots with one leg of his trouser stuck in the top, walking with a stoop and carrying one hand behind his back. I was attracted toward him on account of his appearance, and I inquired of Mr. Ed Thayer, a dry goods merchant, who that gawk was. Mr. Thayer told me he was one of the best lawyers and brightest men in the state. He said, 'You ought to go and hear him plead in court.' I had a chance in a short time to see him handle a murder case and heard him plead."

Like the other fellow-townsmen of Mr. Lincoln, Mr. Stewart was soon numbered "among his most ardent admirers. To know him was to love him. No one could be long with him without being drawn to him. There was something in his smile and kindly look that made you lose sight of his homely face. He was a modest man and a grand companion, full of good humor and anecdote."

Charles Church Tyler

The cousins of Abraham Lincoln moved, a family at a time, from Grayson County, Ky., to Hancock County, Ill.[1] While the migration was going on letters passed between the relatives in the two states. They were written plainly, with here and there a lapse into phonetic spelling. A collection of these letters is in the possession of Mr. Charles Church Tyler of Fountain Green. Mr. Tyler is past 70, a splendid specimen of the Illinois pioneer. He was for his business lifetime the leading merchant of Fountain Green, a partner of the father of Robert W. McClaughrey, warden of the United States Penitentiary of Leavenworth, and penologist of international fame. Mr. Tyler retired from business some years ago, built "The Crow's Nest," a mansion of twenty rooms, in Fountain Green, and lives there, the confidant and the adviser of the whole community.[2] These letters and papers of the Lincolns were placed with him for safe-keeping. They are treasured with a roomful of other historical relics and reminders of early Illinois.

The first of the letters between the Lincolns, cousins of Abraham Lincoln, is dated "Leitchfield, Kentucky, January the 19th, 1831." That was about the time Abraham Lincoln was completing his rail-splitting job on the Hanks farm west of Decatur. This letter was from Mordecai Lincoln, who was still living in Kentucky, addressed to his brother, James B. Lincoln, who had settled in the community which was to become Fountain Green.[3] The reference in the letter to Abraham Lincoln is to the brother, not the cousin, of James and Mordecai. The letter was not inclosed in an envelope, but on the back of the folded sheet Mordecai Lincoln wrote plainly, "Mr. J. B. Lincoln, State of Illinois hancock county the head of the rapids." In the upper left-hand corner is written, "Litchfield, Ky., Jan'ry 28." In the upper right-hand corner is marked in ink the amount of postage paid, "25" cents. The remembrance of that postage was evidently in Mordecai's mind when he told the Illinois Lincolns, "you can all wright one letter."

The letter reads, without correction of the spelling:

Dear brother: I received your letter This evening baring date the 4th of Nov'm last which has been nearly three months on the road. I want you to wright to me again in the Spring as it is likely that the change in the ceason may make a change with father's complaint. I will want to hear from him about that time. We are all well and have been generally since Abm left hear.

You mentioned something in your letter about Montgomery. I have never saw Montgomery since Abraham left Grayson [County], nor I don't expect to see him shortly. So you had better secure your debt in the hands of Abraham in the way you mentioned in your letter to me. I mean out of the horse you spoke of.

Tell Abraham that no sooner was his back turned than J. Vertrees McFerren and others injoined the most of his money in the hands of the sheriff. I went down to Brownville and attended to the business and set aside the attachment tho it cost me three or four dollars. The sheriff had receipts which he produced that reduced the sum to about eighty dollars which I received and receipted to him for and have got the money now. After I had received the money I was garnisheed in twoo cases before I could get away from Brownville. So they detained me two days at the time, and when I got on my own side of Green River on my way home I felt like I was delivered, as it might be from purgatory. While I was there among them they would corcus about among one another, and presently would come Mr. Crump with a garnashee warrant. Well then we would go to trial and I would defeat them. So they would keep me warranted or rather attached all day and keep my ears distracted with their hypocritical prayers nearly all night, and God knows I was glad to get from among them for I dwoo not believe there ever was such another set of hypocritical scoundrels outside of eternal hell.

The very day that Abraham left the claylick fork of bearcreeke, jack Decker sold all his property to his son, bill. I warranted him on the notes I had in my hands. I bursted their sham sale and made the money out of his property and he now begs indulgence on the last payment and I think it would be best to stay the affair after Hart gets a Judgment by making him pay the Interest on the Commonwealths paper debt which would bee four or five dollars. And if Ben has a mind to dwoo so he had better wright to me and instruct me to have it don. It would bee to Bens advantage to dwoo so after we get a Judgment against him. I mean the Interest on the Commonwealths paper which I have collected. Commonwealths is 2 ½ discount now and has been all the fall and winter occasioned by a talk of a relone which has not taken place and we expect it will be nearly at pare by next September. An if ben has a mind to indulge decker on this termes let him wright.

I am always verry well myself. I get as much shoe making as I can dwoo for cash and a tolerable chance of constables business. So one is just a good recreation for the other. I think I am dwooing verry well. I spend the fewest idle hours that I ever did in my life. I am study busy. Nothing more but remain yours &c.

MORDECAI LINCOLN

You can all wright one letter.

[On outside of letter] "M. Lincoln J. Lincoln Ben Mudd And all their families and George Knisley and family

There have been presidents of the United States, several of them, who, in their younger days, did not write and spell better than did Mordecai Lincoln.

Besides the three brothers, James, Abraham and Mordecai Lincoln, who moved from Kentucky to Hancock County, there were sisters who were cousins of the famous Abraham Lincoln. One of the girls was [Mary] Rowena, who married the George Kneisley [Knisley] referred to by Mordecai in his letter.[4] Another was [Martha] Patsy Lincoln. She married George Washington Neighbours, who was living in Leitchfield some years after the rest of the Lincolns had moved to Hancock County.[5] A sister of Ben Mudd, referred to in the letter, was the wife of the Hancock County Abraham Lincoln.[6] The wife of James B. Lincoln, the first squire of Fountain Green, was Francis [Frances] Day, a sister of John Day, one of the pioneers who migrated with the Lincolns from their old home in Kentucky.[7] Between the Neighbors and the Lincolns correspondence was kept up. Two letters in the collection of Mr. Tyler are of more than ordinary interest in their relation to the Lincoln family history. Both were written by George W. Neighbours, the brother-in-law, one to James B. Lincoln and the other to Abraham Lincoln. They reveal the eccentricity, the strain of melancholy which had developed in the life of the other brother, Mordecai Lincoln. The first letter was from Leitchfield, dated "4th of September, 1836." It was addressed to "Abram Lincoln, Carthage Illinois." The custom of the Lincolns was to pronounce Abraham Lincoln as if it was spelled "Abr'm." George Neighbours wrote a flourishing business hand, using plenty of ink. He expressed himself clearly.

Dear sir: I received yours of the 18th of April, inclosing me a power of attn. ratifying the sale of your land. The sale is made good and the purchaser has possession of the premises and I am told is making a tolerable good crop of tobacco, which I hope will turn out well, as he is a poor man, but am in hopes an honest man. If so, I'll work the payments out of him. In your answer to this you will please let me know whether I shall keep the notes or inclose them to you. I have been writing ever since yours came to hand, but would still put it off thinking I would collect something of more importance to write. The season has been very fine here, which has given us a rarity (to-wit), good crops and fine white oak mast.

You will please write particularly how George comes on, and whether he is married or not, and Mary L. Mudd also. News reached us that she was married, but I have put no credance in the report, also helth and prosperity of the connections generally.

I can not close this letter without disclosing the painful circumstances of Mordecai's departure from this place, and request the earliest information of him you can give, not so much on my own account as Patsy's. She is in a delicate state of health and has been so during the summer, and it goes hard with her. He left here in the night as far as I am informed for I was not at home, being on a trip to Lexington with the sheriff assisting him to take a lunatic to the hospital at that place, and never heard anything of the circumstances until the 9th day after he left (on my arriving at home). What makes it the more strange I can't learn anything that happened nor can I conjure anything without it was a little pecuniary embarrassment that he could have got through in six months had he have stuck to the noble resolution he took six or seven months previous. I shall add nothing more but desire that our best respects be given to all the connections, particularly to Mother Lincoln in whose welfare I should like to contribute. Yours with esteem,

G. W. NEIGHBOURS

P.S.—I have layed out $1200.50 for land since I saw you.

"Patsy" referred to in the letter was the sister [Martha] of the three brothers, James, Abraham and Mordecai, and the wife of the writer of the letter. "Mother Lincoln" was the wife of President Lincoln's own uncle. She survived her husband several years, living with her sons in Hancock County.

Not hearing anything to relieve the distress of his wife about her brother, Geo. W. Neighbours, on the 29th of January, 1837, wrote to James B. Lincoln:

Dear friend: I have delayed writing to you in consequence of having but a short time previous to the reception of yours of September last wrote to Abram and requested an answer amediately for reason then assigned and will assign to you. Which was the misterious elopement of Mord. which has not caused me any particular uneasiness, but a member of my family that is very dear to me has suffered verry much which is Patsy. She was in delecate helth when he left and his departure with the many reports that followed seems to have affected her mentally as well as bodily. If he has not reached you please write for her sake, not that it would gratify me to hear from him, but on her account.

With regard to myself, I am wriding sheriff and carrying on my shop with two fires. Patsy wishes some of you to come in the Spring and bring Mother Lincoln with you to remain the summer as we have concluded to return the visit as soon as posable. Times are more lively here than I ever saw them (Money plenty and that thats good) Property high and a market for any and everything the farmer or mechanic has to spear.

You wrote me that Abram left home the 15th of June to return in 5 or 6 weeks and you had not herd from him at the date of your letter, which I am glad to be informed has turned out well as Mr. Jo Bratcher informs me.

I feel very sorry for your late affliction, the long lingering disease your youngest daughter has been afflicted with but feel in great hopes that long since she has been restored with good health in arms of affectionate father and mother. But if on the countrary she has left this life of peril you may rest assured she is in the embraces of the risen Savior.

I have nothing of a general nature that would entertain you. You will be so good as to give our compliments to the connections collectively after taking to yourself and lady a fair proportion. Write to me soon. Give all the particulars if any mariages or deaths that have taken place among any of our connection, what George is doing &c. &c. Yours with esteem.

G. W. NEIGHBOURS.

Mordecai Lincoln was the most interesting of the three cousins of President Lincoln. He left Kentucky suddenly in 1836 and joined the rest of the family in Hancock County, Ill., making a new home near Fountain Green. Mordecai never married. His "elopement," as his brother-in-law, George W. Neighbours, called it, was not with a woman, but, in some degree, on account of a woman. About the time that Abraham Lincoln, in Sangamon County, was going through the sorrow of Ann Rutledge's death, his cousin Mordecai was having an experience of another kind which embittered him against womankind. Later in life Mordecai wrote out the story telling how certain persons in Kentucky had conspired to get him married. Mordecai escaped the plotters; he left Leitchfield between two days. There was one element in the Kentucky town which mourned the departure of "Old Mord," as they called him, not because of age, but from familiarity. Mordecai Lincoln, like his illustrious cousin, was the friend of boys. He owned a house in town and lived by himself. The lower floor was his shoemaking and shoemending shop, and also his office while he was constable. Upstairs was his sleeping room. The small boys frequented the shop. Old Mord gave them little presents and entertained them. He had a fiddle, which was a wonderful instrument. The story the town told about that fiddle was that a revolutionary soldier made it from a piece of sugar-tree wood, having for his only tool a shoe knife. Summer nights Old Mord sat out in front of the house and made music to entertain all Leitchfield. Perhaps distance of time lent enchantment, but it is history that years after Mordecai's unceremonious disappearance Leitchfield people insisted they had never heard anybody play the fiddle equal to Mordecai Lincoln.

With his other worldly possessions, Mordecai Lincoln left his fiddle behind him when he departed from Leitchfield. People who had claims presented them, and all that Mordecai had accumulated was taken and distributed. The life of Mordecai became more eccentric after he settled a short distance from Fountain Green. There was nothing mean or ugly or dangerous about him. To this day the relatives remember that Mord would occasionally come to Grandfather Burrows' house, where there was a violin, enter without a word, pick up the instrument and walk the floor while he played, at the same time crying as if overcome with grief. The music and the spectacle was so melancholy that the womenfolks would cry also. After playing some time Mordecai would put down the violin, and without a word leave the house. The next time he came he would be pleasant and talkative. He was a man who read and wrote a great deal. He was very independent and rather resented advice from his acquaintances. On one occasion the neighborhood attempted to make a temperance man out of Mordecai Lincoln, although it does not appear that his habits were very bad. This effort to reform him prompted Mordecai to issue a formal statement of his position. He didn't date his manifesto from Fountain Green, but from "Jo Duncan," which was a hamlet two miles east. The letter was dated the 16th of August, 1843, and was addressed to one of the leading citizens of Fountain Green:

> Dear Sir—After leaving you yesterday, I felt it my duty to drop you a few
> lines in a neighborly way. You no that you began a conversation with me
> about the conduct of Mr. Langwell. You ast me several questions and I told
> you the truth so far as I went. You then expressed regret by saying that you
> hoped that Langwell, Davis and myself never would drink any more. But, sir,
> how could I hollow (hurra) for Walker all along the road from Nauvoo to
> Andrew Perkinses and to Ramus had I not have drank a we bit of a dram.
> And again, Langwell was preparing a gallos for Mordecai and how would he
> ever have got on it himself had I not have don all that I did do?
>
> As for your hopes or wishes with regard to me they dont interrupt my

mind at all. I claim it as my rite to drink anything I please to drink. And by the same rule I claim it as my wright if I think it best for myself to let it alone. But my dear sir I am of opinion that you would not have card anything about my drinking if Mordecai had have got on the gallos in place of Haman. Now, my good sir, all the hope you may have about me and all the good you can without disfurnishing yourself, and not hope to doo me any harm.

Now my good neighbor, for I can call you nothing else, you have some furniture around your own fireside whose near relationship entitles them to your prayerful hopes and attentions. And I think you should watch as well as hope and pray keep of temptations and tempters. While all I want you to do for me is what I have before stated (to wit) if any person acts mean towards me I dont want you to hope to excuse them at my expense. For instance, old Mrs. Cox acted mean about the grass and she was hope to do so and then they wanted to hope to excuse her. But I would not let them come it over me that way. And without they get somebody else to hope her she will just have to stand and help herself. This may not look so to you nor it may not look so to a man up a tree but all looks exactly so to me. With unchanged respect I remain yours as usual.

MORDECAI LINCOLN.

Mordecai Lincoln lived until after the civil war. He took great interest in the election of his Cousin Abraham in 1860. One day he entered the store of Mr. Tyler in Fountain Green and picked up a copy of Eugene Sue's "The Wandering Jew." He sat down and read for an hour. Then he asked the loan of the book, took it home and read it. The story made a powerful impression on Mordecai's mind. He talked about it. He quoted from it long passages, especially from Father Rodin. He talked and wrote much about "a conspiracy of Jesuits." Many of these Lincoln relatives in Hancock County are members of the Catholic Church. Mordecai Lincoln became incoherent upon the subject of religion, calling all Catholics "Jesuits." On everything but religion he was sensible.

Mordecai Lincoln had a big dog he called Grampus. He would say: "Cuss him, Grampus!" Thereupon Grampus would bark viciously, much to his master's delight.

Third, fourth, fifth and sixth cousins of President Lincoln are numerous in Hancock County. They are descended from the sons and daughters of Squire James Bloomfield [Bradford] Lincoln, the first cousin of Abraham Lincoln of Sangamon County. Among them are the Taylors and Lovelys and Edisons of Burnside, the Nelsons of Fountain Green, the McManus family of Carthage.[8]

The Hancock County cousins of President Lincoln gave him no trouble about the offices. They were interested in their distinguished relation, but not selfishly. They were numerous, but so far as is known at Fountain Green, not one of them filled a federal office. Robert Lincoln, the son of Abraham, who lived at Carthage, went on to Washington and saw the president. He had something in mind. President Lincoln suggested another place. Robert promptly declined what was offered, returned to Carthage and resumed his money lending business.

Mr. Tyler speaks most kindly of Mordecai Lincoln as a man with a remarkable memory, well informed, a good conversationalist and sensible upon all other topics but religion.

"Abraham Lincoln and James Lincoln," Mr. Tyler said, "I never knew personally. They were dead when I came to Illinois. They were both far above the average in natural ability and acquired considerable property for that day. They are still held in high esteem by the older living residents as being among the most desirable pioneers of Fountain Green."

Theophilus Van Deren

I had the pleasure of a conversation with Mr. Theophilus Van Deren,[1] of this city [Charleston], quite recently about the Lincoln and Douglas debate held here, the substance of which, as near as I remember, is as follows:

The Lincoln and Douglas debate attracted to our town the largest assemblage of people that I had ever before or have since then seen here, as it seemed that all of the streets, the highways leading in this direction, with long processions of persons in wagons, carriages and on horseback, with banners flapping in the breeze, were densely packed; and as to the Fair Ground, where the speeches were delivered, it appeared to be filled with a breathing, earnest mass of humanity, with every one of the thousands eager to hear the orators, and in an effort to occupy a position as near as possible to the speaker's stand. Many persons were here from various parts of the State—from Decatur, Sullivan, Shelbyville, Paris, and even from the City of Chicago.

Notwithstanding the intense political excitement, and the usual party prejudice manifested on such occasions, perfect order and harmony prevailed; and I do not think we had a policeman at the meeting, or that we even had such an officer in Charleston. The Democrats and Republicans had, by agreement, appointed as Marshal of the Day Dr. W. M. Chambers, of this place, and who filled the office without partiality, with honor to himself and to the entire satisfaction of all right-minded citizens; though the Doctor told me, a few days since, that Mr. Douglas, in one of his subsequent speeches, referred to him—Chambers—as Lincoln's lieutenant at Charleston; and if Mr. Douglas did so it is evident that he believed the Doctor to be more in sympathy with Mr. Lincoln than with him, and the doctrine which "The Little Giant" advocated; for the Doctor, as well as Mr. Lincoln, had been, previous to that time, an old-time Henry Clay Whig. When I tell you that the Hon. O. B. Ficklin and other prominent citizens occupied seats on the stand, back of the speakers, you must not infer that those were the only distinguished individuals present; for there were numbers of others scattered promiscuously in the vast assembly; and I remember well to have stood beside Gov. Oglesby while Mr. Lincoln was speaking. On passing out through the south gate of the Fair Grounds I saw Mr. Lincoln approaching, accompanied by a number of his warm political friends, and it struck me that I had never seen him appear so tall as on that occasion, and then, in addition to his natural height, he had on a high stove-pipe silk hat which caused him to tower, in appearance, a head and shoulders above those men who surrounded him.

When he entered the gate he was covered from head to foot with dust; his dark suit of clothes, white shirt collar, his hair, eyebrows and cheerful face were, with his silk hat, what might be called a good drab color; but when he spoke, and his usual smile lighted up his countenance, he came back as natural as ever to my memory. Coles County being the home of Mr. Lincoln's father and mother and many other relatives, he did not feel himself a stranger at Charleston; and as he had for many years as a lawyer attended our courts, his acquaintance with our people was very extensive, being universally beloved by even the most bitter partisans; for if he had a personal enemy in this community no one is conscious of the fact.

On arriving at Charleston Mr. and Mrs. Douglas put up at the Bunnel House, where the day after, it being Sabbath, they were visited by a number of gentlemen and ladies, among whom were Hon. O. B. Ficklin and wife, Dr. W. M. Chambers, my brother Dumas J. Van Deren and wife, and myself; but we had scarcely seated ourselves and entered into pleasant conversation when Capt. Sam Goodrich, a man thoroughly versed in the good old-fashioned Illinois dialect, and a great admirer of Mr. Douglas, knocked at the door and said that he wished to see Mr. and Mrs. Douglas, and, his desire having been gratified by an introduction to both, he, addressing himself to Mr.

Douglas, entered into a complete history of his (Sam's) life from infancy to that day. He gave Mr. Douglas to understand that he was from his childhood as well acquainted with Gen. Jackson as with anybody. "Why, Mr. Douglas," said he, "my daddy use to keep tavern on the road the Gineral traveled, and many's the time the old man's tuck me twix his legs and patted me on the head. Yes, sir!" Uncle Sam entertained us the greater part of the evening, having the floor without limit to himself, and shown great respect by Mr. Douglas until the company separated.

Mr. John Ginn, of Moultrie County, a warm friend of Mr. Douglas, had come over with his horses and carriage for the purpose of conveying Mr. and Mrs. Douglas to Sullivan, the county site of Moultrie, at which place, I think, the next debate was to be held, and they arrived at Mattoon in good time for supper and there remained until the next morning. And having myself accompanied the Douglas party to Mattoon, we were together until a late hour that Sabbath night, and though I had met Mr. Douglas several times before, I felt that I had never appreciated the man as he deserved to be, but had regarded him as a shrewd politician—honest as most politicians, whose principal aim is to become popular, and thus to keep in office.

As on that bright, clear and beautiful night Mr. Douglas and I sat alone on the balcony of the Pennsylvania House, looking northward over the grand prairie, with Donati's comet lighting up the clear blue sky, he justified his course and opposition to the Administration of Mr. Buchanan, and I was enabled to see matters differently from what I had before.

Appendix 1

Mrs. Benjamin S. Edwards's Recollections of Abraham Lincoln and Mary Todd

I was so indignant with Mr. Herndon, for the falsity of his statement with regard to Mr. Lincoln's marriage.[1] I am impatient to tell you that all that he says about this wedding—the time for which was "fixed for the first day of January"—is all a fabrication.[2] He has drawn largely upon his imagination in describing something, which never took place.

I know the engagement between Mr. Lincoln and Miss Todd was interrupted for a time, and it was rumored among her young friends that Mr. [Ninian] Edwards had rather opposed it. (Of that I cannot speak with any certainty, but his visits to Mr. E's house ceased and they met at the house of a mutual friend—Mrs. Simeon Francis—whose husband, I think, was the first editor of the *Springfield Journal*) but I am sure there had been no "time fixed" for any wedding, that is no preparations had ever been made until the day that Mr. Lincoln met Mr. Edwards in the street and told him that he and Mary were going to be married that evening. Upon enquiry Mr. L said they would be married in the Episcopal Church to which Mr. E replied—"No, Mary is my ward—and she must be married at my house."

He went home to make the announcement to his wife to whom it came as a *shock*—and surprise.

He then came over to my home—to give an invitation—which was in these words—"My wife wants you all to come to our house this evening"—I enquired what is going on? Then he gave the particulars of his having Mr. Lincoln, etc., adding, "I left Elizabeth crying—but Mrs. Levering (their near neighbor) has gone in to see if she can help her."

Mrs. Edwards told me afterward what a shock the news was to her, and how hurt she had been at Mary's want of confidence in her. She said that after she was composed enough to see Mary and talk with her about it, she seemed very much disinclined to say anything of it, only, when she said "Mary, you have not given me much time to prepare much of a wedding entertainment for our friends. I shall have to send to old Dickey—(the only bakery in town)—for some ginger bread and beer"—jokingly. Mary with

an indignant tip of her head, said—"Well that is good enough for plebe-
ians, I suppose."

This word—it seems—Mr. Edwards, in his very early acquaintance
with Mr. Lincoln[,] had used in giving his opinion of Mr. L, and Mary had
not forgotten it.

If I remember rightly the wedding guests were few, not more than thirty,
and it seems to me all are gone now but Mrs. Wallace, Mrs. Levering and
myself, for it was not much more than a family gathering[;] only two or
three of Mary Todd's young friends were present. The "entertainment"
was simple, but in beautiful taste (for Mrs. Edwards was a notable housekeeper), but the bride had neither veil nor flowers in her hair, with which to
"toy nervously." There had been no elaborate trousseau, for the bride of
the future president of the United States, nor even a handsome wedding
gown, nor was it a gay wedding.

. . . I do not know that I have made things very clear to you, dear Miss
Tarbell, only, I know Mr. Herndon's story is all untrue. I have often
doubted that it was really a love affair between Mr. L and Mary T, but
think it was through mutual friends (?) that the marriage was made up (in
common parlance).

He was deeply in love with Matilda Edwards, a daughter of Mr. Cyrus
E., brother of Gov. E, but the father objected, and it was then, (I heard) that
he almost lost his reason.[3]

Appendix 2

The Accuracy of Newspaper Accounts of the
1858 *Lincoln-Douglas Debates*

In 1858, two Chicago newspapers, the Democratic *Times* and the Republican *Press and Tribune,* employed shorthand reporters to record the words of Stephen A. Douglas and Abraham Lincoln during their seven debates.[1] The Republicans chose Robert R. Hitt, a twenty-four-year-old graduate of Asbury University in Greencastle, Indiana (later renamed Depauw University). Raised in Mount Morris, Illinois, Hitt attended the Rock River Seminary, which his father, the Rev. Thomas S. Hitt, and his uncle helped to found.[2] At the age of fourteen, he became intrigued by "phonetic reform" and taught himself the art of shorthand. "The first fruitful use of it," he later recalled, "was in taking notes of lectures at college. With a little shorthand skill one could distance other students in obtaining credit marks with the professor lecturing, for he naturally thought a student who showed unusual or precise knowledge of his lectures worthy of good marks." After graduating from college, Hitt in 1856 traveled to New Orleans, where medical students offered him large sums to record lectures by an eminent physician. Though too unsure of himself to accept the challenge, he realized that a shorthand reporter could earn a comfortable living and worked hard to improve his command of the then-rare skill. In the autumn of 1857 Hitt moved to Chicago and pursued a career as a law reporter and journalist.[3] According to one source, at the time he "was the only representative of the shorthand art in the Northwest."[4]

That fall Lincoln came to know and admire Hitt's work during the Rock Island Bridge case and the following year hired him to record the debates with Douglas.[5] Early in 1861 Lincoln, who described Hitt as "about the only man he had ever known in his life connected with newspapers in whose honesty he fully believed," asked the young stenographer to accompany him to Washington. "He treated me with the utmost kindness, almost like a father," Hitt wrote at the time.[6] Because of a commitment to cover the Illinois legislature, Hitt declined the offer, but later that year he accepted the post of secretary of the commission which scrutinized John C. Fremont's administration of affairs in Missouri. In 1863 Hitt served as secretary to a U.S. Senate committee investigating naval expeditions led by General Ambrose E. Burnside, and two years later he played a similar role for a commission which negotiated with Indians at the headwaters of the Missouri River. Immediately after the war he worked as a stenographer for military courts in North Carolina and Washington, and in 1871–72 he was secretary to the Congressional Committee investigating the Ku Klux Klan. In 1874 President Grant named him secretary of the American legation in Paris, a post he held for six years. In 1881 he became assistant secretary of state to James G. Blaine, and the following year he won election to the U.S. House of Representatives, where he gained renown as an expert on foreign relations.[7]

Hitt's counterpart for the *Chicago Times* was provided by the editor of the *Philadelphia Press,* John W. Forney, who championed Douglas's cause during the acrimonious fight over the Lecompton, Kansas, Constitution in 1857–58. Forney dispatched one of his shorthand reporters, James B. Sheridan, to aid the Little Giant; the management of the *Chicago Times,* realizing his value, employed him to cover the debates. Sheridan was assisted by Henry Binmore, a twenty-five-year-old native of England who had been a journalist in Montreal, St. Louis and New York. In 1858 the *Missouri Republican* (St. Louis) assigned him to cover Douglas's return to Chicago from Washington. Senator Douglas hired Binmore to help Sheridan; during the debates the latter took down the Senator's remarks while the former recorded the words of the challenger.[8] For the *Press and Tribune* Hitt covered both candidates.

Each paper accused the other of doctoring Lincoln's language. The *Times* claimed that "the Republicans have a candidate for the Senate of whose bad rhetoric and horrible jargon they are ashamed," and that "they called a council of 'literary' men, to discuss, re-construct and re-write" Lincoln's words before allowing them to be printed, for "they dare not allow Lincoln to go into print in his own dress."[9] Those who had heard Lincoln's public addresses, the *Times* remarked, "must know that he cannot speak five grammatical sentences in succession."[10]

The *Press and Tribune* indignantly protested that "[i]f mutilating public discourses were a criminal offence, the scamp whom Douglas hires to report Lincoln's speeches would be a ripe subject for the Penitentiary. . . . Mr. Lincoln's remarks at Galesburg are shamefully and outrageously garbled. Hardly a sentence he uttered has escaped defacement. Not a paragraph has been fairly reported, from the commencement to the conclusion of his speech. Some of his finest passages are disemboweled, and chattering nonsense substituted in their stead." The Republican journal went on to allege that the *Times'* stenographer "undoubtedly defaced and garbled" Lincoln's remarks at the "express orders" of Douglas himself.[11] A Republican newspaper in Galesburg, speaking of the debate in that town, complained of "long passages, where the *Times'* reporter appeared to aim only at the sense, without giving the language" of Lincoln. It maintained that "[t]here is scarcely a correctly reported paragraph in the whole speech! Many sentences are dropped out which were absolutely necessary for the sense; many are transposed so as to read wrong end first; many are made to read exactly the opposite of the orator's intention."[12]

The charge that Douglas ordered the *Times* to misrepresent Lincoln's words is unproven, but during the first debate he certainly did misrepresent Lincoln's role in framing a radical antislavery platform four years earlier. In his closing remarks at Ottawa, the Senator read some resolutions adopted by militant abolitionists in 1854 at Aurora, Illinois, and charged (wrongly) that they had been drafted by Lincoln at the Republican state convention.[13] Hitt exposed the error. As he later recalled, "The discovery was accidentally made by me in writing out my notes, as I took down the resolutions for a time as Judge Douglas was reading them, but observing that he had them before him in print and not doubting that I could readily procure the printed text, I seized the moment for a brief rest from the hard work of that hot day. From that [point] on I took down only the opening and closing lines of the second and third resolutions, but Judge Douglas going away immediately, and I being compelled to take the train quickly, I did not get the printed resolutions, and on coming to write them out I requested the editors of the *Press and Tribune,* Dr. Ray and Mr. Scripps, to look in the files for the easily-ascertained resolutions indicated in my notes. They were soon found, and proved to be resolutions adopted at a meeting held in Aurora." Douglas's friends assured Hitt that the Senator had made an honest mistake, but Douglas himself never said so and "never gave any satisfactory explanation."[14]

The *Times'* account of Lincoln's words certainly is more garbled than the *Press and Tribune*'s. Here are some examples:

> *Times*: the proper question to consider, when we are legislating about a new country which is not *at ready to be beset* with the actual presence of slavery.[15]
>
> *Press and Tribune*: the abstract moral question, to contemplate and consider when we are legislating about any new country which is not *already cursed* with the actual presence of the evil, slavery.

Times: an opportunity has already been afforded, to see our respective views upon a large portion of the speech, *which has not been addressed to you.*[16]

Press and Tribune: There has been an opportunity afforded to the public to see our respective views upon the topics discussed in a large portion of the speech which *he has just delivered.*

Times: All these things were put together and although passed in separate acts as they were, they were nevertheless, as the speeches made upon them will show, made to *defend the one or the other.*[17]

Press and Tribune: All these things were put together and though passed in separate acts, were, nevertheless, in legislation (as the speeches at the time will show) made to *depend on each other.*

Times: But meanwhile the three are *all glad that* an endorsement of his truths and honor by a re-election to the United States Senate.[18]

Press and Tribune: But meanwhile the three are *agreed that each is "a most honorable man."* Judge Douglas requires an indorsement of his truth and honor by a re-election to the United States Senate.

Equally striking are the numerous passages where the *Times* gives a condensed version of the *Press and Tribune*'s text of Lincoln's remarks. Here are some examples of the way that the *Times* compressed Lincoln's remarks at Galesburg:

Times: I have to trust to a reading community to judge whether I advance just views, or whether I state views that are revolutionary or hypocritical.[19]

Press and Tribune: I take it I have to address an intelligent and reading community, who will peruse what I say, weigh it, and then judge whether I advance hypocritical, and deceptive, and contrary views in different portions of the country.

Times: I have insisted that in legislating for a new country where slavery does not exist, there is no just rule other than that of pure morality and pure abstract right.[20]

Press and Tribune: I have never manifested any impatience with the necessities that spring from the actual presence of black people amongst us, and the actual existence of slavery amongst us where it does already exist; but I have insisted that, in legislating for new countries where it does not exist, there is no rule other than that of moral and abstract right!

Times: Judge Douglas turns away from that task.[21]

Press and Tribune: Judge Douglas turns away from the platform of principles to the fact that he can find people somewhere who will not allow us to announce those principles.

Times: Now I have all the while made a wide distinction between this.[22]

Press and Tribune: Now, I have all the while taken a broad distinction in regard to that matter; and that is all there is in these different speeches will show that distinction was made.

Times: I have all the while maintained that insofar as there is a physical inequality between the white and black, that the blacks must remain inferior.[23]

Press and Tribune: I have all the while maintained that insofar as it should be insisted that there was an equality between the white and black races that should produce a perfect social and political equality, it was an impossibility. This you have seen in my printed speeches.

Times: I feel, having regard to all constitutional guards thrown around it, that I do nevertheless desire a policy that shall prevent the enlargement of it.[24]

Press and Tribune: I feel, having regard for its actual existence amongst us and the difficulties of getting rid of it in any satisfactory way, and to all constitutional guards thrown around it, that I do nevertheless desire a policy that shall prevent the enlargement of it as a wrong.

It seems highly unlikely that Lincoln uttered the passages of gibberish and nonsense quoted above from the *Times*. In part the garbling can be explained easily, for transcription blunders hardly bothered the reporters and their editors, who naturally cared more about producing a coherent version of Douglas's remarks than Lincoln's. Horace White, a journalist who accompanied Lincoln on the debate trail, later absolved the Democratic shorthand reporters of the charge of willfully mutilating Lincoln's remarks:

> Sheridan and Binmore took more pains with Mr. Douglas's speeches than with those of his opponent. That was their business. It was what they were paid for, and what they were expected to do. The debates were all held in the open air, on rude platforms hastily put together, shaky, and overcrowded with people. The reporters' tables were liable to be jostled and their manuscript agitated by the wind. Some gaps were certain to occur in the reporters' notes and these, when occurring in Mr. Douglas's speeches, would certainly be straightened out by his own reporters, who would feel no such responsibility for the rough places in Mr. Lincoln's.[25]

Despite White's contention, there is reason to credit the *Press and Tribune*'s charge that the *Times* deliberately mangled Lincoln's words to make him seem inarticulate. Hitt believed that to be the case, as the account he gave to Walter B. Stevens indicates.[26] Hitt was in a good position to know if Binmore deliberately falsified Lincoln's words. Binmore and Hitt had first met in September 1857, during the trial of the Rock Island Bridge case in Chicago. They did not see each other again until July 7, 1858, when Binmore, who was writing abusive articles about the Republican party for the *Missouri Republican,* asked to go into partnership with Hitt. Understandably Hitt felt some reluctance, for Binmore's appearance inspired little confidence. He wore "an old battered wool hat" and "winter clothing though the weather was hot." Moreover, he "was not too nice in his linen and generally looked seedy." Hitt grew more suspicious when Binmore, in quest of cigars, "asked for the loan of a quarter," explaining that "he had nothing but a hundred dollar check with him."[27]

Nevertheless, when the *Press and Tribune* asked Hitt to cover Stephen A. Douglas's speech on July 9, the young man enlisted Binmore's assistance and together they managed to transcribe their notes in time for the morning edition, much to the delight of the management and the astonishment of the city. The next day they collaborated on a report of Lincoln's speech in Chicago. At Binmore's urging, they "formed a partnership after a certain fashion," which lasted till late July, when Douglas hired Binmore "to go around with him throughout the canvass and report when necessary, but principally to occupy himself with writing letters to various papers throughout the state and managing others into silence, to assist in every possible way the election of Douglas." Two years later Hitt and Binmore resumed their partnership as they covered the 1860 Republican national convention in Chicago and the sessions of the state legislature in Springfield the following winter.[28]

Hitt was thus well qualified to judge Binmore, whom he called "a complete little fop and a fool" with "no common sense," a man "hard to get along with" and "always needy."[29] More tellingly, Hitt considered Binmore a liar: "I have . . . seldom known Binmore to tell the truth about his family."[30] Hitt disliked Binmore's "fondness for telling stories about his connections, the amounts of money he has made and the familiarity of his acquaintance with every great man ever named in his presence," all of which caused Hitt "to place but little confidence in many of his assertions." With evident irritation, Hitt recorded that "[n]o land can be mentioned in his presence but he has been there and is perfectly familiar with the greatest men in the country."[31]

Another journalist, Sylvanus Cadwallader, portrayed Binmore unflatteringly. In August 1863, while covering Grant's army for the *Chicago Times,* Cadwallader visited General Stephen Hurlbut's Memphis headquarters, where Binmore was serving as an adjutant. In his memoirs, Cadwallader described Binmore as "a little red-headed English dude or Cockney." When Cadwallader suggested that General Hurlbut's order forbidding him to transmit stories to his paper was perhaps an oversight (Hurlbut had rescinded such a ban earlier), Binmore snapped that "nothing is ever overlooked or forgotten in this office" and threatened Cadwallader with arrest. Beating a hasty retreat, Cadwallader made inquiries about Binmore and "collected a bundle of damaging facts in writing," which included evidence that Binmore had taken an "abandoned woman" from Chicago to Memphis, where he introduced her to Mrs. Hurlbut as his wife; that he refused to pay his laundry bills in Memphis; that he had behaved disreputably in Cairo. Subsequently Binmore was expelled from the service and returned to Chicago to work again for the *Times.* There Cadwallader found that he "was heartily despised by all who knew him but had been engaged on the *Times* as an expert stenographer."[32]

It does not strain credulity to believe that such a man would deliberately misreport the words of Lincoln in 1858.

Even if Binmore had been a model of integrity and had tried to render Lincoln's words accurately, his account would still be untrustworthy, for he could not keep pace with the Republican candidate. According to Hitt, Lincoln, unlike Douglas, was not a speaker easy to cover. Contrasting Douglas's speech of July 9 and Lincoln's of the following day, Hitt confided to his journal that "Douglas spoke slowly, emphatically, delivering each word in a deep bass voice, and with a round fullness that could leave no mistake as to his meaning. Such a speaker it was easy and delightful to report, but Lincoln has a voice that is almost shrill, it is so clear, and he speaks rapidly." Hitt noted that

> so fast did his words follow each other that it was with the utmost difficulty that I could follow him and I was aware all the time that I was not writing my notes in such a neat and legible style as with Douglas. Besides, his sentences were not finished and harmonious like those of Douglas but broken with endless explanations and qualifications and parentheses, which made it difficult to write or read it. Often he repeated what he had to say two or three times and each time qualified it in some new way. His mind seems to be one

of excessive caution and no statement that he makes will he suffer to go forth without a qualification that will prevent all misunderstanding, but which at the same time destroyed [deprived] the statement of its vigorous and independent tone.[33]

Hitt and Binmore both took down Lincoln's July 10 speech in shorthand. The following day, Hitt helped Binmore transcribe his notes and discovered that "there was much matter that Binmore had omitted in his report. These passages were just where I remember Lincoln spoke the fastest."[34] This contemporary evidence suggests that Binmore's version of Lincoln's words in the debates is hardly trustworthy, even if one accepts Horace White's assertion that there was no attempt by either Binmore or the editors of the *Times* to misrepresent them.

The *Press and Tribune* editors touched up their accounts of Lincoln's remarks slightly, as Horace White later acknowledged, "where confusion on the platform, or the blowing of the wind, had caused some slight hiatus or evident mistake in catching the speaker's words." White also italicized passages where Lincoln's "manner of delivery had been especially emphatic."[35] Lincoln himself "never saw the report of any of the debates before printing."[36] Hitt probably did not tamper with the text, for he usually turned his notes over to an assistant named Larminie and first viewed the transcripts of his handiwork when they appeared in print.[37] Whatever cosmetic surgery the Republican editors may have performed, it surely did far less violence to the text than did the carelessness, incapacity, and partisan malice of the *Times*'s reporter and editors. Readers seeking the most authentic texts of Lincoln's words during the debates should consult the version reported in the *Press and Tribune*, not the version reported in the *Times*.[38]

Appendix 3

Lincoln's Meeting with the Missouri Radicals, September 30, 1863

In the Nicolay-Hay Papers at the Illinois State Historical Library the follow-ing notes of the meeting, taken by John Hay and William O. Stoddard, are preserved. The opening pages are by Hay.

The Delegation from Missouri and Kansas arrived here last week and have been preparing their address for some days with care and labor. This morning, Wednesday the 30th of September at 10:30 a.m., Jim Lane & C. D. Drake came up stairs and announced that the Delegation was wait-ing below. They were ushered into the East Room by my order and the re-porters for the Press excluded. The President delaying for a few moments Jim took me down to see the little army as he styled it, and we found them ranged along three sides of the East Room, the North End being open. He introduced me to several of the sovereigns and we waited for the President. The men were simply representative men from Missouri not better than the average. The frowziness of the ungodly Pike was there though it was a decenter and quieter crowd than would have come in the old days of the border murders. An ill combed, black broadcloth, dusty, longhaired and generally vulgar assemblage of earnest men who came to get their right as they viewed it. They say things are in a bad way out there and they came here, a little vaguely, for redress.

The President came in and walked up the hollow square to the South end he faced and stood, straighter than usual. Mr Drake of St. Louis said, "Gentlemen! I have the profound honor of presenting you the President of the United States." The President bowed and the earnest Pikes bowed, stiffly, but with unmistakable respectfulness: legs that thrust out back-ward, some scraping some awkward spreading of the hands: & the Pikes stood erect again, stern and ruminant. An abortive attempt at clapping which expired in its youth. Drake said Mr Prest. we came for purpose of presenting a statement of fact and making certain requests, embodied in an address I hold in my hand. Will it please to hear it now? "It will!" said Pres.

and Mr Drake read the address. After Mr Drake had finished the reading of his address the President said:

I suppose the committee now before me is the culmination of a movement inaugurated by a Convention held in Missouri last month, and is intended to give utterance to their well considered views on public affairs in that state. The purpose of this delegation has been widely published and their progress to the city everywhere noticed. It is not therefore to be expected that I shall reply hurriedly to your address. It would not be consistent either with a proper respect for you, or a fair consideration of the subject involved to give you a hasty answer. I will take your address, carefully consider it and read at my earliest convenience. I shall consider it, without partiality for or prejudice against any man or party: no painful memories of the past and no hopes for the future, personal to myself, shall hamper my judgment.

There are some matters which you have discussed upon which my impressions are somewhat decided, in regard to which I will say a few words, reserving the privilege of changing my opinion even upon these, upon sufficient evidence.

You have alluded to an expression I used in a letter to General Schofield, characterizing your troubles in Missouri as a "pestilential factional quarrel". You do not relish the expression but let me tell you that Govr. Gamble likes it still less. He has written me a letter complaining of it so bitterly that on the representation of my private Secretary I declined reading it & sent a note to him informing him that I would not.

You have much to say in regard to Govr. Gamble's position. You will remember that at the very beginning of the War, your own Governor being disloyal, you elected a Convention, a large majority of whom were Union members, for whom I suppose you yourselves voted. There were at that time no dissentions among Union men in your state. Your convention elected Mr Gamble Governor in place of the disloyal incumbent, seemingly with the universal assent of the Union people of the State. At that time Governor Gamble was considered, and naturally so, the Representative of the loyalty of Missouri. As such he came to Washington, to request the Assistance and support of the general government in the organization of a state militia force. It was considered here a matter of importance: it was discussed in a meeting of the Cabinet, and an arrangement which seemed satisfactory was finally made. No one doubted the proper intentions of those who planned it. The only doubt was whether the arrangement could be properly carried out— whether this Imperium in Imperio would not breed confusion. Several times since [then] Governor Gamble has endeavored to have the troops raised on this basis transferred to the exclusive control of the state. This I have invariably refused. If any new arrangement has been made of enrolling State troops independently of the general government I am not yet aware of it. Such organizations exist in some of the states. I have no more right to interfere with them in Missouri than elsewhere. If they are consistent with your state laws I cannot prevent them. If not, you should redress your proper wrong. I will however give this subject as presented by you, careful consideration.

I am sorry you have not been more specific in the statements you have seen fit to make about Gen. Schofield. I had heard in advance of your coming that a part of your mission was to protest against his administration & I thought I should hear some definite statements of grievances instead of the vague denunciations which are so easy to make and yet so unsatisfactory. But I have been disappointed. If you could tell me what Gen Schofield has done that he should not have done, or what omitted that he should have done, your case would be plain. You have on the contrary only accused him vaguely of sympathy with your enemies. I cannot act on vague impressions. Show me that he has disobeyed orders: show me that he has done something wrong & I will take your request for his removal into serious consideration. He has never protested against an order—never neglected a duty with which he has been entrusted so far as I know. When Gen. Grant was struggling in Mississippi and needed reinforcement no man was so active and efficient in sending him troops as Gen. Schofield. I know nothing to his disadvantage. I am not personally acquainted with him. I have with him no personal relations. If you will allege a definite wrongdoing & having clearly made your point, prove it, I shall remove him.

You object to his order on my recent proclamation suspending the privilege of the writ of Habeas Corpus. I am at a loss to see why an order executing my own official decree should be made a ground of accusation to me against the officer issuing it. You object to its being used in Missouri. In other words that which is right when employed against yr. opponents is wrong when employed against yourselves. Still I will consider that.

You object to his muzzling the press. As to that, I think when an officer in any department finds that a newspaper is pursuing a course calculated to embarrass his operations and stir up sedition and tumult, he has the right to lay hands upon it and suppress it, but in no other case. I approved the order in question after the Missouri Democrat had also approved it.

(*Mem[ber of the] Del[egation.]*) "We thought it was then to be used against the other side."

[*President.*] "Certainly you did. Your ideas of justice seem to depend upon the application of it.

"You have spoken of the consideration which you think I should pay to my friends as contradistinguished from my enemies. I suppose of course that you mean by that those who agree or disagree with me in my views of public policy. I recognize no such thing as a political friendship personal to myself. You insist upon adherence to the policy of the proclamation of Emancipation as a test of such political friendship. You will remember that your State was once excluded from the operation of that decree by its express terms. The Proclamation can therefore have no direct bearing upon your state politics. Yet you seem to insist that it shall be made as vital a question as if it had. You seem to be determined to have it executed there."

[*Delegate.*] "No sir, but we think it a national test question."

[*President.*] "You are then determined to make an issue with men who may not agree with you upon the abstract question of the propriety of that act of mine. Now let me say that I, who issued that proclamation after more thought on the subject than probably any one of you have been able to give it, believe it to be right and expedient. I am better satisfied with those who believe with me in this than with those who hold differently. But I am free to say that many good men, some earnest Republicans, and some from very far North, were opposed to the issuing of that Proclamation holding it unwise and of doubtful legality. Now when you see a man loyally in favor of the Union—willing to vote men and money—spending his time and money and throwing his influence into the recruitment of our armies—I think it ungenerous unjust and impolitic to make his views on abstract political questions a test of his loyalty. I will not be a party to this application of a pocket Inquisition.

You are aware of movements in the North of a different character—interfering with the draft—discouraging recruiting—weakening the war spirit—striving in all possible ways to weaken the Government merely to secure a partizan triumph. I do not take the party of your opponents in Missouri to be engaged in this line of conduct."

Del. "They are."

[*President.*] "In a civil war one of the saddest evils is suspicion. It poisons the springs of social life. It is the fruitful parent of injustice and strife. Were I to make a rule that in Missouri disloyal men were outlawed and the rightful prey of good citizens as soon as the rule should begin to be carried into effect I would be overwhelmed with affidavits to prove that the first man killed under it was more loyal than the one who killed him. It is impossible to determine the question of the motives that govern men, or to gain absolute knowledge of their sympathies."

Del. "Let the loyal people judge."

Prest. "And who shall say who the loyal people are? You ask the disfranchisement of all disloyal people: but difficulties will environ you at every step in determining the questions which will arise in that matter. A vast number of Missourians who have at some time aided the rebellion will wish to return to their homes and resume their peaceful avocations. Even if you would, you cannot keep them all away. You have your state laws regulating the qualifications of voters. You must stand by those till you yourselves alter them."

Del. "Are we to be protected at the polls in carrying out these laws?"

Prest. "I will order Gen. Schofield to protect you at the polls and save them from illegal interference. He will do it you may be assured. If he does not I will relieve him."

Jim Lane at this point burst in boisterously, "Do you think it sufficient cause for the removal of a General, that he has lost the entire confidence of the people."

Presdt. "I think I should not consider it a sufficient cause if he had lost that confidence unjustly, it would [not] be a very strong reason for his removal."

Lane. "General Schofield has lost that confidence."

Presdt. "You being judge!"

A confused murmur of delegates all crying in chorus, confirmation of Lane's statements.

The President very quickly said, "I am in possession of facts that convince me that Gen Schofield has not lost the confidence of the entire people of Missouri."

Delegates. "All loyal people."

Prest. "You being the standard of loyalty."

Lane. "There are no parties and no factions in Kansas—*All* our people demand his removal."

"The massacre of Lawrence, is in the opinion of the people of Kansas, solely due to the embicility of Gen. Schofield."

Prest. "As to that, it seems to me that is a thing which could be done by any one making up his mind to the consequences, and could no more be guarded against than assassination. If I make up my mind to kill you for instance, I can do it and [three?] hundred gentleman could not prevent it. They could avenge but could not save you."

A member from the interior then felt called on to say something and said it. He began in a quiet hesitating way but gradually warmed up with his subject and bellowed like a mad bull, about "the sufferings me and the rest of the board suffers, with the guerillas achasing of us, and we a writing to Mr.

Scovil for help & he not giving it to us, so we couldnt collect the broken
bonds."

Prest. "Who's *us*?" (very quietly but evidently desiring information.)

Del. "The *Board*." (As if that word would strike all questioning dumb.)

Presdt. "What board" (not struck dumb apparently.)

Del. "The Board for collecting the broken bonds." (getting a little nervous
again.)

Presdt. "Who appointed you & by what law, & how were you acting & by
what right did you ask a military force from Gen. Schofield?"

These questions completed the ruin of the unhappy commissioner & he
floundered in a maze of hopeless explanation, which represented him as a
sportive and happy free plunderer on the estates of misguided traitors
passing his time in rapid alternation from stealing secesh cattle to running
from guerillas.

Another plethoric gentleman wailed gloomily for a quarter of an hour
over scenes of cruelty he and a number of his friends had witnessed in their
town and had not the manhood to prevent.

In every instance, a question or two from the President pricked the bal-
loon of loud talk and collapsed it around the ears of the delegate to his no
small disgust and surprise. The baffled patriot would retreat to a sofa &
think the matter over again or would stand in his place and quietly listen in
a bewildered manner to the talk and discomfiture of another.

I was compelled to leave for a little while. When I returned the delegation had departed. I instructed Mr. S[toddard] to take notes in my absence.
He immediately developed them and they are as follows: They contain, he
says only the language of the President.

In reply to an assertion that "We are your friends and the Conservatives
are not" the Presdt. said:

These so called Conservatives will avoid, as a general thing, votes, or any action, which will in any way interfere with or imperil, the success of their
party. For instance they will vote for supplies, and such other measures as are
absolutely necessary to sustain the Government. They will do this selfishly.
They do not wish that the Government should fall, for they expect to obtain
possession of it. At the same time their support will not be hearty: their votes
are not equal to those of the real friends of the Administration. They do not
give so much strength. They are not worth so much. My Radical friends will
therefore see that I understand and appreciate their position. Still you appear
to come before me as my friends *if I agree with you, but not otherwise.* I do

not here speak of mere personal friendship, as between man and man,—when I speak of my friends I mean those who are friendly to my measures, to the policy of the government.

I am well aware that by many, by some even among this delegation,—I shall not name them,—I have been in public speeches and in printed documents charged with "tyranny" and willfulness, with a disposition to make my own personal will supreme. I do not intend to be a tyrant. At all events I shall take care that in my own eyes I do not become one. I shall always try and preserve one friend within me, whoever else fails me, to tell me that I have not been a tyrant, and that I have acted right. I have no right to act the tyrant to mere political opponents. If a man votes for supplies of men and money; encourages enlistments; discourages desertions; does all in his power to carry the war on to a successful issue,—I have no right to question him for his abstract political opinions. I must make a dividing line, some where, between those who are the opponents of the Government and those who only oppose peculiar features of my administration while they sustain the Government.

In the Vallandigham case a commander in the field decided that a certain political enemy of the government had become dangerous in a military point of view, and that he must be removed. I believe that he was justifiable in coming to such a decision. In cases where political opponents do not in any way interfere with or hinder military operations, I have judged it best to let them alone.

My friends in Missouri last winter did me a great unkindness. I had relied upon my Radical friends as my mainstay in the management of affairs in that state and they disappointed me. I had recommended Gradual Emancipation, and Congress had endorsed that course. The Radicals in Congress voted for it. The Missouri delegation in Congress went for it,—went, as I thought, right. I had the highest hope that at last Missouri was on the right track. But I was disappointed by the immediate emancipation movement. It endangers the success of the whole advance towards freedom. But you say that the gradual emancipation men were insincere;—that they intended soon to repeal this action; that their course and their professions are purely fraudulent. Now I do not think that a majority of the gradual Emancipationists are insincere. Large bodies of men cannot play the hypocrite.

I announced my own opinion freely at the time. I was in favor of gradual emancipation. I still am so. You must not call yourselves my friends, if you are only so while I agree with you. According to that, if you differ with me you are not my friends.

But the mode of emancipation in Missouri is not my business. That is a matter which belongs exclusively to the citizens of that state: I do not wish to interfere. I desire, if it pleases the people of Missouri, that they should adopt gradual emancipation. I think that a union of all anti-slavery men upon this point would have made emancipation a final fact forever. Still, I do not assume any control. I am sorry to see anti-slavery men opposing such a movement, but I will take up the subjects you have laid before me, without prejudice, without pique, without resentment, and will try and do what is best for all, as affecting the grand result to which we all are looking.

The Delegation on the whole disappointed me badly. I expected more cohesion more discretion from what Cartter had told me & from what Hawkins Taylor retailed. Their cause, incoherent, vague, abusive, prejudiced, and did no good that I can yet see. They claimed to advocate no man— but asked for Butler—to speak without prejudice—yet abused Schofield like drabs; to ask for ascertained rights and they rambled through a maze of ridiculous grievances and absurd suggestions. In the main ignorant and well meaning, they chose for their spokesman Drake who is neither ignorant nor well-meaning, who covered the marrow of what they wanted to say in a purposeless mass of unprofitable verbiage which they accepted because it sounded well, and the President will reject because it is nothing but sound. He is a man whom only facts of the toughest kind can move and Drake attacked him with tropes & periods which might have had weight in a Sophomore Debating Club. And so the great Western Delegation from which good people hoped so much for freedom, discharged their little rocket, and went home with no good thing to show for coming—a little angry and a good deal bewildered—not clearly seeing why they have failed—as the President seemed so fair and their cause so good.

Notes

Editor's Introduction

1. *St. Louis Globe-Democrat*, 3 January 1909, magazine section, 3.

2. Stevens rewrote some of the reminiscences submitted to the Lincoln Centennial Association but did not change their substance.

3. Charleston IL, correspondence, 4 January 1887, *St. Louis Globe-Democrat*, 6 January 1887, 6.

4. Robert McIntyre, "Lincoln's Friend," *Charleston IL Courier*, n.d., reprinted in the *Paris (IL) Gazette*, reprinted in the *Chicago Tribune*, 30 May 1885. Later Eleanor Atkinson palmed McIntyre's interview off as her own in *The Boyhood of Abraham Lincoln* (New York: McClure, 1908). I am grateful to Paul H. Verduin of Silver Spring, Maryland, for calling Atkinson's literary piracy to my attention.

5. Adlai Stevenson, *Something of Men I Have Known* (Chicago: A. C. McClurg, 1909), 110–11, 275.

6. Prince's account appeared as volume 3 of *Transactions of the McLean County Historical Society* (Bloomington IL: Pentagraph, 1900). Schneider's reminiscences are on pages 91–92 of that volume.

7. Stevens, *Reporter's Lincoln*, 4.

8. Harold Holzer, ed., *The Lincoln-Douglas Debates: The First Complete, Unexpurgated Text* (New York: HarperCollins, 1993).

9. See appendix 2 in this volume, and Douglas L. Wilson, *Lincoln before Washington: New Perspectives on the Illinois Years* (Urbana: Univ. of Illinois Press, 1997), 151–65.

10. Jean Baker, *Mary Todd Lincoln* (New York: W. W. Norton, 1987), 122. For other examples of Mary Todd Lincoln's use of corporal punishment, see Michael Burlingame, *The Inner World of Abraham Lincoln* (Urbana: Univ. of Illinois Press, 1994), 62–63.

11. D. Wilson, *Lincoln before Washington*, 99–132.

12. Charleston IL correspondence, 4 January 1887, *St. Louis Globe-Democrat*, 6 January 1887, 6.

13. Harry E. Pratt, "Lincoln's Jump from the Window," *Journal of the Illinois State Historical Society* 48 (1955): 456–61; Paul E. Stroble Jr., *High on the Okaw's Western Bank: Vandalia, Illinois, 1819–39* (Urbana: Univ. of Illinois Press, 1992), 125–26.

14. William Allen White, *A Puritan in Babylon: The Story of Calvin Coolidge* (New York: Macmillan, 1938), vii, quoted in Donald Ritchie, *Doing Oral History* (New York: Twayne, 1995), 14.

15. J. G. Randall, *Lincoln the President: Springfield to Gettysburg*, 2 vols. (New York: Dodd, Mead, 1945), 2:324–25.

16. D. Wilson, *Lincoln before Washington*, 91–92. See also 21–54, 74–90, 93–98.

17. Ritchie, *Doing Oral History*, 92.

18. "Kindly Caricatures, no. 163," in *The Mirror*, n.d., clipping in Walter Stevens Scrapbooks, no. 79, Missouri Historical Society, St. Louis; postscript to a letter by one A. H. D., n.p., n.d., Miscellaneous Newspapers Collection, Missouri Historical Society, St. Louis.

19. *National Cyclopedia of American Biography* 12 (1904): 11–12.

20. Walter Williams and Floyd Calvin Shoemaker, eds., *Missouri: Mother of the West*, 5 vols. (Chicago: American Historical Society, 1930), 2:552; Floyd C. Shoemaker, *The State Historical Society of Missouri: A Semicentennial History* (Columbia: State Historical Society of Missouri, 1948), 69.

21. Dr. Alexander N. De Menil, quoted in Williams and Shoemaker, *Missouri*, 2:552.

22. *St. Louis Globe-Democrat*, 29 August 1939, 7A; 30 August 1939, 2B; and 7 October 1958, 15; *National Cyclopedia of American Biography* 12 (1904): 11–12.

Dedication

1. King was chief editorial writer for the *Globe-Democrat*. Stevens called him "one of the most polished, forceful writers of his generation." Stevens, "Joseph B. McCullagh," part 8, *Missouri Historical Review* 26 (July 1932): 382.

They Knew Lincoln

1. The town was founded in 1829 but within a decade had virtually ceased to exist. Lincoln lived there from 1831 to 1837.

2. In 1839 Petersburg became the county seat of the newly created Menard County, which had been part of Sangamon County.

3. Ann Rutledge (1813–35) was Lincoln's sweetheart in New Salem. See John Y. Simon, "Abraham Lincoln and Ann Rutledge," *Journal of the Abraham Lincoln Association* 11 (1990): 13–33; D. Wilson, *Lincoln before Washington*, 74–98; and John Evangelist Walsh, *The Shadows Rise: Abraham Lincoln and the Ann*

Rutledge Legend (Urbana: Univ. of Illinois Press, 1993). Those three authors effectively rebut James G. Randall's dismissal of the Ann Rutledge story in *Lincoln the President: From Springfield to Gettysburg*, 2 vols. (New York: Dodd, Mead, 1945), 2:321–42.

4. John Armstrong (1804–54) was the leader of a group of boisterous young men known as the Clary's Grove boys. After their celebrated wrestling match in 1831, Lincoln and Armstrong became good friends.

5. William "Duff" Armstrong (1833–99) was the son of Jack and Hannah Armstrong. In 1858 Lincoln successfully defended him in a murder trial in which an almanac helped determine whether the moon was up at a time when a witness claimed that by moonlight he had seen Armstrong kill someone.

6. The Eighth Judicial Circuit of Illinois from 1843 to 1853 contained fourteen counties. Lincoln spent about four months each year traveling the circuit with his colleagues at the bar trying cases in various county seats. After 1853 it was reduced to seven counties, and after 1857 it was further reduced.

7. Robert Roberts Hitt (1834–1906) represented the Freeport district from 1882 until his death.

8. In 1873 Joseph Burbridge McCullagh (1842–96) founded the *St. Louis Daily Globe*, which merged with the *Missouri Democrat* two years later. McCullagh edited this new hybrid for the rest of his life.

9. In Washington DC, near the White House.

10. James Shields (1806–79) was a prominent Illinois Democrat who challenged Lincoln to a duel in 1842.

11. Lincoln spoke in several New England towns in March 1860.

12. William Keeney Bixby (1857–1931) was a prominent St. Louis industrialist and collector of manuscripts, rare books, and paintings.

Growing Days at New Salem

1. William Franklin Berry (1811–35) and Lincoln bought a store in New Salem which "winked out" after a brief time. Berry, a heavy drinker, died young, leaving Lincoln to pay off large debts. The store was called a grocery because it sold liquor by the drink.

2. According to James Short, "Armstrong & others rolled a man named Jordan down hill at New Salem. Lincoln had nothing to do with any of these wild frolics." Douglas L. Wilson and Rodney O. Davis, eds., *Herndon's Informants: Letters, Interviews, and Statements about Abraham Lincoln* (Urbana: Univ. of Illinois Press, 1998), 74.

3. When Lincoln, his cousin John Hanks, his stepbrother John D. Johnston, and Denton Offutt tried to load some hogs on their flatboat headed for Louisiana in 1831, the animals balked. Corn was strewn on the gangplank, but, according to Mark Delahay, "their ordinary greed was not equal to their distrust, and they refused to appreciate the food, or follow the corn on board." (Delahay may well have heard this story from Lincoln, who was a cousin of Dehalay's wife, Louisiana Hanks.) Offutt (in Lincoln's words) "conceived the whim that he could sew up their eyes and drive them where he pleased. No sooner thought of than decided, he put his hands, including A[braham] at the job, which they completed—all but the driving. In their [the hogs'] blind condition they could not be driven out of the lot or field they were in." Delahay described this scene more fully: "The brilliant genius of the owner finally conceived a new plan to accomplish the purpose. He ordered the hogs driven into a pen, and directed the hands to get needles and thread, and sew up the eyes of the animals, to prevent their seeing the staging [gangplank]. This cruel operation was completed; but even this availed nothing against the 'natural cussedness' of the brute, for which he is so proverbial, and the hogs still would not go on board." Instead they "followed each other round in a continuous circuit to a chorus of their own peculiar and delightful music." Finally, as Lincoln recalled, "they were tied and hauled on carts to the boat." According to John Hanks, Lincoln said "I Can't sew the Eyes up," so instead "He held the head of hogs whilst Offutt did so up their Eyes." Lincoln, autobiography written for John L. Scripps, ca. June 1860, in *The Collected Works of Abraham Lincoln*, ed. Roy P. Basler et al., 8 vols. (New Brunswick NJ: Rutgers Univ. Press, 1953–55), 4:64; Mark W. Delahay, "Abraham Lincoln," unpaginated pamphlet (New York: Daniel H. Newhall, 1939); D. Wilson and Davis, *Herndon's Informants*, 44.

4. Kentucky-born Coleman Smoot (1791- or 1794–1876) was a farmer who served as the first justice of the peace in the Indian Creek precinct near New Salem. His reminiscences of Lincoln can be found in D. Wilson and Davis, *Herndon's Informants*, 253–54.

5. Perhaps Jacob Killian or his son William.

6. Mary S. Owens (1808–77) of Kentucky, sister of Lincoln's friend Elizabeth Abell, was courted by Lincoln sporadically in 1836 and 1837. She rejected his halfhearted proposal of marriage. Lincoln did not disparage "political women"; rather, Mary Owens told William Herndon, "me thinks I hear you say, save me from a *political woman! So say I!*" Owens to Herndon, Weston MO, 22 July 1866, D. Wilson and Davis, *Herndon's Informants*.

7. Rock Creek, a small settlement south of New Salem, hosted regular camp meetings.

8. Johnny Potter (1808–1900) settled with his family in Sangamon County in 1820.

9. Denton Offutt was remembered in Illinois as a garrulous, bibulous, "short, rather stockily built man, of good natured, amiable disposition, free handed and of great sociability—a trader and speculator who always had his eyes open to the main chance." Thomas P. Reep, *Lincoln at New Salem* (Petersburg IL: Old Salem Lincoln League, 1927), 98. Lincoln's friends did not recall Offutt fondly. See D. Wilson and Davis, *Herndon's Informants*, 9, 13, 18, 73. For a biographical sketch of Offutt, see William H. Townsend, *Lincoln and the Bluegrass: Slavery and Civil War in Kentucky* (Lexington: Univ. of Kentucky Press, 1955), 30–45, 150–53, and "Dr. Denton Offutt: Horse Tamer," *Abraham Lincoln Quarterly* 2 (1943): 330–33.

10. This precinct near New Salem was named after John Clary (1793–1860) of Tennessee, who settled there in 1819.

11. The Clary's Grove boys were a hell-raising, prankish set of young men who were "emphatically wild and rough, and were the terror of all those who did not belong to the company." John Todd Stuart, interview with James Q. Howard, May 1860, copy in the hand of John G. Nicolay, John Hay Papers, Brown University.

12. Of all the accounts of this celebrated wrestling match, Johnny Potter's is probably the most reliable. See Douglas L. Wilson, *Honor's Voice: The Transformation of Abraham Lincoln* (New York: Knopf, 1998), 19–51.

13. Edward Potter, husband of Jack Armstrong's sister—Elizabeth (Armstrong) Potter (1805–86)—was one of the earliest settlers in Sangamon County. He owned a celebrated maple grove in Rock Creek. Hugh Armstrong was Jack Armstrong's brother.

14. Actually Lincoln moved to have the petition published in the journal of the House of Representatives, but the motion was defeated. He was more concerned about having the capital moved to Springfield than about having Sangamon County divided. Opinion within the county on the proposal to divide it was mixed. When the county was finally divided in 1839 (with the new counties of Dane, Menard, and Logan shorn off from Sangamon), Lincoln played a leading role in drafting the legislation and shepherding it through the legislature. Harry E. Pratt, "Lincoln and the Division of Sangamon County," *Journal of the Illinois State Historical Society* 47 (1954): 398–409.

15. Attorney William B. Thompson (b. 1845) was the son of Nathaniel B. Thompson (1811–82), who, after leaving Beardstown, established a successful general store in Virginia, Illinois.

16. Beardstown is forty-five miles northwest of Springfield, on the Illinois River.

17. In fact, Lincoln borrowed law books from John Todd Stuart, not from Thompson.

18. In 1835 Parthena Nance (1816–98) of Kentucky married Samuel Hill (1800–1857), store-owner and village postmaster in New Salem. She shared her reminiscences of Lincoln with William Herndon. D. Wilson and Davis, *Herndon's Informants*, 604–5.

19. Bennett Abell of New Salem owned many books that Lincoln evidently borrowed. According to William Butler, Abell's wife, Elizabeth (1804?–?), "was a cultivated woman—very superior to the common run of women about here. Able, who was from Kentucky, had married her rich, and had got broken down there, and in consequence had come out here." Michael Burlingame, ed., *An Oral History of Abraham Lincoln: John G. Nicolay's Interviews and Essays* (Carbondale: Southern Illinois Univ. Press, 1996), 19.

20. She wed Jesse Vineyard in 1841.

21. Benjamin R. Vineyard (1842–1905).

22. Bath is located on the Illinois River, thirty-six miles northwest of Springfield.

23. In May 1860, the sobriquet "rail-splitter" was bestowed on Lincoln at the Illinois Republican State Convention in Decatur.

24. Lincoln's uncle William Hanks (1765?–1851/52) was the father of John Hanks (1802–89), with whom Lincoln split many rails near Decatur in 1830. Lincoln worked for Charles Hanks during part of his sojourn in Decatur.

25. In William Dean Howells's biography of Lincoln, which Lincoln read and corrected, there appears the following statement: "Mr. George Close, the partner of Lincoln in the rail-splitting business, says that. . . . [they] made about one thousand rails together for James Hawks [Hanks] and William Miller, receiving their pay in homespun clothing." W. D. Howells, *Life of Abraham Lincoln* (Bloomington: Indiana Univ. Press, 1960), 24. See James Q. Howard's interview with Close in David C. Mearns, *The Lincoln Papers: The Story of the Collection with Selections to July 4, 1861*, 2 vols. (Garden City NY: Doubleday, 1948), 1:150–51.

26. In his original account of this interview with Mrs. Hill, Stevens asked her about this episode. She replied: "Lincoln wrote something on the subject of religion, which he intended for a pamphlet, and he brought it into the store, which was a great gathering place, and read it out to the crowd. When he got through, Mr. Hill took it out of his hand and threw it into the fire. I think that is the way I heard that it occurred." Petersburg IL, correspondence, 12 September 1886, *St. Louis Globe Democrat*, 14 September 1886.

27. Other sources corroborate Hill's story. See D. Wilson and Davis, *Herndon's Informants*, 61–62, 545. Mentor Graham denied this story, claiming that Lincoln

wrote a defense of "universal salvation," not an attack on Christianity, and that Hill impulsively grabbed and burned a letter about Ann Rutledge, not an essay on religion. Graham to B. F. Irwin, Petersburg IL, 17 March 1874, in *Mentor Graham: The Man Who Taught Lincoln*, by Kunigunde Duncan and D. F. Nikols (Chicago: Univ. of Chicago Press, 1944), 228–29.

Giants in Those Days

1. Frederick William Lehmann (1853–1931) was general attorney for the Wabash Railway Co. before becoming solicitor general of the United States (1910–12).

2. James Alexander McDougal (1817–67) represented California in the U.S. Senate (1861–67). James Shields fought in the Mexican War and the Civil War and represented Illinois, Minnesota, and Missouri in the U.S. Senate. Edward D. Baker (1811–61), a close friend of Lincoln's, was a colonel in the Civil War, not a general. Lyman Trumbull (1813–96) represented Illinois in the U.S. Senate (1855–73). David Davis (1815–86) was a boon companion to Lincoln, who appointed him a Supreme Court justice in 1862. He later represented Illinois in the U.S. Senate (1877–83). Orville Hickman Browning (1806–81) represented Illinois in the U.S. Senate (1861–63) and served as secretary of the interior under Andrew Johnson (1866–69).

How He Broke the Quorum

1. Vandalia was the capital of Illinois from 1819 to 1839.

2. Kaskaskia was the capital of Illinois from 1818 to 1819.

3. Sangamon County at that time was more than twice the size of the state of Rhode Island. Slow and primitive transportation forced people living far from Springfield to spend inordinate amounts of time traveling to that county seat. See "Division of Sangamon County," manuscript essay, Abraham Lincoln Association Files, Illinois State Historical Library, Springfield, summarized in M. L. Houser, *Lincoln's Education and Other Essays* (New York: Bookman, 1957), 90, 111 n. 62; and Pratt, "Lincoln and the Division of Sangamon County."

4. William L. D. Ewing of Vandalia was chosen speaker of the state House of Representatives.

5. Ebenezer Capps, born in London in 1798, settled in Vandalia in 1830 and quickly became the principal storekeeper in the area.

6. This story is badly garbled. See Stroble, *High on the Okaw's Western Bank*, 125–26. On 5 December 1840, to avoid a quorum call, Lincoln stepped from a

window of Springfield's Second Presbyterian Church, which at the time served as the temporary hall of the state House of Representatives. See Pratt, "Lincoln's 'Jump' from the Window," 456–61.

The Duel He Didn't Fight

1. John Davis Whiteside of Monroe County, elected as a Democrat to the Illinois House of Representatives in 1830, 1832, 1834, and 1844, and to the state senate in 1836 from Madison County, became state treasurer in 1837. His family was celebrated for its Indian fighters.

2. Elias H. Merryman was a hot-tempered Whig physician in Springfield whom Lincoln once described as "a very intimate acquaintance and friend of mine." William Butler (1797–1876), clerk of the Sangamon County Circuit Court, befriended Lincoln when he served in the state legislature.

3. Elijah Lott (1806–95), a Whig originally from Ohio, was the postmaster and justice of the peace at Whitehall, Illinois. When he learned about the intended duel, he summoned John J. Hardin (1810–47), a leading Whig politician in Illinois and a friend of Lincoln's, to help settle the quarrel.

4. The *Alton Telegraph*, founded in 1836, was known as the *Telegraph and Democratic Review* from 1841 to 1853.

5. Souther did write an account of the duel that eventually appeared in *The Magazine of History* 4 (September 1906): 145–47. Some of the details given there are also included in Stevens's account, which may be based on it.

6. Dr. Thomas M. Hope was a businessman who served as mayor of Alton (1852–53). He claimed credit for the murder of the abolitionist editor Elijah Lovejoy in 1837. Samuel A. Buckmaster (d. 1878) was a prominent businessman who served as mayor of Alton (1853–54) and as a state senator (1859–61). Dr. Revel Wharton English (1810–94), a prominent Democrat from Green County, was born in Kentucky. After moving to Alton, he became postmaster of the town in the 1850s. He won election to the Illinois House of Representatives in 1836, 1838, and 1840, and to the state senate in 1842.

7. Jacob Bunn established the Springfield Marine and Fire Insurance Company in 1851.

8. This story is garbled; no reliable evidence suggests that Lincoln chivalrously came to the rescue of Mary Todd and Julia Jayne. See D. Wilson, *Honor's Voice*, 265–73.

9. Democrat Josiah Lamborn (1809–47), a lawyer from Jacksonville, served as

attorney general of Illinois from 1840 to 1843. He was unflatteringly described by a colleague at the bar as "wholly destitute of principle," a man who "shamelessly took bribes from criminals prosecuted under his administration. I know myself of his having dismissed forty or fifty indictments at the Shelbyville Court, and openly displayed the money he had received from defendants—He showed me a roll of bills amounting to six or eight hundred dollars, which he acknowledged he had received from them—the fruits of his maladministration. . . . He grew worse and worse towards the latter end of his life, and finally threw himself entirely away, consorting with gamblers and wasting his substance upon them. He gave himself up to intemperance, to the neglect of wife and child, whom he abandoned, and finally died miserably." Usher F. Linder, *Reminiscences of the Early Bench and Bar of Illinois* (Chicago: Chicago Legal News, 1879), 259.

10. George T. M. Davis, who took over the editorship of the *Alton Telegraph* from John Bailhache in 1841, served as mayor of Alton (1844–46).

Duff Armstrong and the "Almanac"

1. James P. Metzgar was injured on 29 August 1857 and died three days later.

2. Hannah Armstrong (1811–90) had been a surrogate mother to Lincoln in New Salem.

3. The collector was Charles F. Gunther (1837–1920), a prosperous candy manufacturer who bought many Lincoln relics and documents in addition to the almanac.

4. J. McCan Davis served as Ida Tarbell's research assistant in Springfield when she was working on her Lincoln biography. In the Tarbell Papers at Allegheny College are three essays by Davis about the Armstrong trial.

5. J. Henry Shaw was the assistant prosecutor in the Armstrong trial.

6. John A. Logan (1826–86) represented Illinois in the U.S. Senate (1871–77, 1879–86). William R. Morrison (1824–1909) ran against Logan for the U.S. Senate in 1885. He represented an Illinois district in the U.S. House (1863–65, 1873–87).

Brand of Whiskey Grant Drank

1. Henry Taylor Blow (1817–75) represented a Missouri district in the U.S. House (1863–67).

2. Julia Dent, daughter of Frederick Dent and Ellen Bray Wrenshall Dent, married U. S. Grant in 1848.

3. The battle of Shiloh took place in Tennessee on 6 and 7 April 1862.

4. Grant captured Fort Donelson in Tennessee on 16 February 1862. It was the first major victory for the North in the war.

5. John Eaton, John A. Dahlgren, and John M. Thayer also claimed that Lincoln told them this story. But according to Albert B. Chandler, the president said "that he had heard the story before [about sending Grant's brand of whiskey to his other generals], and that it would have been very good if he had said it, but that he didn't. He supposed it was charged to him to give it currency. . . . the original of the story was in King George's time. Bitter complaints were made to the King against his General Wolfe in which it was charged that he was mad. The King replied angrily: 'I wish he would bite some of my other generals then.'" In conversation with New York Congressman Moses F. Odell, Lincoln also disclaimed credit for the story. Don E. Fehrenbacher and Virginia Fehrenbacher, eds. *Recollected Words of Abraham Lincoln* (Stanford: Stanford Univ. Press, 1996), 92, 147, 349, 444.

Captain Henry King's Experience

1. This quotation, and the story behind it, are garbled. Seward proposed a final paragraph for the inaugural address, which Lincoln accepted but rewrote extensively.

The "New Party" of the Fifties

1. No such correspondence appears in the Lincoln Papers at the Library of Congress or in Roy P. Basler's edition of Lincoln's works.

2. In fact, Lincoln was eager to return to Congress.

3. No letters from Lincoln to Haworth are extant.

4. Lincoln himself said that, in the early 1850s, he was "losing interest in politics." On his semi-retirement from politics at that time, see Burlingame, *Inner World of Lincoln*, 1–19.

5. In fact, Lincoln did do a great deal to organize the Republican party in Illinois, but starting only in 1854. See Don E. Fehrenbacher, *Prelude to Greatness: Lincoln in the 1850s* (Stanford: Stanford Univ. Press, 1962), 19–47.

6. Richard J. Oglesby (1824–99) was elected governor of Illinois in 1865, 1872, and 1884. Richard Yates (1818–73) served as governor of Illinois (1861–65).

7. Lincoln gave a temperance address on 22 February 1842 before the Washington Society of Springfield.

8. Lincoln in fact openly expressed anger on many occasions. See Burlingame, *Inner World of Lincoln*, 147–235.

9. This quotation suspiciously resembles Lincoln's language in a letter to Louisiana Governor Michael Hahn, dated 13 March 1864: "They would probably help, in some trying time to come, to keep the jewel of liberty within the family of freedom." Basler, *Collected Works of Lincoln*, 7:243.

A Drink and a Sunrise

1. This informant was perhaps Benjamin Smith (b. 1814), who was "a successful fruit grower and leading agriculturalist." Edward Bryan Landis, "The Influence of Tennessee in the Formation of Illinois," *Transactions of the Illinois State Historical Society* 30 (1923): 141.

The Eighth Circuit

1. Lincoln actually spent about four months a year on the circuit.

2. Stephen Trigg Logan (1800–1880) was Lincoln's second law partner. Daniel Wolsey Voorhees (1827–97) represented an Indiana district in the U.S. House (1861–65, 1869–73) and later served in the U.S. Senate (1877–97). John Palmer Usher (1816–89) of Indiana served as secretary of the interior (1863–65). Democrat Norman Higgins Purple ran unsuccessfully for the Illinois legislature in 1840; he was a Democratic presidential elector in 1844. Theophilus Lyle Dickey (1811–85) was a prominent attorney in Ottawa, Illinois.

3. Ezra Morton Prince (1831–1908) edited a voluminous account of the 1856 Republican Convention in Bloomington: *Meeting of May 29, 1900, Commemorative of the Convention of May 29, 1856, That Organized the Republican Party in the State of Illinois*, vol. 3 of *Transactions of the McLean County Historical Society* (Bloomington IL: Pentagraph, 1900). Prince's account of the eighth circuit appears on pages 18–20 of that volume.

4. John Todd Stuart (1807–85), a native of Kentucky, was Lincoln's law partner from 1837 to 1841. A fellow member of the bar described Stuart as "the handsomest man in Illinois," with "the mildest and most amiable expression of countenance." He was ever "cheerful, social and good-humored" and "had the reputation of being the ablest and most efficient jury lawyer in the State." Stuart was especially effective "in trespass and slander cases, preventing the recovery of large damages for the plaintiff when he was for the defendant." See Linder, *Reminiscences of the Early Bench*, 348. In an 1860 campaign biography of Lincoln, John Locke Scripps noted that during the 1834 canvass, "Lincoln was thrown considerably into the company of Hon. John T. Stuart. . . . To Lincoln's great surprise, Mr. Stuart warmly urged him to study law. Mr. Stuart was a gentleman of education, an able

lawyer, and in every respect one of the foremost men of the State. Advice of this character, tendered by one so competent to give it, could not be otherwise than gratifying to a young man, as yet unknown to fame outside of New Salem precinct, and being accompanied by a generous offer to loan him whatever books he might need, Lincoln resolved to follow it. As soon as the election was over, he took home with him a few books from the law library of Mr. Stuart, and entered upon their study in his usually earnest way." Scripps, *Life of Abraham Lincoln*, ed. Roy P. Basler and Lloyd Dunlap (Bloomington: Indiana Univ. Press, 1961), 69–70. Scripps received almost all of his information about Lincoln's early life from Lincoln himself. William Henry Herndon (1818–91) was Lincoln's third law partner (1844–61). Not mentioned by Prince was Stephen T. Logan, Lincoln's second law partner (1841–44).

5. Leonard Swett (1825–89) of Bloomington, a close friend and political ally of Lincoln's, worked hard to secure his nomination for president in 1860.

6. Jesse Wilson Fell (1808–87) requested that Lincoln write an autobiography in 1859; the request was honored. He worked hard to help Lincoln win the presidential nomination in 1860.

7. Lincoln to Fell, 20 December 1859, enclosing his autobiographical sketch, in Basler, *Collected Works of Lincoln*, 3:511–12.

8. Fell sent the information to Joseph J. Lewis, who published a biographical account of Lincoln in the *Chester County Times* (West Chester PA), 11 February 1860.

9. Adlai Ewing Stevenson (1835–1914) of Bloomington was vice president under Grover Cleveland (1893–97).

10. Lincoln's grandfather was killed by Indians in 1786.

11. This is a slightly inaccurate version of the autobiography Lincoln prepared for Fell. See Basler, *Collected Works of Lincoln*, 3:511–12.

12. In 1860 Lincoln wrote another autobiographical sketch at the request of John L. Scripps of the *Chicago Tribune*. Lincoln appointed Lawrence Weldon (1829–1905) of Bloomington U.S. district attorney for southern Illinois; in 1883 Weldon became a judge of the U.S. Court of Claims.

The Bloomington Convention

1. Paul Selby (1825–1913) of Jacksonville was one of the most prominent leaders in the formation of the Republican party in Illinois. He edited the *Quincy Whig Republican* in the late 1860s and early 1870s and the *Springfield Illinois State Journal* from 1874 to 1889. The *Morgan Journal* became the *Jacksonville Journal* in 1858.

2. With Joseph Medill, Charles Henry Ray (1821–70) owned the *Chicago Tribune* and worked hard to secure Lincoln's nomination for president in 1860.

3. Isaac C. Pugh, who had commanded a company in the Black Hawk War, ran unsuccessfully for the Illinois legislature in 1838. Harvey C. Johns was president of the Illinois Agricultural Society. Major E. O. Smith is perhaps the mechanic Edward O. Smith (b. 1817) of Decatur, who served in the Illinois state senate as a Whig (1848–50).

4. Basler, *Collected Works of Lincoln*, 2:333.

5. William Harrison Bissell (1811–60) represented an Illinois district in the U.S. House (1849–55) and served as governor of Illinois (1857–60).

6. George Schneider (1823–1905) edited the *Chicago Staatszeitung* (1851–62) and was appointed consul to Elsinor, Denmark, by Lincoln (1861).

7. These remarks are reprinted from Prince, *Transactions of the McLean County Historical Society*, 3:88–91.

8. Joseph Oscar Cunningham (1830–1917) of Urbana was admitted to the bar in 1856 and served as judge of the Champaign County Court (1861–65).

9. Jesse Kilgore Dubois (1811–76) was a close friend and political ally of Lincoln's.

10. On 21 May 1856, a mob of more than seven hundred supporters of slavery burned the Free State Hotel and destroyed the offices of two Free Soil newspapers in Lawrence, Kansas, provoking indignation throughout the North.

11. Andrew H. Reeder (1807–64) of Pennsylvania had served as governor of the Kansas Territory (1854–55).

12. This account appeared in Prince, *Transactions of the McLean County Historical Society*, 3:91–92. A similar account can be found in Cunningham, "The Bloomington Convention of 1856 and Those Who Participated in It," *Transactions of the Illinois State Historical Society for the Year 1905* (Springfield: Illinois State Journal, 1906), 101–10.

13. Elisha P. Ferry (1825–95) was mayor of Waukegan; in 1889 he was elected governor of Washington.

14. "Egypt" refers to southern Illinois.

15. John McAuley Palmer (1817–1900) of Carlinville became a Republican in 1856 after breaking with the Democrats over the Kansas-Nebraska Act of 1854.

16. Cf. Cunningham's recollections in a speech delivered in Norwalk, Ohio, on 4 July 1907, in *Lincoln among His Friends: A Sheaf of Intimate Memories*, ed. Rufus Rockwell Wilson (Caldwell ID: Caxton, 1942), 118–19.

17. James Stanley Emery (b. 1826) of Maine was a magistrate of the peace in Kansas and an ardent foe of slavery. In January 1856 he was selected as one of the four emissaries dispatched by the Free Soilers to appeal for help throughout the North. In 1864 Lincoln named him district attorney for Kansas.

18. This appears in Prince, *Transactions of the McLean County Historical Society*, 3:93–94. It was originally written for a Kansas newspaper.

19. The abolitionist Owen Lovejoy (1811–64) of Princeton, Illinois, represented his district in the U.S. House (1857–64).

20. Joseph M. Medill (1823–99) edited the *Chicago Tribune* (1855–99).

21. Wendell Phillips of Massachusetts (1811–84) was a leading abolitionist.

22. Burton C. Cook (1819–94) represented an Illinois district in the U.S. House (1865–71); he nominated Lincoln at the 1864 Republican national convention in Baltimore. Archibald Williams (1801–63) of Quincy was a leading Illinois Whig who helped organize the Bloomington convention in 1856. He did not give a speech at that event. He served in the state legislature (1832–40) and was a U.S. district attorney (1849–53). Isaac N. Arnold (1815–84) of Chicago served in the U.S. House of Representatives (1861–65).

23. Thomas Jefferson Henderson (1824–1911) of Princeton represented his Illinois district in the U.S. House (1875–95). His remarks are taken from Prince, *Transactions of the McLean County Historical Society*, 3:81.

24. In 1854 Owen T. Reeves (b. 1829) left his native Ohio and moved to Bloomington, where he served as city clerk and city attorney. In 1877 he won election as a circuit court judge, a post he held until 1891, when he became dean of the Bloomington Law School.

25. Mrs. Robinson was the wife of Charles Robinson (1818–94), who in 1856 became governor of Kansas.

26. George Perrin Davis (1842–1917).

27. The German-born John George Nicolay (1832–1901) served as Lincoln's chief personal secretary (1860–65). John Milton Hay (1838–1905) served as Lincoln's assistant personal secretary (1861–65). Nicolay and Hay wrote *Abraham Lincoln: A History*, 10 vols. (New York: Century, 1890).

Lawyer, Philosopher, Statesman

1. The trial of Isaac Wyant was held between 31 March and 4 April 1857.

2. John Howard Burnham (1834–1917) edited the *Bloomington Pentagraph* from 1864 to 1867. He had moved to Illinois from Massachusetts in 1855 and studied at the State Normal University in Bloomington, from which he graduated in 1861.

3. Asahel Gridley (1810–81), a prominent merchant, banker, and lawyer in Bloomington, became a brigadier general of militia during the Black Hawk War and served in the state legislature.

4. On another occasion Reeves recalled Lincoln's words somewhat differently:

"Reeves, I have just been up on Grove street to see Gridley's new mansion, and it strikes me that he is making a mistake building such a fine house in his own town." "Judge Reeves' Lincoln Stories," typescript, McLean County Historical Society, Bloomington IL. In that document appears a story about Lincoln not included in Stevens's interview:

> In the year 1856 one Thompson was engaged in buying hogs in McLean County and depended for prices on telegrams from the firm to whom he shipped in Chicago. On a certain day he received over the Illinois & Mississippi Telegraph Company from his Chicago firm a telegram giving him the price for hogs. The telegram, as delivered, fixed the price at 50 cents per hundred pounds higher than the figure written in the original telegram by the firm, and in consequence Thompson suffered a loss of several hundred dollars. He employed Mr. Lincoln to bring suit, which he did in the circuit court in this city. Judge Dickey, of Ottawa, appeared for the telegraph company. The case was tried before a jury and the only defense which the company put up was a provision printed on the blank upon which the telegram was sent— only liable if there was a mistake when the receiver of the telegram should have it repeated back for verification and pay one-half the charge.
>
> When Mr. Lincoln came to reply to Judge Dickey's defense, he told the jury that the judge's argument reminded him of the story of an old farmer who was induced by his merchant to buy his first snuffers and when on his return home after candle lighting he called to his wife to bring him his new snuffers, that he wanted to snuff his candle. He took the new fangled snuffers in one hand and with the bare fingers of his other separated a section of the wick, as he had been accustomed to do, and then opened the snuffers and placed the portion of the wick he had removed in them, turned to his wife and said, "you see, wife, these are very handy little things." Mr. Lincoln laughed and the jury also laughed and that was the end of Judge Dickey's defense. The jury promptly brought in a verdict in favor of Mr. Lincoln's client for the full amount of the demand.

Reeves gave further reminiscences of Lincoln in "Personal Recollections and Estimates of Lincoln," in *Abraham Lincoln by Some Men Who Knew Him*, ed. Paul M. Angle (Chicago: Americana House, 1950; originally published in 1909), 20–35.

5. The Northwest Ordinance of 1787 forbade slavery in the old Northwest Territory, consisting of the states of Ohio, Indiana, Illinois, Michigan, and Wisconsin.

6. The Missouri Compromise forbade slavery in that part of the Louisiana Purchase Territory above the latitude of 36 degrees and 30 minutes.

7. John Charles Fremont (1813–90) nearly won the 1856 presidential election.

William L. Dayton (1807–64) of New Jersey served as U.S. minister to France during the Civil War.

8. Norman Buel Judd (1815–78) of Chicago, chairman of the Illinois State Republican State Central Committee (1856–61), was instrumental in helping Lincoln win the nomination in 1860.

Wells H. Blodgett's Experience

1. A St. Louis railroad attorney, Wells Howard Blodgett (1839–1929) won the Congressional Medal of Honor for bravery in the Civil War. On Lincoln as a mentor for younger men see Burlingame, *Inner World of Lincoln*, 6–7, 73–77.

2. *Hurd v. Rock Island Bridge Co.* (familiarly known as the *Effie Afton* case) ended in a hung jury in 1857. Lincoln's associates in the case were Norman B. Judd of Chicago and Joseph Knox of Rock Island.

A Land Case

1. Jonathan H. Cheney (1833–1920) was a prominent railroad manager.

The "Lost Speech"

1. Reuben Moore Benjamin (1833–1917) began practicing law in Bloomington in 1856 and served as a county judge (1873–86).

2. Lewis Cass (1782–1866) represented Michigan in the U.S. Senate (1845–48, 1849–57). Charles Sumner (1811–74) represented Massachusetts in the U.S. Senate (1851–74). William M. Gwin (1805–85) represented California in the U.S. Senate (1850–55, 1857–61). Andrew Pickens Butler (1796–1857) represented South Carolina in the U.S. Senate (1846–57). James M. Mason (1798–1871) represented Virginia in the U.S. Senate (1847–61). William Henry Seward (1801–72) represented New York in the U.S. Senate (1849–61). Salmon P. Chase (1808–73) represented Ohio in the U.S. Senate (1849–55, 1861). Judah P. Benjamin (1811–84) represented Louisiana in the U.S. Senate (1853–61).

3. George Mason (1725–92) of Virginia was a leading statesman of the Revolutionary era.

4. John Wickizer (1821–89) was born in Pennsylvania and in 1847 settled in Bloomington, where he became mayor in 1852. He served in the Illinois General Assembly and was a partner of Gridley for several years. His reminiscences of Lincoln can be found in D. Wilson and Davis, *Herndon's Informants*, 423–24, 516.

5. "Long John" Wentworth (1815–88) of Chicago served as a Democrat in the U.S. House (1843–51) and as the Republican mayor of Chicago (1857–61).

When He was Just "Bob's Father"

1. Marshall Solomon Snow (1842–1916) served as dean of Washington University from 1876 to 1912.

2. Robert Todd Lincoln (1843–1926) graduated from Exeter in 1860.

3. Address at Cooper Institute, 27 February 1860, in Basler, *Collected Works of Lincoln*, 3:522–50.

4. Born and educated in New York, John Curtiss Underwood (1809–73) was an active Republican whom Lincoln named fifth auditor of the U.S. Treasury in 1861 and judge of the U.S. district court for Virginia in 1864.

They Heard the Final Debate

1. John H. Yeager (1833–1911) served in the Illinois House of Representatives (1866–68).

2. Henry Guest McPike (1825–1910), mayor of Alton (1887–91), moved from Indiana to Alton, where he was a prominent businessman. His grandfather, Captain James McPike (1751?–1825), served as a sergeant in the Fourth Pennsylvania Line during the Revolutionary War.

3. Henry W. Billings was mayor of Alton (1851–52).

4. Irish-born Robert P. Tansey (1833–99), a close friend of Douglas's, was paymaster of the Alton & Sangamon Railroad. He became president of the St. Louis Merchants Exchange in 1871. Thomas Dimmock (1820–1909) edited the *Alton National Democrat*.

5. Zephaniah Job served in the Illinois House of Representatives (1858–60).

6. Cyrus Edwards (1793–1877) was defeated for governor of Illinois in 1838. He served in the state legislature (1832–38, 1840–42, 1860–62) at first as a Whig and later as a Republican. Friend S. Rutherford (d. 1864), a Democrat who became a Republican leader in Alton, superintended the state penitentiary, and, during the Civil War, commanded the 97th Illinois Volunteers. George T. Brown (1821–80) edited and owned the *Alton Courier*, served as mayor of Alton (1846–47), led the Republican party in southern Illinois, and became sergeant-at-arms of the U.S. Senate in 1861. John Mills Pearson (1832–1910) owned a book store.

7. This event took place on 25 July 1856.

8. Martin P. Sweet was a Whig lawyer from Freeport.

9. Horace White (1834–1916) covered the 1858 Lincoln-Douglas debates for the *Chicago Tribune*.

Impressions Made on J. S. Ewing

1. James S. Ewing (1835–1918) was the first cousin and law partner of Adlai Stevenson, vice president under Grover Cleveland, who appointed Ewing minister to Belgium. Most of what Ewing says here is also given, along with much else, in his speech to the Illinois Schoolmasters' Club, Bloomington, 12 February 1909, in Angle, *Lincoln by Some Men Who Knew Him*, 36–59.

2. Samuel H. Treat (1815–1902), a St. Louis attorney, sat on the U.S. District Court (1857–87).

3. William G. Ewing (b. 1839).

The Lincoln Scrapbooks

1. James Nicholas Brown of Island Grove served in the Illinois House of Representatives (1840–44, 1846–48, 1852–54).

2. Lincoln to Brown, Springfield, 18 October 1858, in Basler, *Collected Works of Lincoln*, 3:327–28.

3. Washington correspondence, 14 January 1892, *St. Louis Globe-Democrat*, 17 January 1892, 28.

4. Joshua R. Giddings (1795–1864) represented an Ohio district in the U.S. House (1842–59). Frederick Douglass (1817–95), a former slave, was the most prominent of the black abolitionists.

5. James B. Sheridan was a reporter for the *Philadelphia Press*, whose editor, John W. Forney, vigorously supported Douglas in his quarrel with President Buchanan. Forney had sent Sheridan west to help Douglas win reelection.

6. In fact, Douglas's speeches are longer than Lincoln's.

7. Henry Binmore was a twenty-five-year-old native of England who had been a journalist in Montreal, St. Louis, and New York. He was hired to assist Sheridan. See appendix 2.

8. In 1860 James Washington Sheahan published a campaign biography of Douglas, who in 1854 had induced him to leave his post as a Washington correspondent and assume the editorship of the *Chicago Times*.

9. In 1848 William Bross came to Chicago, where he bought the *Herald of the Prairies* and changed its name to the *Prairie Herald*. In 1852 he joined with John L. Scripps to found the *Democratic Press*, which merged with the *Chicago Tribune* in 1858.

10. The actor James H. McVicker (1822–96) was noted for his impersonation of Yankee characters. He also managed an important theater in Chicago.

11. Herman Kreismann became city clerk of Chicago in 1858.

12. Ichabod Codding was a prominent Illinois abolitionist.

13. John Locke Scripps (1818–66) joined the *Tribune* in 1852.

14. Judah P. Benjamin (1811–84) represented Louisiana in the U.S. Senate (1853–61). In the Confederate Cabinet he served at different times as secretary of state, secretary of war, and attorney general.

15. John F. Farnsworth (1820–97) represented an Illinois district in the U.S. House (1857–61, 1863–73).

16. Richard M. Johnson (1780–1850), Martin Van Buren's vice president (1837–41), had two daughters by his mulatto mistress, Julia Chinn.

17. The church paper was published in Chicago (1855–61). William W. Patton of Chicago led a delegation of clergymen to the White House in September 1862. Samuel C. Bartlett was pastor of the New England Congregational Church in Chicago. Joseph Edwin Roy was pastor of the Plymouth Congregational Church of Chicago (1855–59).

How He Studied German

1. Luman Burr (1836–1921) of Connecticut moved to Bloomington in 1856 and spent the rest of his life there.

2. The following account is similar to, but not identical with, Luman Burr's statement, dated Bloomington, 25 January 1909, Lincoln Centennial Association Files, Illinois State Historical Library, Springfield.

3. Winston Churchill (1871–1947) wrote a novel entitled *The Crisis* (1901), which, according to Burr, "pictures Mr. Lincoln as a clown." Burr indignantly asserted that the author "had not the faintest conception of Mr. Lincoln's character, and the book is a burlesque so far as it attempts to portray his manner." Burr's statement, dated Bloomington, 25 January 1909.

4. William McCullogh (1812–62) served as sheriff of McLean County for three terms starting in 1840; he then won four consecutive elections to the post of clerk of the county court. In the Civil War he was lieutenant colonel of the 4th Illinois Cavalry. After McCullogh was killed in battle, Lincoln wrote his daughter Fanny an unusually eloquent letter of condolence. Basler, *Collected Works of Lincoln*, 6:16–17.

5. William H. Hanna (1823–70) left Indianapolis to settle in Bloomington, Illinois, in 1846. John M. Scott (b. 1823), a Bloomington attorney who became chief justice of the Illinois State Supreme Court, wrote a revealing sketch entitled "Lincoln on the Stump and at the Bar." It is enclosed in Scott to Ida Tarbell, Bloom-

ington IL, 14 August 1895, Tarbell Papers, Allegheny College, Meadville PA. Ward Hill Lamon (1828–93), an attorney in Danville, was a close friend of Lincoln's.

The Bowl of Custard

1. Mrs. Bradner's first husband, who died in 1857, was a good friend of Lincoln's in Bloomington. Much of the material in the following paragraphs comes from Mrs. Bradner's letters, dated Bloomington, 27 June and 1 July 1908, written to James R. B. Van Cleave, secretary of the Lincoln Centennial Association, in the files of the association, Illinois State Historical Library, Springfield. Cf. her interview, "Mr. Lincoln in the Social Life of His Period," *Bloomington Pentagraph*, 6 February 1909, in *Intimate Memories of Lincoln*, ed. Rufus Rockwell Wilson (Elmira NY: Primavera, 1945), 120–22.

2. Mrs. Capt. Bradford was perhaps the wife of John S. Bradford, who had been state printer of Illinois.

3. Elsewhere Mrs. Bradner identified her sister as Mrs. John A. Jones. See Bradner, "Mr. Lincoln in the Social Life of His Period," 122. A native of Georgetown, in the District of Columbia, John Albert Jones moved to Illinois in 1835 and became a lawyer in Tremont. According to his daughter, Jones and Lincoln were "fast friends." See Eugenia Jones Hunt, "My Personal Recollections of Abraham Lincoln and Mary Todd Lincoln," *Abraham Lincoln Quarterly* 3 (1945): 235.

4. In her letter of 27 June 1908, Mrs. Bradner quotes Mary thus: "Shut your mouth. Never tell that again."

Albert Blair's Three Vivid Impressions

1. Albert Blair (b. 1840), a corporation lawyer in St. Louis, grew up in Barry, Illinois, where his father, William Blair, was a political leader.

2. Amos Tuck (1810–79) was a prominent New Hampshire Republican leader whom Lincoln appointed naval officer for the port of Boston.

The Friend of the Boys

1. Fred Thomas Dubois (1851–1930) represented Idaho in the U.S. Senate (1891–97).

2. Illinois State University at Springfield.

3. William N. Reynolds taught at Pennsylvania College in Gettysburg before

moving to Springfield, Illinois, in 1854. George Delachaumette Reynolds (1841–1921) was U.S. attorney for the eastern district of Missouri (1889–93) before becoming a judge in 1908.

4. Quinn "Peachy" Harrison was tried in 1859 for the murder of Greek Crafton, a young lawyer.

5. Peter Cartwright (1785–1872) was a well-known Methodist preacher who ran unsuccessfully for Congress against Lincoln in 1846.

6. The prosecutors in the Harrison trial were J. B. White, John M. Palmer, N. M. Broadwell, and Isaac Cogdal. James H. Matheney Sr. (1818–90) of Springfield, known as a "silver-tongued" attorney, served as county judge of Sangamon County (1873–90). He was a member of the 1847 constitutional convention and during the Civil War served as the colonel of the 130th Illinois regiment.

7. Milton Hay (1817–93), uncle of John Hay, was a Springfield lawyer and friend of Lincoln's.

8. John Alexander McClernand (1812–90) of Shawneetown represented his district in the U.S. House (1843–51, 1859–61) and served as a general in the Civil War.

9. James C. Conkling (1816–99) was a friend and neighbor of Lincoln's.

10. Davis's father told him in 1854 that "Mr. Lincoln enquires for you affectionately, whenever I meet him. He recollects your ride with Old Buck to Danville." David Davis to George Perrin Davis, Bloomington IL, 17 April 1854, David Davis Papers, Chicago Historical Society.

11. David B. Campbell (d. 1855) was a Democrat who for many years served as attorney general of Illinois.

12. William Knox Patrick (b. 1841) was a businessman who had served as a paymaster in Union army during the Civil War. William Hyde (1836–98) joined the *Missouri Republican* (St. Louis) in 1857 and became its editor-in-chief in 1866. He was appointed postmaster of St. Louis in 1885.

The Bixby Collection

1. Journalist Eugene Field (1850–95) wrote whimsical verse.

2. These cousins included James B., Abraham, and Mordecai Lincoln, sons of Mordecai Lincoln, the brother of the president's father, Thomas Lincoln. They lived in Fountain Green, Hancock County, Illinois.

3. The Bixby Historical Autograph Collection is housed in the Washington University Library in St. Louis.

4. Hudgins's letter, dated 27 January 1865, was addressed to Congressman Austin A. King, not Lincoln.

5. Austin A. King (1802–70), who had served as governor of Missouri (1848–53), represented a Missouri district in the U.S. House (1863–65).

6. Lincoln to James Speed, 28 February 1865, in Basler, *Collected Works of Lincoln*, 8:324.

7. Memorandum dated 13 December 1861. George May resided in Plattsmouth, Nebraska, and was recommended for a Utah judgeship. See Basler, *Collected Works of Lincoln*, 5:68.

8. James Harlan (1820–99) represented Iowa in the U.S. Senate (1857–65). James Falconer Wilson (1828–95) represented an Iowa district in the U.S. House (1861–69). James Wilson Grimes (1816–72) represented Iowa in the U.S. Senate (1859–69).

9. This endorsement, dated 27 January 1864, was sent to Edward Bates. Solomon P. McCurdy became associate justice for Utah Territory in April 1864.

10. General Green Clay Smith (1826–95) represented a Kentucky district in the U.S. House (1863–66) and was governor of the Montana Territory (1866–69). William Duke was a brother-in-law of Green Clay Smith.

11. These documents, dated 27 August 1863, are in Basler, *Collected Works of Lincoln*, 6:414.

12. This endorsement, sent to Benjamin B. French and dated 30 September 1861, appears on a letter from the Rev. Mr. E. P. Phelps, Baltimore Conference, Methodist Episcopal Church, 28 September 1861, recommending B. W. Ferguson for a post with the commissioner of public buildings.

13. Joseph Mosley Root (1807–79) of Norwalk, Ohio, served in the U.S. House (1845–51) as a Whig. Lincoln was a fellow Whig in the House (1847–49). In 1861 Root was named U.S. attorney for the northern district of Ohio. This document does not appear in Basler, *Collected Works of Lincoln*.

14. A slightly different version of this document appears in Basler, *Collected Works of Lincoln*, 8:370.

15. A slightly different version of this document appears in Basler, *Collected Works of Lincoln*, 8:346.

16. Basler gives the following version of this document, dated Springfield, 29 June 1857: "When I went to Bloomington . . . I saw Mr. Price and learned from him that this note was a sort of 'insolvent fix-up' with his creditors—a fact in his history I have not before learned of." Basler, *Collected Works of Lincoln*, 2:410.

17. Mary Ann Cuthbert was a stewardess at the White House during the Civil War. She complained that Mary Todd Lincoln had confiscated her wages and left her impoverished. Orville Hickman Browning, manuscript diary, entry for 12 April 1866, Illinois State Historical Library, Springfield: "Met Mrs Cuthbert, housekeeper at the White House in President Lincolns time. Met her on the steps of the

Capitol. She stopped me to ask me to aid in getting her some employment. She said she was very destitute and in distress. That Congress allowed $600 per annum for the Stewardess at the White House, but that she never got it—it was all taken and appropriated by Mrs Lincoln, and she was left pennyless." For other evidence of Mary Lincoln's ethical misconduct in the White House, see Michael Burlingame, *Honest Abe, Dishonest Mary* (Racine WI: Lincoln Fellowship of Wisconsin, 1994). "Aunt Mary" Dines was a black nurse employed by the Lincolns.

The Courtship and Home Life

1. Albert S. Edwards (1839–1915) served as custodian of the Lincoln home from 1897 until his death.

2. Ninian Wirt Edwards (1809–89), who served as a Whig in the Illinois House of Representatives (1837–41) and Senate (1844–52), had, according to Usher F. Linder, "inherited from his father so much vanity and egotism that it made him offensive to most of his acquaintances." He was "naturally and constitutionally an aristocrat" and "hated democracy . . . as the devil is said to hate holy water." Linder, *Reminiscences of the Early Bench*, 279, 280.

3. Ninian Edwards (1775–1833) served as governor of Illinois Territory (1809–18) and represented Illinois in the U.S. Senate (1818–24).

4. Elizabeth P. Todd (1813–88) married Ninian W. Edwards in 1832.

5. In 1836 Frances Jane Todd (1817–99) wed Dr. William Wallace (1802–67) in Springfield. In 1846 Ann Maria Todd (1820–91) married Clark Moulton Smith, a Tennessee native who became a successful merchant in Springfield.

6. Dr. Gershom Jayne (1791–1867) was a prominent physician in Springfield, where he settled in 1820. His son William Jayne (1826–1916), who worked closely with Lincoln in politics, was also a physician.

7. William F. Elkin (b. 1792?) won election to the Illinois House of Representatives in 1828, 1836, and 1838. Vermont-born Daniel Stone served in the Ohio legislature before moving to Illinois. He was elected to the Illinois House of Representatives from Sangamon County in 1836. The following year he joined with Lincoln to issue a protest against slavery. Virginia-born farmer John Dawson (1791?–1850), a veteran of the War of 1812, served in the Illinois House of Representatives (1830–32, 1834–40). Andrew McCormick (b. 1801), a stonecutter who weighed nearly three hundred pounds, won election to the General Assembly in 1836 and 1838. Robert L. Wilson (1805–80) of Athens, near New Salem, was elected to the General Assembly in 1836.

8. Archer Gray Herndon (1795–1867), a leading Democrat, served in the Illi-

nois Senate (1836–42). He sired Lincoln's law partner and biographer, William Henry Herndon. Job Fletcher, who had settled in Sangamon County in 1819, won election from there to the Illinois House of Representatives in 1826 and 1844 and to the Illinois Senate in 1835 and 1836.

9. Matilda Rachel Edwards (1824–51).

10. There was in fact much more to the story than Edwards believed. See D. Wilson, *Lincoln before Washington*, 99–132.

11. This description appears in a letter from Mrs. Elizabeth Humphreys Norris to Emilie Todd Helm, Garden City KS, 28 September 1895, photocopy, James G. Randall Papers, Library of Congress.

12. Dr. John Ward was an Episcopal minister who ran a coeducational academy in Lexington.

13. Margaret Wickliffe, young Mary Todd's best friend, was the daughter of Robert "Duke" Wickliffe, one of the richest men in Lexington. William Preston (1816–87) of Kentucky served as a brigadier general in the Confederate Army.

14. Robert Smith Todd (1791–1849) served as clerk of the Kentucky House of Representatives and later became a Kentucky state senator.

15. The father of Eliza Ann Parker Todd (1794?–1825) died in 1800.

16. Herndon made no such mistake.

17. In 1831 in Springfield, Simeon Francis (1796–1872) founded the *Sangamo Journal*, which became the *Illinois State Journal*.

18. This account of the courtship is badly garbled. See D. Wilson, *Honor's Voice*, 213–30.

19. Herndon, basing his story on statements given by Elizabeth Edwards, was wrong about the bereft bride left standing at the altar by the defaulting groom.

20. Benjamin Stephenson Edwards (1818–87), the youngest son of governor Ninian Edwards, studied law with Stephen T. Logan and was the law partner of first Edward D. Baker and then John Todd Stuart. John Todd (1787–1865), Mary's uncle, served in the War of 1812 as surgeon general of Kentucky troops. In 1827 he became register of the U.S. Land Office in Springfield, Illinois. He married Elizabeth Smith, who bore him six children.

21. In 1844 Charles Dresser, who was born in Connecticut and moved to Illinois from Virginia because of his distaste for slavery, sold the Lincolns the house he owned at 8th and Jackson Streets in Springfield.

22. The newlyweds lived at the Globe Tavern for $4 per week.

23. In fact, Lincoln's domestic life was miserable. See Burlingame, *Inner World of Lincoln*, 268–326.

24. Emilie Todd Helm, quoted in Katherine Helm, "Mary Todd Lincoln," *McClure's Magazine* 11 (September 1898): 479.

25. Frances Todd Wallace declared to a journalist that her sister Mary enjoyed a happy marriage: "I don't see why people should say Mr. Lincoln's home life was unhappy. He was devoted to his home, and Mrs. Lincoln thought everything of him. She almost worshipped him." Mrs. Wallace's reliability is somewhat compromised by her statement later in this interview: "And then they say that Mrs. Lincoln was an ambitious woman. But she was not an ambitious woman at all." Interview dated 2 September 1895, in William E. Barton, *The Women Lincoln Loved* (Indianapolis: Bobbs-Merrill, 1927), 244–48.

26. Norman F. Boas, "Unpublished Manuscripts: Recollections of Mary Todd Lincoln by Her Sister Emilie Todd Helm; An Invitation to a Lincoln Party," *Manuscripts* 43 (Winter 1991): 25.

27. See Burlingame, *Inner World of Lincoln*, 308–13, 325.

William T. Baker

1. William T. Baker's recollections of Lincoln's days as a rail-splitter and soldier appeared in the *St. Louis Globe-Democrat*, 10 January 1909, magazine section, 3.

2. In 1897 J. Otis Humphrey (1850–1918) was appointed judge of the U.S. Court for the Southern District of Illinois. In 1909 he helped found the Lincoln Centennial Association and served as its president (1909–18).

3. Joseph G. Cannon (1836–1926) represented an Illinois district in the U.S. House (1873–91, 1893–1913, 1915–23) and was speaker of that body (1903–11).

4. William Hanks (1765?–1851?), Lincoln's great-uncle, was the father of John Hanks (1802–89), a cousin of Lincoln's mother. In the mid-1820s, William settled in Spencer County, Indiana, where he was a neighbor of the Lincolns briefly. He moved to Macon County, Illinois, in 1829. Between 1830 and 1831, he was once again a neighbor of the Lincolns. On and off between 1822 and 1826 John Hanks lived in the Lincolns' cabin in southwest Indiana. He and Lincoln split rails together in Macon County, Illinois, in 1830.

5. In June and July 1832, James Baker, like Lincoln, served in Captain Jacob Early's company of mounted volunteers.

6. Baker's recollection of Lincoln's boat appeared in the *St. Louis Globe-Democrat*, 31 January 1909, magazine section, 3.

7. This misadventure took place in late April 1831.

8. This event in 1860 drew thousands, including Lincoln; he declined to give a speech. Baker's comments on the rally appeared in the *St. Louis Globe-Democrat*, 3 January 1909, magazine section, 6.

9. For the significance of this remark, see the recollections of Martin L. Bundy.

10. Baker's comments on Lincoln and drinking appeared in the *St. Louis Globe-Democrat*, 17 January 1909, magazine section, 3.

Orville F. Berry

1. Orville F. Berry was an amateur historian and active member of the Illinois State Historical Society. His reminiscences appeared in the *St. Louis Globe-Democrat*, 4 April 1909, magazine section, 3.

2. The Military Tract was an area of approximately 3,500,000 acres, enclosed between the Illinois and Mississippi Rivers, which Congress set aside as bounty land to reward veterans of the War of 1812.

3. Samuel Lincoln (1619?–1690) left Hingham, England, for Massachusetts in 1637.

4. Levi Lincoln (1749–1820) served as governor of Massachusetts (1808–9).

5. The younger Levi Lincoln (1782–1868) served as governor of Massachusetts (1825–34).

6. Enoch Lincoln (1788–1829).

7. Mordecai Lincoln Sr. (1657–1727) was actually the great-great-great-great grandfather of President Lincoln.

8. Mordecai (1686–1736) and Abraham (1688?–1745) had a brother named Isaac and a sister named Sarah.

9. Abraham Lincoln (1744–86) was President Lincoln's grandfather.

10. Mordecai Lincoln (1771?–1830) was President Lincoln's uncle. Thomas Lincoln (1776?–1851) was President Lincoln's father.

11. According to John L. Nall, grandson of Mordecai's sister Nancy, "Old men who knew Uncle Mordecai said that he was a very smart man and exceedingly popular; but was a sporting man and somewhat reckless." See Henry C. Whitney, *Lincoln the Citizen*, ed. Marion Mills Miller (New York: Baker & Taylor, 1908), 8 n. Lincoln's friend Usher F. Linder, who from boyhood knew Mordecai Lincoln, called him "naturally a man of considerable genius . . . of great drollery. . . . [He] was quite a story-teller, and they were generally on the smutty order, and in this Abe resembled his Uncle Mord. . . . He was an honest man, as tender-hearted as a woman, and, to the last degree charitable and benevolent. . . . Lincoln had a very high opinion of his uncle, and on one occasion said to me: 'Linder, I have often said that Uncle Mord had run off with all the talents of the family.' . . . Old Mord . . . had been in his younger days a very stout man, and was quite fond of playing a game of fisticuffs with any one who was noted as a champion. . . . His sons and daughters were not talented, like the old man, but were very sensible people, noted

for their honesty and kindness of heart." Linder, *Reminiscence of the Early Bench*, 38–39.

12. His third son was named James Bradford Lincoln (1802?–1837?).

13. In fact, the shiftless Thomas Lincoln portrayed by traditional biographers is much closer to the truth than the virtuous pillar of the community that revisionists like Louis A. Warren have imagined. See John Y. Simon, *House Divided: Lincoln and His Father* (Fort Wayne IN: Louis A. Warren Library and Museum, 1986). A neighbor of Thomas Lincoln's in Illinois, George B. Balch, declared that Thomas supposedly "was a farmer, and such he was, if one who tilled so little land by such primitive modes could be so called. He never planted more than a few acres, and instead of gathering and hauling it [his crops] in a wagon he usual[l]y carried it to his [reception?] in a basket or large tray." Balch characterized Thomas as "uneducated, illiterate, and contented with a 'from hand to mouth' living," in sum, "an excellent spec[imen] of poor white trash," "rough . . . lazy & worthless." He owned "few sheep" and "talked an[d] walked slow." Balch added, "[s]everal anecdotes of his ignorance and singularity might be related, but we for bear." George B. Balch, "The Father of Abraham Lincoln," manuscript pasted into a copy of Francis Fisher Browne, *The Every-Day Life of Abraham Lincoln*, Lilly Library, Indiana University, Bloomington; Balch's interview with Jesse W. Weik [1886?], in D. Wilson and Davis, *Herndon's Informants*, 597. Cf. Browne, *Every-Day Life of Abraham Lincoln* (New York: N. D. Thompson, 1886), 85–86.

14. The record of Thomas Lincoln's landholdings suggests that he inherited some money, which he used to buy land, but he managed his farm so badly that he was soon impoverished. See Wayne C. Temple, "Thomas and Abraham Lincoln as Farmers," pamphlet (Racine WI: Lincoln Fellowship of Wisconsin, 1996), 12–28; Charles H. Coleman, *Abraham Lincoln and Coles County, Illinois* (New Brunswick NJ: Scarecrow Press, 1955), 19–49; William E. Bartelt, "The Land Dealings of Spencer County, Indiana, Pioneer Thomas Lincoln," *Indiana Magazine of History* 87 (1991): 211–23.

15. In fact, Thomas Lincoln seems to have been a mediocre carpenter at best. An Illinois neighbor deemed him "a cheap carpenter that could put doors, windows, and floors in log houses." George Balch paraphrased in Dr. W. H. Doak, Martinsville IL, to his nephew, Dr. W. D. Ewing of Cambridge OH, n.d., *Terre Haute IN Star*, 11 February 1923. He was "versed only in the skill of a rude carpenter," one Hoosier wrote. See "Abraham Lincoln's Boyhood," anonymous manuscript written on the stationery of the Spencer County Assessor's Office, assessor Bartley Inco, 189—, copy, Francis Marion Van Natter Papers, Vincennes University, Vincennes IN. Bartley Inco's wife was the daughter of Lincoln's friend James Grigsby. In 1807 Denton Geohegan complained of Thomas's "unworkmanlike manner" in hewing

timbers: seven of the twenty-five logs were either too long or too short for Geo-hegan's sawmill. When Geohegan refused to pay, Thomas sued him and won. See Louis A. Warren, *Parentage and Childhood: A History of the Kentucky Lincolns Supported by Documentary Evidence* (New York: Century, 1926), 162–64.

16. Indicted was President Lincoln's first cousin, Abraham Lincoln (1797?–1852), a farmer who migrated from Kentucky to Fountain Green, Illinois, around 1828. He and his wife, Elizabeth Mudd, had seven children.

17. James Bradford Lincoln (1802?–37?) was a cabinet maker who served as the first justice of the peace in Hancock County, as well as a county commissioner and U.S. land commissioner.

18. Robert Lincoln (1826?–68) was described by John Hay in 1867 as a hard-drinking, hard-chewing, "rather rough farmer-looking man" who was dying of consumption. Hay diary, Brown University (entry for 17 June 1867). Hezekiah Lincoln (1829–88), a farmer, lawyer, and merchant, settled in La Harpe, Illinois. He married Phoebe Ann Brewer in 1869. Nicholas Lincoln (1834–88) never married.

19. Abraham Lincoln had four daughters: Ellen, Pricilla, Parmelia, and Mary Jane.

20. Thomas L. Purvis argues that Lincoln was proud of his cousins who belonged to the local elite of Hancock County. No evidence supports this conclusion. Purvis, "The Making of a Myth: Abraham Lincoln's Family Background in the Perspective of Jacksonian Politics," *Journal of the Illinois State Historical Society* 75 (1982): 148–60.

Francis E. Brownell

1. Francis E. Brownell was corporal of the guard in the Ellsworth Zouaves. Elmer Ephriam Ellsworth (1837–61), a kind of surrogate son to Lincoln, was killed on 24 May 1861 in Alexandria, Virginia, shortly after he hauled down a Confederate flag from the roof of a hotel. When Ellsworth was shot, Brownell immediately killed the assassin, who tried to shoot Brownell after felling Ellsworth. Brownell's reminiscences of the event were taken from Washington correspondence, 28 May 1888, *St. Louis Globe Democrat*, 3 June 1888, 29. See also Walter B. Stevens, "Ellsworth's Diary," *St. Louis Globe-Democrat*, 27 May 1888, 29, and an article not signed by Stevens, "Ellsworth and Jackson," *St. Louis Globe-Democrat*, 12 September 1886, 9.

2. James W. Jackson was the proprietor of the Marshall House, a hotel in Alexandria that in 1861 flew the Confederate flag.

3. Soldiers in the Eleventh New York Regiment were recruited in April 1861 by Ellsworth from among the volunteer firemen of New York City.

4. The United States Zouave Cadets, a group of young men from Chicago who had been recruited and trained by Ellsworth in 1860, attracted much attention during their national tour that year.

5. In Chicago Ellsworth had entered the patent-soliciting business with a partner who betrayed him and left him penniless.

6. Henry C. Whitney noted that a "relation like that of knight and squire of the age of chivalry existed between the two" and that Lincoln had an "almost fatherly affection" for Ellsworth. Whitney, *Lincoln the President*, ed. Marion Mills Miller (New York: Baker & Taylor, 1908), 87–88. A biographer of Ellsworth concluded that Lincoln regarded him "with a father's love." See Ruth Painter Randall, *Colonel Elmer Ellsworth: A Biography of Lincoln's Friend and First Hero of the Civil War* (Boston: Little, Brown, 1960), 261. See also John R. Turner Ettlinger, "A Young Hero—Elmer Ellsworth, 1837–1861," *Books at Brown* 19: 23–68 (1963), and Charles A. Ingraham, *Elmer E. Ellsworth and the Zouaves of '61* (Chicago: Univ. of Chicago Press, 1925).

7. John E. Wool (1784–1869) commanded the Department of the East at the beginning of the war.

8. In 1847 Edwin D. and Henry A. Willard took over Fuller's City Hotel, which stood two blocks from the White House at 14th Street and Pennsylvania Avenue, remodeled it, and named it the Willard Hotel. Nathaniel Hawthorne said that "it may much more justly be called the center of Washington and the Union than . . . the Capitol, the White House, or the State Department."

Martin L. Bundy

1. Martin L. Bundy (b. 1818) served as a colonel in an Indiana regiment during the Civil War. His reminiscences appeared in the *St. Louis Globe-Democrat*, 3 January 1909, magazine section, 6.

2. Robert Toombs (1810–85) represented a Georgia district in the U.S. House (1845–53) and served in the U.S. Senate (1853–61). Alexander H. Stephens (1812–83) represented a Georgia district in the U.S. House (1843–59) and served as vice president of the Confederacy (1861–65).

3. Attorney Horatio M. Vandeveer was clerk of the Christian County Circuit Court.

Stephen R. Capps

1. Stephen R. Capps's comments appeared in the *St. Louis Globe-Democrat*, 14 February 1909, magazine section, 3.

2. There, on 11 February 1859, Lincoln lectured on the topic "Discoveries and Inventions." See Basler, *Collected Works of Lincoln*, 3:356–63.

John Carmody

1. John Carmody's reminiscences appeared in the *St. Louis Globe-Democrat*, 24 January 1909, magazine section, 3.

2. James C. Robinson (1823–86), a Springfield lawyer who unsuccessfully ran for governor in 1864, served in the U.S. House of Representatives (1859–65, 1871–75). Usher F. Linder regarded him "as a very remarkable man" and likened him to Lincoln "in that he has risen to high distinction in spite of the deficiencies of his education, by the force of his native intellect." Linder, *Reminiscences of the Early Bench*, 132. Norman M. Broadwell (1825–93) studied law with Lincoln in 1852 and served as a Sangamon County judge, a member of the state legislature, and mayor of Springfield. Christopher C. Brown (1834–1904) was a prominent Springfield attorney. William Henry Herndon (1818–91) was Lincoln's biographer and third law partner.

3. James Lea Lamb was a prominent Springfield merchant.

4. John M. Palmer (1817–1900) was a lawyer from Carlinville who represented Illinois in the U.S. Senate (1891–97).

5. Carmody doubtless means Ninian W. Edwards (1809–89), husband of Lincoln's sister-in-law Elizabeth. He was the son of Ninian Edwards (1775–1833), governor of Illinois Territory (1809–18).

Augustus H. Chapman

1. Augustus H. Chapman (1822–98), husband of Dennis Hanks's daughter Harriet, served as an officer in the Civil War and in 1865 became agent for the Flathead Indians in Montana. He gave William Herndon several valuable statements about Lincoln. Chapman's reminiscences here were taken from Charleston IL correspondence, 4 January 1887, *St. Louis Globe-Democrat*, 6 January 1887, 6.

Jonathan H. Cheney

1. Jonathan H. Cheney's comments and copy of Lincoln's speech appeared in the *St. Louis Globe-Democrat*, 3 January 1909, magazine section, 3.

2. There are at least three other versions of this speech. See Basler, *Collected Works of Lincoln*, 3:190–91.

Enos Clarke

1. Enos Clarke's reminiscences of Lincoln's meeting with the Missouri delegation appeared in the *St. Louis Globe-Democrat*, 14 March 1909, magazine section, 3.

2. William Cullen Bryant (1794–1878), a celebrated poet, edited the *New York Evening Post*.

3. The battle of Chickamauga, Georgia, was fought 19–20 September 1863. There Union General William S. Rosecrans was defeated.

4. Confederate General Braxton Bragg (1817–76) commanded the Army of Tennessee.

5. Between 4 and 14 July 1863, Gen. George Gordon Meade failed to pursue vigorously Lee's beaten army, which escaped across the Potomac, much to the dismay of Lincoln and his constituents.

6. Hamilton R. Gamble (1798–1864) was the Unionist governor of Missouri (1861–64).

7. General Benjamin F. Butler (1818–93) of Massachusetts had won the admiration of Radicals by declaring that fugitive slaves reaching his lines were "contraband of war." General John M. Schofield (1831–96) commanded the Department of Missouri (May 1863–January 1864).

8. Odon Guitar was a leading guerrilla fighter.

9. Charles D. Drake represented Missouri in the U.S. Senate (1867–70) and served as chief justice of the court of claims (1870–85).

10. Benjamin F. Loan (1819–81) of St. Joseph served in the U.S. House (1863–69). Joseph W. McClurg (1818–1900) represented a Missouri district in the U.S. House (1865–68) and served as governor (1869–71).

11. Emil Preetorius (1827–1905) edited the *St. Louis Westliche Post* for forty years.

12. Charles Philip Johnson (1836–1920), a leading member of the St. Louis bar, was elected lieutenant-governor of Missouri in 1872.

13. John Hay and William O. Stoddard took notes on this important meeting, which are reproduced in appendix 3.

14. Samuel R. Curtis (1817–66) was relieved as commander of the Department of Missouri in May 1863.

15. Lincoln to Gamble, Washington, 23 July 1863, in Basler, *Collected Works of Lincoln*, 6:344.

James D. Conner

1. James D. Conner's recollections of traveling with Lincoln appeared in the *St. Louis Globe-Democrat*, 7 February 1909, magazine section, 3, 7.

2. Stevens's account is based on Conner's letter to James R. B. Van Cleave, Winona Lake IN, 6 July 1908, files of the Abraham Lincoln Association, folder 2, "Reminiscences," Illinois State Historical Library, Springfield.

3. Oliver P. Morton (1823–77) served as governor of Indiana (1861–68).

4. General George K. Steele, an Indiana state senator, was chairman of the committee of Indiana legislators that accompanied the president-elect through the Hoosier State.

Shelby M. Cullom

1. Shelby M. Cullom's reminiscences about Lincoln appeared in the *St. Louis Globe-Democrat*, 17 January 1909, magazine section, 3.

2. Shelby M. Cullom (1829–1914) of Springfield served in the Illinois legislature (1856–62), the U.S. House (1865–71), and U.S. Senate (1883–1913).

3. Cf. Mrs. Seymour Moody to Lincoln, Springfield, 19 July 1861, Lincoln Papers, Library of Congress. In July Lincoln appointed John Armstrong postmaster of Springfield.

4. John George Nicolay (1832–1901) was Lincoln's principal private secretary.

5. James G. Blaine of Maine served as speaker of the U.S. House (1869–75).

6. James A. Garfield (1831–81) of Ohio was elected president in 1880 and assassinated in 1881.

7. Andrew Johnson (1808–75) was elected vice president in 1864.

George T. M. Davis

1. George T. M. Davis, *Autobiography of the Late Gen. T. M. Davis* (New York: Mrs. Ellen D. Cady and Mrs. Susan Train Guluger, 1891). This section on Lincoln's letter to Davis appeared in the *St. Louis Globe-Democrat*, 21 February 1909, magazine section, 3.

2. The full text of this letter appears in Basler, *Collected Works of Lincoln*, 4:132–33.

3. Stevens's article on Lincoln and the governorship of Oregon appeared in the *St. Louis Globe-Democrat*, 7 March 1909, magazine section, 3. In 1849 Lincoln was at first offered the post of secretary of Oregon Territory; when he turned that down, he was offered the governorship. The inside story of this episode was told by John Todd Stuart to John G. Nicolay:

When Mr. Fillmore [Zachary Taylor] became President, a number of his friends here who felt that Mr. Lincoln was entitled to some recognition at the hands of the Administration, signed and sent to Washington a request to the President to appoint him Commissioner of the General Land Office. Mr. [Justin] Butterfield had however got an inkling of what was going on, and made haste to get the appointment through the influence of Mr. [Daniel] Webster, as it was thought at the time.

The Administration however did not entirely forget the matter, and evidently thinking that the paper which had been sent forward was one which ought not to be neglected, determined to appoint him Governor of the Territory of Oregon.

We were at Bloomington attending Court together, when a special messenger came up there who had been sent from here with the information that this appointment had been tendered him. On our way down from Bloomington he talked the matter over with me, and asked my opinion about it. I told him I thought it was a good thing: that he could go out there and in all likelihood come back from there as a Senator when the State was admitted.

Mr. Lincoln finally made up his mind that he would accept the place if Mary would consent to go.

But Mary would not consent to go out there.

[Joshua] Speed told me that Lincoln wrote to him that if he would go along, he would give him any appointment out there which he might be able to control. Lincoln evidently thought that if Speed and Speed's wife were to go along, it would be an inducement for Mary to change her mind and consent to go.

But Speed thought he could not go, and so the matter didn't come to anything.

Mary had a very violent temper, but she had more intellectual power than she has generally be[en] given credit for.

Interview dated 24 June 1875, in *An Oral History of Abraham Lincoln: John G. Nicolay's Interviews and Essays*, ed. Michael Burlingame (Carbondale: Southern Illinois Univ. Press, 1996), 15.

4. Simeon Francis (1796–1872) had founded the *Sangamo Journal* in 1831. In 1849 Lincoln worked in vain to win him the post of secretary of Oregon Territory.

5. Wayne C. Temple has suggested that Mary Todd seduced Lincoln at the home of Simeon Francis and thus got him to marry her. Temple, *Abraham Lincoln: From Skeptic to Prophet* (Mahomet IL: Mayhaven, 1995), 27.

6. Over the years Lincoln contributed many anonymous and pseudonymous pieces to the *Sangamo Journal*. See Simeon Francis to Anson G. Henry, 14 July 1855, Henry Papers, Illinois State Historical Library, Springfield; memo by William Henry Bailhache, San Diego, 14 January 1898, and statement of Col. J. D. Roper, 22 October 1897, enclosed in J. McCan Davis to Ida M. Tarbell, Springfield, 27 November 1897, Tarbell Papers, Allegheny College, Meadville PA; Albert J. Beveridge, *Abraham Lincoln: 1809–1858*, 2 vols. (Boston: Houghton Mifflin, 1928) 1:183–84; William E. Barton, "Abraham Lincoln, Newspaper Man," typescript, and "Lincoln Editorials," handwritten memo, Springfield, 28 December 1928, and undated typescript of the same title, Barton Papers, University of Chicago; Audus Walton Shipton, "Lincoln's Association with the Journal" (pamphlet, 1939); Andy Van Meter, *Always My Friend: A History of the State Journal–Register and Springfield* (Springfield: Copley Press, 1981), 48–49, 67–68; William E. Baringer, *Lincoln's Vandalia: A Pioneer Portrait* (New Brunswick NJ: Rutgers Univ. Press, 1949), 62; Albert J. Beveridge to J. C. Thompson, 5 March 1925, copy, Beveridge Papers, Library of Congress; Harry E. Pratt, "Lincoln in the Legislature," pamphlet (Madison: Lincoln Fellowship of Wisconsin, 1947), 6; Robert S. Harper, *Lincoln and the Press* (New York: McGraw-Hill, 1951), 2, 14–15; Glenn H. Seymour, "'Conservative'—Another Lincoln Pseudonym?" *Journal of the Illinois State Historical Society* 29 (1936): 135–50; [Paul M. Angle], "Lincoln—Author of the Letters by a Conservative," *Bulletin of the Abraham Lincoln Association*, no. 50 (Dec. 1937), 8–9. James G. Randall agreed with Glenn Seymour's conclusion that the "Conservative" letters were probably by Lincoln. Seymour's thesis "is ingeniously presented, and the reasoning seems pretty sound. . . . The main arguments for Lincoln's authorship seem to be his connection with the *Journal* and the test of literary style. The letters do seem to have a kind of Lincoln tang." Randall to Arthur C. Cole, 20 March 1936, copy, James G. Randall Papers, Library of Congress. According to William Herndon, Lincoln had "undisputed use" of the columns of that paper, whose name was eventually changed to the *Illinois State Journal*. Herndon said, "I frequently wrote the editorials in the *Springfield Journal*, the editor, Simeon Francis, giving to Lincoln and to me the utmost liberty in that direction. Occasionally Lincoln would write out matter for publication." Both men wrote for the *Journal* until 1860. See Angle, *Herndon's Lincoln*, 184, 296, 197. James Matheny, the best man at Lincoln's wedding, recalled that when he served as deputy postmaster in Springfield in the mid-1830s he "got to Know Lincoln's hand writing as such P. M—He Lincoln used to write Editorials as far back as 1834—or 5 for [Simeon] Francis—[editor of] the *Sangamon Journal*—took hundreds of such Editorials from Lincoln to the *Journal* office." James H. Matheny, interview by William Herndon, November 1866, in D. Wilson and Davis, *Herndon's Informants*, 431. In fact,

between 1834 and 1837, when Lincoln left New Salem for Springfield, the *Sangamo Journal* printed scores of anonymous and pseudonymous contributions that Lincoln probably wrote.

7. John Addison was a clerk in the Interior Department.

Thomas Dowling

1. Thomas S. Dowling married Dennis Hanks's daughter Sarah Jane (1822–1907). His comments about Lincoln are taken from Charleston IL, correspondence, 4 January 1887, *St. Louis Globe-Democrat*, 6 January 1887, 6.

2. Henry Pelham Holmes Bromwell (1823–1903), a law partner of Usher F. Linder, represented his district in the U.S. House (1865–69).

3. Lincoln did express anger rather more than is commonly thought. See Paul M. Angle, "Abe Lincoln Had a Temper," *Midwest: Magazine of the Chicago Sunday Times*, 12 Feb. 1956, 6; and Burlingame, *Inner World of Lincoln*, 145–235.

4. Stephen Trigg Logan (1800–80) was Lincoln's second law partner. When he began studying law, Lincoln borrowed books from John Todd Stuart, who in 1836 became his first law partner.

Mrs. Benjamin S. Edwards

1. He was actually worth about $15,000. Mrs. Benjamin S. Edwards's reminiscences about Lincoln appeared in the *St. Louis Globe-Democrat*, 21 February 1909, magazine section, 3.

2. When he left for Washington, Lincoln withdrew $400 from his bank account, which left a balance of $600. He did not have to borrow money.

3. Lucian Tilton, president of the Great Western Railroad, rented the Lincoln home from 1861 until 1869, when he and his family moved to Chicago.

4. Mrs. Benjamin S. Edwards, nee Helen K. Dodge (1818–1909), grew up in Kaskaskia, New York City, and New Haven. She met her future husband when he was a student at Yale; they were married in 1839 and settled in Springfield the following year. She became friendly with Mary Todd, whom she called "a great reader" who possessed "a remarkably retentive memory. Her brilliant conversation, often embellished with apt quotations, made her society much sought after by the young people of the town. She was quick at repartee and when the occasion seemed to require it was sarcastic and severe." She had "a fine mind and cultivated tastes." After the assassination of her husband, Mary Lincoln told Mrs. Edwards "of her fear lest Mr. Lincoln should be defeated in his re-election [in 1864], adding: 'I could have gone down on my knees to ask votes for him and again and again he

said: "Mary, I am afraid you will be punished for this overweening anxiety. If I am to be re-elected it will be all right; if not, you must bear the disappointment.'" Mary Edwards Raymond, ed., *Some Incidents in the Life of Mrs. Benjamin S. Edwards* (privately printed, 1909), 11–12, 16.

Orlando B. Ficklin

1. Democrat Orlando Bell Ficklin (1808–86) represented the Charleston district in the U.S. House (1843–49, 1851–53). This article on Ficklin's reminiscences on Lincoln is taken from Charleston IL correspondence, 4 January 1887, *St. Louis Globe-Democrat*, 6 January 1887, 6. For further Lincoln reminiscences by Ficklin, see William Melvin McConnell, *The Classmate*, 6 February 1926, clipping, Lincoln Museum, Fort Wayne IN.

2. Charles Maltby, Lincoln's assistant in Denton Offutt's New Salem store, recalled that Lincoln would, after studying hard for two or three hours, relax and "take up Burns' poems, which he read much and admired greatly. He read with that hilarity which usually was so peculiar to him, some of the most humorous productions of that versatile poet, his favorite selections being Tom O'Shanter, Address to the Dial, Highland Mary, Bonny Jeane and Dr. Hornbrook. Having a very retentive memory he soon became familiar with these poems and many others; and his frequent quotations from them indicated the humorous inclination of his mind in his early life. There were times, however, when his countenance and actions indicated more serious thoughts, and memory was busy with incidents of his boyhood days. He then would read the Cotter's Saturday Night, or Gray's Elegy, or one of Cowper's poems. The reading of the poets was subordinate to his general studies. He often said that he only read them as a relish or dessert after taking the more solid and substantial food." Maltby, *The Life and Public Services of Abraham Lincoln* (Stockton CA: Daily Independent Steam Power Print, 1884), 31–32. Milton Hay, who worked in Lincoln's law office in 1839 and 1840, said that at that time "Burns and Shakespeare were his favorites. He could nearly quote of [sic] all of Burns' Poems from memory. I have frequently heard him quote the whole of 'Tam O'Shanter,' 'Holy Willies prayer' and large parts of [']the Cotter's Saturday Night' from memory only. He had acquired the Scotch accent, and could render Burns perfectly." Milton Hay to John Hay, Springfield, 8 February 1887, Hay Papers, Brown University. Scottish poet Thomas Campbell (1777–1844) wrote "The Last Man."

3. Lincoln denounced President Polk for provoking the war, but he supported all appropriations for the troops prosecuting it.

4. Lincoln's criticism of the way in which the Mexican War began did not hurt him politically. See Gabor Boritt, "A Question of Political Suicide: Lincoln's Oppo-

sition to the Mexican War," *Journal of the Illinois State Historical Society* 67 (1974): 79–100; and Mark E. Neely Jr., "Lincoln and the Mexican War: An Argument by Analogy," *Civil War History* 24 (1978): 5–24.

5. On 3 March 1837, Lincoln and another member of the Illinois General Assembly, Dan Stone, filed a protest against a resolution condemning abolitionists that the legislature had passed six weeks earlier by the lopsided vote of 77 to 6, with Lincoln and Stone among the minority. That popular resolution declared that Illinois legislators "highly disapprove of the formation of abolition societies, and of the doctrines promulgated by them," that "the right of property in slaves is sacred to the slave-holding States by the Federal Government, and that they cannot be deprived of that right without their consent," and that "the General Government cannot abolish slavery in the District of Columbia, against the will of the citizens of said District without a manifest breach of good faith." State of Illinois, *House Journal, 1836–37*, 241–44. In their protest, Lincoln and Stone stated their belief "that the institution of slavery is founded on both injustice and bad policy; but that the promulgation of abolition doctrines tends rather to increase than to abate its evils." The document further stated its authors' belief that "the Congress of the United States has the power, under the constitution, to abolish slavery in the District of Columbia; but that power ought not to be exercised unless at the request of the people of said District." See Basler, *Collected Works of Lincoln*, 1:74–75. Lincoln had tried to amend the original resolution to permit abolition in the District with the consent of the people living there. What is striking about the Lincoln-Stone protest is not its unfavorable comments about abolitionism; in 1837 the overwhelming majority of Illinoisans—indeed, of white Americans in general—were hostile to abolitionists. What is truly remarkable about Lincoln was his willingness to vote against the resolution condemning them and then, in a public document, to brand slavery unjust. In 1860, Lincoln declared that this 1837 protest "briefly defined his position on the slavery question; and so far as it goes, it was then the same that it is now." See Lincoln, autobiography for John Locke Scripps, ca. June 1860, in Basler, *Collected Works of Lincoln*, 4:65.

William Fisher

1. William Fisher's account of the Henry Clay Convention appeared in the *St. Louis Globe-Democrat*, 14 March 1909, magazine section, 3.

2. Fisher's comments on Lincoln's temperance lecture appeared in the *St. Louis Globe-Democrat*, 17 January 1909, magazine section, 3.

3. In Springfield on 22 February 1842, Lincoln gave a temperance address. See Basler, *Collected Works of Lincoln*, 1:271–79.

Mrs. Annie C. Fox

1. Mrs. Annie C. Fox's reminiscences appeared in the *St. Louis Globe-Democrat*, 7 February 1909, magazine section, 3.

2. The *National Era*, published in Washington and edited by Gamaliel Bailey, was a leading abolitionist newspaper.

Thomas Goodwin

1. Thomas Goodwin was a preacher in the Disciples of Christ denomination with a reputation as "a great man to 'holler.'" See Coleman, *Lincoln and Coles County*, 133. Goodwin's reminiscences were taken from Charleston IL correspondence, 4 January 1887, *St. Louis Globe-Democrat*, 6 January 1887, 6.

2. John D. Johnston (1815–54) was Abraham Lincoln's step-brother.

Dennis Hanks

1. The interview with Dennis Hanks is taken from Charleston correspondence, 4 January 1887, *St. Louis Globe-Democrat*, 6 January 1887, 6. Though Stevens claims to have conducted this interview, his text is virtually a verbatim reproduction of an interview by Robert McIntyre that appeared first in the *Charleston IL Courier*, n.d., was reprinted in the *Paris IL Gazette*, and was reprinted again in the *Chicago Tribune*, 30 May 1885.

2. A full statement by Christopher Columbus Graham (1784–1885) about the wedding of Thomas Lincoln and Nancy Hanks can be found in Ida M. Tarbell, *The Early Life of Abraham Lincoln* (New York: S. S. McClure, 1896), 231–36.

John B. Henderson

1. John B. Henderson (1826–1913) represented Missouri in the U.S. Senate (1862–69). His reminiscences are taken from Washington correspondence, 16 January 1888, *St. Louis Globe-Democrat*, 18 January 1888, 6. Cf. Henderson, "Emancipation and Impeachment," *Century Magazine* 85 (December 1912): 196–209; and Henderson's funeral oration, delivered in Louisiana MO, 23 April 1865, uni-

dentified clipping (ca. 3 May 1865, probably from a St. Louis paper), John Hay scrapbooks, 55:31, Hay Papers, Library of Congress.

2. Trusten Polk (1811–76) represented Missouri in the U.S. Senate (1857–62).

3. Benjamin Franklin Wade (1800–78) represented Ohio in the U.S. Senate (1851–69). Zachariah Chandler (1813–79) represented Michigan in the U.S. Senate (1857–75, 1879).

4. For other versions of this story, see Titian J. Coffey in Rice, *Reminiscences of Lincoln*, 237–38; Adlai E. Stevenson, *Something of Men I Have Known* (Chicago: A. C. McClurg, 1909), 352–53; and Francis B. Carpenter, *Six Months at the White House with Abraham Lincoln* (New York: Hurd and Houghton, 1866), 256–57.

J. F. Humphreys

1. J. F. Humphreys's impressions of the "lost speech" appeared in the *St. Louis Globe-Democrat*, 24 January 1909, magazine section, 3.

James T. Jones

1. James T. Jones's impressions of Lincoln's storytelling appeared in the *St. Louis Globe-Democrat*, 3 January 1909, magazine section, 3.

2. Jones's further impressions of Lincoln appeared in the *St. Louis Globe-Democrat*, 14 March 1909, magazine section, 3.

Lyman Lacey

1. Lyman Lacey's impressions of Lincoln's storytelling appeared in the *St. Louis Globe-Democrat*, 3 January 1909, magazine section, 3.

2. In 1873 Democrat Lyman Lacey (b. 1832) was elected judge of the Illinois state appeals court, a post he held for twenty-four years. In 1857–58 he assisted Lincoln during the trial of Duff Armstrong. See Lacey to John T. Hobson, Havana IL, 22 August 1908, in J. T. Hobson, *Footprints of Abraham Lincoln* (Dayton OH: Otterbein Press, 1909), 45–47.

3. William Walker moved in 1865 from Illinois to Lexington, Missouri, where he served as a county judge.

4. Lacey's impressions of Lincoln and Douglas appeared in the *St. Louis Globe-Democrat*, 10 January 1909, magazine section, 3.

5. This exchange actually took place during the first of the joint debates, held at Ottawa.

Edward F. Leonard

1. Edward F. Leonard's recollections of Lincoln's departure for Washington appeared in the *St. Louis Globe-Democrat*, 7 February 1909, magazine section, 3. Stevens's account is based on Leonard's letter to James R. B. Van Cleave, Amherst MA, 8 January 1909, Abraham Lincoln Association files, folder 2, "Reminiscences," Illinois State Historical Library, Springfield.

2. In 1857 Edward F. Leonard (1837–1915) went from Massachusetts to Springfield, where he read law with William Herndon and John A. McClernand. He then worked in the office of the state auditor, Lincoln's friend Jesse K. Dubois. After the Civil War he served as secretary of the St. Louis, Alton and Terre Haute Railroad and eventually became president of the Toledo, Peoria, and Western Railroad. When Shelby Cullom was elected governor, he chose Leonard to be his personal secretary.

3. William S. Wood was appointed superintendent of public buildings in 1861, but his nomination was withdrawn when unethical conduct on his part came to the attention of Congress and the president.

4. F. M. Bowen was the superintendent of the Great Western Railroad, according to Victor Searcher, *Lincoln's Journey to Greatness* (Philadelphia: John C. Winston, 1960), 8.

5. Basler, *Collected Works of Lincoln*, 3:194–96.

Thomas J. Lincoln

1. This account of the Lincoln extended family appeared in the *St. Louis Globe-Democrat*, 7 February 1909, magazine section, 5. Lincoln's cousins are described in William E. Barton, *The Lineage of Lincoln* (Indianapolis: Bobbs-Merrill, 1929), 99–123.

2. James Bradford Lincoln in 1821 married Frances Day, daughter of William and Frances Day. Abraham Lincoln's daughter Nancy married William Brumfield (1778–1858) and bore him four children.

3. Abraham Lincoln (1744–86) was the son of John and Rebecca Flower Morris Lincoln.

4. Samuel Haycraft (1752–1823) came to the Elizabethtown area around 1779 and built one of the three forts that constituted the original settlement.

5. Mordecai Lincoln moved his family from Washington County to Grayson County in 1811. Nineteen years later he migrated to Illinois.

6. Mordecai's son Abraham was born ca. 1797.

7. In fact, there is abundant evidence that the Lincolns were regarded by their

relatives and by their frontier neighbors as unusually poor. See D. Wilson and Davis, *Herndon's Informants*, 86–87, 176–77, 240–41, 245, 658; J. Edward Murr, "Lincoln in Indiana," *Indiana Magazine of History* 14 (1918): 13; Bess V. Ehrmann, *The Missing Chapter in the Life of Abraham Lincoln* (Chicago: Walter M. Hill, 1938), 92–93.

8. Major Ben Helm (1767–1858) was a prosperous merchant, farmer, and town clerk. He founded his store with Duff Green, who in time became a trusted adviser to Andrew Jackson.

9. John B. Helm (1797–1872) was a leading merchant and lawyer in Elizabethtown. In 1852 he moved to Hannibal, Missouri, where he became a judge of the Court of Common Pleas.

10. John B. Helm's story does not jibe with other accounts, including Lincoln's. See R. Gerald McMurtry, *A Series of Monographs Concerning the Lincolns and Hardin County, Kentucky* (Elizabethtown KY: Enterprise Press, 1938), 31–34.

11. Captain Thomas Helm settled in the area of Elizabethtown around 1779. He was one of the three original settlers.

12. John L. Helm (1802–67) served as governor of Kentucky (1850–51, 1867).

13. In 1856 Benjamin Hardin Helm (1831–63) married Emilie Todd (1836–1930), Mary Todd Lincoln's half-sister.

14. The minister was David Elkin, whom a historian of Kentucky Baptists called "uncultivated, being barely able to read," "extremely poor, as to this world's goods," "very indolent and slovenly in his dress." Elkin's reputation was "somewhat sullied in his latter years, perhaps from too free a use of strong drink." See J. H. Spencer, *A History of Kentucky Baptists from 1769 to 1885*, 2 vols. (Cincinnati: J. R. Baumes, 1885), 1:336.

15. Around 1850 Lincoln did, famously, declare to his law partner, William H. Herndon: "All that I am or hope ever to be I get from my mother—God bless her." Herndon to Ward Hill Lamon, 6 March 1870, Lamon Papers, Huntington Library, San Marino CA. In his correspondence and other writings, Herndon never quotes Lincoln referring to his "angel" mother. That expression originated in an interview Herndon gave to George Alfred Townsend, who reported that Lincoln "broke out once to Mr. Herndon, as they were returning from court in another county: 'Billy, all I am or can be I owe to my angel-mother.'" *New York Tribune*, 15 February 1867. Cf. "The Lincoln Mother Controversy," *Lincoln Lore*, no. 832 (19 March 1945).

16. In 1806 Sarah Bush (1788–1869) married Daniel Johnston, who died in 1818.

17. Matilda, John, and Sarah.

18. Thomas Jefferson Lincoln (1822–1914) married Martha Jane Burres in 1851.

19. In the spring of 1839, William Fraim was convicted of murder and executed.

20. Keokuk, Iowa, is located across the Mississippi River from Carthage, county seat of Hancock County.

21. Emily Susan Lincoln (1830–92).

Mrs. James Judson Lord

1. Mrs. Kate Lord was the daughter of Charles Smalley, a prosperous merchant. She recounts her husband's recollections of Lincoln in the *St. Louis Globe-Democrat*, 7 February 1909, magazine section, 3.

2. Dr. James Judson Lord wrote the dedicatory poem read at the unveiling of the Lincoln national memorial in October 1874. He gave a statement to Herndon about Lincoln. D. Wilson and Davis, *Herndon's Informants*, 358. Lord was listed in the 1860–61 Springfield directory as "proprietor of Dr. Topping's Alternative Sirup." He wrote books about Lincoln that were never published. Franklin Lord (nephew of J. J. Lord) to William E. Barton, n.p., n.d., Barton Papers, box 9, folder 5, University of Chicago.

Robert W. McClaughry

1. Major Robert Wilson McClaughry (1839–1920) served in the 118th Illinois regiment during the Civil War. He was warden of the Illinois state prison in Joliet (1874–88) and the federal prison in Leavenworth, Kansas (1899–1913). His recollections of Lincoln appeared in the *St. Louis Globe-Democrat*, 21 February 1909, magazine section, 3. McLaughrey's reminiscences originally appeared in the *Springfield Illinois State Journal*, 29 January 1909, reprinted in R. Wilson, *Intimate Memories of Lincoln*, 55–58.

2. McClaughry's recollections of Lincoln's funeral procession appeared in the *St. Louis Globe-Democrat*, 21 February 1909, magazine section, 3.

3. A historian observed that Lincoln's death "burdened every black with a personal sense of loss." Benjamin Quarles, *The Negro in the Civil War* (Boston: Little, Brown, 1953), 345. The day after Lincoln died, a black preacher in Troy, New York, declared: "We, as a people, feel more than all others that we are bereaved. We had learned to love Mr. Lincoln as we have never loved man before. We idolized his very name. We looked up to him as our saviour, our deliverer. His name was familiar with our children, and our prayers ascended to God in his behalf. He had taught us to love him. The interest he manifested in behalf of the oppressed, the weak and

those who had none to help them, had won for him a large place in our heart. It was something so new to us to see such sentiments manifested by the chief magistrate of the United States that we could not help but love him." Jacob Thomas of the African Methodist Episcopal Zion Church, quoted in David B. Chesebrough, *"No Sorrow like Our Sorrow:" Northern Protestant Ministers and the Assassination of Lincoln* (Kent OH: Kent State Univ. Press, 1994), 18. See also Carpenter, *Six Months at the White House*, 345; Howard K. Beale, ed., *The Diary of Gideon Welles, Secretary of the Navy under Lincoln and Johnson*, 3 vols. (New York: Norton, 1960), 2 (19 April 1865): 293; and B. F. Winslow to his grandfather, Washington DC, 18 April 1865, S. Griswold Flagg Collection, box 2, Sterling Library, Yale University.

Thompson Ware McNeely

1. Thompson Ware McNeely's reminiscences appeared in the *St. Louis Globe-Democrat*, 21 February 1909, magazine section, 3.

2. Thompson Ware McNeely (1835–1921), son of Robert T. McNeely, who owned land in New Salem, attended law school in Louisville, Kentucky. In 1862 he served as a delegate to the Illinois State Constitutional Convention. In 1866 he shared his reminiscences of Lincoln and New Salem with William Herndon. See D. Wilson and Davis, *Herndon's Informants*, 424–25.

3. Most historians doubt the story about Lincoln's prophetic "hit it hard" statement, for its source, John Hanks, was not with Lincoln at the time.

4. On Lincoln's depressions, see Burlingame, *Inner World of Lincoln*, 92–122.

Henry Guest McPike

1. Henry Guest McPike's reminiscences of Lincoln and his son Tad appeared in the *St. Louis Globe-Democrat*, 10 January 1909, magazine section, 3.

John F. Mendonsa

1. John F. Mendonsa's reminiscences of Lincoln appeared in the *St. Louis Globe-Democrat*, 12 February 1909, 3. Stevens based this article on Mendonsa's letter to James R. B. Van Cleave, Springfield, 2 July 1908, Lincoln Centennial Association's vertical files, folder 3, "Reminiscences," Illinois State Historical Library, Springfield.

2. Mary Lincoln's stinginess is examined in Burlingame, *Inner World of Lincoln*, 274–76.

Joseph B. Messick

1. Joseph B. Messick's recollections of Lincoln appeared in the *St. Louis Globe-Democrat*, 4 April 1909, magazine section, 3.

2. Born in Green County, Kentucky, in 1807, Alexander Sympson migrated to Illinois in 1836 and settled in Carthage eight years later. Lincoln called Sympson a "confidential friend." See Basler, *Collected Works of Lincoln*, 4:43.

Ezra M. Prince

1. Ezra M. Prince's recollections of his journey with Lincoln appeared in the *St. Louis Globe-Democrat*, 7 February 1909, magazine section, 3. A typescript of Prince's essay, "A Day and a Night with Abraham Lincoln," from which this excerpt was taken by Stevens, is in the Herndon-Weik Papers, Library of Congress.

Addison G. Proctor

1. Addison G. Proctor's recollections of Lincoln's nomination for president appeared in the *St. Louis Globe-Democrat*, 7 February 1909, magazine section, 3. See also Proctor's account of the 1860 convention in R. Wilson, *Lincoln among His Friends*, 201–9.

2. John C. Heenan, a native of Troy, New York, was called "the Benicia boy" because he first came to prominence in Benicia, California.

3. Jacob Collamer (1791–1865) represented Vermont in the U.S. Senate (1855–65).

4. Edward Bates (1793–1869) of Missouri served as Lincoln's attorney general (1861–64).

5. Andrew Gregg Curtin (1815?–94) was governor of Pennsylvania (1861–65). Henry Smith Lane (1811–81) was elected governor of Indiana in 1860. Samuel J. Kirkwood (1813–94) was elected governor of Iowa in 1859.

John W. Proctor

1. John W. Proctor moved to Sangamon County in 1824 and became a banker in Lewiston IL. His recollections of Lincoln appeared in the *St. Louis Globe-Democrat*, 3 January 1909, magazine section, 3. See also Proctor to James R. B. Van Cleave, Canton IL, 1 July 1908, Abraham Lincoln Association Vertical Files, Illinois State Historical Library, Springfield.

2. Lincoln spoke in Vermont on 27 October.

Owen T. Reeves

1. Owen T. Reeves's commentary on Lincoln and Judge David appeared in the *St. Louis Globe-Democrat*, 21 February 1909, magazine section, 3.

2. Thomas Ewing (1829–96) of Leavenworth commanded the District of the Border during the Civil War and served in Congress (1877–81).

3. John James Ingalls (1833–1900) of Atchinson represented Kansas in the U.S. Senate (1873–91).

4. Reeves's insights on Lincoln's high fee appeared in the *St. Louis Globe-Democrat*, 14 February 1909, magazine section, 3.

James P. Root

1. James P. Root (b. 1830) was a lawyer in New York before moving to Chicago in 1854, where he became an active Republican and was named Cook County attorney in 1873. His reminiscences of Lincoln appeared in the *St. Louis Globe-Democrat*, 3 January 1909, magazine section, 3.

2. John McLean (1785–1861) was a justice of the U.S. Supreme Court (1830–61). Thomas Drummond (b. 1809) was a judge of the U.S. district court for Illinois (1850–69).

3. A native of New Hampshire and an alumnus of Williams College, Justin Butterfield (1790–1855) practiced law in New York before moving to Chicago, where he became a prominent lawyer. From 1841 to 1844 he was U.S. district attorney in Chicago. In 1849 Butterfield won the commissionership of the general land office, a post for which Lincoln had fought hard.

Henry M. Russell

1. Henry M. Russell's account of Lincoln's game of billiards appeared in the *St. Louis Globe-Democrat*, 31 January 1909, magazine section, 3. Stevens based his account on Russell's letter to James R. B. Van Cleave, Urbana IL, 14 August 1908, files of the Abraham Lincoln Association, folder 2, "Reminiscences," Illinois State Historical Library, Springfield.

2. At various times in his early adulthood in Urbana, Henry M. Russell (b. 1826) taught school, worked at a hotel, and drove a stage.

3. Jarius Corydon Sheldon came from Ohio to Urbana in 1853 and began to study law in 1855. Lincoln examined him when he applied for admission to the bar.

Benjamin F. Shaw

1. Benjamin F. Shaw (1831–1900) served an apprenticeship in the office of the *Rock Island Advertiser* (1848–51) before becoming editor and publisher of the *Dixon Telegraph and Lee County Herald* in 1851. He remained at that post until his death. His reminiscences of Lincoln appeared in the *St. Louis Globe-Democrat*, 14 February 1909, magazine section, 3. Stevens reproduced these remarks from Prince, *Transactions of the McLean County Historical Society*, 3:69–71.

John Q. Spears

1. John Q. Spears's account of his grandmother's impression of Lincoln appeared in the *St. Louis Globe-Democrat*, 24 January 1909, magazine section, 3.

2. John Quincy Spears (1828–1911), son of George Spears (1805–92), was "a wealthy farmer" in Tallulah in Menard County. See *Chicago Inter Ocean*, 13 April 1881. Spears shared his reminiscences of Lincoln with William Herndon in D. Wilson and Davis, *Herndon's Informants*, 705.

3. Spears's recollection of Lincoln and the formation of the Republican party appeared in the *St. Louis Globe-Democrat*, 3 January 1909, magazine section, 3, 6.

Adlai E. Stevenson

1. Adlai E. Stevenson (1835–1914) was vice president under Grover Cleveland (1893–97). His reminiscences about Lincoln appeared in the *St. Louis Globe-Democrat*, 28 March 1909, magazine section, 3. Stevens alleges that Stevenson's remarks were made during an interview with Stevens, but some of the text comes verbatim from Stevenson's autobiography, *Something of Men I Have Known* (Chicago: A. C. McClurg, 1909), 110–11, 275.

2. See Harry E. Pratt, "Abraham Lincoln in Bloomington, Illinois," *Journal of the Illinois State Historical Society* 29 (1936–37): 42–69.

3. No such debates took place between Lincoln and Cartwright.

4. According to Lincoln's friend, Congressman H. P. H. Bromwell, this episode involved Judge J. P. Cooper, a Republican from Marshall County, Illinois, and Dr. A. Goodell, a Democrat. In September 1856, Lincoln and Cooper spoke at Grandview, in Edgar County. Dr. Goodell repeatedly interrupted Cooper, not Lincoln. Exasperated, Cooper finally screamed, "Well, doctor, I'll take anything in the world from you; but for God's sake don't give me any of your pills." Undated clipping from the *Daily Beacon*, reprinted as "Recollections by Hon. H. P. H. Bromwell," in *Memoirs of Abraham Lincoln (in Edgar County, Illinois)*, by the Edgar

County Historical Society (Paris IL: Edgar County Historical Society, 1925), 23–26.

5. Noah Brooks recalled an episode in 1856 when Lincoln put down a heckler deftly: "He was always good-humored, witty and ready with a repartee for all those foolish fellows who will persist in making asses of themselves by interrupting a public speaker. Said he to one 'irrepressible' muggins who had been unusually impertinent and persistent: 'Look here, my friend, you are only making a fool of yourself by exposing yourself to the ridicule which I have thus far succeeded in bringing upon you every time you have interrupted me. You ought to know that men whose business it is to speak in public, make it a part of their business to have something always ready for just such fellows as you are. You see you stand no show against a man who has met, a hundred times, just such flings as you seem to fancy are original with yourself; so you may as well, to use a popular expression, "dry up" at once.' The individual was obliged to see the force of the remark and at once subsided." Brooks, "Some Reminiscences of Abraham Lincoln," *Marysville CA Appeal*, 4 November 1860, describing a speech Lincoln gave on 17 July 1856, in Dixon, Illinois.

6. Douglas spoke in Bloomington on 16 July with Lincoln in the audience. Lincoln spoke there on 4 September.

J. G. Stewart

1. J. G. Stewart's recollections of Lincoln appeared in the *St. Louis Globe-Democrat*, 28 March 1909, magazine section, 3. This gentleman is unmentioned in the literature on Lincoln photographs. He is perhaps the person alluded to in the following letter by Ezra M. Prince: "I saw Mr. Stewart yesterday. He is very loath to part with the pictures but is perfectly willing to give you copies of them. He also has a photo of Robert Lincoln given him by Mr. Lincoln in 1881. . . . He said Mrs. Lincoln had an ungovernable temper. How much one can rely on him I do not know, as I never met him until yesterday, and you know the memory of things fifty or sixty years ago is apt to play one queer tricks. What we think ought to have happened we are apt to remember that it did happen & old time gossip is fact which we firmly remember. It requires a trained mind at any time to tell the truth. To remember things as they actually took place is very rare. He repeated the old story that she was a 'Southern sympathizer' until the latter part of the war. That was old gossip to me but I think no one has repeated one word of hers that justifies anything of the kind." Prince to Truman H. Bartlett, Bloomington IL, 18 August 1907, Bartlett Papers, Boston University. Six weeks later Prince reported that "the picture of Robert was taken by C. E. Bell Photographer Washington DC in 1883 & sent by Robert to

Mr. Stewart. The pictures of Willie & Tad were sent by Mrs. Lincoln to Mrs. John W. Gray, Mother of Mrs. J. G. Stewart." Prince to Bartlett, Bloomington IL, 2 October 1907, Bartlett Papers.

Charles Church Tyler

1. This article on the exchange of letters among Lincoln relatives appeared in the *St. Louis Globe-Democrat*, 7 February 1909, magazine section, 5–6.

2. Charles Church Tyler was born in Marietta, Ohio, in 1837. Four years later his family settled in Carthage. See Tyler, "Reminiscences of Fountain Green, Illinois," *Journal of the Illinois State Historical Society* 8 (1915): 55–64.

3. Mordecai died in Fountain Green in 1867.

4. With George Knisley (or Nicely), Mary Rowena Lincoln had three children, Mary, John, and James.

5. George Washington Neighbors served as acting sheriff of Grayson County.

6. In 1819 President Lincoln's cousin Abraham married Elizabeth Lucretia Mudd, daughter of Hezekiah Mudd of Washington County, Kentucky.

7. Frances Day (1799–1844) of Grayson County, Kentucky.

8. Mary Rowena Lincoln, daughter of James B. Lincoln, married William Lovely and bore him a son, William.

Theophilus Van Deren

1. Theophilus Van Deren's recollections of attending a Lincoln and Douglas debate are taken from Charleston IL correspondence, 4 January 1887, *St. Louis Globe-Democrat*, 6 January 1887, 6.

Appendix 1

1. These recollections of Abraham Lincoln and Mary Todd are taken from Mrs. Benjamin S. Edwards to Ida M. Tarbell, Springfield, 8 October 1895, copy, Ida M. Tarbell Papers, Allegheny College, Meadville PA. See also Edwards's accounts in T. G. Onstot, *Pioneers of Menard and Mason Counties* (Peoria IL: J. W. Franks, 1902), 34–37, and in Raymond, *Some Incidents in the Life of Mrs. B. S. Edwards*, 5, 13–16.

2. See D. Wilson, *Lincoln before Washington*, 99–132.

3. See D. Wilson, *Lincoln before Washington*, 99–132.

Appendix 2

1. This is an expanded version of an article that appeared in the *Lincoln Herald* 96, no. 1 (fall 1994): 18–23.

2. Murat Haltead, "The Hon. R. R. Hitt," *Harper's Weekly*, 5 May 1895; biographical sketch of Hitt, corrected by Hitt, dated 25 June 1902, enclosed in Knickerbocker Publishing Co. to Hitt, New York, 25 June 1902, Hitt Papers, Library of Congress.

3. Otis E. Goodall, "Hon. Robert Roberts Hitt," *Phonographic Magazine* (Cincinnati), 1 June 1893, 205–6.

4. *Ogle County Portrait and Biographical Album* (1886), copy, Hitt Papers, Library of Congress. Cf. *New York Herald*, 29 May 1904, in *The Lincoln-Douglas Debates of 1858*, ed. Edwin Earle Sparks (Collections of the Illinois State Historical Library, vol. 3; Lincoln Series, vol. 1; Springfield: Illinois State Historical Library, 1908), 79.

5. Goodall, "Hon. Robert Roberts Hitt," 206–7.

6. Transcript of Hitt's shorthand journal, undated entry (ca. February 1861), 272–74, Hitt Papers, Library of Congress.

7. Biographical sketch of Hitt, corrected by Hitt, dated 25 June 1902, enclosed in Knickerbocker Publishing Co. to Hitt, New York, 25 June 1902, Hitt Papers, Library of Congress.

8. Sparks, *Lincoln-Douglas Debates*, 80–82; R. R. Hitt, journal, Hitt Papers, Library of Congress.

9. *Chicago Times*, 25 August 1858, quoted in Sparks, *Lincoln-Douglas Debates*, 83.

10. *Chicago Times*, 25 August 1858, in *Abraham Lincoln: A Press Portrait*, ed. Herbert Mitgang (Chicago: Quadrangle, 1971), 110.

11. *Chicago Press and Tribune*, 11 October 1858, 1.

12. Sparks, *Lincoln-Douglas Debates*, 83.

13. Douglas's reply at Ottawa, 21 August 1858, in *Abraham Lincoln: Speeches and Writings, 1832–1858*, ed. Don E. Fehrenbacher (New York: Library of America, 1989), 527–32.

14. Charles S. West, "The Lincoln-Douglas Debates," part 2, *Phonographic Magazine* (Cincinnati), 1 December 1896, 361–62.

15. Holzer, *Lincoln-Douglas Debates*, 254. Emphasis added in this and subsequent quotations from the debates.

16. Holzer, *Lincoln-Douglas Debates*, 252.

17. Holzer, *Lincoln-Douglas Debates*, 257.

18. Holzer, *Lincoln-Douglas Debates*, 261.

19. Holzer, *Lincoln-Douglas Debates*, 254.

20. Holzer, *Lincoln-Douglas Debates*, 254.

21. Holzer, *Lincoln-Douglas Debates*, 255.

22. Holzer, *Lincoln-Douglas Debates*, 254.

23. Holzer, *Lincoln-Douglas Debates*, 254.

24. Holzer, *Lincoln-Douglas Debates*, 258.

25. White quoted in Sparks, *Lincoln-Douglas Debates*, 594–95.

26. In addition to Stevens's interview with Hitt in this volume, see also West, "Lincoln-Douglas Debates," part 2, 360.

27. Hitt's journal, 23 July 1858, Hitt Papers, Library of Congress.

28. Hitt's journal, entries for 23, 26, and 28 July 1858, and undated entry, 240.

29. Hitt's journal, undated entries, 238, 265, 269.

30. Hitt's journal, 265.

31. Hitt's journal, entry for 28 July 1858.

32. Cadwallader, *Three Years with Grant*, ed. Benjamin P. Thomas (New York: Alfred A. Knopf, 1955), 128–31.

33. Hitt's journal, entry for 23 July 1858. Thirty-eight years later, Hitt shared his memories of the debates with an author, who, evidently paraphrasing those recollections, contrasted the speaking styles of Douglas and Lincoln:

> When reading the utterances of Mr. Douglas, one is led to believe that he was a rapid speaker. But he was not. His bass voice was incapable of great speed. His deep tones filled in the space between his words, and gave the listener the impression of rapid speaking, but he rarely used more than 120 to 125 words per minute, and these were spoken at an even and measured pace. His sentences were short, and he made long pauses between them. He was the stenographer's delight, as well as the delight of his hearers.
>
> But with Lincoln it was different. In speaking he seemed to be imbued with a desire to impress upon his audience the point which he was trying to make, rather than to please them with his manner of speaking. His voice was shrill, almost squeaky, although his words were distinct and easily understood. He would dwell upon and emphasize several important words, perhaps in the middle of a sentence, and the rest of it would be spoken with great rapidity, and quickly followed by another sentence in the same manner, convincing to his hearers, but annoying and fatiguing to the reporters. Taken altogether, he spoke much more rapidly, using many more words in a given time, than did Douglas.

Charles S. West, "The Lincoln-Douglas Debates," part 1, *Phonographic Magazine* (Cincinnati), 15 November 1896, 346.

34. West, "Lincoln-Douglas Debates," 1:346.

35. White in Sparks, *Lincoln-Douglas Debates*, 77.

36. Hitt, quoted in Goodall, "Hon. Robert Roberts Hitt," 207.

37. West, "Lincoln-Douglas Debates," 2:362; Goodall, "Hon. Robert Roberts Hitt," 207.

38. Sparks, *Lincoln-Douglas Debates*, indicates where Lincoln modified slightly the language in the *Press and Tribune* when he had the debates published in 1860. Most subsequent editions have been based on Lincoln's 1860 volume. The *Times*'s version is found in Holzer, *Lincoln-Douglas Debates*.

Index